THE
EVERYDAY
COOKBOOK

Published by Lansdowne, Sydney
a division of RPLA Pty Limited
176 South Creek Road, Dee Why West, N.S.W., Australia,
2099.
First published 1974
6th Impression 1983
7th Impression 1984
© Copyright RPLA Pty Ltd
Produced in Australia by the Publisher
Typeset in Australia by Filmset Centre Pty Limited, Brisbane
Printed in Hong Kong by South China Printing Co.

**National Library of Australia
Cataloguing-in-Publication Data**

Fulton, Margaret.
   The everyday cookbook.

   First published as: The complete Margaret Fulton
   cookbook. Sydney: Hamlyn, 1974.
   Includes index.
   ISBN 0 7018 1682 1.

   1. Cookery. I. Title.

641.5

THE
EVERYDAY
COOKBOOK

MARGARET FULTON

Lansdowne
Sydney·Auckland·London·New York

contents

introduction

One of the happiest periods of my life has been the time devoted to working on this book. We had just moved into a new home on Sydney harbour, surely one of the most beautiful harbours in the world. My garden boasted native trees which attracted some of the sweetest songbirds of the Australian bush and to cap it all, I had a brand new kitchen.

Large and airy, this kitchen was reminiscent of the huge farmhouse kitchens, where as a very young girl I had my first taste of cooking. It houses modern equipment alongside a battery of pots, pans, knives and other special pieces I have gathered over the years, including a 200-year-old cake dish from Germany and a 100-year-old mortar and pestle from Finland. It was a kitchen that cried out to be used to its fullest.

My daughter Suzanne had just returned from the Cordon Bleu School of Cookery in London where she had graduated with a diploma and where she had worked in the famous restaurant of that name. It soon became apparent that Suzanne had not only inherited my love of cooking but had returned with many new skills. Her year away had given her a chance to put into practice all that she had learnt as a student and best of all the assurance of a cook who knows what she's doing. Why not combine our forces and work together!

The idea appealed to Suzanne (now Suzanne Gibbs) and we set to work on a new book of cookery, complete with everything we had ever learnt.

The pattern of our daily lives took on a new shape. Shopping locally and at markets for fish, fruit and vegetables, talking to butchers, green grocers, shopkeepers, we literally worked our way through the four seasons. Each day we cooked, tasted and recorded. We found ourselves typing recipes and making notes into the wee small hours of the night. It soon became obvious that if this wasn't to take a lifetime we would need some help.

We were joined by Barbara Small who had studied at the Cordon Bleu in Paris and had cooked in many parts of the world. She contributed enthusiasm and a love of good food and wine. Susan Whitter, the youngest member of our team with a Diploma of Home Science and tremendous energy, completed the work force.

We needed a photographer and Warren Croser proved ideal. Talented and with an appreciation of the work that went into the preparation of each dish, he photographed delicate soufflés, tender omelets, juicy steaks or garden salads while each was still at its peak, never letting a skin form on a sauce, a slice of roast beef dry out or a salad lose its freshness. Nothing suffered and the illustrations speak for themselves, showing our lovely food to best advantage.

I like to think that this is not only a recipe collection, it is also a book that explains the basic principles of cooking. It is to be hoped that the information preceding each recipe will be read before it is made. It always helps to really understand what you are doing.

6

To begin at the beginning—there are stocks and sauces and herbs and spices. Each chapter is stocked full of recipes, and each recipe contains instructions on the techniques and principles of the cooking method used.

Todays trend in cooking seems to be international. British households no longer confine their cooking to English foods nor do Italians eat only Italian style. Take any one street in any one city of the world and you find a different cuisine being prepared in every second kitchen. With this in mind, it seemed logical that each section would have to include recipes from all over the world. Soups, for example, include Minestrone from Italy, Short Soup from China, the French soup so often served at weddings, Madreline, and Mulligatawny from India. After much testing and tasting it was only the very best that made the grade regardless of the country of origin.

We've spared a thought for slimmers and for those with a budget. There are recipes for hot days and cold days, for picnics, parties, good family style eating and stylish entertaining. For many of us these recipes are interchangeable, the simplest food you automatically give your family may well be one of the best dishes you could serve an honoured guest.

I would like to stress the importance of following a recipe carefully. Once a dish has been mastered, give it the stamp of your own personality by adding a favourite flavour or your choice of garnish. Cookery is after all one of the creative arts and one by which we can all express our individuality.

I hope that new cooks will learn from these recipes and experienced cooks will enjoy my interpretation of the many classical recipes included in this book.

Happy cooking and good eating.

Margaret Fulton

Crab Soufflé (see recipe on page 116)

Cooking terms and helpful hints

- To test if oil temperature is hot enough add a small cube of bread. The temperature is right when bread browns in less than 1 minute.

- It's a great help when breadcrumbing food to lightly flour it and then to hold it between two spoons before dipping it in the beaten egg and breadcrumbs. This does make the job a good deal easier and cleaner.

- Always hang a Christmas pudding in a dark dry place to prevent it becoming mouldy and to allow it to mature in the best way possible. A cool kitchen cupboard is an ideal place for both the pudding and the Christmas mincemeat, which should first be covered by an airtight lid.

- Adding silver coins to the Christmas pudding is an old fashioned custom we can no longer indulge in as the present day currency is not suitable. However, if you do wish to add some silver coins, wrap some 5c pieces in aluminium foil and press them into the hot pudding just before you take it to the table.

- Don't worry if a little mould forms on the pudding cloth. Just wipe it off if possible and boil the Christmas pudding as instructed in the recipe. **Never, never** place the pudding in a clean cloth. This will only let the water in as soon as you boil it, ruining your pudding.

- A cold soufflé should be made the day before it is to be eaten to give it a chance to set properly.

- To remove the skins from pistachio nuts, first shell them and place into a bowl. Pour over boiling water, allow to stand three minutes and then remove and gently rub off the loosened skin.

- A goose does not go as far as a turkey of the same size because the breast is shallow. However, the flesh of the goose is very rich and may be served in smaller portions.

- To split a sponge finger without breaking it, is a delicate job. The best way to do it is to saw through it with a serrated edged knife.

- The secret of cooking pork to a golden crisp finish (for Sweet and Sour Pork) is double frying. Cubes of pork are fried in peanut oil until almost cooked and then drained. Oil must be brought back to boiling point and then pork is returned for five seconds only, until it is golden and crisp.

- To prepare hazelnuts for garnishing cakes and desserts, first place the shelled nuts on a shallow tray in a moderate oven (350°F—170°C) for about 5 minutes or until their papery skins crack. Remove them and rub in a teatowel to remove their skins. Toast them under a hot grill or in a hot oven (400°F—200°C) until a deep golden all over.

- Hot Chinese mustard is frequently but sparingly used as a table condiment. It is made by blending a little English mustard with water to form a paste and a pinch of salt and 2 drops of vinegar are added. Leave at least 15 minutes for flavour to develop.

- Skinning a fish: Cover a board with a piece of greaseproof paper. Place the fish skin-side down with the tail facing you. Make a small cut across the tip of the tail. Slide the knife under the skin to separate it from the flesh. Dip the fingers in salt and hold the skin firmly. Pull it towards you with the left hand and, with the other, ease knife along the fillet removing skin.

- Clarified butter: This is clear butter—fat with the milk solids and salt removed. It can be heated to a greater temperature without burning, and is used for frying, giving especially good colour and flavour to the dish. It may be purchased in cartons (marketed as "ghee") from most supermarkets. If you wish to make it yourself, melt 250 g (½ lb) of butter gently until a good foam comes to the top. Cook for a few more seconds, remove from the heat and skim the top well. Pour into a bowl.

- Overcooking potatoes or cutting them too small makes them waterlogged and they lose all flavour. They should break under pressure of a fork when cooked but should not be a mush. Adding cold milk to potatoes makes them stodgy.

- To prepare the potatoes ahead of time: Cook them as described, then mash and press down well in the saucepan with a potato masher. Add the butter, spoon about 4 tablespoons of the hot milk over the top and cover with a well-fitting lid. Stand in a warm place. Before serving, beat well, adding more hot milk if necessary. Potatoes will keep for up to 20 minutes in this way.

- For gratin potato dishes, wash potatoes after peeling but do not leave them to soak. If they are left in water, potatoes lose their starch, which gives this dish its characteristic creaminess. It is best to prepare this dish and cook it straight away so that the potatoes will not discolour. If, however, you wish to make preparations ahead of time, pour on the milk and add the cheese and cover with some plastic wrap.

- To blanch almonds: Place them in a bowl and pour over boiling water to cover. Allow to stand for a few minutes and then lift out of the hot water and remove the skin. Almonds bought with their skins on have a better flavour then those already blanched.

- To sweat vegetables: This is a term you will soon become familiar with. Simply allow the vegetables to cook gently in butter in a covered pan until they are quite soft. The butter will absorb the flavour of the vegetables and transfer it to the rest of the dish.

- Luting Paste is thick flour and water paste used for sealing lids on terrines and other oven-baked meats. Foil can be used but the paste provides a superior seal, and allows less shrinkage of the meat. To make luting paste, mix 1 cup flour with 4 tablespoons water.

- To make lining of jam roll tin take two sheets greaseproof paper about 5-8 cm (2-3 in) larger all round than the tin. Fold up 2-3 cm (1-1½ in) on side and ends, secure corners with a paper clip. Sit paper case inside tin.
- Jam roll tin and lining paper must be well greased if cake is to come out easily.
- Egg yolks must be beaten until really thick and creamy—this will take a good 10 minutes.
- For best results, chill cream well before whipping and whip in a chilled bowl over a pan full of ice cubes.
- For decoration use a 1 cm (1½ in) star pipe and a nylon piping bag. Fill with cream and twist top, forcing cream down. Make sure bag and cream are very cold as in summer the heat of your hand can cause cream to curdle as you pipe it. Squeeze the cream out of the tube, swirl and lift your hand at the same time. Release pressure on the bag and the cream flow will stop.

- Salad greens and vegetables won't discolour if cut with a stainless steel knife. Many vegetables contain acid which will stain carbon steel knives and cause an unpleasant taste.

- Tossing green beans while still warm in dressing allows them to absorb more of the flavour.
- Do not use too much dressing—allow 2-3 tablespoons for tossing warm green beans and 3-4 tablespoons for tossing completed salad.
- Other dried beans such as lima and soy beans can be used to make this salad. Canned beans may also be used— red kidney, lima, butter and green beans are readily available. Drain and rinse in fresh water before using.

- Test the oil before the fritters are added. Place a few drops of batter into the hot oil. If it sizzles and quickly rises to the surface, the oil is at the correct temperature.
- Immediately fritters are removed from the oil, drain on crumpled kitchen or brown paper, dust with icing or caster sugar and serve at once.
- If it is necessary to keep the fritters standing, place them in a low oven (200°F—90°C).
- To give fritters a truly exquisite flavour, first macerate the pieces of fruit in sugar and liqueur or other suitable alcohol for at least 30 minutes before dipping them in the batter.

- To slake: This term refers to mixing arrowroot or cornflour with a small amount of cold water before using as a thickening agent. Use 1 teaspoon of arrowroot or cornflour to 2 tablespoons of cold water.

- When frying in deep hot fat keep a lid to the pan beside you in case the fat catches alight. This lid will block out the oxygen and kill the fire.

- Saffron is expensive and may be omitted but it does give beautiful colour and flavour.
- Turmeric can be added for colour but it has little flavour.

- To bake blind: Line the pastry case with greaseproof paper and fill with dried beans or peas. Bake in a moderately hot oven (375°F—190°C) for about 15 minutes until the pastry is set. Remove the paper and the dried beans. Return the pastry case to the oven for a further 5 minutes to dry out the base. Allow to cool. This baking ensures a good crisp crust and prevents the pastry from becoming soggy when the filling is added.

- Chicken Stock-Pot: It is a good idea to get into the habit of keeping a stock-pot going when you are cooking.
  Start the stock-pot as you begin preparing the meal. Throw such things as mushroom peelings and stalks, parsley stalks, vegetable trimmings (onions, carrots, turnips and celery, for example) into a saucepan as you prepare the vegetables.

Add the bird's neck, giblets and feet if you have them. The gizzard should be cut open with a pair of scissors and the yellow residue removed, as this can make the stock bitter. Cover with cold water and add 1 sliced onion, 1 sliced carrot, a few peppercorns, a bunch of herbs and a good pinch of salt. Bring to the boil. Skim the surface carefully and allow to simmer half-covered for 3 to 4 hours, or longer.

- Mushroom Duxelles is a mixture of finely chopped shallot and mushrooms cooked in butter. Used as a basis for sauces, meat, fish and eggs.
- Court Bouillon is an aromatic liquid, mainly used to poach seafood.

- When making Bombe Favourite make sure the springform cake tin is perfectly clean and free from rust, as the cream will absorb the rust flavour. If your tin should be rusty, line first with aluminium foil.

- Apples for use in pies, puddings and compotes should not be put into cold water after slicing, this may preserve their whiteness but at the expense of flavour.
- Avoid getting apples too pulpy when cooking, if they are very juicy remove the lid soon after they start to cook, and heat rapidly to reduce the liquid. They will continue to soften even when removed from the heat so take care not to overcook.

- The perfume of the vanilla bean is unequalled for flavouring desserts, cakes and custards.
  For flavouring custards and other sweet sauces, the bean is steeped in warm milk and left until it cools a little, then removed, washed and dried.
  Cakes and desserts are more often flavoured with vanilla sugar. Store the vanilla bean in an airtight jar containing caster sugar and while the sugar preserves the bean it takes up its perfume at the same time.

- Flouring meat can be done cleanly and effortlessly if you place a little seasoned flour into a plastic bag, add the meat and shake until it is well coated.
- Meat should be at room temperature when put into oven. If it has been frozen it should be thawed completely.
- Baste meat every 15-20 minutes to keep it moist. This does not apply to pork as basting pork will prevent the crackling becoming crisp.
- Allow meat to rest in a warm place for about 15 minutes before carving. This allows the meat to firm, making it easier to carve.
- "Boiled" meat is a misnomer. It must never be boiled but simmered gently until tender. This method of cooking is ideal for the less expensive cuts. It preserves their natural juices and imparts the flavour of the vegetables, herbs and spices added with the meat.
- Skim liquid of Brawn and Potted Hough while cooking to give a clear jelly. The meat for Brawn and Potted Hough is chopped roughly to keep the meat moist and to give it a more attractive appearance when sliced.
- Cool and store boiled meats in their liquid to keep moist. They are best kept in an airtight container. All cold meats should be removed from the refrigerator for about 10 minutes before serving as chilling dulls their flavour.
- When pressing tongue allow it to cool slightly. When cold it is difficult to press into a good shape.
- The look of Spiced Beef and Pumped Leg of Lamb is made more attractive if the cooked meat is first wiped with a warm damp cloth to remove any surface fat and then brushed with a little of the cooled liquid. The liquid will form a nice glaze.
- It's a well-known fact the only safe knife is a sharp knife. Avoid cutting cold meats with serrated edged knives. Boiled and jellied meats are best cut into generous slices.
- For outdoor eating, use a stainless steel knife to cut meat because a carbon steel knife easily discolours when allowed to stand unwashed for any length of time.

- Marinate: To steep before cooking in liquid, usually containing acid such as vinegar, lemon juice or wine, to flavour and tenderise.
- Dégorger: A process of extracting indigestible juices from vegetables. Usually done by sprinkling with salt and leaving to stand.

- Veal and fillet steaks, chicken breasts etc may be easily flattened to the required size by placing them between two sheets of plastic and beating them with a wooden or metal meat tenderiser or the heavy end of a bottle.

stocks, sauces and pickles

Stocks

Let's give honour where honour is due . . . the wonderful flavour of good French food is mostly the result of the stock used in its cooking, its flavouring or its sauce.

To a good cook, stock is everything. The French refer to stocks as the "fonds de cuisine" which literally means the "foundation of cooking."

Stock is the liquid obtained from the simmering together of meat (or fish or chicken) bones, trimmings and vegetables, seasonings and water. Sometimes this liquid is strained and simmered gently until it is boiled down so that you get a concentration of flavours.

Stocks are extremely simple to prepare and once they are set over a low heat they simmer gently requiring little attention from the stock.

All stocks should be strained through a fine strainer or fine cheesecloth and chilled so that the fat which rises to the top can be lifted off as the stock is required.

They may be frozen in quantities you are likely to use:
- for most soups.
- for thickened gravies and sauces.
- for enriching many casseroles and stews.
- for savoury jellies or aspics.
- for the basic sauces: Velouté, brown sauce or espagnole.

White Stock

500 g (1 lb) chicken or veal bones or a
    combination of both
3 litres (5 pints) cold water
1 teaspoon salt
1 carrot, cut in half
2 medium onions
bouquet garni (1 celery stalk, 3 sprigs
    parsley, 1 sprig thyme, 1 bay leaf
    tied together)
1 teaspoon black peppercorns

Place the bones into a large, heavy saucepan. Cover with cold water and add the remaining ingredients. Bring to the boil and skim the surface carefully. Simmer very slowly for 3 to 4 hours. Strain and cool. Refrigerate until needed.

The fat on the surface seals in the flavoured jelly underneath. When chilled this fat sets hard and is easily removed. This stock will keep for a week in the refrigerator.

Makes about 6 cups of stock and is used for velouté sauces, white sauces and soups.

Fish stock

1 fish head and bones (a snapper head
    is ideal)
5 cups water
1 cup white wine
$\frac{1}{2}$ teaspoon salt
1 onion
1 carrot, cut in half
bouquet garni

Place all the ingredients into a large saucepan and bring to the boil. Skim the surface and then boil gently for 20 minutes. Strain. Makes about 4 cups of fish stock. Used for fish velouté and in many fish sauces and soups.

Brown Stock

1 kg (2 lb) beef bones (shank, marrow bone or rib bones)
1 carrot, sliced thickly
2 onions, sliced thickly
2 teaspoons salt
3 litres (5 pints) water
bouquet garni (2 celery stalks, 4 sprigs parsley, 1 sprig thyme and 1 bay leaf tied together)
1 teaspoon black peppercorns

Place the bones in a roasting pan with the carrot and onion and roast in a moderately hot oven (400°F—200°C) until a good dark brown. Put them into a large saucepan. Rinse out the roasting pan with a little water and add to the bones. Add the remaining ingredients and bring slowly to the boil. Skim the surface and cook slowly 4 to 8 hours uncovered. Strain through a fine sieve and store in the refrigerator when cool. Makes about 6 cups.

Use for brown sauces and soups.

To clarify stock: 6 cups cold stock; 2 egg whites, lightly beaten; 2 egg shells.

Remove all the fat from the stock and place in a saucepan with the egg whites and egg shells. Bring slowly to the boil, whisking occasionally. Allow the liquid to rise in the pan and then lower the heat. Simmer very gently for 20 minutes.

As the egg whites cook they attract and hold the particles of fat and the residue that clouds the stock. Strain through a colander lined with butter muslin.

This clear stock is the basis of many clear soups.

Sauces
White Sauces

These are light in colour usually creamy white or a light straw-colour and delicate in taste and smooth as satin. This smooth texture is achieved by a well-made roux and liquid carefully added.

The two basic white sauces are Béchamel and Velouté. Béchamel is made with butter, flour and milk, flavoured with aromatics and should form a light coating over the food. It may be served "as is", and is also the foundation for other sauces. Sauce Mornay enriched with cream and egg yolks and flavoured with cheese is one of the best known variations.

Velouté is made with butter, flour and white stock. The stock may be veal, chicken or fish according to what food it accompanies and this sauce is often enriched with egg yolks and cream. Sometimes a knob of butter is swirled into the sauce at the last moment for extra richness. When the butter is added, the pan is moved in a circular motion spreading the butter through the sauce. It is then taken from the heat and served immediately.

Sauce Mornay

Used to coat fish, vegetables, chicken or eggs before glazing under a hot griller or in a hot oven.

Béchamel sauce—1 quantity
45 g (1½ oz) grated Parmesan cheese, gruyère or a dry sharp cheddar
1 egg yolk (optional)
1 teaspoon cream (optional)

To the hot Béchamel sauce add the cheese gradually. The sauce will become glossy. If a richer sauce is required combine the cream with the egg yolk and add a little of the hot sauce. When thoroughly combined stir this back into the hot sauce. Do not allow to boil again.

15

Creamy smooth Béchamel Sauce

16

Béchamel Sauce

This is the basis of many other sauces. Its flavour comes from the butter in the roux and the aromatic vegetables and herbs infused in the milk.

2 cups milk
1 slice of onion
8 peppercorns
1 bay leaf
1 small celery stalk
blade of mace
2 tablespoons butter
2 tablespoons plain flour
salt
freshly ground pepper
nutmeg

Put the milk into a saucepan with the onion, peppercorns, bay leaf, celery and mace. Place on a low heat to infuse but do not allow the milk to boil. Remove from the heat and strain. Cool.

Melt the butter in a heavy saucepan and when it is sizzling, stir in the flour. Lower the heat and cook gently for 1 minute, stirring all the time. Remove the pan from the heat and stir in the milk almost all at once, stirring until a smooth sauce is obtained. Place the sauce back on the heat and stir continually until it boils. Lower the heat and allow the sauce to cook very gently for 15 minutes, stirring frequently. Season with salt, pepper and a hint of nutmeg.

Cream Sauce

Used for any food that is served "creamed"—eggs, chicken, veal.

1 quantity of Béchamel sauce
¼ cup cream
few drops lemon juice

Heat the Béchamel sauce and add the cream. Bring to the boil and add the lemon juice.

A tablespoon of capers and a teaspoon of finely chopped parsley added to this sauce goes well with boiled or grilled fish.

Variations:
Mushroom Sauce: To 2 cups of Béchamel sauce add 125 g (4 oz) sautéed, diced mushrooms. Serve with lamb grills, poultry, eggs and fish.
Mustard Sauce: To 2 cups of Béchamel sauce add 1 tablespoon of English mustard blended with a little water. Serve with boiled meats and fish.
Onion Sauce: Finely chop 4 white onions. Boil until tender and drain. Add to 2 cups of hot Béchamel sauce. Serve with eggs, fish, veal and lamb dishes.
Parsley Sauce: To 2 cups of Béchamel sauce add 4 tablespoons of finely chopped parsley and a few drops of lemon juice. Serve with corned beef, tripe, boiled chicken, fish and eggs.
Horseradish Sauce: To 2 cups of Béchamel sauce add 4 tablespoons of prepared horseradish. Serve with boiled meat such as lamb's tongue.

Velouté Sauce

This is a sauce made with a blond roux. The liquid used is a light stock of some sort, depending on the food it accompanies. Sometimes the stock is combined with milk. Egg yolks and cream are often added to enrich the sauce and give it its characteristic velvety texture. Ideal with chicken or veal and when fish stock is used for fish dishes.

1 tablespoon butter
1 tablespoon plain flour
1¼ cups of stock (chicken, veal, fish)
salt
freshly ground pepper
few drops lemon juice (optional)
1 egg yolk
1 tablespoon cream

In a heavy saucepan melt the butter and stir in the flour.

Cook over a low heat stirring all the time until the roux becomes straw-coloured.

Remove from the heat and gradually stir in the cold stock. Place back on the heat and stir until boiling. Cook over a low heat for 15 minutes, stirring from time to time. Season with salt and pepper and a little lemon juice. Combine the egg yolk with the cream and a little of the hot sauce and then add to the sauce. Stir until well combined but do not allow the sauce to boil.

● Take care when adding lemon juice to sauces. A few drops are delicious but too much can be ruinous.

When sauces are made in advance, cover them with some buttered or wet greaseproof paper or plastic wrap to prevent a skin from forming on top. Most sauces can be reheated. Place the pan containing the sauce in a pan of hot water and stir the sauce until it reaches the desired temperature.

Parsley Sauce

Used for fish, eggs, veal and chicken.

1 quantity of Velouté sauce (using the
appropriate stock)
finely chopped parsley

Stir the parsley in the finished Velouté sauce and serve.

Sauce Aurore

1½ tablespoons tomato purée
1 quantity of Béchamel sauce
1 tablespoon butter

Stir the tomato purée into the hot Béchamel sauce and then swirl in the butter.

Brown Sauces

Brown sauces have always been important in French cooking. They are a rich brown in colour. Their base is a brown roux made from butter and flour cooked slowly until hazelnut brown. Brown stock is added and sometimes tomatoes and wine. The sauce is highly seasoned. In a brown sauce the liquid reduces and the flavours blend together and become more concentrated.

Brown sauces may be made in several ways:
- In the cooking pan scraping up all the crusty meat juices.
- With the cooking liquid from stews thickened with beurre manié.
- In a saucepan with a brown roux (butter or oil and flour mixed together) and brown stock.

For a good brown sauce:
- Stir the roux (butter and flour) all the time over a very low heat until it becomes hazelnut brown. The roux is very easy to scorch which can make the sauce bitter and spotty.
- Stir the sauce. Whisking quickly lightens the colour.
- Before storing a brown sauce pour over a small quantity of sherry.
- Remember a good wine makes a good sauce. Do not use a wine you would not drink.

Brown Sauce

3 tablespoons olive oil or clarified butter
1 small carrot, finely diced
1 small onion, finely diced
1 small stick celery, finely diced
1 tablespoon flour
2¼ cups brown stock
few mushroom peelings (optional)
1 tablespoon tomato purée
bouquet garni
5 peppercorns

Place the oil and diced vegetables in a heavy saucepan. Cook over a low heat until the vegetables are golden. Stir in the flour and continue to cook very slowly stirring all the time until the roux is a hazelnut brown.

Remove from the heat and add 1½ cups brown stock stirring all the time. Add the remaining ingredients. Bring to the boil and half cover with a lid. Simmer for 25 minutes. Add half of the remaining stock. Allow to reboil and skim the surface. Add the remaining stock. Bring to the boil and skim the surface once more. This "dépouillement" removes the fat that rises to the surface and gives the sauce a glossy appearance. Strain the sauce through a fine sieve and use as required.

Sauce Poivrade

A sharp-flavoured sauce used for grills.

1 tablespoon tarragon vinegar
1¼ cups brown sauce
1 teaspoon capers
1 teaspoon finely chopped parsley
1 teaspoon tomato purée

Reduce the vinegar to 1 teaspoonful and add to the brown sauce with the remaining ingredients. Bring to the boil. Remove from the heat and serve.

Madeira Sauce

Used for the best cuts of beef, veal, ham or poultry.

2 cups brown sauce
¼ cup of Madeira

Cook the brown sauce until it is reduced to 1 cup and stir in the Madeira. Allow to heat to boiling point but do not allow to boil again.

- **"Dépouiller"**: This term means to remove the scum or fat which rises to the surface during the long simmering of a brown sauce. This is helped by the addition of a little cold stock at the end of the simmering period.

  This reserved stock is added in two parts and the sauce is allowed to reboil each time before skimming thoroughly. If the pan is tilted slightly the fat will rise to the surface on one side only and can easily be removed.

  When the dépouillement is completed the sauce should be clear with a glossy appearance.

Bordelaise Sauce

Used for grilled or sautéed steaks.

2 shallots, finely chopped
½ cup red wine
1 cup brown sauce
2 tablespoons beef marrow
½ teaspoon chopped parsley

Put the shallots and wine into a saucepan and reduce to ¾ of its original volume. Add the brown sauce and cook for 10 minutes. Just before serving add the beef marrow which has been cut into small dice, poached in warm water for a few minutes and drained. Stir in the parsley.

- Beef marrow is the fat contained in the marrow bones. When buying the bones ask the butcher to split them so that the marrow may be easily removed.

Sauce Chasseur

Used for grills, entrées and roasts.

15 g (½ oz) butter
1 shallot, finely chopped
60 g (2 oz) small mushrooms, finely sliced
½ cup dry white wine
2 teaspoons tomato purée
1¼ cups brown sauce

Melt the butter in a heavy saucepan and add the shallot. Cook over a low heat until it is soft but not coloured. Add the mushrooms and cook until they turn golden. Pour on the wine and allow it to reduce to half. Add the tomato purée and brown sauce and stir until well combined. Allow to simmer for 2 minutes.

Rich Butter Sauces

These are known as emulsified sauces because they are thickened with an emulsion of egg yolks and butter. They also contain some acid (vinegar, white wine or vermouth or lemon juice) which helps to stabilise them. The most important of these sauces are Hollandaise and Bearnaise. They are not difficult to make if certain rules are observed:
- Use a double boiler. Do not allow the water in the bottom pan to boil during cooking.
- Add the butter a little at a time. Make sure each portion of butter is thoroughly incorporated before adding more.
- Stir the sauce continually until it is finished.
- If the sauce does curdle, place an egg yolk into a clean saucepan (off the heat) and add the curdled mixture whisking it in gradually.

Bearnaise Sauce

Served with grilled and sautéed steaks, roast fillet of beef, shellfish and some vegetables.

$\frac{1}{4}$ cup of white wine vinegar or
  dry vermouth
1 shallot, finely chopped
4 crushed peppercorns
1 sprig tarragon, finely chopped
1 bay leaf
1 sprig thyme, finely chopped
2 egg yolks
125 g (4 oz) butter
1 heaped teaspoon chopped tarragon
  or parsley (optional)
freshly ground pepper

Place the white wine vinegar or vermouth in a saucepan with the finely chopped shallot, peppercorns, tarragon, crushed bay leaf and thyme and reduce to 1 tablespoon.

Add the reduced mixture to the egg yolks and place in the top of a double boiler, beat until the egg yolks have thickened slightly.

Add the butter gradually in small pieces. Whisk the sauce until the butter is thoroughly combined and the consistency resembles whipped cream. Stir in the finely chopped tarragon or parsley and season with pepper.

Paloise Sauce

This is made in the same way as Bearnaise sauce except that finely chopped mint leaves are substituted for the tarragon or parsley and thyme. Serve with grilled lamb and poultry.

Hollandaise Sauce

This rich but delicate sauce is good with salmon, asparagus, vegetables, fish and eggs.

1 tablespoon water
2 egg yolks
125 g (4 oz) unsalted butter
small pinch salt
few drops lemon juice

In the top of a double boiler place the water and egg yolks and whisk over hot water until they are light and fluffy. Do not allow the water in the bottom pan to boil. Add a spoon of cold water frequently to keep it below boiling point. Add the butter to the egg yolks (see steps for Bearnaise sauce) whisking it in well until the butter is melted and the sauce starts to thicken. Continue adding the butter and stirring constantly until all has been added. Add the salt and flavour with a little lemon juice. Be very careful. Too much lemon juice can ruin the sauce.

The 'Naturals' . . .

Bread Sauce

Serve with roast poultry.

1 small onion, chopped
1 cup milk
1 blade mace
1 cup soft white breadcrumbs
salt, freshly ground pepper

Place onion, milk and mace in a small heavy saucepan. Cover and simmer until the onion is tender. Strain the milk. Stir enough breadcrumbs into milk to make a thick sauce. Season with salt and pepper and place over a very low heat for about 10 minutes, stirring frequently.

Mint Sauce

Serve with roast lamb or mutton.

½ cup fresh mint, finely chopped
½ tablespoon caster sugar
salt, freshly ground pepper
1 tablespoon hot water
vinegar

Combine the mint with the sugar and season with salt and pepper. Add the hot water and stir in sufficient vinegar to give the desired consistency.

Apple Sauce

Serve warm or cold with roast pork or duck.

4 large cooking apples, peeled and sliced
2 tablespoons water
2 tablespoons sugar
3 cloves
30 g (1 oz) butter

Place the apples, water, sugar and cloves on a very low heat. Cover and cook until the apple is very soft. Remove the cloves. Stir the apple and then add the butter in small pieces.

Tomato Sauce

Serve with grilled meats, pasta and green vegetables. A few tablespoons give a boost to casseroles and sauces.

3 tablespoons olive oil
½ stalk celery
1 small onion, finely chopped
1 clove garlic, crushed
500 g (1 lb) ripe tomatoes OF
470 g (15 oz) tin tomatoes
½ cup tomato purée
1 tablespoon tomato paste
salt, freshly ground pepper
1 bay leaf
**1 small bouquet of herbs, (oregano,
   parsley or marjoram)**

Heat the oil in a saucepan, add the celery, onion and garlic and brown lightly. Add the tomatoes, tomato purée and tomato paste. Season with salt and pepper. Add the bay leaf and bouquet of herbs. Cook gently for 45 minutes to 1 hour. Remove the bay leaf and bouquet and strain through a fine sieve.

A selection of mouthwatering pickles.

Sauces for Cold Meats

"Sauce" is one of those French words that was introduced into the English language by the conquering Normans and remains unchanged to this day. Although the English have adopted many French culinary words and some of the French cookery methods, they have excelled in creating their own sauces that go so well with cold meats.

Apple and Horseradish Sauce

3 cooking apples
1-2 tablespoons water
2 tablespoons sugar
1 strip lemon rind
2 tablespoons horseradish

Peel and core apples. Cut into quarters, then slice. Put into a small pan with the water, sugar and lemon rind. Cover and cook gently to a pulp. Allow to cool. Remove the lemon rind and mix in the horseradish.

Serve with pressed tongue, pickled pork.

Gribiche Sauce

3 hardboiled egg yolks
1 teaspoon French mustard
½ teaspoon salt
freshly ground white pepper
1½ cups olive oil
½ cup white wine vinegar
3 hardboiled egg whites, finely chopped
½ cup capers and gherkins, finely chopped
1 tablespoon mixed parsley, tarragon and
    finely chopped

Rub hardboiled egg yolks through a fine sieve. Mix with the mustard, salt and pepper. Add the olive oil gradually as if making a mayonnaise and then add the vinegar stirring constantly. Finally add the egg whites, capers and gherkins and finely chopped herbs.

This is a rich sauce resembling mayonnaise and is good with cold beef, tongue, chicken and shellfish.

Sour Cherry Sauce

½ cup sugar
2 teaspoons cornflour or arrowroot
1 500 g (16 oz) can pitted sour red cherries
1 tablespoon port

Mix the cornflour or arrowroot with 1 tablespoon cherry juice. Combine the sugar, cornflour or arrowroot and cherries and stir over a low heat until the syrup is thick and clear. Add the port. Serve hot or cold.

This sauce is delicious with tongue or pickled pork.

Spiced Mustard Sauce

2 tablespoons brown sugar
3 tablespoons cider or white wine vinegar
4 tablespoons olive oil
1 teaspoon prepared English mustard
½ teaspoon salt
ground black pepper
pinch ground cloves

Combine ingredients. This is excellent with corned beef, tongue or brawn.

Cumberland Sauce

3 tablespoons red currant jelly
1 tablespoon lemon juice
1 tablespoon orange marmalade
2 tablespoons port
1 teaspoon prepared English mustard or
  2 teaspoons French mustard

Put all ingredients into a bowl and mix together quickly. The mixture will be rough textured but this is one of the nice features of the sauce.

  This is one of the best cold sauces to serve with cold meats and game.

For Veal

¼ cup brandy
¼ cup port
2 tablespoons olive oil
1 small carrot sliced
1 small onion sliced
bouquet garni

Combine ingredients for marinade in a bowl. Add the meat and turn in the marinade from time to time. Sufficient for 1 kg (2 lb) of meat.

Sweet Sauces

A sauce is very often the making of a pudding, bringing out and enhancing the flavour.

  Many of the combinations are traditional but perhaps the best known is custard sauce. It is worthwhile learning to make this as it should be made—our recipe calls for egg yolks only. The left-over whites may be stored for many weeks in a covered jar in the refrigerator and used for meringues.

Rum Butter Sauce

This provides an ideal accompaniment to mince pie, baked apples and rich steamed puddings.

90 g (3 oz) butter
½ cup brown sugar
little grated orange rind
a squeeze of orange juice
¼ cup rum

Cream the butter thoroughly, beat in the sugar gradually with the grated orange rind and orange juice. Add rum to flavour.

Sauce Mousseline

Serve with steamed or baked sponge puddings.

1 whole egg
1 egg yolk
2 tablespoons caster sugar
3 tablespoons sherry, rum, orange juice
  or strong coffee

Place all ingredients together in a bowl. Whisk over hot water until thick and frothy. Use as soon as possible but if the sauce must wait, whisk it for a minute just before serving.

Hard Sauce

Serve with all steamed puddings

90 g (3 oz) butter
1 cup icing sugar
2 teaspoons brandy or more to taste
1 egg white, beaten stiffly

Cream the butter until soft. Sift icing sugar and add to butter and beat until light and creamy. Beat in the brandy and then fold in stiffly beaten egg white. Chill before serving.

Note: Substitute $\frac{1}{4}$ cup ground almonds for $\frac{1}{4}$ cup of the icing sugar for a variation, or flavour with:

- Grated orange rind and tablespoon or orange juice instead of brandy.
- Grated lemon rind and tablespoon of lemon juice instead of brandy.
- Coffee essence instead of brandy.
- Cinnamon and mixed spices (nutmeg, cardamom and mace).
- 2 tablespoons of fresh strawberry purée instead of brandy.

Custard Sauce

Serve with all hot puddings.

4 egg yolks
$\frac{1}{3}$ cup sugar
2 cups scalded milk
1 teaspoon vanilla or brandy to taste

Beat the egg yolks with the sugar until light and thick. Gradually stir in the scalded milk. Return this mixture to the saucepan and stir over a very low heat or in the top of a double boiler until the custard coats the back of a spoon. Remove from the heat and flavour with vanilla or brandy.

Apricot Sauce (1)

$1\frac{1}{2}$ cups apricot jam
$\frac{1}{2}$ cup water
2 tablespoons sugar
2 tablespoons kirsch or other liqueur

Combine apricot jam, water and sugar in a saucepan and bring to the boil. Cook slowly 5 to 10 minutes, stirring frequently to prevent scorching. Rub through a sieve and add the liqueur.

Apricot Sauce (2)

250 g (8 oz) dried apricots
$\frac{1}{2}$ cup sugar
1 stick cinnamon (optional)

Soak apricots for several hours in enough water to cover. Bring to boil with cinnamon stick and simmer until soft. Remove the cinnamon stick. Rub through a sieve and add the sugar. Return to the heat and cook until the sugar is dissolved. A little more water may be added if the sauce is too thick.

Spoon apricot sauce over poached apples and pears or lightly brush over fruits which are to be flamed with liqueur. Serve with Apple Charlotte and use as a glaze for fruit tarts.

Melba Sauce

250 g (8 oz) raspberries
3-4 heaped tablespoons sifted icing sugar

Rub the raspberries through a sieve and beat the icing sugar into the purée a little at a time, adding enough to thicken the purée.

Traditionally served with ice cream and peaches poached in a vanilla-flavoured syrup but may be used over ice cream or other poached fruit.

Sauce au Vin Rouge

1 cup red wine
2 tablespoons sugar
3 tablespoons of thick purée of cooked
   dried apricots or apricot jam

Boil the red wine with the sugar for 2 to 3 minutes and add the apricot purée or jam. Stir until well combined.

Serve with fruit fritters, steamed puddings and dessert cakes.

Pickles and Chutneys

Pickled Orange Wedges

4 medium oranges
¼ teaspoon bicarbonate of soda
1 teaspoon whole allspice
12 whole cloves
2 cups malt vinegar
8 cm (3 in) cinnamon stick
2 cm (1 in) piece fresh ginger
2 cups sugar

Wash oranges and cut each into 8 wedges. Put into a saucepan, add water to cover and the bicarbonate of soda. Bring to the boil and simmer gently for 15 minutes. Place remaining ingredients in another pan and bring to the boil, stirring until the sugar is dissolved. Drain orange wedges and place into vinegar syrup. Cover and simmer for 20 minutes. Remove orange wedges with a slotted spoon and pack into hot dry jars. Boil the syrup and top up jars. Cover and seal. This pickle will be ready in a week.

Sour Pickled Lemons

12 lemons
3 tablespoons rock salt
1 tablespoon paprika
3 bay leaves
12 peppercorns
½ cup olive oil

Boil the whole unpeeled lemons for 20 minutes. Drain. Cut each lemon into quarters and layer in a large jar with the salt, paprika, bay leaves and peppercorns. When the jar is full, pour on the olive oil. Cover. The lemons will be ready in 6 months. One red chilli may be added for a hot pickle.

Pickled Quinces

2 quinces
1 cup sugar
2½ cups spiced vinegar

Peel quinces, cut each into 8 sections and remove cores. Heat sugar and vinegar and add the quinces. Cover and simmer gently for 1 hour or until the quinces are tender and pink in colour. Spoon quince sections into hot, dry jars. Bring syrup to the boil and pour over fruit. Cover and seal. The fruit will be ready to eat in a week.

Pickled Onions

2 kg (4 lb) pickling onions (brown or
   white)
250 g (8 oz) salt
2 red chillies
½ cup sugar, optional
4 cups spiced vinegar

Cut ends off onions, then peel. Stir salt into 8 cups of water to dissolve and pour over onions. Leave to soak for 18-24 hours. Drain and pack lightly into jars. Add chillies to jar. Dissolve the sugar (if used) in the cold spiced vinegar and pour over onions. Cover and store for several weeks before using.

Spiced Vinegar

Malt or cider vinegars give a good flavour. For a clear pickle use distilled white vinegar.

Spices used for flavouring pickles must be fresh and whole as ground spices darken the pickles and when stale, they impart a dusty flavour. The spices can be tied in muslin for easy removal but we prefer to leave the spices in the vinegar to give a lasting flavour, although this may cloud the pickles slightly.

4 cup vinegar (cider, malt or white wine)
6 black peppercorns
6 cloves
1 cinnamon stick
5 blades of mace
2 teaspoons whole allspice

Place vinegar in saucepan with spices. Bring slowly to boiling point, then remove pan from heat and cover with lid. Leave for 2 hours. Strain if desired. Use spiced vinegar cold. Makes 4 cups.

Variations can be made by adding one of the following: 1 tablespoon celery seeds or mustard seeds; 5 cm (2 in) fresh ginger; 1 garlic clove; 3 bay leaves.

Coconut Sambol

1 cup desiccated coconut
½ teaspoon chilli powder, optional
1 onion, finely chopped
1 to 2 tablespoons hot milk
3 tablespoons paprika, 1 teaspoon salt
1 tablespoon lemon juice

Combine all ingredients in a bowl and mix well. Garnish with sliced chillies.

Banana Chutney

10 dates
¼ cup water
6 large bananas
1 tablespoon lime juice, lemon juice or
    vinegar
2 tablespoons thick coconut milk or sour
    cream
¾ cup desiccated coconut
good pinch ground mustard
2 medium onions, finely chopped
2 teaspoons mint, finely chopped
½ teaspoon paprika
¼ teaspoon cayenne

Stone dates and simmer in water until soft. Peel and mash bananas. Combine the dates and mashed bananas with remaining ingredients to make a thick chutney. Chill before serving.

This chutney can also be made with beetroot instead of bananas, with the addition of a good pinch nutmeg and ¼ teaspoon black pepper.

Mint Chutney

120 g (4 oz) fresh mint
1 medium onion
juice of 1½ limes or lemons
4 tablespoons finely chopped parsely or
    coriander
½ teaspoon cayenne, 1½ teaspoons salt
3 teaspoons sugar

Wash and shake the mint dry. Use only the leaves, except for about half a dozen stalks. Finely chop onion and mint and place in a bowl, add remaining ingredients and mix well. Chill before serving.

Tomato Chutney

1 lb (500 g) tomatoes
Rind of ½ lime or lemon thinly pared
1 teaspoon freshly ground black pepper
¼ teaspoon basil, ¼ teaspoon paprika
1 grated medium onion
5 cm (2 in) green ginger finely chopped

Peel and finely chop tomatoes. Place in a bowl and mix with remaining ingredients. Chill before serving.

Cucumber in Sour Cream

2 cucumbers
salt
¼ teaspoon grated ginger
1 clove garlic, crushed
1 cup sour cream
paprika

Peel cucumbers and slice very thinly. Sprinkle with salt and let stand 20 to 30 minutes. Drain off all the liquid, add ginger, crushed garlic and sour cream. Mix well and add more salt if necessary. Chill and sprinkle with paprika.

Tomato and Onion Sambol

6 firm red tomatoes
1 onion
1 clove garlic, crushed
4 tablespoons olive oil
2 tablespoons white vinegar
dash tabasco
salt and pepper to taste

Slice tomatoes and onion and place in serving dish. Combine remaining ingredients. Pour over tomatoes and onions and toss lightly to mix.

Dhal (Lentil Purée)

Dhal is a simple dish of lentil purée. It is often included in curry meals as a change or an extra flourish. Different lentils may be used—red, yellow, or brown will all give their own distinctive flavour and colour.

250 g (8 oz) lentils
$\frac{1}{2}$ teaspoon ground chilli
1 teaspoon salt
$\frac{1}{4}$ teaspoon turmeric
3 tomatoes
2 onions
30 g (1 oz) butter

Put lentils, chilli, salt and turmeric into a saucepan with $4\frac{1}{2}$ cups of boiling water and cook until tender.

Quarter tomatoes, finely chop onions and fry in the butter until golden. Add to lentils. Cook for 5 minutes. The dhal should have the consistency of a thick sauce and is best eaten with boiled rice. Serves 2.

Coconut Milk

Coconut milk is an essential flavouring for many types of curry.

3 cups desiccated coconut
3 cups milk

Put coconut into a saucepan, pour milk over and bring slowly to the boil. Allow to cool slightly. Put into blender and blend at high speed 2 to 3 minutes. Strain. Alternatively, heat milk, add coconut and steep.

Pour into a sieve over a bowl and knead the coconut well to extract all the milk. This is the first extract or thick milk. Repeat process with the same coconut and 3 cups fresh milk. This will give thinner milk, which will still have good flavour.

Top left and right: Pickles and chutneys, superb accompaniments to any meal.
Bottom: Any of these dishes give an extra flourish to a curry.

Marinades

A marinade is a seasoned liquid, cooked or uncooked, in which foods (mainly meat and fish) are steeped.

The purpose of marinating is to season the food by impregnating it with the flavours of the herbs and spices used in the liquid. The length of time the food should be left in the marinade depends on its size and texture

In winter, large cuts of meat can be marinated for 5 to 6 days. In summer, they should be marinated for no longer than 24 hours or, if they are placed in the refrigerator, allow 48 hours.

Marinating softens the fibres of some kinds of meat and enables it to keep longer. Useful in the summer months for camping or fishing holidays.

Wine Marinade

This marinade is suitable for any meat. When marinating red meats, use red wine. Use whites for white meats.

1 cup wine
4 tablespoons olive oil
4 parsley sprigs
2 thyme sprigs or $\frac{1}{2}$ teaspoon of dried thyme
1 tablespoon brandy
1 teaspoon peppercorns
1 bay leaf
3 whole cloves
1 onion, sliced
1 carrot, sliced
2 garlic cloves, peeled and cut in half

Place the meat in a glass or enamel container. Add all other ingredients, cover and chill several hours or overnight. Sufficient for 1 to 1.5 kg (2 to 3 lb) of meat.

Note: For large joints to be roasted or pot roasted, increase wine by 2 cups. It is preferable to use olive oil for marinades because of its fruity flavour.

For Lamb or Beef

1 cup red wine
$\frac{1}{4}$ cup wine vinegar
2 tablespoons olive oil
1-2 bay leaves

Combine ingredients in a bowl and add the meat. Turn in the marinade from time to time. Sufficient for 1 to 1.5 kg (2 to 3 lb) of meat.

For Lamb or Pork

$\frac{1}{2}$ cup olive oil
2 tablespoons lemon juice
freshly ground black pepper and rock salt
2 garlic cloves peeled and cut in half
1 bay leaf
1 sprig of rosemary (optional)

Mix ingredients together in a bowl and add the meat. Cover the bowl. Turn the meat 3 or 4 times during its marination period.

Note: This marinade is also suitable for lamb kebabs. Leg steaks 2.5 cm (1 in) thick cut into cubes are marinated for several hours. Thread the meat on to skewers and grill for 10 to 12 minutes, turning and basting with the marinade as they cook.

Mustard Coated Spareribs

Mustard Coated Spareribs

These meaty pork spareribs baked brown and crisp are lemon flavoured with a spicy hint of mustard.

1 kg (2 lb) pork spareribs
4 teaspoons dry mustard
2 teaspoons sugar
¼ cup lemon juice
freshly ground pepper

Place the spareribs in a flat glass, china or enamel dish. Mix the remaining ingredients and pour over the spareribs. Leave to marinate for at least 2 hours, turning over once. If necessary, they may be left in the refrigerator overnight.

Place the spareribs in a roasting pan, pour over the marinade and bake in a hot oven (425°F—220°C) for about 1 hour or until tender, basting frequently.

To serve carve into sections and accompany with lemon wedges and small new potatoes sprinkled with parsley.

herbs and spices

Herbs

To dry herbs: Tie herbs in bunches and hang in the open air for 2 to 3 weeks. When dry, strip the leaves from the stalks and place into clean airtight jars labelling them carefully. You can make your own particular blend.

Basil is one of the most useful and delightfully aromatic herbs and was supposed to have been found growing on the site of the crucifixion in Jerusalem.

Sweet Basil has large leaves and pungent perfume.

Bush Basil likes a warm, sunny position and it thrives when its buds are picked frequently. Basil is an indispensable herb in many Italian and Mediterranean dishes. It is the perfect herb accompaniment for tomatoes — in a fresh tomato salad or a tomato sauce. It is delicious with cucumber, in a potato salad, a rice salad or chopped and sprinkled over beans.

Bay Leaves are the leaves of a small tree and are one of the ingredients of the bouquet garni used to flavour marinades, stocks, soups and many other dishes. Bay leaves are usually sold in packets but they can sometimes be bought on a branch. A bay leaf is often placed on top of a terrine or pâté before it is cooked or they are added to pickles and olives.

Bay leaves may be used fresh or dried but should be kept stored in an airtight jar.

They were made into wreaths to crown the heads of the first Olympians, emperors and victorious generals in the days of ancient Greece and Rome. They were also reputed to protect people from lightning.

Fresh Coriander resembles parsley and is sometimes known as Chinese Parsley. It is added to many eastern and Mexican dishes and finely chopped may be used in a chutney for curries.

Dill is an annual herb with feathery leaves which have a delicate aniseed flavour. It seasons many Scandinavian dishes and some central and eastern European dishes. It is good with cucumber, with salmon and other fish, with pickles, and finely chopped, it adds flavour to sauces.

Fennel is a hardy perennial plant with a bright yellow head of tiny flowers and green feathery leaves. It is easy to grow and is often seen growing wild in country areas. Its dried seeds flavour cakes, bread and cheese, and grilled fish acquires its aromatic aniseed scent when flamed on a bed of dried fennel twigs.

Florence Fennel is the thick white bulbous stem which is sliced thinly into salads or cooked and served in a parsley or mornay sauce or a herb butter. In a vinaigrette dressing it is delicious with cold chicken, fish or shellfish and its crisp texture adds interest to a green salad. It is used in stuffings for pork and fish and adds its fresh aniseed flavour to mayonnaise and to various alcoholic aperitifs. Fennel is supposed to be very kind to the digestion and according to some authorities aids slimming. If chewed after meals it sweetens the breath.

Marjoram is a perennial herb with small greyish-green leaves which have a strong perfume. It is used in sauces, soups, stews or finely chopped in salads and combined with other herbs to flavour an omelet.

Mint is a perennial herb, hardy and liking a fairly rich soil with plenty of water and space to grow. Most useful are the **Common Mint** with curly leaves, and the **Spearmint.** Mint is delicious with citrus fruits and pineapple, with new potatoes, peas and carrots, in tomato sauces, mint jellies, curries and middle eastern food. Its cool, clean flavour takes the edge off rich, spicy food. **Mint Leaves** give a refreshing taste to summer drinks and mint is the base of the liqueur, Crème de Menthe.

Oregano is wild majoram with a far more pungent perfume than sweet marjoram. It is widely used in Italy, flavouring tomato sauces, pizzas, olives, salads and shellfish and meat dishes.

Parsley is the best loved and most widely used herb. It is a biennial and likes a good soil and plenty of water, sun and space.

It would hardly be an exaggeration to say parsley may be used in, or as a garnish for, almost every dish which isn't sweet. It is one of the aromatic herbs of the bouquet garni and with finely chopped chives makes Fines Herbes, giving a professional touch to an omelet or scrambled eggs. Finely chopped and mixed with butter, it forms a sauce for grills and adds a fresh touch to a salad. Parsley should be rinsed well before it is used, then squeezed dry in a towel and chopped on a wooden board with a sharp knife.

There's an old saying that if parsley seeds are sown on Good Friday they will bring happiness and good fortune to all around.

Rosemary is a hardy evergreen bush which flourishes best near the sea. The oil in its leaves is very pungent so it is wise to use it discreetly. A few leaves heated in butter or oil will release enough flavour so that the leaves can be removed and the cooking continued in the rosemary-scented butter. Rosemary is delicious with roast lamb and rabbit. It can be most agreeable in robust chicken and shellfish dishes or added to spinach or pea soup.

The spiky leaves can be tough when fresh but when they are dried they become brittle and are easy to chop or crumble. In ancient times rosemary was used to ward off black magic and placed on the brow to relieve headaches.

Sage is a perennial herb with a grey-green leaf which has a powerful and slightly musty flavour indispensible in the sage and onion stuffing for goose and duck. The English are very fond of sage and use it to flavour their sausages and various meat dishes. The Italians enjoy its flavour and add it to veal, game and liver. A little finely-chopped sage is excellent mixed with cream cheese or cooked with poached leeks.

Sage-flavoured honey is a speciality from Dalmatia which honey connoisseurs consider the best in the world.

Winter and Summer Savory are Mediterranean herbs. Summer savory is an annual and winter savory is a perennial. Both have a peppery aromatic flavour which is used in meat and fish dishes, in stuffings and with beans. It is sometimes used to flavour a fresh tomato sauce or home-made sausages.

Salad Burnet was a herb greatly favoured in Elizabethan England. It has little saw-tooth leaves which have a smell not unlike cucumber. It may be crushed and added to summer drinks or finely chopped and added to ravigote sauce or mayonnaise.

Tarragon is a perennial with long slender leaves which likes plenty of sunlight and is all the better for being picked frequently. There are two varieties but it is the **French Tarragon** which possesses the tart, aromatic flavour so prized by good cooks. Tarragon is used in sauces, soups, egg, seafood, chicken and veal dishes. It is the perfect herb, when used sparingly, for delicate foods. It can be stored in vinegar—then the flavoured vinegar is used to make a great vinaigrette dressing. A little tarragon goes a long way—its flavour is strong and quickly diffuses through hot dishes.

Thyme is a powerfully aromatic perennial and one of the great European culinary herbs. It is most important in the bouquet garni and used in bread stuffings and to flavour terrines. There are many varieties of thyme but the most popular is the grey shrubby garden thyme. The green leaf lemon-scented thyme is so lovely when added to chicken while it is cooking. There is even a honey fragrant with wild thyme.

Chives belong to the onion family but their delicate grass-like leaves have a far more delicate flavour. They are a great asset in many seafood, cheese and egg dishes and are almost indispensable in a potato and rice salad. In fact they are a herb which improves most salads. Try them with cucumber or snipped over beans or beetroot. They are finely chopped and added to cold sauces such as rémoulade and ravigote.

Chives should be picked frequently so that the plant will grow vigorously and the leaves develop a better flavour.

Garlic Chives may be used in much the same way as ordinary chives. They have coarser leaves, faintly scented with garlic.

Spices

Allspice is not, as those who only buy it ground may think, compounded of several spices. It is the tiny dried berries of a tree of the myrtle family. It has an aroma resembling a combination of cinnamon, cloves and nutmeg. Whole berries are used in pickling spice and in pickling herrings in Scandinavia. The berries may be ground in a pepper mill but their aroma is strong and a separate grinder should be kept for this purpose. When ground, Allspice is used sparingly to flavour marinades, terrines, meat dishes, cakes and puddings.

Cardamom Pods are a creamy green which have to be split open to release their highly aromatic seeds. These seeds are added whole to rice pilafs and Indian lentil dishes and one is often stuffed into the long spouts of the brass coffee pots the Bedouins use, giving the coffee an exotic flavour. Ground Cardamom is one of the spices which makes garam masala, an indispensable flavouring in many Indish dishes, and unusual though it may seem, is used often in Scandinavian cookery in their cakes, biscuits and desserts. This spice is most expensive and loses its aroma quite quickly when ground. Like all spices it should be stored in an airtight jar, bought in small quantities and replenished frequently.

Caraway Seeds taste of aniseed and are used a great deal in various parts of Europe to flavour breads, cakes, cheeses, cabbage dishes and even liqueurs. They are reputed to have a soothing effect on the digestion.

Cayenne is the ground product of various species of the chilli pepper and is extremely fiery. Used sparingly it gives a piquant taste to seafood dishes, egg and cheese dishes and some sauces. Not so long ago it was quite common to find a pot of cayenne pepper on the table alongside the pepper and salt.

Chillies are small hot peppers used a great deal in eastern food. There are many varieties. They may be added whole, fresh or dried to curries, chutneys and pickles and many eastern specialities and are often included in a good pickling spice. They are used lavishly in Mexican food, both whole and powdered.

Cinnamon is the bark of a tree native to Ceylon. It has a wonderful warm flavour and is bought in slim cinnamon-brown quills rolled up like a cigarette russe biscuit. **Cinamon Bark** is responsible for flavouring rice, curries, and many eastern and middle eastern dishes and is added while apples and apricots are cooking. **Ground,** it flavours creams, cakes and desserts, is perfect with chocolate, delicious sprinkled on cream in coffee or combined with sugar on hot buttered toast. It adds an aromatic quality to brandied fruits and to creamy rice desserts. Look for bark which is pale in colour and unbroken.

Cloves are the flower buds of an evergreen tree from Zanzibar. Cloves have a strong piercing flavour and must be used sparingly. A few cloves are often added while apples are cooking and a pinch of **Ground Clove** is most interesting in terrines and meat loaves and quite indispensable in Christmas mincemeat and puddings. A clove is often stuck into an onion to flavour a stock and in the scored fat of the Christmas ham which is then glazed. Cloves are spiked into oranges which, with other spices, form a pomander to scent clothes cupboards. They flavour hot wine toddies and gluwein greatly appreciated on cold winter evenings. Cloves contain a volatile oil which many of us have been thankful for when a toothache has proved too much.

Coriander are the dried seeds of a small plant. They have an aromatic orange flavour which is particularly favoured in eastern countries. **Ground Coriander** is used in most curries, and often flavours sausages and pickling mixtures.

Ginger is the aromatic root of the tuberous ginger plant. It is used a great deal in all eastern food. It has a spicy hot flavour which is delicious ground and rubbed into pot roasts and mixed with other spices for the famous English spiced beef. The English have a great liking for this spice and it turns up frequently in their cakes, biscuits and puddings. It flavours ginger beer, ginger ale and even a wine. **Root Ginger** preserved in a sweet syrup makes a delicious sweetmeat after dinner, especially when surrounded by dark chocolate. **Stem Ginger** is delicious sliced and mixed into a fresh fruit salad or into sweetened cream cheese, ice cream and cream desserts.

Green ginger may be successfully stored in the refrigerator for quite a long time tied securely in a plastic bag. When you wish to use it, peel a little and grate it or peel a quantity of root ginger, cut into chunks and store in dry sherry.

Juniper Berries grow on a shrub belonging to the cypress pine family. They take three years to ripen to their deep blue colour, then they are picked and dried. They impart a sweet aromatic and slightly sharp flavour to stews, game, sauerkraut and other cabbage dishes, terrines, pork and stuffings for goose and duck. They are the most important of the aromatics in gin which takes its name from the Latin for Juniper Berry, "ginepro".

Mace is the lacy cage surrounding the nutmeg. After it is removed, it is pressed flat and dried and its colour changes from scarlet to an orange brown. Its flavour is similar to nutmeg but more refined and it is much more expensive to buy. Mace may be added to sauces, soups, stews, stuffings, meat and shellfish cakes and desserts. **Oil of Mace** was once reputed to cure insomnia.

Mustard seeds come from the mustard plant. The whole seeds are excellent in cabbage and potato salads and are essential in a pickling spice. Ground mustard is blended to form **mustard powder** and a pinch adds piquancy to cheese dishes, shellfish and bland sauces. Mustard is added to vinaigrette and other salad dressings; it helps stabilise a mayonnaise; it is sometimes spread on meats which are to be breadcrumbed and fried; it is added to rabbit dishes, oxtail, smoked fish, pigs trotters and it is universally used with ham and sausages. French mustards are more aromatic and kinder and less pungent than English mustard.

Mustard plasters and footbaths were once a popular remedy for colds, fevers and sciatica.

Nutmeg is the hard-dried seed of a tropical tree. It has a distinct aromatic quality which is easily lost when the nutmeg is ground. It is best to buy **whole nutmeg** which may be dark brown or white, caused by the lime used to discourage insects. There are small graters made especially for nutmeg so that the required amount can be grated freshly each time you wish to use it. Years ago the housekeepers of the great English country houses wore a silver nutmeg grater attached to a chain around their waist and, up to the end of the 19th century, no fastidious traveller would venture forth without a nutmeg and a grater so he could personally flavour his food or drink. Today nutmeg is an almost indispensable flavouring. The Italians adore it, as is witnessed by their food, the French and the English both use it in sauces, to heighten the flavour of cheese dishes, with fish, savoury and veal dishes, with spinach and carrots, in egg-nogs, cakes and many desserts. It is also widely used in the Middle and Far East and is supposed to have a soothing effect on the digestive system.

Paprika is the ground seed of the sweet pepper. The best quality comes from Hungary where there are many grades ranging from mildly hot, mild and sweet. A good quality paprika should be a rich, bright red with a warm, sweet aroma. One could call it the national spice of Hungary where it is used everywhere to flavour and colour. It flavours cheeses, sauces, egg dishes, chicken, seafoods, vegetables and hors d'oeuvres and its warm colour sprinkled on pale, creamy dishes looks most attractive.

Peppercorns come from a tropical vine. The **black** peppercorns are gathered immature and green. When dried they have a highly aromatic flavour. **White peppercorns** are the inner part of the ripe red berry after the husk has been removed. They are far hotter and more pungent than black peppercorns.

To appreciate the aromatic qualities of pepper at its best the peppercorns should be ground fresh from a pepper mill. Black pepper is the pepper preferred for everyday use. White pepper is often used for flavouring pale-coloured dishes such as white sauces and chicken, but mostly for aesthetic reasons only.

When buying peppercorns, make sure the grains are of an even size and colour and keep them in an airtight jar. Some cooks prefer the flavour of a mixture of black and white which is sometimes known as **Mignonette Pepper.** Pepper like many other spices is a stimulant and is an aid to digestion.

Poppyseed is widely used throughout Europe and especially in Jewish cookery. It flavours breads, meat and vegetable dishes, biscuits, cakes and puddings. **Ground Poppyseed** is used in some curries where its function is partly to flavour and partly to improve the texture and thicken the gravy.

Pickling spice usually comprises mustard seed, bay leaf, allspice, cinnamon bark, coriander seed and black peppercorns. Sometimes dried ginger root, chilli and mace are added. The proportions vary in different recipes but many people rely on one of the excellent ready-mixed pickling spices packaged by well-known spice companies.

Saffron comes from the stigmas of the saffron crocus. The stigmas are gathered by hand and it is estimated that between 75,000 and a quarter of a million flowers are necessary to produce 500 g (1 lb). Needless to say saffron is exceedingly expensive, but a pinch is sufficient to colour a dish golden and flavour it with its incredible perfume. Its warm, haunting scent is an essential ingredient in Bouillabaisse, Paëlla, many Mediterranean fish stews and soups, rice pilafs, eastern spiced meat dishes and the famous risotto from Milan. In England one can still buy saffron buns.

The tiny orange saffron stigmas look a bit like tobacco and they may be bought like this or in powdered form which is very expensive and one packet is only sufficient to flavour one dish. Cheap saffron does not exist. When adding saffron to a dish first infuse it in a small quantity of boiling water or stock until it has turned the liquid a deep bright orange.

In Elizabethan times saffron was a popular hair dye and was reputed to cure fainting fits and palpitations of the heart.

soups

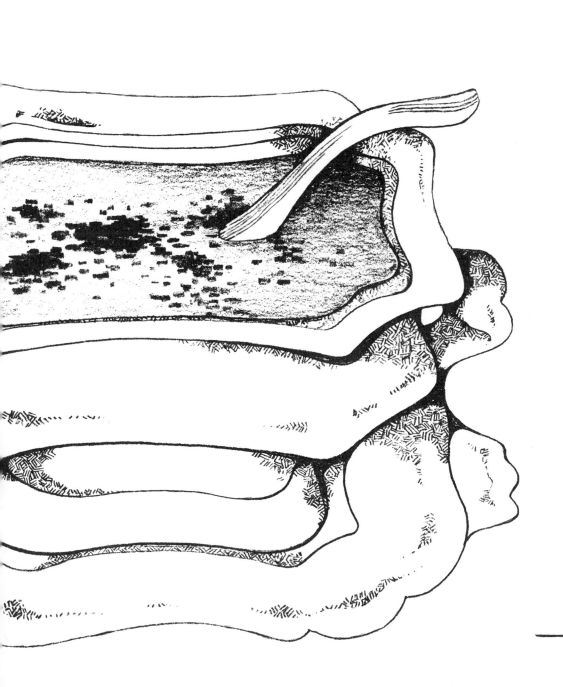

Mushroom Soup

Soups

Mushroom Soup

A delicious old-fashioned mushroom soup which, you'll probably agree, is the best you've ever tasted.

375 g (12 oz) mushrooms
60 g (2 oz) butter
1 clove garlic, crushed
1 tablespoon parsley, finely chopped
salt
freshly ground pepper
grated nutmeg
1 thick slice of bread with the crusts
   removed
4 cups chicken stock or water and stock
   cubes
½ cup cream
extra parsley, finely chopped

Rinse the mushrooms in cold water and wipe dry with a damp cloth. Do not peel or remove stalks. Chop into small pieces. Heat the butter in a heavy-based saucepan and add the mushrooms. Allow them to cook gently until soft. After a few minutes add the garlic, parsley and season with salt, pepper and a little nutmeg. Cook for a further few minutes.

Soak the bread slice in a little of the stock and then squeeze out all the moisture and add to the mushrooms. Stir to combine the bread with the mushrooms. Heat the stock and add to the mushrooms. Cook the soup for 15 minutes.

Place the soup in a blender and blend at high speed until it is smooth—or rub through a sieve. Return it to the saucepan and when reheated add the cream. Serve in bowls garnished with finely chopped parsley. Serves 4.

Pondicherry Soup

Delicious leek soup with a subtle taste of curry.

6 leeks
30 g (1 oz) butter
1 teaspoon curry powder
90 g (3 oz) rice
4½ cups chicken stock
1 cup milk
salt
freshly ground pepper
1 egg yolk ⎫ beaten together
¼ cup cream ⎭

Split the leeks down to the white part and wash well. Cover with cold water and bring to the boil. Allow to boil gently for 10 minutes. Drain under running cold water and then chop them finely. Melt the butter in a large heavy pot, add the leeks and fry them gently for a few minutes. Remove from the heat and stir in the curry powder.

Add the rice, chicken stock and milk. Season with salt and pepper. Return the pot to the heat and cook the soup over a low heat for 30 minutes. Push through a sieve or purée in an electric blender. Return the purée to the heat and adjust the seasoning. Stir a little of the hot soup into the egg yolk and cream mixture and then add this to the remaining soup stirring all the time. Do not allow the soup to boil once the egg yolk and cream mixture has been added. Serve hot.

Pumpkin Soup

Trust the frugal French to make the most of a simple vegetable like pumpkin. This is a beautiful soup which often costs a fortune in good restaurants but which can be made at home for little more than a song.

60 g (2 oz) butter
4½ cups peeled, chopped pumpkin
½ cup finely chopped onion
3 cups water
30 g (1 oz) butter
2 tablespoons plain flour
1 cup milk
1 egg yolk (optional)

Melt 60 g (2 oz) butter in a heavy pan and add the pumpkin and the onion. Cook for 10 minutes stirring constantly. Add the water and cook gently until the pumpkin is very tender.

Press through a sieve or purée in an electric blender with a little milk.

Melt 30 g (1 oz) butter and then stir in the flour, add the pumpkin purée and milk gradually stirring constantly until well blended. Simmer for 20 minutes. Just before serving combine the egg yolk with a little of the pumpkin soup. Stir into the remaining soup. Serves 6.

Onion Soup

Onion soup is the French classic, which, traditionally, was served in the early hours of the morning at Les Halles, the main Paris markets.

This soup is thick with onions and bread and although it is usually made with beef stock sometimes it is made with a mixture of milk and water—sometimes just water. It's very filling and can be served as a meal (make sure you have enough for second-helpings)—or a small bowl as a first course.

45 g (1½ oz) butter
1 tablespoon oil
750 g (1½ lb) onions, thinly sliced
1 teaspoon salt
2 tablespoons plain flour
7 cups beef stock
½ cup dry white wine
freshly ground pepper
rounds of French bread, cut into 2.5 cm
** (1 in) slices**

Melt the butter and the oil in a large, heavy saucepan. Add the onions and allow them to cook very slowly until softened and golden, stirring occasionally. Do not allow them to brown. Sprinkle with salt and stir in the flour. When blended allow to cook over a moderate heat for 3 minutes. Remove from the heat and stir in the stock. Add the wine. Season with pepper. Cover the pot and allow to simmer for 30 to 40 minutes skimming the surface of the soup occasionally.

While the soup is cooking, bake the bread slices on a baking sheet in a moderately slow oven (325°F—160°C) for about 30 minutes until crisp and lightly coloured.

If desired the bread can be brushed with a little olive oil halfway through cooking, and after baking each slice rubbed lightly with a cut clove of garlic.

Onion Soup Gratinée

onion soup (as above)
rounds of French bread, baked or toasted
250 g (8 oz) gruyère or emmenthaler
** cheese, finely sliced**

Bring soup to the boil. Place prepared bread into a soup tureen or bowls. Pour boiling soup over the bread. Scatter the cheese over the top and place under a hot griller until the cheese melts and browns lightly. Serve straight away.

Mulligatawny

A highly spiced dish which is not really a soup. This dish has a great deal of sauce and is usually served in a large old-fashioned soup plate with boiled rice spooned into the centre of each plate.

Sometimes a bowl of rice is served on the side, then guests may spoon the rice at will into the spicy mixture.

3 pints strong stock

60 g (2 oz) butter

3 medium onions, sliced

12 curry leaves (optional)

4 teaspoons curry powder or curry paste

1 cup thinly sliced celery

1½ cups diced cooked meat or chicken

2 cups coconut milk

lemon wedges

Make a well-flavoured stock with beef bones, lamb shanks or chicken, or use stock cubes of any flavour. Heat butter in a large saucepan and gently fry onions until golden. Add curry leaves and curry powder and fry a minute longer. Add stock and celery and simmer for 20 minutes. Add meat or chicken and the coconut milk and bring almost to boiling again. Taste for seasonings. Serve with lemon wedges which are squeezed over the soup just before eating.

Sometimes Mulligatawny is served with hot boiled rice. Put a spoonful of rice into each bowl first and ladle the Mulligatawny over. Serves 6 to 8.

Tomato and Orange Soup

A delicate soup flavoured with orange juice and slivers of orange rind.

1 kg (2 lb) ripe firm tomatoes

1 onion, peeled

1 carrot, sliced

1 strip of lemon peel

1 bay leaf

6 peppercorns

4½ cups chicken stock

good pinch of salt

45 g (1½ oz) butter

3 tablespoons flour

rind and juice of half an orange

½ cup cream

Wash the tomatoes, cut in half and squeeze them to remove their seeds. Put them in a saucepan with the onion, carrot, lemon peel, bay leaf, peppercorns, stock and salt. Cover the pan and cook for about 30 minutes until the tomatoes are soft and pulpy. Rub through a sieve. Clean the saucepan, melt the butter and then stir in the flour. Cook over a low heat for 1 minute stirring all the time. Take off the heat and stir in cold tomato stock gradually. Return to the heat and bring to the boil and simmer for five minutes.

Cut the orange rind into needle thin shreds. Blanch in boiling water and drain in a sieve. Add the orange juice to the soup and season with salt and pepper.

Just before serving stir the cream into the hot soup. Pour it into a tureen or bowls and sprinkle with orange rind.

Vegetable Soup

2 cups diced vegetables in season
(carrots, onion, celery)

45 g (1½ oz) butter

2 tablespoons flour

4 cups stock

salt and freshly ground pepper

finely chopped parsley or herbs in season

Chop the vegetables into small dice. Melt the butter and fry the vegetables gently but do not allow them to colour. Sprinkle with flour and cook for a few minutes.

Add the stock, season with salt and pepper and simmer the soup for 15 to 20 minutes. Adjust seasoning and sprinkle with finely chopped parsley.

Stock: See page 14 or use good instant soup stock powder. "Continental" market a variety in 100 g (3¼ oz) jars. For this soup try beef or chicken.

Minestrone

Minestrone

A hearty Italian vegetable soup which differs from region to region. It's said minestrone should be so thick a spoon will stand up in it. Though this recipe is not quite as thick as that, it is still a rich, thick hearty soup.

90 g (3 oz) red kidney beans
1 kg (2 lb) shin of beef on the bone
5 litres (8 pints) water
1 large brown onion, sliced
12 peppercorns
salt
2 large tomatoes, skinned
1 tablespoon olive oil
1 stalk celery, sliced
1 carrot, chopped
1 clove garlic, crushed
125 g (4 oz) pork belly, diced
1 tablespoon tomato paste
125 g (4 oz) cauliflower (coarse stalk removed)
freshly ground pepper
60 g (2 oz) fine spaghetti
grated parmesan cheese

Soak red kidney beans in some cold water overnight. Put the shin of beef in a large saucepan with the water and simmer covered with the onion, peppercorns, drained kidney beans and 2 teaspoons of salt for 2 hours or until the meat is very tender. Skim the surface occasionally to clear the stock. Strain it. Remove the meat from the bone and add to the stock. Cool and then refrigerate. When the fat has set on the surface, remove it.

Cut the tomatoes in quarters and sauté in hot olive oil with the celery, carrot and garlic for 10 minutes until the vegetables are golden brown.

Add the stock to the vegetables and the diced pork, the tomato paste and cauliflower broken into small pieces. Season with salt and pepper and simmer the soup for 45 minutes. After 30 minutes cooking add the spaghetti.

Serve with a bowl of grated parmesan cheese.

Zuppa alla Pavese

This soup was first prepared for Francis I, King of France, during the battle of Pavia. He had stopped by at a local farmhouse and the cook, realising she had a royal person in the house, turned her minestrone into this light and elegant soup.

8 thick slices of French loaf
60 g (2 oz) butter
8 eggs
4 tablespoons freshly grated parmesan cheese
salt
4 cups clear stock

Fry the bread quickly in butter until golden brown on both sides but still soft inside. Place 2 slices of bread into each soup bowl which has been heated.

Break 2 eggs carefully into each bowl, sprinkle with a tablespoon of parmesan cheese and a pinch of salt. Bring the stock to the boil and swiftly, but as carefully as possible, pour a cup of this into each bowl. Allow the stock to continue to boil as you fill the bowls. This is important as the stock must be so hot that it cooks the eggs. Serve immediately.

Tomato Savory Soup

This is a rich, thick tomato soup subtly flavoured with winter savory.

3 large tomatoes, peeled
1 medium onion, sliced
1 small clove garlic, peeled
1 teaspoon salt
¼ teaspoon freshly ground pepper
2 sprigs winter savory
1 tablespoon tomato paste
¼ cup cold water
½ cup cooked macaroni
1 cup chicken stock
¾ cup cream

Slice the tomatoes into a saucepan. Add the onion, garlic, seasonings, winter savory, tomato paste and water. Bring to the boil, cover and simmer for 12 to 15 minutes. Transfer to an electric blender. Add the macaroni. Cover and blend at high speed. Uncover and add the stock and half the cream. Blend once more. If you do not have a blender push the soup through a sieve.

Serve hot with the remaining cream swirled in at the last moment.

Variations:
- Finely chopped peeled tomato may be added for a garnish.
- Fresh dill may be substituted for winter savory.
- Fresh lemon thyme or 1 teaspoon of dried dill may also be substituted.

Broccoli Soup

A vegetable soup, green in colour with the wonderful flavour of fresh broccoli.

30 g (1 oz) butter
1 onion, finely sliced
1 carrot, finely sliced
1 celery stalk, finely sliced
1 bunch broccoli (fresh or frozen)
4 cups chicken stock
salt and cayenne pepper
¾ cup cream
1 egg yolk
1 tablespoon snipped chives

Melt the butter in a saucepan, add the onion, carrot and celery and sauté gently until soft (about 4 minutes). Trim the woody ends of the broccoli stalks and roughly cut up the heads and remaining stalk. Add the broccoli to the pan with the chicken stock and season with salt and cayenne pepper. Bring to the boil, cover and simmer for about 25 minutes or until the broccoli is tender.

Rub vegetables through a sieve and then work them to a cream or purée in an electric blender. Return to the saucepan and heat until lightly boiling. Remove from the heat, stir a little of the hot purée into the cream which has been mixed with the egg yolk and then add this to the remaining purée. Return to the heat and stir until the soup has thickened slightly. Serve immediately, sprinkled with chives.

Lettuce and Sorrel Soup

1 small lettuce heart
6 sorrel leaves
4½ cups good chicken stock
salt
freshly ground pepper

Shred the lettuce and sorrel leaves very finely and drop into boiling water. After two minutes drain in a colander and reserve. Heat the chicken stock gently until it comes to the boil. Season to taste and just before serving add the blanched lettuce and sorrel. Heat through and serve.

Variations:
- Serve over thin slices of French bread which have been dried in a slow oven.
- Purée the soup in a blender. Place back on the heat and stir in 2 egg yolks which have been lightly beaten with ½ cup of cream. Do not allow this soup to boil or the egg yolks will curdle.

Note: Two silverbeet leaves may be used in place of sorrel.

Top: Tomato Savory Soup
Below: Broccoli Soup

Spinach Soup

500 g (1 lb) fresh spinach, well washed and
  trimmed
45 g (1½ oz) butter
1 tablespoon flour
5 cups milk
½ cup cream
freshly grated nutmeg
salt, freshly ground pepper

Cook the spinach in salted boiling water until tender. Drain and push through a sieve.

Melt the butter in a heavy saucepan and when the foam has subsided, blend in the flour and stir over a low heat for 1 minute to cook the roux. Remove from the heat and stir in the milk gradually and, when smooth, return to the heat and stir until it comes to the boil, allow to simmer 5 minutes and add the spinach purée and the cream. Bring to the boil, season with nutmeg, salt, and pepper. Serve hot with croûtons.

Slimmers' Yoghurt Soup

½ cup natural yoghurt
2½ cups tomato juice
½ garlic clove, crushed
salt
freshly ground pepper
60 g (2 oz) prawns, peeled
Garnish:
extra yoghurt
prawns, peeled
1 tablespoon finely chopped chives

Place the yoghurt, tomato juice and half garlic clove in a blender. Blend at high speed until smooth. Season with salt and pepper and place in a bowl with the prawns. Chill.

Serve in individual bowls garnished with a small spoonful of yoghurt, a few prawns and a sprinkling of finely chopped chives.

Variations:
- Substitute finely chopped basil for chives.
- Flavour the soup with orange. Add ¼ cup of orange juice to 2¼ cups of tomato juice.
- Garnish with finely sliced green pepper instead of chives or diced tomato and finely chopped mint leaves.

Chicken Broth with Tripolini

This soup gets its name from the small Italian pastina that is used. Tripolini are small egg bows. Other shapes that may be used are alphabet shapes, tiny squares of egg flakes called tagliarini, small shells (conchigliette) or little peppercorns (acini di pepe).

¾ cup small egg noodles
4 cups chicken stock
grated parmesan cheese

Cook the egg noodles in 4 cups of boiling salted water for 10 minutes. Drain. Meanwhile bring the chicken stock to the boil. Gradually add the drained egg noodles.

Serve immediately with a bowl of grated parmesan cheese.

Oyster Soup

30 g (1 oz) butter
2 tablespoons plain flour
3½ cups fish stock (page 14)
2 dozen oysters
½ cup cream

Melt the butter in a heavy saucepan. Stir in the flour and cook over a gentle heat for about 1 minute. Pour on the stock and bring to the boil stirring constantly. Allow to simmer for 15 minutes.

Place the oysters and cream in a soup tureen or soup bowls and pour the boiling soup over them. Season to taste.

Cucumber Soup

Cucumber and mint flavour this refreshing soup which may be served hot in winter and chilled in the summer.

2 cucumbers, peeled and sliced
½ cup chopped shallots
4 cups chicken stock
30 g (1 oz) butter
15 g (½ oz) plain flour
salt
freshly ground pepper
1 egg yolk
¼ cup cream
2 tablespoons mint, finely chopped

Slice the cucumbers into thick pieces. Place with the shallot and chicken stock into a large saucepan. Bring to the boil and then simmer for 20 minutes.

Rub through a sieve or purée in an electric blender. Rinse the saucepan, melt the butter and then stir in the flour. Cook over a low heat for 1 minute and then add the cucumber purée. Stir the soup, season with salt and pepper and allow it to come to the boil. Simmer gently for 10 minutes.

Just before serving, mix the egg yolk with the cream in a small bowl. Combine with a little of the hot soup and then slowly pour the egg yolk mixture into the soup. Stir until it thickens slightly but don't boil again. Stir in the finely chopped mint.

Short Soup

A bowl of soup is always part of the simplest Chinese meal. For this soup it is better to use a good, home-made chicken stock.

3 dozen Won Ton (page 84)
6 to 8 cups chicken stock
sliced shallots to garnish

Have the Won Ton ready. Heat chicken stock and season well to taste with salt. When boiling add the Won Ton and simmer for 5 to 8 minutes. Serve in bowls with few slices of shallot on each.

Sweet and Sour Short Soup

Prepare the Sweet and Sour Sauce on Page 189. Deep fry the Won Ton in hot oil until golden and cooked, then drain and place on serving dish. Pour the hot sauce over and serve immediately.

● When adding Won Ton to the simmering stock, add a few at a time, otherwise, they will fall to bottom of pan and stick. Give a few gentle stirs at beginning of cooking.

Pea Soup

Thanks to the English and Dutch we have thick, wholesome pea soup flavoured with a hambone. Pea soup has been immortalised in many nursery rhymes and is a great favourite.

500 g (1 lb) split green peas, soaked in
water overnight
2 litres (3 pts) water
1 ham bone
salt
freshly ground pepper
1 Bratwurst sausage or 6 frankfurts

Bring the ham bone, peas and water to the boil. Season with a little salt and pepper. Simmer for 30 minutes. Remove the ham bone and cut off the pieces of ham. Strain soup through a sieve. Reheat and add the ham pieces and slices of sausage which have been heated gently in a little water. Season again to taste.

Borsch (see recipe on page 56)

Pondicherry Soup (see recipe on page 45)

55

Borsch

Borsch is one of the three basic Russian soups but there are so many versions it would take months to try them all. This one came to us via a Swiss—which may seem unusual—but we respect his good judgment.

4 to 5 beetroot
2 medium potatoes, peeled and diced
8 cups of well-flavoured beef stock
juice of 1 lemon
freshly ground pepper
reduced sour cream
finely chopped chives

Place the beetroot (leaving some of the stems on) in 10 to 12 cups of cold salted water, bring slowly to the boil, cover the pot and simmer for 20 minutes. Cool, then peel and grate into medium thick shreds.

Place the shredded beetroot and diced potatoes into the beef stock and cook until the potatoes turn to a pulp. Add lemon juice to taste. Season with a little pepper. Serve with a dollop of sour cream and some finely chopped chives or, better still, swirl the sour cream into the Borsch just before serving and serve a bowl of chopped chives.

Note: This soup may be made in advance and then gently reheated and the sour cream swirled in at the last moment.

Sherry Flavoured Consommé

A consommé made with strongly flavoured clear stock with a rich brown colour. It may be served hot or jellied and is usually garnished.

4 cups cold brown stock (page 15)
2 egg whites, lightly beaten
2 egg shells
250 g ($\frac{1}{2}$ lb) finely minced lean beef
$\frac{1}{4}$ cup dry flor sherry

To clarify consommé: Remove any fat from the stock and place in a saucepan with the egg whites, egg shells and beef. Bring slowly to the boil, whisking occasionally. Allow the liquid to rise in the pan and draw it aside. Boil up carefully once more, taking care not to break the crust which will form on the top. Draw aside, lower the heat and then simmer the soup very gently for 30 minutes. This slow simmering will extract all the flavour from the meat.

Strain through a colander lined with butter muslin holding back the egg white crust with a spoon and then at the end, sliding it out on to the cloth. The consommé should now be clear. Return to the heat and add $\frac{1}{4}$ cup of dry sherry and the garnish.

A little sherry can make a consommé but too much can break it. Use a good dry flor sherry—1 to 2 teaspoons for each serving according to your taste. Sherry flavoured consommé is excellent on its own but it is often garnished and takes its name from the particular garnish.

Consommé Royale

Custard: Break up 1 egg white with a whisk or fork but do not make it frothy. Add 4 tablespoons cream and season with salt and white pepper. Pour into a small mould or cup and steam or poach this custard for 30 minutes or until set. Allow to cool completely and then turn out. Slice into strips or cut into shapes. Add to soup (recipe above) just before serving.

Consommé Celestine

Very finely slice a pancake which has been rolled up tightly and add to hot consomme just before serving.

Consommé Madrilene

Technically speaking, a Madrilene is a clear soup strongly flavoured with tomato. This version is not clear but still uses the traditional chicken stock and tomato.

1 medium onion, finely chopped
30 g (1 oz) butter
8 cups strong chicken stock
1 × 425 g (15 oz) tin of tomatoes
1 large bouquet garni containing a strip
    of lemon peel
salt and freshly ground pepper
½ cup sherry
1 tablespoon arrowroot
lemon juice
cream for garnishing
chopped chives

Soften the onion in the butter and add the stock, tomatoes and bouquet garni. Season with salt and pepper. Cover and simmer for 40 minutes. Rub through a sieve. Rinse the pan out, add the sherry, reduce by half and then add the sieved soup. Slake the arrowroot with 2 tablespoons of water or stock and thicken the soup. Reboil and add a few drops of lemon juice. Adjust the seasoning and serve with a spoonful of cream swirled into each cup and a sprinkling of chopped chives.

Note: The soup should be quite thin with a well spiced flavour. It may also be served iced with a slice of lemon in each cup. In this case, omit the cream.

Iced Soups

Iced Cucumber Soup

Iced cucumber soup is the kind of first course which is ideal for Christmas dinner in Australia where so often heatwave conditions prevail.

6 small white onions
4 large cucumbers
3 tablespoons butter
3 teaspoons plain flour
6½ cups chicken stock
salt and freshly ground pepper
lemon juice
Angostura bitters
2 egg yolks
1 cup cream
finely chopped mint, chives, parsley or dill
1 cucumber cut into tiny dice but
    unpeeled for garnish

Peel the onions and chop them finely. Peel the cucumbers and cut into chunks. Melt the butter and cook the onions and cucumber in a covered pan until soft. Blend in the flour, gradually add the stock and season with salt and pepper. Cover and simmer for about 20 minutes.

Remove from the heat, adjust the seasoning and add a little lemon juice and a few drops of Angostura bitters. Blend in an electric blender or push through a fine sieve. Return to the saucepan and reheat.

Beat the egg yolks with the cream, blend in a few spoonfuls of the hot soup.

Add the egg and cream mixture to the soup in the pan and cook until it thickens but do not allow it to boil. Remove from heat, cool and then chill in the refrigerator.

Serve scattered with finely chopped mint, chives, parsley or dill and tiny cucumber dice.

Gazpacho

A soup from Spain that could well have been created to combat summer heat waves.

500 g (1 lb) tomatoes
1 cucumber
2 cloves garlic, crushed
3 shallots, finely chopped
12 black olives, stoned and halved
1 green pepper, blanched and chopped
2 tablespoons olive oil
1 tablespoon vinegar
salt and freshly ground pepper
pinch cayenne pepper
4 slices brown bread
1 tablespoon chopped parsley
1 cup iced water
ice cubes

Peel tomatoes, cutting out the core, and chop them finely, almost to a purée. Peel cucumber and cut in small dice. Put tomato and cucumber in a large bowl or soup tureen, with garlic, shallots, olives, and green pepper.

Measure in oil and vinegar, season with salt and pepper to taste and add cayenne.

Remove crusts from bread and cut into small cubes. Add to soup with the parsley, iced water and ice. Stir well and serve immediately.

● The Spanish often choose Gazpacho for an easy to eat and reviving mid-day meal. Chopped hard-boiled egg may be sprinkled over each serving, and sometimes a glass of wine is used in place of water, making it more of a meal.

Iced Cream of Curry Soup

A smooth and creamy soup flavoured delicately with curry, chicken and apples. This soup is equally delicious served hot or cold. For summer meals, however, serve well chilled.

2 onions
30 g (1 oz) butter
2 teaspoons curry powder
2 cooking apples
1 teaspoon plain flour
2 cups chicken stock
1 cup dry white wine
pinch cayenne pepper
salt and ground white pepper
1 cup cream
½ cup finely diced, cooked chicken
   (optional)

Chop the onions. Heat the butter and add the onions and curry powder and cook gently (sweat) over a low heat until the onions are soft and transparent.

Peel and slice apples thinly. Add to the pan and cook until they become transparent. Stir in the flour and cook over a slightly higher heat for 5 minutes, stirring constantly. Add the stock, wine, cayenne, salt and pepper. Bring to the boil and simmer for 10 minutes, stirring occasionally.

Sieve the soup or purée in an electric blender. Cool and chill. Just before serving, stir well-chilled cream and diced chicken into the soup or garnish with wafer-thin slices of lemon.

Gazpacho

Cream Soups

Crème Olga

This beautiful cream soup preserves the full flavour of the mushrooms, by adding them raw just before serving.

4 tablespoons butter
2 bunches of shallots
1 garlic clove
salt and freshly ground white pepper
4 tablespoons flour
3 cups chicken stock
2 cups of flat field mushrooms, sliced
½ cup cream
pinch of tarragon

Melt the butter in a pan. Slice the shallots, using their green stems as well, and add them with the garlic to the pan. Season with salt and pepper. Allow the vegetables to sweat in the butter but not to brown. When the vegetables are soft, blend in the flour and stir while adding stock. Bring to the boil and then simmer for a few minutes. Rub through a sieve with the raw mushrooms, then return soup to the pan. Add the cream and tarragon, reheat and serve.

Cream of Broccoli Soup

This wonderful creamy soup with the fresh flavour of broccoli may be made all the year round. Make it with the fresh broccoli in season, and use frozen broccoli at other times of the year.

1 medium onion, sliced
1 medium carrot, sliced
1 small celery stalk, sliced
1 garlic clove
½ cup water
2 cups cooked broccoli, coarsely chopped
1 teaspoon salt
pinch cayenne pepper
½ cup cooked macaroni
1 cup chicken stock
½ cup cream
sour cream

Place the onion, carrot, celery, garlic and water in a saucepan. Bring to the boil and then lower the heat and simmer for 10 minutes. Transfer to an electric blender and add the broccoli, salt, cayenne pepper and macaroni. Blend at the highest speed. Add the stock and cream and blend. It you haven't got a blender push the soup through a sieve.

Chill and serve with a spoonful of sour cream.

Cream of Chicken Soup

A lovely old-fashioned soup, relying for its flavour on a good chicken stock. This is a basic cream soup to which you can add garnishes such as finely sliced chicken meat, fine slices of ham, small cubes of avocado, etc.

6 cups chicken stock
$\frac{1}{2}$ cup cream
$\frac{1}{2}$ cup milk
2 tablespoons butter
2 tablespoons plain flour

Heat the chicken stock, add the cream and milk and bring to the boil.

Cream the butter with the flour and add gradually to the soup. Stir until the flour and butter are incorporated and the soup thickened slightly. Do not allow it to boil.

Garnish as desired with chopped parsley, finely shredded ham, sliced celery, finely sliced chicken or cubed avocado.

Pea Soup (see recipe on page 53)

Slimmers' Yoghurt Soup (see recipe on page 52)

appetisers

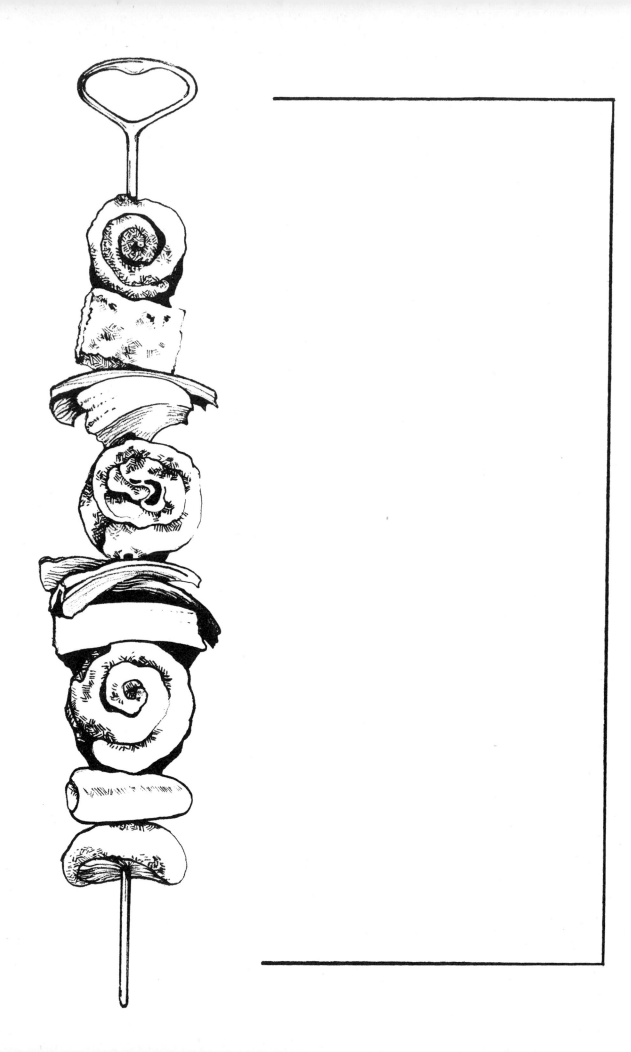

Cold Appetisers

Hors d'oeuvres Variés

Hors d'oeuvre originated in Russia as a host of small, lavish dishes devised to stimulate the appetite. Today the aim is still the same but there is no need for lavish preparation. This is a course which may be prepared on the spur of the moment from the refrigerator and kitchen cupboard, or by taking a quick trip to the delicatessen. Its success depends on the imagination used in selecting the ingredients and on their preparation.

As a guide, we list below a selection of ingredients suitable for hors d'oeuvre:

- Italian or other varieties of salami. Slice thinly and fold or roll loosely before arranging on a dish.
- Coppa ham, prosciutto or ham deluxe. Slice paper thin, roll loosely, fold or arrange in overlapping slices.
- Artichoke hearts in oil—these are obtainable in small jars in continental delicatessens and should be drained before using and seasoned with some freshly ground black pepper. If using artichokes packed in brine, wash well, drain and marinate in a well seasoned vinaigrette for at least 1 hour. Drain, cut in half if large, and sprinkle with chopped herbs.
- Pickled mussels (these are sold in 200 g (6½ oz) jars). Drain, add squeeze of lemon juice and freshly ground black pepper or marinate in vinaigrette dressing and drain before serving.
- Tomato—choose medium-sized ripe, firm tomatoes. Cut into thick slices and sprinkle with a little vinaigrette dressing and chopped herbs or chopped, blanched shallots or garnish with a spoon of thick sour cream and chives or red or black lumpfish roe.
- Feta cheese—cut in 1 cm (½ in) cubes.
- Black or green olives—there are many varieties to choose from—the pointed Calamata olives from Greece, the Spanish olives, stuffed olives, or large Queen olives, for example.

For marinated olives: Pack black olives into a jar with 2 crushed garlic cloves, a few parsley stalks and 1 small chilli pepper. Fill the jar with good olive oil and marinate for a few days before using. Drain to serve.

- Baby beetroot—available in jars from delicatessens. Scoop out the top of each with a melon baller and garnish with mayonnaise or formosa butter and sprinkle with chopped herbs or shallots.
- Asparagus spears—select slim white variety which have good flavour, and are tender but do not break up. Drain, season with vinaigrette and sprinkle with chopped parsley.
- Radish—trim the stalk end by cutting a thin slice off the top of the radish. Garnish with 1 teaspoon of mayonnaise or formosa butter and chopped herbs.
- Cucumber—peel and score the cucumber by running a fork down the surface. Cut in thick slices, salt lightly and leave for half an hour. Drain and wash under running cold water, dry with paper towels and garnish with a mound of sour cream and some Danish lumpfish roe or chives. Danish lumpfish roe (Danish caviar) is available in small 45 g (1½ oz) jars in either red or black variety.
- Baby mushrooms—obtainable in jars packed in brine. Wash well, drain and marinate for 1 hour in vinaigrette dressing, well-flavoured with herbs.
- Green, red or yellow peppers—slice off top, remove seeds and cut into thin rings.
- Formosa Butter—cream 60 g (2 oz) butter and blend with the sieved yolks of 2 hard-boiled eggs. Flavour with ½ teaspoon of dry mustard, salt and freshly ground pepper. This may be piped through a rose tube or dropped from a teaspoon.

To arrange the ingredients for a plate of hors d'oeuvre, consider the balance of colour, texture and flavour. For example, the soft, juicy texture, sweetness and colour of a ripe tomato combines with the crispness of a green pepper, the saltiness of black olives. The crisp, fresh taste of cucumber is good with the richness of sour cream which in turn is dressed attractively with a sprinkling of salty tasting red or black lumpfish roe.

Artichokes

To prepare artichokes for cooking: Remove the tough outside leaves and then cut one-third off the top of the artichoke and trim the stalk and outer leaves.

As each one is prepared, place into a bowl of cold water to cover into which is squeezed plenty of lemon juice to prevent them from discolouring. This method of preparing them gives a most attractive shape. Or the sharp points of the leaves may simply be trimmed with scissors and the stalk cut off level with the base. Place in water with lemon juice as you prepare them.

To cook: Place them in boiling salted water with a slice of lemon and boil gently for 30 to 45 minutes depending on the age and size. When cooked, drain and with a sharp-pointed knife cut the centre leaves out—this should reveal the fuzzy choke. Remove this carefully with a small teaspoon; the sauce or dressing may then be put into this cavity. Place the artichoke on an individual serving plate with the centre leaves beside it. Serve warm with melted butter, hollandaise, rémoulade or mayonnaise or warm or cold with vinaigrette dressing. A little finely chopped parsley may be scattered over them before serving.

How to eat an artichoke: Pull the leaves off one at a time and dip the tender fleshy base into the sauce and eat this choice morsel. Provide finger bowls filled with warm water and ample napkins.

Rémoulade Sauce

To 1 cup of mayonnaise add 1 good teaspoon of French mustard and 1 tablespoon of chopped gherkins, capers, parsley and tarragon mixed together. When thoroughly combined, stir in a few drops of anchovy essence.

The regal globe artichoke should not be confused with the small cream tuberous Jerusalem artichoke which is a winter vegetable, most often puréed and used to make an excellent soup.

Italian Artichokes in Wine

Cut the artichokes lengthwise into quarters. Put into cold water to cover with some lemon slices as you prepare them. Drain on paper towels. Heat a little olive oil in a heavy pan with a sprig of fresh or a pinch of dried oregano and 1 clove of garlic. Add the artichokes and cook over a moderate heat, turning and tossing the artichokes until they are burnished and crispy on the outside. Remove garlic clove. Add ½ cup of white wine, season with some salt and freshly ground pepper, cover the pan and simmer gently until the artichokes are tender, about 10 to 15 minutes. Serve warm as a first course.

Note: At the beginning of the season the elongated Italian artichokes are available. They have hardly any choke and what choke they do have, is not worth worrying about.

Avocado Seafood

Cut the flesh of 1 ripe medium-sized tomato and 1 ripe avocado into cubes. Combine with two green shallots finely chopped and half a cup of shelled prawns, crayfish or crab or a seafood combination. Season with salt and pepper and toss with two tablespoons of vinaigrette dressing. Serve chilled and sprinkled with finely chopped herbs.

Guacamole

Cut two avocados in half, remove seeds and flesh. Cut flesh into chunks and blend at high speed until smooth or push through a sieve. Crush 1 small clove of garlic with 1 teaspoon of salt and add to the avocado purée with two teaspoons of finely-chopped onion and a few drops of tabasco sauce. A few rashers of crumbled crisp cooked bacon may be added for a variation. Cover and chill. Serve with crackers as a dip or spread it on cold poached chicken breasts, cold poached fish or seafood.

Les Crudites

Avocado Salad

Cut 1 medium ripe peeled tomato and the flesh of 1 avocado into good size pieces, mix with two finely chopped shallots and toss with 2 tablespoons of vinaigrette mixed with a little canned pimento which has been rubbed through a sieve. Serve chilled on a glass dish, in a crisp lettuce leaf or piled back into a scooped out avocado shell. Accompany with a lemon slice and some finely chopped herbs.

Les Crudites (raw vegetables)

One of the favourite hors d'oeuvres of provincial France is a simple arrangement of crisp, young and fresh raw vegetables. The prepared vegetables should be crisped in iced water. Once crisped they will keep well in any air-tight container. Arrange the vegetables as simply as you like, we used a wire basket. Serve crudites with aioli, Provence's famous garlic mayonnaise, and vinaigrette dressings for dipping. (Recipes for these dressings on page 273).

Preparing Vegetables

Celery: Wash and cut stalks in 12 cm (5 in) lengths. "Fray" ends by making 2 cm (1 in) cuts, 5 mm ($\frac{1}{4}$ in) apart, lengthwise at each end of stalk. Use a stainless steel knife. Drop into a large bowl of iced water and leave for 45 minutes to 1 hour to allow stalks to curl and become crisp.
Carrots: Wash, peel and trim small young carrots, then cut each one in quarters. If only large carrots are available, cut each one in two, across, then quarter each half lengthwise. Drop in iced water to crisp.
Radishes: Use only small, round, firm ones which are bright red. Trim top leaves, leaving small leaf intact. (The one leaf left makes it easier for guests to eat the radish in their fingers). Wash radishes well. For radish roses use a small, sharp knife and shave thin, petal-shaped strips of the red peel from the radish tip to within 5 mm ($\frac{1}{4}$ in) of the base— without detaching the peel from the radish. Put radishes in iced water and the "roses" will open. A second layer of petals can be cut under the first to make a fuller rose.
Shallots: Wash, remove outside leaf and trim off root and green tops, about 5 cm (2 in) above the fork of the leaves. Keep in iced water until ends curl.
Tomatoes: Use very firm small tomatoes, preferably the cherry tomato variety. Wash and chill. If using larger tomatoes halve or quarter them.

Asparagus Milanese

Wrap 2 to 3 freshly cooked (or canned) asparagus stalks in a thin slice of ham or prosciutto. Lay in small bundles in a buttered ovenproof dish and season with freshly ground pepper. Spoon over 6 tablespoons of thick cream and sprinkle with $\frac{1}{4}$ cup of freshly grated Parmesan cheese and 60 g (2 oz) of butter cut into tiny cubes and dust with nutmeg. Bake in a hot oven (425°F—215°C) for 5 minutes or place under a hot grill until the cheese melts and turns golden brown. Serve immediately.

Freshly boiled asparagus served cold makes a wonderful first course. Serve it in a vinaigrette dressing, with mayonnaise mixed with finely chopped chives or with sour cream flavoured with tarragon or other herbs.
Note: This is one time when it is acceptable to eat with your fingers at the table. Provide a small bowl of warm water with a slice of lemon in it for each guest to clean his fingertips.

Fresh Asparagus

Fresh asparagus has something about it. Boiled to perfection, glistening with melted butter, it looks almost too beautiful to eat. Maybe the fact that it's a slender lily has something to do with it.

Asparagus has an all-too-short season. The local varieties are the first to appear with thick white and purple stalks—which is the way the French like them. Soon after, the slender green New Zealand variety is flown in, packed in special cartons to protect the delicate tender tips.

Cooking asparagus is a simple matter as long as you can find some suitable utensils so that they can stand up with their heads above water. The delicate tips should only steam while the firmer stalks cook in boiling salted water.

To boil asparagus: Allow 6 to 8 stalks per person and carefully snap off the hard woody stalk end. This will break off cleanly where the tender part begins. It may also be necessary to pare the stalk with a small knife depending on the variety and age. Place the asparagus into a large bowl of cold salted water as you prepare them.

Tie the asparagus in two places into a firm bundle and stand in boiling salted water with the tips just above the surface. Cook until the stalks are tender, which might take from 12 to 20 minutes depending on the thickness and freshness of the asparagus. Lift out at once, remove the string and drain well on absorbent kitchen paper.

Pile on to heated dishes and serve in the simplest way with melted butter and lemon juice or with a hollandaise sauce (page 21).

Asparagus Polonaise

Boil 1 large bunch of asparagus and drain well. Chop 2 hard-boiled eggs finely and sprinkle with some finely chopped parsley over the asparagus tips. Fry 2 tablespoons of fine white breadcrumbs in 60 g (2 oz) of butter until the butter turns a light nut brown, add the juice of $\frac{1}{4}$ of a lemon and some freshly ground pepper and pour over the asparagus tips. Serve more butter separately.

Asparagus Mousse

This delicate mousse is very simple to make and preserves the fine flavour of good asparagus. It can be made in advance and is perfect for a light summer luncheon. It is also a good addition to the buffet table.

1 envelope (or 3 teaspoons) gelatine
$\frac{1}{4}$ cup water
1 500 g (1 lb) can asparagus spears
$\frac{3}{4}$ cup cream
salt and white pepper
2 egg whites
tomatoes for garnish

Sprinkle gelatine over water and leave to soak. Drain asparagus and rub the spears through a sieve or purée in a blender, then rub through a sieve to remove any stringy stalk.

When gelatine is soaked dissolve over simmering water and quickly stir into asparagus. Whip chilled cream lightly and fold in. Season to taste with salt and white pepper. When on the point of setting, fold in the stiffly beaten egg whites. Pour into a 2-cup mould which has been lightly oiled. Chill.

To serve, turn out on to a plate. Garnish with tomato quarters tossed in vinaigrette dressing.

To prepare tomatoes: Pour boiling water over three small tomatoes in a bowl. Count to 12 and immediately transfer to iced water. The skins will peel off easily. Quarter tomatoes, remove stalk ends, scoop out seeds and strain them reserving the juice to add to the dressing. Toss tomato in a dressing made by mixing together 1 tablespoon white vinegar with $\frac{1}{2}$ teaspoon French mustard, 1 tablespoon tomato juice, clove garlic crushed with salt and freshly ground pepper to taste. Add 3 tablespoons olive oil and whisk until thick. Arrange tomato in centre and sprinkle with chopped parsley.

Jellied Tomatoes

Jellied tomatoes can be made from the kitchen cupboard; fresh tomatoes when they are very ripe, red and sweet are naturally the best but for those times when they are not available, canned tomatoes make an excellent substitute.

1 × 425 g (15 oz) can peeled tomatoes
strip of pared lemon rind
a few peppercorns
1 clove garlic, crushed slightly
1 bayleaf
pinch of salt
½ cup of water
1 tablespoon gelatine

Add the tomatoes to a pan with the lemon rind, peppercorns, garlic, bay leaf and salt. Bring slowly to boil, and simmer for a few minutes. Cool slightly and pass through a nylon sieve.

Meanwhile put the measured water into a pan, sprinkle over the gelatine and allow the gelatine to swell, about 2 minutes. Dissolve over a gentle heat until it is quite clear. Stir into tomato mixture until well combined, and check the seasoning, adding freshly ground pepper if necessary. Rinse out individual jelly moulds or a ring mould with cold water and pour in the tomato mixture. Place in a refrigerator and allow to set. Turn out on to a plate, dipping the mould in hot water for 1 second to make it easier.

Serve with asparagus spears, sliced cucumber in yoghurt, celery, and parsley sprigs.

Tomatoes Piperade

Ripe peeled tomatoes filled with a delicious creamy egg mixture combining onions, green and red peppers and tomato. These are served cold and may be prepared well in advance. The Piperade mixture may also be served hot with a thick slice of grilled or baked ham or by itself surrounded by a few fried croutons.

12 even-sized ripe red tomatoes
2 large onions
1 large green pepper
1 large red pepper
1 tablespoon olive oil
125 g (4 oz) butter
6 eggs
salt and freshly ground pepper
2 tablespoons freshly chopped herbs
**   (parsley, chives and basil)**
2 tablespoons vinaigrette dressing

Peel the tomatoes, carefully remove the core then turn them over and slice the top off each tomato. Using a small sharp knife remove the pulp from each tomato and place in a bowl for later use. Place the tomato shells in the refrigerator.

Slice the onions finely, cut the peppers in half, remove the core and seeds and shred finely. Heat the oil in a frying pan and then add 30 g (1 oz) of the butter. When hot add the onions, peppers and reserved tomato pulp. Cover the pan and cook slowly until the vegetables are very soft. Remove from heat and add herbs.

In a saucepan melt 45 g (1½ oz) of butter and when the foam has subsided pour in the eggs which have been lightly beaten with a fork and seasoned with salt and pepper.

Stir with a wooden spoon until they are cooked but still very creamy. Take off the heat and add the remaining butter which has been cut into small pieces.

Combine the eggs with the vegetable mixture, adjust the seasoning if necessary and allow to cool.

Fill each tomato with the Piperade mixture placing the tomato 'cap' on top. Brush with vinaigrette dressing. Serve chilled.

Hors D'Oeuvres Variés (see recipes on page 66)

72

Mushrooms Coriander (see recipe overleaf)

73

Tomatoes Nicoise

Ripe sweet tomatoes filled with a delicious colourful combination of crisp vegetables flavoured with vinaigrette dressing.

4 ripe tomatoes
1 green pepper
60 g (2 oz) black olives
4 tablespoons shallots
3 tablespoons vinaigrette dressing
parsley, finely chopped

Peel the tomatoes and slice a thin cap off each. Cut the pepper into shreds and blanch in boiling water for 2 minutes. Cut the olives into fine shreds and slice the shallots diagonally.

Using a teaspoon remove the seeds from the tomatoes, strain them in a sieve and add the juice to the vinaigrette. Scoop out a little of the tomato flesh and reserve.

Combine the green pepper, olives, shallots and scooped-out tomato with the vinaigrette. Fill the tomatoes piling the mixture up and chill. Just before serving sprinkle with chopped parsley.

Mushrooms Coriander

The combined flavours of the orange-scented coriander and the bay leaves are the secret of this dish. It may be served cold or hot and can be stored in the refrigerator for a few days.

500 g (1 lb) small white mushrooms
   (quartered or whole)
juice 1 lemon
2 teaspoons coriander seeds
4 tablespoons olive oil
3 bay leaves
salt
freshly ground pepper

Clean the mushrooms with a cloth dipped in water and lemon juice. Trim the stalks. Slice the mushrooms into quarters and squeeze some lemon juice over them.

Crush the coriander seeds in a mortar or with a rolling pin.

Heat the olive oil in a heavy frying pan over a low heat. Add the coriander seeds and allow to heat through. Add the mushrooms and bay leaves. Season with salt and pepper. Cook 1 minute. Cover the pan and allow the mushrooms to cook for a further 5 minutes over a very low heat.

Place the mushrooms in a dish and cool. Serve with crusty French bread to mop up the juices.

Mushrooms à la Grecque

"A la Grecque" refers to foods cooked Greek-style. Vegetables cooked in this way are often served chilled as a first course or as a luncheon dish with crusty French bread to mop up the juices. They also go well with grills.

500 g (1 lb) button mushrooms
1 tablespoon tarragon, chopped or
   1 teaspoon dried tarragon
1 tablespoon lemon juice
1 clove garlic, crushed
1 tablespoon parsley, finely chopped
1 tomato, peeled and seeded
pinch dried thyme
salt and freshly ground black pepper
1 bay leaf
$\frac{1}{4}$ cup olive oil
1 cup water

Carefully wash mushrooms, trim off stems and place in a heavy saucepan. Add the remaining ingredients. Cover the pan and bring to the boil. Reduce the heat and simmer for 8 to 10 minutes. Allow to cool, then chill.

● **Zucchini may be substituted for mushrooms.** Use 500 g (1 lb). Just cut them into 1 cm ($\frac{1}{2}$ in) diagonal slices, add remaining ingredients and cook for 10 minutes. Allow to cool and chill.

Brandade de Morue

In France, cod is usually eaten salted and dried, and Brandade, which is almost a fish pâté, is one of their favourite ways of preparing it. This dried salt cod, or ling fish as some call it, is sold in almost every Italian delicatessen in Australia, and with our young garlic (so necessary in a Provençal recipe), good olive oil and milk, we have all the ingredients for making this delicious dish right here.

Following overnight soaking, then poaching, the cod is pounded and beaten with warmed oil and milk to a consistency of creamy mashed potato.

It can be served warm or cold. Usually it is mounded up in a dish, surrounded with black olives and served with hot toast for an entrée or light luncheon. We found it ideal for parties when spooned into tiny, crisp, hot puff pastry cases.

1 kg (2 lb) dried salt cod
1 large clove garlic, crushed
½ cup olive oil
½ cup milk

Soak salt cod for 24 hours or overnight. Drain and wash well under cold running water. Place in a saucepan with water to cover, bring to the boil and simmer 5 minutes. Drain.

Remove skin and bones and place flaked fish in a saucepan with crushed garlic. Place over low heat and pound well with a wooden spoon, a pestle, or the end of a rolling pin.

Just warm oil and milk in separate saucepans. Alternately add spoonfuls of the oil and milk to the fish, pounding and stirring constantly to make a smooth cream. There will still be fibres, quite characteristic of this dish, in the purée. An electric blender may be used at this stage if a smoother cream is preferred.

Add seasoning to taste, but be sparing. Pile Brandade in a large dish, mounding and shaping with the flat of a knife or spatula. Surround with black olives and accompany with hot toast.

Brandade may also be served in warmed puff pastry cases—ideal for individual servings or for cocktail parties.

- Dried salt cod must be soaked for a minimum of 12 hours —if possible under a trickle of running water, or in very frequent changes of water. The soaking process not only softens the fish, but also washes away much of the saltiness.
  After soaking and cooking cod, taste first before adding additional seasoning.
  Do not soak dried cod in a metal container—enamel or earthenware is best.

Avocados Vinaigrette

Cut a ripe avocado in two, lift out the stone and fill the hollow with a well-flavoured vinaigrette. Sprinkle with some finely-chopped herbs and serve with a twist of lemon and a pepper mill for those who like the special flavour of freshly-ground pepper.

Avocados with Seafood

Avocados with Seafood

Small school prawns marinated in a garlic-flavoured vinaigrette with a piquant touch of Tabasco, fill fresh ripe avocados.

500 g (1 lb) prawns, preferably school prawns
2 ripe avocados
freshly chopped parsley
1 lemon
Vinaigrette Dressing:
1 tablespoon wine vinegar
1 small clove of garlic, crushed with a little salt
4 tablespoons olive oil
salt, freshly ground black pepper
dash of Tabasco sauce

Peel the prawns and remove the vein along the back. Mix all ingredients for the Vinaigrette Dressing in a small bowl and pour over the prawns. Cover and chill for at least 1 hour. Chill the avocados.

Halve the avocados, remove the seeds and place on individual plates. Spoon some marinated prawns into each half and sprinkle with chopped parsley. Serve with wedges of lemon.

● To remove the seed from an avocado half without damaging the flesh, pierce the seed with the point of a sharp knife holding the avocado carefully with one hand and gently ease the seed out.

Seafood Cocktail

There is hardly a restaurant which does not feature a seafood cocktail among its first courses. The seafood used should be the freshest you can find. The glass dish as well as the ingredients should be well chilled and the cocktail assembled at the last moment.

For each serving allow:
½ cup shelled and de-veined prawns
2 chilled plump oysters
crabmeat or crayfish (optional)
finely shredded lettuce
cocktail sauce

Cocktail sauce:
½ cup tomato purée
dash of tabasco
½ teaspoon salt
squeeze of lemon juice
1 teaspoon horseradish or grated onion

Chill the seafood. Shred the lettuce finely and place a little in each chilled glass dish to form a bed for the seafood. Combine the seafood with the cocktail sauce and then pile onto the lettuce bed and serve.

Blend all the ingredients together and chill. This amount of sauce is ample for 4 servings.

Note: For best results, combine ingredients for seafood cocktail at the last moment. All ingredients may be prepared beforehand.

Cheese and Onion Piroshki

Piroshki with one of their varied fillings are the most delicious accompaniment we know to light soups. They should be served piping hot. Piroshki may be made and baked and then stored in aluminium foil in the freezer until needed. Just reheat them, still in the foil package, in a moderate oven for 15 to 20 minutes.

30 g (1 oz) compressed yeast
2½ tablespoons sugar
3 cups plain flour
1¼ cups milk
125 g (4 oz) butter
2 teaspoons salt
1 egg yolk
beaten egg to glaze
Filling:
1 large onion, finely chopped
30 g (1 oz) butter
freshly ground pepper
60 g (2 oz) well matured cheddar cheese

Combine the yeast with ½ tablespoon of sugar in a small bowl. Stir until yeast is dissolved, sprinkle with 1 teaspoon of flour and leave in a warm place. Heat the milk, butter, salt and remaining sugar to blood heat.

Sift flour into a large mixing bowl, make a well in the centre, and pour in milk mixture, yeast and egg yolk which has been lightly beaten. Gradually incorporate flour, then beat dough by hand for 3 minutes until smooth and elastic. Sprinkle with a little flour, cover with a teatowel and place in a warm spot until doubled in bulk. Turn on to a floured board and knead lightly.

Tear off pieces of dough the size of a large tablespoon. Place ½ teaspoon of the onion filling and a cube of cheese in the middle of each piece, fold the edge over and then mould into little balls.

Place on lightly greased baking trays and leave in a warm place to rise for 15 minutes. Brush with beaten egg and bake in a very hot oven (450°F—230°C) for 10 to 15 minutes until golden brown. Slide on to a clean tea towel to keep warm.

Filling: Cook the onion in melted butter until soft and transparent. Season with pepper. Cut the cheese into 5 mm (¼ in) cubes.

Hard boiled Eggs with Tapenade

Tapenade is an interesting mixture of olives, fish and capers which are pounded to a paste with olive oil and lemon juice. Hard boiled egg yolks are then added with a touch of brandy. This mixture is piled into the hollows of hard boiled egg whites which are reshaped and served with a refreshing tomato salad. The tapenade may also be packed into tiny pots and eaten with toast like pâté.

6 hard-boiled eggs
24 stoned black olives
8 anchovy fillets
2 heaped tablespoons capers
1 × 99 g (3½ oz) can of tuna
¼ cup olive oil
juice of ½ lemon
brandy or cognac

Shell the eggs and leave in a bowl of cold water. Chop the olives and place in a bowl with the anchovy fillets, capers and tuna fish. Pound with a pestle or the end of a rolling pin to form a thick purée. Gradually work in the olive oil. Season with lemon juice and brandy.

Halve the hard-boiled eggs and take out the yolks. Sieve the yolks into the tapenade mixture and beat well. Fill the centre of the egg whites with this mixture and spread additional mixture on one half of each egg.

Reshape the egg and scrape off any excess mixture with a palette knife, wipe eggs clean with dampened tea towel.

Dolmades

Dolmades or dolmas belong to Turkish cookery. Though they are loved by gourmets to whom cost means nothing, they are a boon to housewives on a budget. Whatever your reasons for making them, they are good eating.

If you can get hold of young, fresh grape vine leaves do try this dish, if not use the canned leaves. They can also be made with cabbage leaves.

The size of dolmades may vary from thin short cigar shapes to round and squat, depending on the size of the leaves. Tiny dolmades, made with small grape leaves, make a delicious hors d'oeuvre. Omit the tomato paste and molasses from the recipe. When cooked allow to cool and serve with cubes of feta cheese or with lemon wedges; the lemon gives a good fresh flavour.

1 onion
2 tablespoons olive oil
500 g (1 lb) lean minced steak
1 egg, beaten
⅓ cup rice
2 teaspoons chopped fresh mint
2 cups stock
salt and pepper
cabbage or vine leaves
1 teaspoon molasses (optional)
1 tablespoon tomato paste

Chop onion and fry in oil until soft. Mix together meat, egg, onion, rice, mint, 1 teaspoon salt and a good grinding of black pepper.

Remove core from cabbage and carefully remove leaves. Drop cabbage or fresh grape leaves into a large pan of boiling water for 2-3 minutes to soften. Drain and rinse with cold water. Cut off any tough stems. Place a spoonful of meat mixture on leaf and roll up, folding ends in to seal in filling. Vine leaves will take only 1 teaspoonful of mixture. Arrange, folded side down, in saucepan making more than one layer if necessary. Mix molasses, tomato paste and stock (may be made with stock cubes) and pour over dolmades. Cover and simmer for 45 minutes.

When serving dolmades hot, transfer to a serving plate and keep warm. Blend 2 teaspoons cornflour with a little cold water, add to stock in pan, stirring over heat until mixture thickens. Serve over dolmades. Serves 4-6.

● Dolmades have a special flavour when made with grape leaves. Pick very young leaves from vines and boil as described in recipe. When filling, place leaves shiny side down.

Canned grape leaves are available from continental delicatessens. The canned leaves must be rinsed in cold water. They do not require boiling.

Steak Tartare Balls

Little Steak Tartare Balls are very special. The beef is rolled in finely chopped parsley and served straight from the refrigerator.

500 g (1 lb) round steak
1 teaspoon grated onion
4 tablespoons chopped parsley
2 tablespoons capers, finely chopped
1 teaspoon Worcestershire sauce
½ teaspoon prepared English mustard
salt and freshly ground pepper

Using a soup spoon with the rounded side uppermost scrape away the soft flesh of the meat. This may seem tedious but it minces the steak very finely.

Combine with the onion and 1 tablespoon of the chopped parsley and then add the capers, Worcestershire sauce and mustard and season well with salt and pepper. Form into small balls and roll in the remaining finely chopped parsley. Chill well before serving.

Note: This amount will make about 40.

Top left: Artichokes (see page 67)
Top right: Dolmades (see recipe previous page)   Above: Asparagus Mousse (see recipe on page 70)

Taramasalata

Taramasalata is a Greek dish made from tarama, the pounded dried eggs of the grey mullet. Tarama is sold in jars in some good delicatessen shops. If you find it difficult to get, the smoked cod's roe or mullet roe which is readily available from most fish shops, may be used. It is stronger in flavour. This unusual fish roe paté is served with Melba toast or fingers of hot toast for an hors d'oeuvre or as a first course.

12 slices white bread
2 cups milk
250 g (8 oz) tarama or cod's roe
**   (obtainable in jars)**
½ cup lemon juice
1 large onion, peeled and grated
2 garlic cloves, crushed
1½ cups olive oil

Cut the crusts off the bread slices and soak in the milk for 5 minutes, then squeeze dry. Place in a large mortar or bowl with the cod's roe, finely chopped. Pound this with a pestle or the end of a rolling pin until the mixture is smooth and creamy. Beat in the lemon juice, the grated onion and crushed garlic and work the mixture until all the ingredients are thoroughly combined.

Add the oil gradually, beating it in one tablespoon at a time, making sure that it is well combined before adding more. Beat hard until the Taramasalata holds its shape. Season to taste with freshly ground pepper and more lemon juice if necessary. Pile into a bowl and chill in the refrigerator. Serve garnished with a black olive with Melba toast or hot toast.

Note: This recipe may be made quickly and easily in an electric blender.

Pineapple Japonaise

It's often a difficult thing to find the right course to precede a very rich dish. Pineapple Japonaise is an excellent choice on such an occasion. It has a refreshing taste, is not too heavy—each pineapple chunk coated with the merest suggestion of light cream dressing.

1 large ripe pineapple
caster sugar
lemon juice
Dressing:
1 large egg
3 tablespoons tarragon vinegar
2 tablespoons caster sugar
pinch salt
3 tablespoons lightly whipped cream

Cut the pineapple in two lengthways, remove the core carefully with a grapefruit knife and cut out the flesh. Cut into chunks and arrange in the shells. Sprinkle with caster sugar and lemon juice. Allow to stand while preparing the dressing.

Dressing: Beat the egg and add the vinegar and sugar with a pinch of salt. Cook in the top of a double boiler over gently simmering water and stir continually until thick. Remove and allow to cool. When quite cold fold in the whipped cream and adjust the seasoning. Just before serving, spoon over the pineapple.

Note: This cream dressing is delicious with chilled pears which have been peeled and quartered.

Hot Appetisers

Devils on Horseback

Prunes and chicken livers wrapped in bacon and grilled are delicious and very popular—they are quick to prepare and need only a few minutes under the grill before they are served piping hot.

plump dessert prunes, stone removed
lean streaky bacon, rind removed

Wrap each prune in half a rasher of bacon. Secure with a toothpick. Place under a hot grill for 3 minutes on each side and serve piping hot.

Chicken Livers on Horseback

plump chicken livers
salt, freshly ground black pepper
lean streaky bacon, rind removed

Season the chicken livers and wrap each one in half-rasher of bacon. Secure with a toothpick. Grill for 3 minutes each side under a hot grill. Serve hot.

Angels on Horseback

plump fresh oysters
bacon rashers, with rind removed
freshly ground pepper

Wrap an oyster well seasoned with pepper in a half-rasher of bacon, fasten with a toothpick and grill under a high heat for 3 minutes each side.

Grilled Grapefruit

A simple hot first course or a good starter to a brunch. Choose fruit which is heavy and as thin-skinned as possible.

Grapefruit
dry sherry
caster sugar

Allow half a grapefruit per person. Chill grapefruit to make it easier to cut into segments.

Cut the grapefruit in half and cut around the outside, slipping the knife under the central core and removing any pips. A curved serrated-edged grapefruit knife is especially made for this purpose.

Cut in between the grapefruit segments, loosening them completely and then remove the membrane between each and the core.

Sprinkle each grapefruit half with 1 tablespoon of dry sherry and dust liberally with caster sugar. Place under a pre-heated grill and leave until the sugar has caramelised. Serve hot.

Stuffed Peppers

6 sweet peppers
6 slices of white bread with the crusts
    removed
milk
1 × 198 g (7 oz) tin of tuna, flaked and
    drained
125 g (4 oz) black olives, coarsely chopped
⅓ cup olive oil
2 tablespoons drained capers
2 tablespoons parsley, finely chopped
1 clove garlic, crushed
salt
freshly ground pepper
⅓ cup chicken stock, or water and stock
    cubes

Slice the tops off the peppers. Remove the seeds and ribs and parboil in gently boiling water for 5 minutes. Drain on paper towels.

Soak bread slices in a little milk. Squeeze dry. Combine with the tuna, olives, olive oil, capers, parsley, garlic and season with salt and pepper. Stuff the peppers with this mixture and place them close together in a baking pan. Pour the stock into the pan and bake the peppers in a moderately slow oven (325°F—160°C) for about 30 minutes.

Tiropites

Tiropites are tiny triangular Greek pastries filled with spinach and feta cheese. Serve them piping hot with drinks at any time of the day. The Greek filo pastry comes in tissue thin sheets from Greek delicatessens and pastry shops.

250 g (8 oz) filo pastry packet
1 × 315 g (10 oz) packet frozen spinach
2 onions, finely chopped
30 g (1 oz) butter
½ cup finely chopped shallots
250 g (8 oz) feta cheese, chopped
1 teaspoon ground nutmeg
½ cup finely chopped parsley
salt
freshly ground black pepper
125 g (4 oz) unsalted butter
3 eggs, beaten

Lay the filo pastry flat on a damp tea towel and cover with a second damp tea towel so that the pastry will not dry out. Cook the spinach according to the packet directions but do not add any butter. Drain it thoroughly and press lightly with a spoon to remove all the excess liquid. Fry the onions in the butter until golden brown. Combine the eggs, shallots, cheese, nutmeg and parsley. Add the onions, spinach and season with salt and pepper to taste. Cut each sheet of filo pastry in half lengthwise.

Fold each piece in two lengthwise and brush with melted butter. Place a teaspoon of the filling in one corner of the pastry strip. Fold corner of pastry over the filling until it meets the folded edge forming a triangle.

Continue to fold pastry over in triangles until you have come to the end of the pastry strip. Brush the top of the triangle with melted butter.

Place on an ungreased baking tray and cook in a moderately hot oven (375°F—190°C) for 45 minutes or until puffed and golden brown.

Vol-au-vents

Small, light, flaky pastry cases filled with ham, mushrooms and pimiento in a creamy sauce. They are easily made now that such good quality puff pastry is sold commercially and may be filled with a variety of good things.

250 g (8 oz) puff pastry
500 g ($\frac{1}{2}$ lb) leg ham
125 g ($\frac{1}{4}$ lb) button mushrooms
Sauce:
1 cup milk
a few parsley stalks, a few slices of onion,
   carrot, a bayleaf and a few peppercorns
30 g (1 oz) butter
30 g (1 oz) flour
1 canned pimento cap
salt
freshly ground pepper

Roll out the pastry about 0.5 cm ($\frac{1}{4}$ in) thick and cut in half. With a round 6 cm ($2\frac{1}{2}$ in) fluted cutter, cut out rounds from one half and place on a baking tray which has been lightly sprinkled with flour. Brush the edge of the pastry with beaten egg. Using the same cutter cut round from the other half of the pastry. With a 5 cm (2 in) fluted cutter cut the inside of these rounds away leaving a pastry ring.

Place these on the circles on the baking tray. Brush the top with beaten egg and bake in a hot oven (425°F—215°C) for 15 minutes.

Prepare the filling. Infuse the milk with the seasonings. Melt the butter in a small saucepan and blend in the flour off the heat. Cook for a minute on a gentle heat and add a little of the milk, blend and add the rest of the milk. Stir until boiling and allow to simmer for 2 minutes.

Season with a little pepper and salt and add the pimento cap which has been puréed in a blender or pushed through a sieve. Shred the ham finely. Wipe the mushrooms with a cloth dampened with water and a little lemon juice. Slice them finely and sauté them in a little butter. Add these with the ham to the sauce. Reheat slightly and fill the hot vol-au-vent cases. Serve immediately.

Won Ton

Sometimes called Chinese Ravioli or Cloud Swallows, Won Ton are served boiled in Short Soup or fried until golden for hors d'oeuvre and Sweet and Sour. The wrappings can be brought, already cut into squares from Chinese food stores and some restaurants, but it is a good idea to order in advance.

250 g (8 oz) Won Ton skins
egg white
oil for deep drying
Filling:
125 g (4 oz) each pork fillet and raw
   prawns
6 canned water chestnuts
4 shallots
3 dried mushrooms, soaked in warm
   water for 20 minutes
3 teaspoons salt
1 teaspoon sugar
2 teaspoons Soy sauce

Prepare the filling first. Finely mince pork, peeled prawns, water chestnuts, shallots and drained mushrooms (stalks removed). Season with salt, sugar and Soy Sauce, combining thoroughly.

Keep the Won Ton skins covered with a damp cloth to prevent them drying out. Place $\frac{1}{2}$ teaspoon of the filling on one corner of each square of pastry and, holding the square of pastry in the left hand, roll dough over filling with the aid of a chopstick until half way, then dampen opposite corners with egg white and join together.

Keep the Won Ton covered until all are made and use in soups or deep fry in hot oil and serve hot as an hors d'oeuvre.

Steamed Dim Sims

Dim Sims are little pastries with a flavoursome filling, steamed to serve as hors d'oeuvre. Bamboo and metal steamers, available at Chinese stores, are made up of three layers, so you can cook a large number at one time. Or you can have different foods steaming in each section.

125 g (4 oz) Won Ton skins
fillings for Won Ton

Keep the skins covered with a damp cloth to prevent them drying out as you make the Dim Sims.

Put 1 small teaspoon filling in centre of each square of pastry so it resembles a money bag.

Rub base of each tier of steamer with a little oil and place the dim sims in steamer, leaving a space between each.

Place steamer in a wok or saucepan with about 2.5 cm (1 in) of simmering water. Cover and allow to steam for 15 minutes or until filling cooks through. The best way to test is to cut one of the dim sims in half. Serve hot.

Pâté

Chicken Liver Terrine

155 g (5 oz) butter
2 tablespoons shallots, finely chopped
1 clove garlic, finely chopped
500 g (1 lb) chicken livers
1 bay leaf
pinch of thyme
salt
freshly ground pepper
2 tablespoons brandy
1 truffle (optional)
60 g (2 oz) chicken fat
few sage leaves

Heat 30 g (1 oz) butter in a frying pan. Add the shallots and garlic and fry gently until softened.

Remove the sinews from each chicken liver and discard any livers that have discoloured. Add the chicken livers to the pan with the bay leaf and thyme. Season with salt and pepper. Fry for about 3 minutes until the livers are stiffened and lightly browned but still pink inside.

Remove the bay leaf and blend the livers in a liquidiser in three portions, then push this mixture through a sieve. If you do not have a liquidiser mash the livers with a fork and then sieve.

Add the brandy to the pan in which the livers were cooked and reduce over a high heat until 1 tablespoon remains.

Cream the remaining butter and gradually mix into the liver mixture. Slice the truffle very thinly and fold into the pâté with the brandy.

Spoon the pâté into a 3-cup earthenware terrine or other china or glass container.

Cut the chicken fat into small pieces and melt it with the sage leaves over a low heat. Strain the fat into a jug and pour over the pâté. When cool cover with a lid and place in the refrigerator. This pâté will keep for 1 week and is best made a few days before it is eaten.

Terrine with Pork Fillets

Terrine with Pork Fillets

A terrine, that most tempting and savoury of cold meat dishes, is to a Frenchman an essential part of everyday eating. The word terrine covers both the earthenware dish in which the food is cooked as well as the food itself. A terrine is usually a mixture of finely minced meat well seasoned and with one special ingredient hidden in the centre to add flavour interest. If you don't have a terrine, any ovenproof dish of attractive shape will do.

500 g (1 lb) pork fillets
¼ cup brandy
pepper and salt
2 shallots
pinch thyme
1 clove garlic
250 g (8 oz) fresh pork fat back or fat from pork loin
750 g (1½ lb) pork and veal mince
1 teaspoon salt
pepper
1 tablespoon brandy
grated rind of ½ lemon
1 bayleaf, optional

Slice pork fillets in two lengthwise. Place between two sheets plastic wrap and batter with a flat mallet until very thin.

Mix brandy with a good grinding of pepper, pinch salt, chopped shallots, thyme, crushed garlic. Lay fillets in a shallow dish, pour brandy mixture over and leave to marinate for 2 hours.

Slice pork fat into 3 mm (⅛ in) strips or sheets.

Arrange lengthwise in 2.5 litre (4 pint) terrine (ovenproof dish) completely covering bottom and sides, leaving a sheet of pork fat for the top. Place remaining ingredients, except bayleaf, in a bowl and mix thoroughly with a wooden spoon. Spoon one third of pork and veal mixture into prepared dish.

Lay half of the prepared pork fillets, drained of marinade, on top of mince. Repeat layers.

If using bayleaf place on top of meat and lay slice of pork fat over all.

Cover with foil and lid, or seal lid with a flour and water paste. Place terrine in a baking dish of hot water and bake in a moderate oven (350°F—175°C) for 1½ hours. Take from oven, remove lid and place a weight on top. Leave until cool and set.

Turn the finished terrine out of mould and serve.

Chicken Liver Ramekins

Several small pots of chicken liver pâté well sealed with clarified butter or chicken fat is just the thing for the Festive Season! A small pot can be taken from the refrigerator when the occasion arises and used generously knowing that there are more little pots on hand. Serve with Melba Toast (this could be made weeks ahead) or if you prefer, spread on fingers of hot toast.

1½ cups chicken livers
⅔ cup finely chopped mushrooms
4 egg yolks, lightly beaten
4 tablespoons cream
sprig of thyme, finely chopped
1½ tablespoons melted butter
salt and cayenne pepper
freshly ground black pepper
2 tablespoons brandy
clarified butter for sealing the pâté

Trim chicken livers of fibres, place in the blender with the mushrooms, egg yolks, cream, thyme, melted butter and season with salt, cayenne and black pepper. Blend until reduced to a purée. Stir in the brandy.

Butter 4 to 6 small ramekins and pack them with the liver mixture.

Cover each with a disc of buttered wax paper and place in a pan of water. Bake in a moderate oven (350°F—170°C) for 30 to 40 minutes. Remove and allow to cool.

Place a herb sprig for decoration in the centre of each ramekin and seal with melted clarified butter. Place in the refrigerator to set.

fish

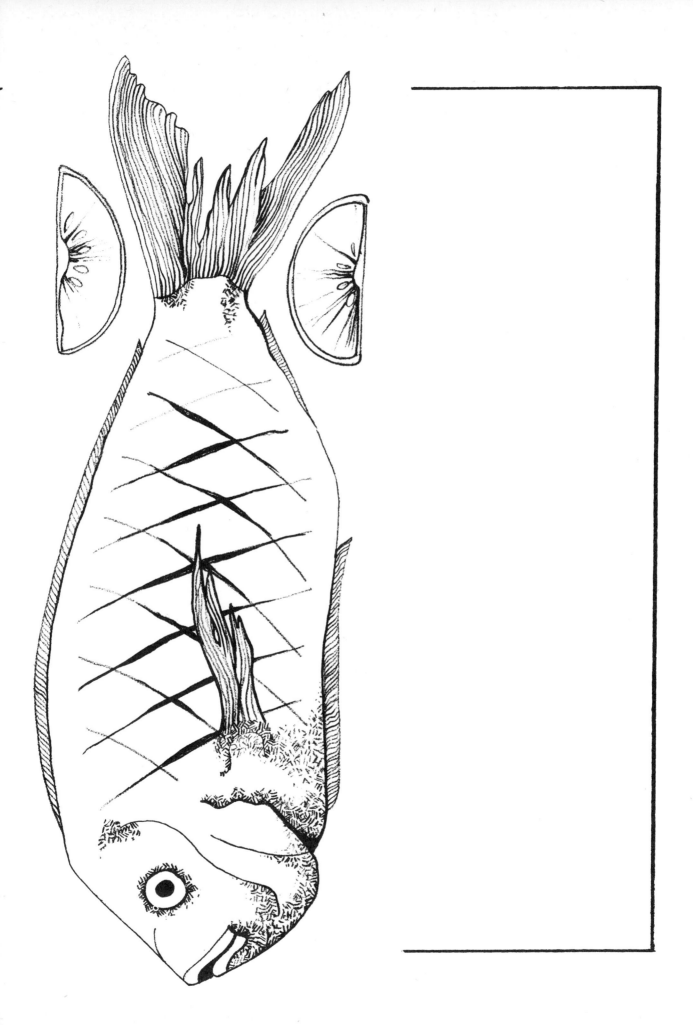

Fish

Baked Whiting with Olives and Capers

4 whiting, weighing 250 g—375 g
  (8—12 oz) each
2 tablespoons capers
8 black olives
salt
¼ cup olive oil
125 g (4 oz) butter
2 teaspoons dried oregano crumbled or
  1 sprig of fresh oregano
black pepper
2 tablespoons lemon juice

Clean and scale the fish but leave their heads and tails on. Drain the capers and cut each olive into three slices, cutting around the stones. Wash the fish well and dry with paper towels. Season the inside with salt. Heat the olive oil with 30 g (1 oz) of butter and when it begins to sizzle add the oregano and a little pepper. Dip the fish in this seasoned oil and butter and then place in a baking dish and bake in a moderately hot oven (375°F—190°C) for 20-30 minutes basting them frequently during the first 15 minutes.

Arrange the baked fish on a heated serving dish and keep warm. Heat the remaining butter until it turns a light brown. Add the capers and olives. Remove from the heat, add the lemon juice and pour over the fish.

Grilled Whole Fish

Choose a fish weighing about 500 to 750 g (1 to 1½ lb) or smaller (snapper, morwong, whiting, flathead).

Make about 4 diagonal incisions 2.5 cm (1 in) apart on each side of the fish. Brush the fish liberally with butter or oil and season with salt and pepper.

Lower the grill rack (the larger the fish the further away it should be from the heat) and grease it lightly. Cook the fish under a moderate heat on each side. Baste it frequently with some butter or oil.

- The skin of the whole fish to be grilled is slit to enable the heat to penetrate without bursting the skin.

Grilled Fish Cutlets

4 thick fish cutlets (blue-eyed cod,
  snapper, kingfisher, jewfish)
melted butter or olive oil
salt
freshly ground pepper

Brush some oil over the grill rack. Preheat the griller. Brush the fish cutlets liberally with melted butter or oil (or a combination of both). Season with salt and pepper and place on the grill rack.

Grill on one side for 3 to 4 minutes. Turn the fish over, baste with more butter or oil and grill a further 3 to 4 minutes. Lower the heat and cook until the flesh turns creamy white and comes away from the bone easily.

Baked Whiting with Olives and Capers

Flounder Veronique

Poached flounder fillets with peeled grapes make a delightful combination. Any table grapes may be used, but muscats are our choice. The fish is coated with white wine sauce, one of the most useful of the wine sauces. This sauce is good with other fish dishes. If seafood is cooked in a Court Bouillon it's a pity not to use such a wonderfully flavoured liquid in a sauce.

15 g (½ oz) butter
2 whole flounders each cut into 4 fillets
   or substitute sole or bream
salt and freshly ground white pepper
185 g (6 oz) grapes
little white wine
Court Bouillon:
1 cup dry white wine
1 cup water
1 bay leaf
4 peppercorns
2 parsley stalks
1 onion, sliced thickly
1 small carrot, sliced thickly
1 celery stalk, cut into pieces
1 teaspoon salt
White wine sauce:
30 g (1 oz) butter
2 tablespoons plain flour, sifted
1 cup milk
salt, freshly ground white pepper
2 eggs yolks
4 tablespoons cream

Place all the ingredients for the Court Bouillon into a saucepan. Bring to the boil, lower the heat and simmer for 15 minutes, strain and cool.

Melt the butter in a shallow ovenproof dish. Lightly season the fish with salt and pepper, fold into three and arrange in the pan. Pour over the Court Bouillon, cover with buttered paper and poach in moderate oven (350°F—170°C) for 8 to 10 minutes. Place the fish on to a dish and keep warm.

Strain the cooking liquid into a saucepan and cook rapidly until reduced to 1 cup. Peel the grapes, remove the pips and sprinkle with a little white wine. Keep in a warm place while preparing the sauce.

Sauce: Melt the butter, stir in the flour and cook over a low heat for 1 minute. Remove from the heat and gradually stir in the milk. Cook until the sauce thickens, stirring all the time. Add the reduced fish liquor, season and simmer for 8 to 10 minutes. Beat the egg yolks with the cream, add a little hot sauce, mix well and then stir into remaining sauce. Stir over heat for 1 minute but do not boil.

Arrange the fish around a mound of grapes on a heated serving dish and spoon over the sauce. Serve immediately.

White Wine Sauce may be used for fish, shellfish, chicken, veal or vegetables. Once you have mastered the basic principles of this sauce it is only a matter of substituting the appropriate stock—veal for a veal dish, chicken for a chicken dish and so on. The flavour of this sauce may also be varied by using different wines. It may be made, and usually is, with a dry white wine but experiment with a soft, full-bodied white wine.

Crumbed Cod Steaks

Serve with lemon wedges and fried parsley.

4 thick cod or other fish steaks
flour seasoned with salt and freshly
   ground pepper
1 egg beaten with 1 teaspoon olive oil
fine white breadcrumbs
oil for frying

Dry the cod steaks thoroughly with paper towels. Lightly coat them in flour and then brush with egg and coat in breadcrumbs.

Fry the cod in ½ cm (¼ in) of hot oil for 2 to 4 minutes on each side. Drain on crumpled paper and serve with lemon wedges and fried parsley.

Fried Fish

Fried fish is a great favourite all over the world whether eaten in the traditional manner from a newspaper bag or from a china plate with fried parsley and lemon wedges.

4 thick bream fillets, skinned or other
   good fish
flour
Batter:
1 cup plain flour
pinch salt
2 tablespoons melted butter
2 eggs, beaten lightly
1 cup beer or soda water
1 egg white, stiffly beaten

Batter: Sift the flour with the salt into a bowl. Make a well in the centre, stir in the butter and eggs. Add the beer gradually. Stir until the mixture is smooth. Cover the bowl and allow the batter to stand in a warm place for 1 hour. Just before you are ready to use it, fold in the stiffly beaten egg white.

Dry the fish on paper towels. Flour lightly. Heat $\frac{1}{2}$ cm ($\frac{1}{4}$ inch) of oil in a large frying pan. Dip fillets in batter. Place the fish in the hot oil and allow 2 to 4 minutes for each side according to the thickness of the fish. Drain on crumpled kitchen paper. Serve as soon as possible.

Note: If cooking a number of fillets, the cooked pieces may be kept hot in warm oven with the door open.

John Dory Meunière

4 fish fillets (John Dory, bream, sole)
flour seasoned with salt and freshly
   ground pepper
60 g (2 oz) butter
juice of $\frac{1}{2}$ lemon
1 tablespoon parsley, finely chopped

Remove the dark skin from the fish fillets. Dry the fillets on a paper towel. Lightly flour them.

Heat 30 g (1 oz) of butter in a frying pan. When it is foaming place the fish in it and cook for about 2 minutes on each side until they are delicate brown.

Add the lemon juice and 30 g (1 oz) of butter to the frying pan and let it brown lightly. Sprinkle the fish with the parsley and spoon the hot pan juices over the fish. Serve immediately.

Another method: Place the cooked fish on a hot platter. Throw away the butter in the frying pan and add fresh butter with the lemon juice. Heat until the butter turns a hazelnut colour. Sprinkle fish with parsley and pour sizzling butter over the top.

Fish Teryaki

750 g ($1\frac{1}{2}$ lb) fish fillets
$\frac{1}{2}$ cup soy sauce
2 tablespoons sake or sherry
1 tablespoon sugar
$\frac{1}{2}$ teaspoon grated fresh ginger
1 clove garlic, crushed

Slice fish into thin strips. Combine remaining ingredients, pour over fish and leave to marinate for 30 minutes. Thread fish on bamboo skewers and grill for 3–4 minutes, turning once. Alternatively place Japanese hibachi with glowing coals on table, arrange fish on plate and allow each person to cook their own portion of fish over the hot coals. Serves 6.

Top: Tiny Fresh Sardines
Above: Garlic Prawns (see recipe on page 98)

94

Fresh Sardines

Sardines are found in many parts of the world, although the only variety considered a "true" sardine comes from Mediterranean waters. These small fish are delicious fresh, crisp-fried and served whole. The bones are soft enough to eat, making the preparation quite simple.

500 g (1 lb) sardines
3 to 4 tablespoons plain flour
salt and pepper
oil for deep frying
lemon wedges

Cut heads away from body using a small sharp knife and gently pull out the stomach. Wash in cold water and dry on paper towels. Many Italian cooks and restaurants do not remove the head and stomach, but we consider this gives the fish a more delicate flavour.

Roll sardines in plain flour seasoned with salt and pepper. Heat 2.5 cm (1 in) oil in a pan and add the fish. When golden, lift out of pan and reheat oil. Return sardines for 30 seconds to crisp the coating. Drain and serve immediately with lemon wedges.

Baked Snapper

1 × 2 kg (4 lb) snapper, cleaned
1 lemon
salt
extra 30 g (1 oz) butter, softened
freshly ground pepper
¼ teaspoon paprika
Stuffing:
1 onion, finely chopped
30 g (1 oz) butter
1½ cups soft breadcrumbs
¼ cup dry white wine
1 sage leaf, finely chopped
1 tablespoon finely chopped parsley
salt
freshly ground pepper

Stuffing: Fry the onion in the butter until soft but not coloured. Remove from the heat and stir in the breadcrumbs, white wine, sage, parsley and season with salt and pepper.

Rub the snapper with lemon juice and sprinkle the cavity with a little salt. Stuff the fish and skewer the opening. Spread the fish with the extra 30 g (1 oz) of butter and season with salt, pepper and paprika. Place the snapper into a buttered ovenproof dish, cover the buttered foil or greaseproof paper and bake in a hot oven (400°F—200°C) for about 20 minutes, basting occasionally with the pan juices. Serve with lemon wedges and a watercress salad.
Note: The cooking time will depend on the thickness of the fish.

Norwegian Fish Bake

4 fish fillets (bream, whiting, flathead,
    blue-eyed cod etc.)
1 teaspoon butter
salt
freshly ground pepper
lemon juice
1 cucumber
2 tomatoes
½ cup fresh dill or 2 teaspoons
    dried dill

Remove any bones from the fish and skin it. Lightly butter an ovenproof dish. Place the fish in it and season to taste with salt and pepper and a squeeze of lemon juice.

Peel the cucumber and cut in two lengthways and remove the seeds. Cut the cucumber into chunky pieces and drop into boiling water for 2 to 3 minutes. Drain and spoon over fish. Cut the tomatoes in thick slices and arrange on top of cucumbers. Sprinkle generously with salt, pepper and dill. Bake in a moderate oven (350°F—170°C) for 15 to 20 minutes.

Serve with crisp Melba Toast.

Rainbow Trout

Rainbow trout are one of the great delicacies. They are found in the swift running mountain streams of the Snowy River district. Only skilled anglers or the occasional lucky ones hook these beauties. They may be caught only at certain times of the year and tickling them under the banks is sternly frowned upon.

These trout are delicately coloured with a smattering of tiny black speckles over the head and flesh that turns a beautiful salmon pink when cooked. Once you taste this incredible fish, the memory of it will stay with you forever.

Trout can be cooked almost any way but maybe they are best baked whole, liberally spread with butter inside and out or stuffed with breadcrumbs, herbs, lemon and butter. But they are also delicious cut into steaks and poached, then served with a creamy Hollandaise sauce. They are good eaten cold too. A few asparagus stalks and a bowl of mayonnaise is all you need to accompany them.

1 to 1.25 kg (2 to 2½ lb) rainbow trout
90 g (3 oz) butter
salt
freshly ground pepper

Scale the trout and clean it. Season the inside of the fish and place 30 g (1 oz) butter inside. Smear the remaining butter over the fish and wrap in aluminium foil. Place in a baking dish and cook in a slow oven (300°F—150°C) for about 30 minutes or until the flesh flakes easily. Serve with its own juices, some lemon wedges and a watercress salad.

Squid

These are a distant cousin to the octopus but are much easier to prepare and have an opaque flesh with a delicate flavour. Choose small squid for this quick method of cooking and serve immediately—the flesh seems to toughen on standing.

500 g (1 lb) small squid
3 tablespoons plain flour
salt and pepper
3 tablespoons olive oil
lemon wedges for serving

To prepare the squid, gently pull the tentacles from the hood (pocket-like part) of the squid, and then hold under cold running water to completely rinse away the ink. Use a little salt to remove any stubborn pieces of ink.

Slide out the piece of cuttle which forms the backbone. Peel skin from the squid and slice squid into rings. Cut away and discard the hard "beak" from the tentacles. The tentacles are delicious to eat and also add to the appearance of the finished dish.

Dry squid on paper towels, then toss in flour seasoned with salt and pepper. Heat oil in a frying pan and cook squid, just a few at a time, for about 4 minutes, turning them occasionally. Drain and serve with lemon wedges.

● There are many kinds of squid available. Some have a very white backbone known as cuttle, thus the name cuttlefish. These are not quite as tender as the squid with the transparent backbone but are still delicious cooked this way.

Fillets of Bream Bonne Femme

This is a famous classic fish dish usually made with Dover sole but is an excellent recipe for all delicate white fish.

8 fillets of bream, sole or other fine
   textured white fish
250 g ($\frac{1}{2}$ lb) button mushrooms
$\frac{1}{2}$ cup chopped shallots
salt
freshly ground pepper
1 cup dry white wine
1 tablespoon lemon juice
water to cover fish
Sauce:
45 g ($1\frac{1}{2}$ oz) butter
3 tablespoons plain flour
strained fish liquid
$\frac{1}{2}$ cup cream
1 tablespoon lemon juice
salt and pepper
30 g (1 oz) softened butter

Remove the skin from the fish fillets. Arrange the fillets folded in three in a buttered ovenproof dish. Wipe the mushrooms and trim the stalks. Reserve eight for garnish. Slice the remaining mushrooms and scatter over the fish with the shallots. Season with salt and pepper.

Pour the wine and lemon juice over the fish, adding enough water to just cover. Cover with buttered greaseproof paper or foil and bake in a moderate oven (350°F—170°C) for 10 minutes.

Remove from the oven and spoon off all the liquid. Keep the fish in a warm place. Make the sauce. Cook the reserved mushroom caps in a little butter until lightly browned. Spoon the sauce over the fish and arrange the mushroom caps on top.
Sauce: Melt the butter in a heavy saucepan, remove from the heat and stir in the flour. Cook the roux for a minute over a gentle heat. Remove from the heat and stir in the cooking liquid.

Place back on the heat and stir until the sauce comes to the boil. Simmer for 3 minutes and then gradually add the cream until the sauce becomes thinner but will still coat the back of a spoon. Season with lemon juice, salt and white pepper. Simmer gently for 5 minutes stirring occasionally. When you are ready to serve the fish, remove the sauce from the heat and whisk in the softened butter.

Whitebait Fritters

Whitebait are silvery-white transparent fish about 3 cm ($1\frac{1}{4}$ in) long. They are eaten whole and are regarded as a great delicacy. In the winter months they can be purchased fresh at a reasonable price from the fish markets and selected fish shops and throughout the year are available in small tins.

Look for the tinned New Zealand whitebait. They tend to be larger and more flavourful than the Japanese variety and are stocked by delicatessens and supermarkets.

One of the most delicious ways of serving these tiny fish is in light, crisp fritters.

2 eggs
1 cup fresh whitebait or 2 tins
salt, freshly ground black pepper
peanut oil for frying

Beat the eggs in a bowl and add the whitebait. Stir until they are combined and season with salt and pepper.

Heat enough peanut oil to cover the base of the pan with a thin film. When the oil begins to smoke, spoon in sufficient whitebait mixture to form a large fritter. Fry for 2 minutes on each side or until golden. Serve with lemon wedges and a sprig of parsley. Makes 4 to 6 large fritters.

Prawns

Prawn Cocktail

8-12 medium prawns or mixture
  of cooked fish and shellfish
½ cup natural yogurt
1 teaspoon tomato paste
few drops hot pepper sauce, optional
1 teaspoon horseradish relish
lemon juice
salt and pepper
shredded lettuce

Shell and de-vein prawns and if large cut into pieces. If using cooked fish remove any skin or bones and break into bite-size pieces. Lucky enough to have lobster? Cut it in slices or chunks. Crabmeat should be flaked and any bony tissue removed.

Put yogurt in a bowl and stir until smooth. Add other ingredients and mix well. Fold in seafood, chill until serving time. Arrange on a bed of shredded crisp lettuce and serve very cold. A thin slice of brown bread and butter may accompany the cocktail. Serves 1.

Garlic Prawns

500 g (1 lb) green prawns
6 tablespoons olive oil
4 garlic cloves
2 tablespoons finely chopped shallots
½ teaspoon chopped chilli pepper OR
  a pinch of chilli powder

Shell the prawns. Heat the oil in 4 flameproof dishes. Chop the garlic finely and combine with the shallots and chilli and divide equally between the dishes. Add the prawns, toss in the garlic mixture and place in a moderately hot oven (375°F—190°C) until the prawns turn pink. Serve immediately with crusty French bread to mop up the garlic juices.
Note: If green prawns are not available use cooked prawns. Heat gently in a large frypan in the garlic flavoured oil, place in heated dishes and then serve immediately.

Prawn and Orange Cocktail

250 g (8 oz) cooked prawns
3 oranges
1 small onion
1 lemon
2 canned pimento
3 canned tomatoes
salt
freshly ground black pepper

Shell and de-vein prawns and if large cut into pieces. Place in a bowl with the juice of 2 oranges and chill for an hour or longer. Chop onion very finely and combine with lemon juice in a small bowl. Let stand for an hour.

Put pimento and canned tomatoes (seeds removed) in container of electric blender with lemon juice strained from the onion and ¼ cup of the orange juice. Blend until smooth. Season to taste with salt and pepper.

Peel remaining orange and cut into sections, removing all pith. Arrange prawns and orange sections in serving dish, spoon the sauce over and sprinkle with the chopped onion. Serve with thin brown bread and butter. Serves 2.

Scandinavian Prawns

Fresh green prawns may be hard to come by so they are worth cooking with care. Cook them in dill and celery-flavoured wine for a few minutes only and then allow them to cool in this liquid.

1 cup dry white wine
1 tablespoon dill weed
2 sticks of celery, chopped
1 teaspoon salt
750 g (1½ lb) green prawns
Sour cream or mayonnaise

Bring the wine, dill weed, celery and salt to the boil. Drop in the prawns.

Stir until the prawns take on a pink tinge then cover and simmer gently for 2 to 3 minutes. Allow to cool in the liquid.

Shell and de-vein. Serve chilled with a bowl of salted sour cream or mayonnaise.

Fresh dill weed may be snipped over the prawns.

Potted Prawns

Potted Prawns is a very simple but memorable first course—small prawns tossed in a spiced butter and then poured into a pot and chilled till firm.

500 g (1 lb) prawns (peeled weight)
185 g (6 oz) butter
¼ teaspoon each ground mace and nutmeg
pinch cayenne
1 teaspoon ground mixed spice
freshly ground black pepper

Cut the prawns into small pieces. Melt the butter in a large frying pan and when the foam subsides add the prawns and the mace, nutmeg, cayenne, mixed spice and pepper. Toss in the butter for a few minutes.

Spoon or pour into a pot. Press lightly, then cover with a round piece of aluminium foil and chill in the refrigerator. Serve with Melba Toast.

Braised Prawns with Snow Peas

750 g (1½ lb) raw prawns
1 tablespoon Chinese wine or dry sherry
1 teaspoon cornflour
1 teaspoon soy sauce
4 oz snow peas
5 to 6 tablespoons oil
Seasonings:
1 tablespoon salt
½ teaspoon sugar
1 teaspoon soy sauce

Shell and de-vein prawns. If large, cut in two. Put into a bowl with wine, cornflour and soy sauce. Mix well, then cover and chill for at least 30 minutes.

String the snow peas. Mix all ingredients for seasoning together.

Heat 4 tablespoons oil in a wok or frying pan and cook prawns, stirring over a high heat until the colour changes. Remove. Add further 1 to 2 tablespoons oil to wok and fry snow peas for 2 minutes.

Return prawns to wok and add seasonings. Toss until heated though and serve immediately.

The combination of prawns and snow peas is not exactly pleasing to the eye but a delight to eat. The crisp texture and sweet flavour of the peas compliments the delicate and tender prawns.

During the winter months, snow peas can be purchased from Chinese stores and markets. When not in season use 1½ cups sliced celery or some sliced, canned water chestnuts.

If using the cooked prawns for this dish, add to mixture at end of cooking and just heat through. Long cooking will toughen the prawns.

King Prawn Cutlets

One of the best known and widely enjoyed Chinese dishes. It is necessary to use raw prawns which can be purchased, already peeled with tails left on, from Chinese stores and some fish shops. Five to six pound frozen blocks of raw, peeled prawns are also available from some Chinese stores.

12 raw king prawns
2 eggs
1 tablespoon soy sauce
pinch of salt
cornflour
fine dry breadcrumbs
oil for deep frying
lemon wedges

If prawns are not already peeled, do so leaving tails intact.

With a sharp knife, slit prawns down the back being careful not to cut right through. Beat eggs with soy sauce and salt.

Dip prawns in cornflour to coat lightly, then into egg mixture and lastly in the breadcrumbs.

Press the cut side of prawns gently with palm of hand to flatten. Deep fry the cutlets in hot oil until golden brown, taking care not to overcrowd pan. Drain on absorbent paper. Serve immediately with lemon wedges.

● When pressing the crumb-coated prawns with the palm of your hand, take care not to press too firmly. This will make the prawns too thin and they will become tough by the time the coating browns when cooking.

Prawn Pilau

This is almost a meal in itself. Serve accompanied by sambols, chutney and a choice of pickle. For some people, additional seasonings will not be necessary.

125 g (4 oz) butter
1 tablespoon curry powder or curry
  paste
2.5 cm (1 in) stick cinnamon
2 bay leaves
6 cardamom pods
3 cloves garlic
½ teaspoon ground black pepper
500 g (1 lb) long grain rice
3½ cups chicken stock OR water and
  stock cubes
salt to taste
¾ cup yogurt
500 g (1 lb) prawns
1 tablespoon lemon juice
4 hard boiled eggs
chopped mint

Heat butter, add curry powder, cinnamon, bay leaves, cardamom pods, crushed garlic and pepper. Cook, stirring for 5 minutes. Add rice and cook until grains are coated with mixture.

Stir in stock, salt and yogurt. Bring to the boil, stir once then cover and cook over low heat for about 20 minutes. Top with shelled prawns, sprinkle with lemon juice, cover and leave another 5 minutes until rice is tender. Toss with a fork and serve.

Garnish with quartered hard boiled eggs and chopped mint.

Oysters Rockefeller (see recipe on page 102)

Oysters

Oysters on Rock Salt

Sydney rock oysters are renowned all over the world and their delicate flavour is best appreciated when served slightly chilled with lemon, black pepper and thin brown bread and butter. However, many people enjoy them with a piquant sauce and we think it's always wise to serve it.

2 doz oysters on their half-shell
rock salt
1 lemon cut into quarters
2 thin slices brown bread
butter
Cocktail Sauce:
$\frac{1}{2}$ cup tomato purée
dash Tabasco sauce
squeeze lemon juice
2 tablespoons cream
salt
freshly ground pepper

Chill the oysters. Place some rock salt on two plates and a small bowl for the sauce in the centre of each. Cut the lemon into quarters. Remove the crusts from the bread, butter it lightly and cut each slice into four. Arrange on a small plate. Fill the small bowls with cocktail sauce. Arrange the oysters on the rock salt bed and place two lemon quarters on each plate.

Cocktail Sauce:
Combine the tomato purée, tabasco, lemon juice, cream and season with salt and pepper.

Note: Horseradish may also be used to flavour this sauce.

Oysters Rockefeller

This most delicious way of serving cooked oysters is known the world over. The recipe originated in New Orleans and was aptly named, being considered as rich as Rockefeller.

1 dozen oysters on the shell
$\frac{1}{2}$ cup sour cream
2 cloves garlic crushed with a little salt
freshly ground pepper
$\frac{1}{2}$ cup cooked spinach, finely chopped (fresh, frozen or canned)
2 tablespoons grated cheddar cheese
3 tablespoons fine white breadcrumbs
15 g ($\frac{1}{2}$ oz) butter

Remove oysters from the half-shell. Mix half of the sour cream with half of the crushed garlic and season with pepper. Place a teaspoon of the mixture in the bottom of each shell and place the oyster back in each shell.

Combine the spinach with the remaining sour cream and garlic, season with pepper and place a tablespoon of this mixture on each oyster.

Sprinkle with grated cheese and breadcrumbs. Arrange oysters on rock salt in an ovenproof dish and place a small piece of butter on each oyster.

Place under a preheated grill for about 4 minutes or until the breadcrumbs are golden brown. Serve hot.

Oysters Kilpatrick

Although their origin is not definite, Oysters Kilpatrick appear to have originated in Australia and most restauranteurs will tell you that they seem to be Australians' favourite way of eating cooked oysters.

1 dozen oysters on the shell
1 tablespoon Worcestershire sauce
15 g ($\frac{1}{2}$ oz) butter
2 lean bacon rashers
freshly ground pepper

Heat the Worcestershire sauce and butter in a small saucepan until the butter has melted and the sauce has begun to simmer. Grill the bacon rashers until golden and crisp. Spoon a little of the Worcestershire sauce and butter mixture on each oyster. Chop the bacon finely and sprinkle over each oyster. Season with freshly ground pepper and place on a bed of rock salt in an ovenproof dish—or directly on the grill.

Place under a preheated grill for 3 to 4 minutes and serve immediately.

Crayfish

Crayfish Mayonnaise

This dish depends for its success on the freshness and tenderness of the cooked crayfish and the perfection of the mayonnaise. It is one of the most luxurious dishes and makes a particularly good luncheon.

1 × 1.25 kg (2$\frac{1}{2}$ lb) cooked crayfish
$\frac{1}{2}$ cup mayonnaise
1 tablespoon tomato purée
2 tablespoons cream
freshly ground pepper
1$\frac{1}{2}$ to 2 cups cooked rice
pinch salt
4 tablespoons vinaigrette dressing
2 tomatoes, peeled and sliced
2 tablespoons freshly chopped parsley

Cut the crayfish flesh into thick slices (called medallions).

Add the tomato purée, cream and crayfish mustard to the mayonnaise and season with pepper.

Toss the crayfish pieces in the mayonnaise and arrange in the empty tail shell.

Toss the cooked rice with the vinaigrette dressing, adding salt if necessary and then mix with 1$\frac{1}{2}$ tablespoons of the parsley. Arrange the rice gently heaped into the centre on an oval serving dish and place the filled crayfish shell on this bed.

Place the tomato slice along one side of the dish and garnish the crayfish with the remaining chopped parsley. The crayfish head may be washed and used to garnish crayfish mayonnaise, if wished.

Alternatively, the crayfish may be served in its shell garnished with parsley, the tomato cut into wedges and tossed with the rice which is served on one side with lemon wedges.

To prepare cooked crayfish

Split through the middle of the shell underneath the crayfish taking care not to cut the flesh. Peel the shell away. Pull the flesh out of the tail. Snap off the shell being careful not to spoil the shape and then pull the shell of the body apart to release the tail flesh with the body flesh.

Remove the sac from the crayfish head leaving the mustard. Spoon the mustard from the crayfish head into a bowl and place on one side to be added to the mayonnaise.

Mussels

Moules Marinière

1 kg (2 lb) fresh mussels
4 shallots, finely chopped
4 parsley stalks
1 bay leaf
sprig of thyme
freshly ground black pepper
60 g (2 oz) butter
2 cups dry white wine
1 teaspoon flour
little chopped parsley

Scrape and clean mussels in several changes of water, discarding any that are not shut tightly. Put into a wide pan with shallots, herbs, pepper, half the butter and the wine. Cover the pan and cook over a high heat for 5 minutes, shaking the pan now and then. Remove the mussels as soon as they open, discarding half of each shell. Arrange the mussels in the remaining shells on warm soup plates. Strain liquid through a sieve, return to the pan with the remaining butter mixed with the flour and boil rapidly until thickened slightly. Pour over the mussels and sprinkle with chopped parsley. Serve at once with crusty bread, creamy butter and dry white wine.

Variations
Mussels with Cream: Replace the butter with $\frac{1}{2}$ cup of cream. Add to the reduced mussel liquid and boil rapidly for several minutes before pouring over mussels.
Mussels with Pernod: Prepare as for Mussels with Cream, adding 2 tablespoons of Pernod to the pot along with the wine. Rich, but delicious.

- Thoroughly scrub one by one to remove mud, seaweed or any dirt that may cling to them. Use a good stiff brush and plenty of water. Pull off the beard that clings around the edges. Soak them in water—they should disgorge any sand.
- Don't overcook. Most recipes call for aromatics (onions, a few herbs, a bay leaf) and a little wine or water. The mussels are cooked in this brew just long enough for them to open their shells. They are then ready for eating.
- Reduce the cooking liquor by placing over a high heat. This is then poured over the mussels which are served on the half shell.

True devotees eat the mussel with a small fork, drink the sauce from the shell and then mop up the remaining liquor with some crusty bread. A chilled white wine is the perfect accompaniment.

Moules Marinière

Scallops

Scallops à la Parisienne

Scallops are a great delicacy, so it is worthwhile treating them with great care. They are available all the year round. This recipe involves some of the most important methods in seafood cookery and although the list of ingredients might seem formidable, don't let this put you off—it's really quite simple. The scallops sit on a bed of Mushroom Duxelles and are covered with a creamy rich sauce made from the scallop liquid.

500 g (1 lb) scallops
Court Bouillon:
1 small celery stalk, sliced
½ small carrot, sliced
½ small onion, sliced
bouquet garni, comprising 2 parsley
  stalks, 1 bay leaf, 1 sprig of thyme
  and a few peppercorns
½ cup dry white wine
¾ cup of water
Mushroom duxelles:
125 g (4 oz) mushrooms, finely chopped
1 shallot, finely chopped
30 g (1 oz) butter
freshly ground pepper and salt
Velouté sauce:
1 tablespoon butter
1 tablespoon flour
¾ cup scallop stock
salt and freshly ground white pepper
1 egg yolk
1 tablespoon cream
4 tablespoons breadcrumbs
2 tablespoons butter

Remove the beard from the scallops. Place all the ingredients for the Court Bouillon in a saucepan and bring to the boil, simmer gently for 20 minutes. Add the scallops and allow to poach for 5 minutes. Remove the scallops and strain the liquid.
Mushroom Duxelles: Melt the butter in a pan and add the shallot. Cook for a minute and then add the mushrooms. Season with salt and pepper and cook for a further 3 minutes. Spoon mixture into 4 scallop shells.

Arrange the scallops on this Mushroom Duxelles bed.

Make the sauce. Melt the tablespoon of butter and stir in the flour. Cook for 1 minute and then add the scallop liquid, gradually stirring all the time. Season with pepper and salt and allow the sauce to cook gently for 10 minutes. Combine the egg yolk with the cream and stir into the sauce. Stir for 1 minute over the heat but do not allow the sauce to boil. Remove sauce from the heat and spoon over the scallops.

Melt butter in a pan and toss the breadcrumbs in it until they are golden and crisp. Sprinkle over the prepared scallop shells.

Place in a hot oven or under the griller to heat through until golden. Serve piping hot, garnished with parsley and lemon wedges.

Crab

Crab Cakes

Lightly devilled crab is the base of this delicious fried entrée. Serve with a tartare sauce and lemon wedges.

185 g (6 oz) crabmeat, canned or fresh
1 small garlic clove, crushed
dash of cayenne
½ teaspoon Worcestershire sauce
1 teaspoon powdered mustard
salt, freshly ground pepper
½ cup fine white breadcrumbs
1 egg, beaten
flour for dusting
2 tablespoons olive oil
30 g (1 oz) butter
freshly chopped parsley for garnishing

Combine flaked crabmeat, garlic, cayenne, Worcestershire sauce, mustard, salt, pepper and breadcrumbs. Bind this mixture with the beaten egg. Shape into 4 cakes and dust lightly with flour.

Heat oil in a large pan and add the butter. When the butter foam has subsided, add the Crab Cakes and fry for 3 minutes on each side or until golden brown all over.

Serve with lemon wedges and Tartare sauce.

Crab Croquettes

These are more delicate than the Crab Cakes and take a little more time to prepare. They, too, are served with tartare sauce and lemon wedges.

185 g (6 oz) crabmeat, canned or fresh
1 cup warm Béchamel sauce
1 small garlic clove, crushed
dash cayenne
½ teaspoon Worcestershire sauce
1 teaspoon powdered mustard
salt and freshly ground pepper
flour, egg and fine white breadcrumbs
   for coating
oil for frying

Lightly mix the crabmeat with the Béchamel sauce, garlic, cayenne, Worcestershire sauce, mustard and salt and pepper.

Spread on to a plate or tray, brush with melted butter, cover with wax paper or plastic wrap and chill until firm.

Cut the mixture into 8 portions. Dust each with flour and then coat in egg and breadcrumbs shaping into a roll like a cork. Chill once more.

Heat 2.5 cm (1 in) oil in a saucepan and when very hot and a a blue haze appears, add the Croquettes and fry until golden brown. This should take 2 to 3 minutes. Drain on kitchen paper and serve hot with tartare sauce and lemon wedges.
Béchamel Sauce: Make a thick Béchamel using these proportions—60 g (2 oz) butter, ⅓ cup flour and 1 cup milk. (page 17).

egg dishes

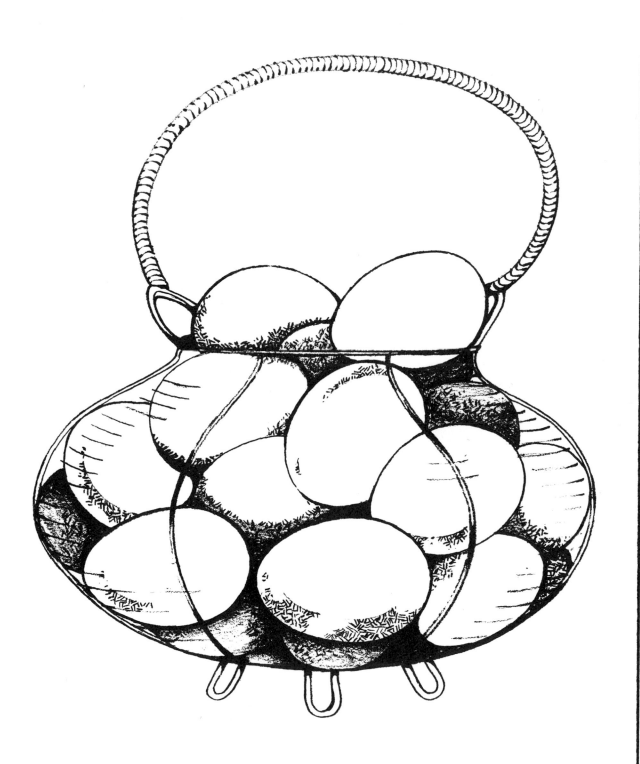

Eggs

Poached Eggs Florentine

1 cup milk
¼ small onion
6 peppercorns
1 bayleaf
30 g (1 oz) butter
30 g (1 oz) flour
60 g (2 oz) Parmesan cheese, grated
500 g (1 lb) spinach
salt, freshly ground pepper
30 g (1 oz) butter
pinch of grated nutmeg
4 eggs

Infuse the milk with the onion, peppercorns and bay leaf. Melt the butter in a saucepan and stir in the flour. Pour on the infused, strained milk. Stir constantly until the sauce comes to the boil and allow it to simmer for 2 minutes. Just before using, stir in the cheese carefully. Wash the spinach and cook in a covered saucepan for 5 minutes. Do not add any water (the water remaining on the leaves after washing is ample). Season with salt and freshly ground pepper. Remove the spinach, chop it finely and add the butter and the grated nutmeg. Return to a low heat to warm through.

Boil some water in a shallow pan. Break each egg into a cup and slide the egg into the water separately. Allow the water to come just to the boil. Turn off the heat and leave the eggs for about 5 minutes to cook.

Arrange the spinach on a gratin dish or an individual oven-proof dish and place the eggs on the spinach.

Coat each egg with the sauce and place under a pre-heated grill or in the oven for a few minutes to glaze the sauce and reheat the eggs.

Chinese Tea Eggs

These spiced eggs with their beautiful marbled appearance resembling antique porcelain are ideal for hors d'oeuvres or, if left in their shells, are excellent for picnics. They may be stored in the refrigerator for several days.

6 eggs
water to cover
3 tablespoons black tea
1 tablespoon salt
1 piece mandarin peel
4 cloves star anise* or 1 teaspoon
    ground anise
¼ cup soy sauce
1 cinnamon stick

Place eggs in water to cover and bring to the boil. Allow them to cook gently 7 minutes. Remove the eggs and reserve the cooking water. Cool eggs thoroughly under cold running water.

Tap the cooled eggs lightly with a spoon cracking the shell. Do not remove the shell.

Boil the water in which the eggs were cooked and add tea leaves, salt, mandarin peel, anise, soy sauce and cinnamon stick. Gently lower the cracked eggs into the spiced tea water and simmer covered until the egg shells turn brown about ½ an hour. Turn off the heat and allow the eggs to stand still covered for a further ½ hour.

Drain the eggs. Allow them to cool and remove the shells. Serve them either cut in halves or quarters.

*Anise can be purchased from Chinese grocery stores.
Note: The cracked egg shells allow the spiced tea water to soak through flavouring the eggs and giving them a marbled effect.

Stuffed Eggs

Even if you're planning to eat soon after your dinner guests arrive, it's a good idea to have a hors d'oeuvre to offer. A dish of olives or crisp radish requires no preparation but if you have the time it's nice to make something yourself. Stuffed Eggs are simple, quick and delicious.

6 eggs
3 tablespoons mayonnaise
1 tablespoon French mustard
salt to taste
pinch cayenne pepper
strips of red pimento to garnish

Lower eggs into a saucepan of gently boiling water to which a good pinch of salt has been added. Cook gently for 10-12 minutes. Stir the eggs for the first 8 minutes so that the yolks will be centred. Remove from the heat and plunge immediately into cold water.

When the eggs are completely cold shell them and cut in half lengthwise using a stainless steel knife (other metals will discolour the egg). Remove the yolks carefully and push through a sieve. Mix in remaining ingredients except the pimento. If the mixture is too thick for piping add a little more mayonnaise. Using a 1 cm ($\frac{1}{2}$ in) plain rosette tube pipe the mixture into egg whites and decorate with strips of pimento.

Variations:

Chicken and mushrooms: Prepare eggs as described above. To the yolk mixture add 60 g (2 oz) minced chicken and 60 g (2 oz) of button mushrooms finely chopped. Pipe into whites and garnish with finely sliced mushrooms.

Anchovy: Pound three anchovy fillets in a mortar or chop very finely on a board and stir into the yolk mixture. Pipe into whites and garnish with anchovy fillets.

Caviar: Omit cayenne pepper and add 1 teaspoon lemon juice to the yolk mixture. Pipe into whites and garnish with black caviar.

Smoked salmon: Pound 2 slices of smoked salmon in a mortar or mash with a fork and stir into the yolk mixture. Pipe into the whites and garnish with a strip of smoked salmon.

Ham and capers: Very finely chop 1 slice of ham and 1 teaspoon of capers and add to the yolk mixture. Pipe into the whites and garnish with capers.

Ham and horseradish: Omit the French mustard and cayenne pepper from the basic recipe and add 2 teaspoons of horseradish to the yolk mixture with 1 slice of finely chopped ham. Pipe into whites and garnish with fine slivers of ham.

Prawns: Pound 60 g (2 oz) of prawns in a mortar or chop them very finely on a board and then stir into the yolk mixture. Add a pinch of nutmeg. Pipe into whites and garnish with a whole small prawn.

Plain Omelet (see recipe overleaf)

Bacon and Eggs

2 bacon rashers
2 eggs

Remove the rind and the rust from the bacon. Heat a frypan and add the bacon. Allow it to cook slowly for 4 to 5 minutes. If you prefer crisp bacon, pour off excess fat from the pan from time to time. Push the bacon to the side of the pan or place on a plate and keep warm. Break the eggs into a cup. With the frypan still on the heat, slide the eggs into the pan. A fried egg should be cooked gently, and basted occasionally with the pan fat. When the white is set and the yolk is still soft remove the eggs with an egg slice to the warm plate with the bacon.

The "rust" on the bacon is the dark edge opposite the rind. When cooked this can become tough, so is best removed. Spread the bacon out with the flat of a knife to prevent the bacon from shrivelling up.

Baked Eggs

15 g ($\frac{1}{2}$ oz) butter
60 g (2 oz) ham
2 eggs
2 tablespoons cream

Butter a small fireproof dish and place the ham, cut into fine strips in the bottom of the dish. Break the eggs on top.

Pour the cream over the eggs, put the dish into a pan of water and place in a moderate oven (350°F--170°C) for 6 to 7 minutes or until the whites are set and the yolks still soft. Serve with hot buttered toast.

Variations:

Follow the same method but use 60 g (2 oz) of any of the following in place of the ham:

- Finely sliced green peppers. Blanch in boiling water for 1 minute and drain under cold water to preserve their bright green colour.
- Finely sliced mushrooms. Toss in a little hot butter until soft.
- Peeled and chopped tomato.
- Potatoes and onions, fried together.

Scotch Eggs

Scotch Eggs need no introduction. Generations of picnickers—not only Scottish ones—have known the delights of spicy meat-coated, hard-boiled eggs.

6 hard-boiled eggs
few drops hot pepper sauce
few drops Worcestershire
500 g (1 lb) sausage mince
$\frac{1}{2}$ cup plain flour
salt and freshly ground white pepper
beaten egg
breadcrumbs
oil for deep frying

Shell the eggs. Mix the sausage mince with the hot pepper sauce and Worcestershire sauce. Divide the meat into 6 equal portions. Dust the eggs lightly with flour mixed with salt and pepper, cover each egg with sausage mince, pressing and moulding on well. Brush with beaten egg and roll in breadcrumbs. Chill for at least 1 hour. Heat oil for deep frying and cook eggs until golden brown. Remove and drain on absorbent paper. Cool and chill.

Omelets

Omelets

The perfect omelet should be plump and golden with a soft and creamy centre. Omelets should be cooked in a well-seasoned pan kept, if possible, just for omelets and never washed with soap and water. Just wipe it out after use and then smear with a little oil.

Place the omelet pan on the heat. Beat three eggs with a fork until the white and the yolk are barely combined. Add the salt, pepper and 1 tablespoon of water. Place a good teaspoon of butter in the hot pan and when melted, pour in the eggs and leave for 10 seconds to allow them to set on the bottom of the pan.

Stir round slowly with a fork, allowing the raw egg to drop back on to the hot pan, shaking the pan while you stir. The omelet will now resemble underdone scrambled eggs.
Add the finely chopped herbs (or the desired filling).

Start to fold the omelet by tilting the pan away from you. Change your grip on the handle so that the handle runs across the palm between the finger and thumb. Holding the hot dish in the other hand, tilt the omelet on to it in one quick movement. Serve at once.

Soufflé Omelet

4 large eggs
2 tablespoons cream
2 tablespoons caster sugar
15 g ($\frac{1}{2}$ oz) butter
strawberry or raspberry jam for filling
icing sugar

Separate the eggs. Beat the yolks with the cream and sugar. Whisk the egg whites until stiff and pour over yolk mixture. Fold in carefully with metal spoon.

Melt the butter in an omelet pan and when the butter is foaming pour in the mixture. Leave on the heat for 1 minute to brown the bottom of the omelet. Quickly place the pan in a preheated moderate oven (375°F—190°C) for a few minutes or put under a hot grill to brown the top.

Heat the jam and spread over the omelet. Cut a slash down the centre of the omelet to help the omelet fold.

Fold in half using a metal spatula and slide on to a warm dish. Dust with sifted icing sugar.

Have some metal skewers ready which have been made red hot by placing them on the electric elements or gas stove. Mark the top of the omelet decorating it in a lattice pattern. The heat makes the sugar caramelise. Alternatively, the omelet may be dusted with caster sugar and served immediately.

Variations:
- Rum omelet—heat 3 tablespoons of rum but do not allow to boil. Set the rum alight and pour while still flaming over the omelet.
- Banana—slice 1 banana diagonally and lightly fry in butter with sugar and rum added. Place filling into omelet and proceed as in above recipe.
- Mix $\frac{1}{2}$ cup of strawberries or raspberries with 1 tablespoon of redcurrant jelly and fill omelet.
- Poach a peach in syrup, add some brandy. Slice. Fill the omelet. Heat some brandy and pour while flaming over the omelet.

Omelet Arnold Bennett

This superb richly-flavoured omelet was named after Arnold Bennett the English literary critic who started his career on a women's magazine. After a stay in France he married a Frenchwoman which may have accounted for his great love of good food.

250 g (8 oz) smoked haddock
75 g (2½ oz) butter
¾ cup cream
5 large eggs
salt, freshly ground pepper
3 tablespoons grated Parmesan cheese

Place the haddock in a saucepan, cover with cold water, bring slowly to the boil and then lower the heat and poach for 5 to 10 minutes depending on the thickness of the fish. Remove carefully from the water and allow to cool. Remove the skin and bones and flake the flesh. Toss the haddock over a quick heat with half the butter and 3 tablespoons of the cream and then allow to cool.

Separate the eggs, beat the yolks with a tablespoon of the cream and season with salt and pepper. Whip the whites stiffly and fold into the yolks with the haddock and half the grated cheese.

Melt the remaining butter in a large frying pan or copper dish, oval for preference, and while still foaming pour in the mixture, stir once or twice over a moderate heat and then leave for about one minute to allow the bottom to brown. Sprinkle with the remaining cheese and cream and slip the pan under a moderately hot grill or into a hot oven (400°F—200°C) to set the omelet. When lightly browned and puffed, serve immediately.

Sufficient for 6 people.

Note: This recipe may be doubled when cooking brunch for a crowd and the omelet cooked in a baking dish.

Spanish Omelet

2 large potatoes
30 g (1 oz) butter
1 medium onion, chopped finely
½ green pepper, cut into thin shreds
2 bacon rashers, diced
8 eggs
salt and freshly ground pepper
3 tablespoons olive oil

Boil the unpeeled potatoes. Peel and cut into a large dice. Melt the butter in a frypan, add the potatoes and onion and brown gently, tossing frequently. Add the green pepper and the bacon and toss for 1 minute in the pan. Beat the eggs (using a whisk) and season with salt and pepper. Add the potato mixture. Heat the olive oil in a large frypan, about 25 cm (10 in) in diameter and when hot pour in the omelet mixture. Stir a few times and then leave to set. Place the pan under a pre-heated griller so the top of the omelet will brown slightly or turn it over in the pan and allow to cook for a minute.

Run a knife around and underneath the omelet to loosen it and slide it on to a warm plate. Garnish with finely chopped parsley. This dish is also delicious cold.

Dessert Omelets

These are soufflé omelets, sweetened with sugar and flavoured with fruit, liqueur or a good fruit jam.

The yolks are beaten with sugar and cream and the stiffly beaten egg whites are folded in. Pour the mixture into sizzling butter in a hot omelet pan and allow it to set on the bottom. Place under a hot griller or into a hot oven to cook the top. Add the filling and fold in two. Serve straight away on a hot dish. For a decorative effect, dust the omelet with icing sugar and then score with red hot skewers to caramelise the sugar—or simply dust with caster sugar.

Savoury Soufflés

Mushroom Soufflé

A most impressive soufflé encrusted with cheese and mushrooms.

250 g (8 oz) small mushrooms
15 g (½ oz) butter
1 shallot, finely chopped
1 teaspoon chopped mixed herbs
**   (marjoram, chives and tarragon)**
1 heaped teaspoon finely chopped parsley
1½ cups Béchamel sauce
3 egg yolks
90 g (3 oz) grated Parmesan cheese
2 tablespoons cream
pinch ground mace
salt
freshly ground pepper
4 egg whites
1 tablespoon grated Parmesan cheese

Wash the mushrooms, peel and cut off stalks. Chop these trimmings very finely. Slice the mushrooms. Melt half the butter in a frying pan and cook the mushrooms briskly for about three minutes. Remove to a plate.

Add the remaining butter to the pan, the chopped mushroom trimmings and the shallot, cook for a few minutes and then add the herbs. Stir continuously whilst cooking.

Add this mixture to the warm Béchamel sauce. Add the egg yolks, one at a time and then add the cheese. When well mixed, stir in the cream and mace and adjust the seasoning.

Whisk the egg whites stiffly, stir 1 tablespoon into the basic mixture and then fold in the remaining egg whites. Pour a third of this mixture into a greased 4-cup soufflé dish, scatter over half the mushrooms, pour in another third of the mixture and then the remaining mushrooms, reserving a few for the top. Cover with the rest of the soufflé mixture. Sprinkle top with sliced mushrooms and the grated cheese.

Bake in a moderately hot oven (375°F—190°C) for 25 to 30 minutes until well risen and the top well browned and firm. Remove from the oven, place on a heated dish and serve immediately.

Béchamel Sauce

45 g (1½ oz) butter
3 tablespoons plain flour
1½ cups flavoured milk
salt and pepper

Melt the butter, stir in flour and cook this roux for 1 minute. Remove the saucepan from the heat and stir in the cool flavoured milk. Return to the heat and stir until the sauce thickens and boils. Lower the heat and simmer for 7 to 10 minutes. Season with salt and pepper.

Crab Soufflé

Grease a 4-cup soufflé dish and tie a band of double buttered greaseproof paper around the dish.

30 g (1 oz) butter
1 teaspoon paprika
1 teaspoon curry powder
185 g (6½ oz) can crab meat
few drops Tabasco sauce
salt
freshly ground pepper
½ cup Béchamel sauce
2 tablespoons cream
3 egg yolks
4 egg whites
1 tablespoon grated cheese
1 tablespoon browned breadcrumbs

Melt the butter and add the paprika and curry powder. Cook for 1 minute. Remove from the heat, add the crab meat and tabasco sauce and season with salt and pepper.

Return to the heat to warm the crab and then add the Béchamel sauce and cream.

Take the pan from the heat and mix in the egg yolks. Whisk the egg whites until they stand in stiff peaks and cut and fold into the crab mixture. Turn into the prepared soufflé dish.

Sprinkle the top with the cheese and browned crumbs and bake in a moderate oven (350°F—170°C) until well risen and firm to the touch—about 20 to 25 minutes.

Cheese Soufflé

45 g (1½ oz) butter
30 g (1 oz) flour
4 egg yolks
5 egg whites
45 g (1½ oz) each of grated Parmesan
   and Cheddar cheese
1 cup milk
pinch cayenne pepper
pinch paprika
dried crumbs, browned in the oven

Lightly grease a 5-cup soufflé dish and tie a collar of greased paper around the outside. This should be about 8 cm (3 in) higher than the dish and holds the soufflé as it rises.

Melt the butter in a medium-sized saucepan, stir in the flour to form a roux. When thoroughly blended pour on the milk, a little at a time, stirring until it comes to the boil forming a thick white sauce. Allow to cool slightly. Beat the egg yolks, one at a time, into the sauce. Season with salt, cayenne pepper and paprika and then work in the cheese.

Whisk the egg whites with a pinch of salt in a dry warm bowl until very stiff and standing in peaks. Using a metal spoon stir a spoonful of egg white into the cheese sauce to soften the mixture and then carefully fold and cut in the remaining egg white.

Pour the mixture into the prepared soufflé dish, sprinkle with browned crumbs and a little extra grated Parmesan cheese. Cut a circle around the inside of the soufflé with a metal spoon to form a top hat. Place the dish on a heated baking tray and bake in a moderately hot oven (375°F—190°C) for about 25 to 30 minutes.

Soufflé is cooked when it is well-risen and a crisp crust has formed on top. Remove from oven, take off paper collar and serve immediately.

Spinach Soufflé

Spinach flavoured with nutmeg is the basis of this delicious, light vegetable soufflé.

1 bay leaf
6 peppercorns
1 onion stuck with 2 cloves
1 cup milk
30 g (1 oz) butter
2 tablespoons plain flour
salt
freshly ground pepper
8 spinach or silver beet leaves
½ teaspoon salt
nutmeg
4 egg yolks
5 egg whites, stiffly beaten

Butter a 15 cm (6 in) soufflé dish and tie a buttered paper collar around the outside.

Place the bay leaf, peppercorns, onion and milk in a saucepan. Bring to the boil. Remove from the heat and cool. Strain. Melt the butter, add the flour and cook for 1 minute. Do not allow the roux to colour. Remove from the heat and gradually stir in the cooled flavoured milk. Return to the heat and stir until it boils and thickens. Cook gently for 10 minutes. Season with salt and pepper.

Meanwhile wash the spinach very well under running water. Pack into a saucepan, sprinkle with salt and cover tightly. Cook for about 6 minutes shaking the pan from time to time. Drain the spinach in a sieve pressing out the excess moisture. Chop very finely and add to the basic sauce. Season with nutmeg. Add the egg yolks.

Beat a tablespoon of the egg white into the basic soufflé mixture and then carefully fold the mixture into the remaining egg white. Spoon into the prepared dish. Cook in a moderately hot oven (375°F—190°C) for about 25 minutes or until well puffed and delicately browned. Serve immediately.
Note: This may be served in individual soufflé dishes. Cook for 12 to 15 minutes.

Grand Marnier Soufflé (see recipe overleaf)

Hungarian Pancakes (see recipe on page 124)

Dessert Soufflés

Grand Marnier Soufflé

A dessert soufflé with the wonderful orange flavour of Grand Marnier liqueur.

45 g (1½ oz) butter
2 tablespoons plain flour
1 cup milk
¼ teaspoon salt
½ cup sugar
½ teaspoon vanilla essence
4 egg yolks
2 tablespoons Grand Marnier liqueur
5 egg whites
sifted icing sugar

Grease the inside of a 5-cup soufflé dish. Sprinkle with caster sugar and remove excess sugar by turning the dish upside down and tapping it gently. Tie a band of double greased greaseproof paper or aluminium foil around rim of the dish.

Melt the butter in a saucepan, stir in flour and cook for 1 minute. Remove from the heat and gradually stir in the milk. When smooth, add the salt, sugar and vanilla.

Return the saucepan to the heat and bring to the boil, stirring continuously. When the sauce is thick and smooth remove it from the heat and allow to cool. Stir in lightly beaten egg yolks and the Grand Marnier. Lastly fold in the stiffly beaten egg whites.

Pour immediately into the prepared soufflé dish and bake in a moderate oven (350°F—170°C) for 35 minutes, or until well risen and golden. Dust with a little icing sugar and serve immediately.

Ginger Soufflé

Ginger is often given as a Christmas gift and this recipe is a delicious way of putting some of it to good use.

2½ cups milk
6 egg yolks
125 g (4 oz) caster sugar
4 teaspoons ground ginger
2 tablespoons gelatine soaked in
  ½ cup water
1 cup cream, lightly whipped
4 tablespoons preserved ginger, sliced
6 egg whites
1 cup cream, whipped
few extra slices of ginger for decoration
60 g (2 oz) pistachio nuts, finely chopped

Tie a double-thickness band of greased greaseproof paper around the outside of a 5 to 6 cup soufflé dish so that it stands 7.5 cm (3 in) above the rim of the dish.

Scald the milk. Beat the egg yolks with the sugar and ground ginger until thick and light in colour. Pour on the hot milk, stirring until the mixture thickens and will coat the back of a metal spoon. Strain into a bowl.

Soften the gelatine in the water and then dissolve over a low heat. Add to the custard mixture, cover the bowl to prevent a skin from forming on top of the custard, and cool.

Chill the custard until it begins to thicken and then fold in the cream and ginger with a metal spoon. Whisk the egg whites until they stand in stiff peaks and fold in quickly and lightly. Turn into the prepared soufflé dish and place into the refrigerator to set.

When set, peel away the paper around the soufflé dish. Decorate with the remaining cream which has been whisked until it is stiff, ginger slices and finely chopped pistachio nuts which are pressed very gently around the sides.

Note: The soufflé mixture should come about 5 cm (2 in) above the rim of the dish. If there is too much mixture, fill a small soufflé dish.

Chocolate Soufflé

90 g (3 oz) dark cooking chocolate
1¼ cups cream
1 envelope (1 tablespoon) gelatine
4 tablespoons water
3 eggs, separated
¾ cup caster sugar
chocolate leaves for decoration
whipped cream and nuts for decoration

Prepare a 4-cup soufflé dish with oiled paper collar. Chop chocolate and melt in a small bowl over a pan of hot, not boiling, water. Sprinkle gelatine over water in a small saucepan.

Put egg yolks into a large bowl and gradually beat in sugar. Place over a pan of simmering water and beat until very thick and lemon coloured. Remove bowl from pan of water and continue beating until bowl is cold. Place gelatine over a low heat to dissolve, but do not boil.

Using a large metal spoon, stir dissolved gelatine, then cooled melted chocolate, gently into beaten egg yolk mixture. Whip cream until it just begins to hold its shape, and fold into mixture. Whip egg whites until stiff but not dry, then fold into chocolate cream mixture. Immediately pour into prepared soufflé dish and chill until set.

Remove paper collar and press finely crushed plain sweet biscuits or nuts around sides of soufflé. Pipe swirls of stiffly whipped, well-chilled cream around edge. Decorate with chocolate leaves. Serves 6.

Strawberry Soufflé

1 punnet strawberries or 1 packet
  frozen strawberries
1 envelope (1 tablespoon) gelatine
¼ cup cold water
4 eggs, separated
pinch salt
¾ cup sugar
1¾ cups cream
few drops red food colouring
whipped cream and strawberries for
  decorating

Prepare a 4-cup soufflé dish with an oiled paper collar. Wash strawberries, reserve a few for decoration and hull the rest. Purée in an electric blender or push through a sieve. If using frozen berries, thaw according to package directions before you purée them. Sprinkle gelatine over water in a small saucepan.

Put egg yolks into a bowl and gradually beat in two-thirds of measured sugar. Place over a pan of simmering water and beat until very thick and lemon coloured. Remove bowl from heat. Place gelatine over a low heat to dissolve, but do not allow to boil. Add gelatine to beaten egg yolks, stirring to combine well. Allow to cool, stirring occasionally. Mix in strawberry purée.

Beat egg whites with pinch of salt until they hold soft peaks, then gradually beat in remaining sugar. Continue beating until egg whites are shiny and hold a definite peak. Whip cream lightly and gently fold into strawberry mixture when it is just on the point of setting. Fold in egg whites, adding a little food colouring to give a deeper pink colour. Immediately pour into prepared dish and chill.

Remove paper collar and decorate soufflé with swirls of whipped cream and reserved strawberries.

Serves 6.

Liqueur Soufflé

$1\frac{1}{2}$ envelopes ($1\frac{1}{2}$ tablespoons) gelatine
$\frac{1}{2}$ cup water
5 eggs, separated
$\frac{1}{2}$ cup caster sugar
$\frac{3}{4}$ cup brandy
$\frac{1}{2}$ cup sweet sherry
1 tablespoon lemon juice
1 tablespoon Benedictine or
   Grand Marnier
$1\frac{1}{4}$ cups cream
toasted ground hazelnuts for decoration

Prepare a 7-cup size soufflé dish with an oiled paper collar. To have the soufflé standing above the dish, a collar is wrapped around it. Cut off a sheet of greaseproof paper long enough to wrap once around the soufflé dish. Fold in half lengthwise, then turn up about 5 cm (2 in) of the folded edge and crease to form a hem. Wrap collar around dish, hem inside. Tie with string. The hem balances the rim of the dish, ensuring the paper wraps smoothly without a crease.

Lightly smear a little oil inside the collar of paper extending above the dish so it will peel away smoothly once the mixture has set.

(For some soufflés, the dish is lined with sponge fingers. Cut fingers level at one end so they will stand straight against the side of the dish.)

Sprinkle gelatine over water in a small saucepan and leave to soak.

In a large bowl over a pan of warm or gently simmering water, beat egg yolks and sugar, using an electric mixer or rotary beater, until thick and lemon coloured. Gradually beat in sherry, brandy, lemon juice and Benedictine. When thick, remove bowl from pan of water and continue beating until mixture is cold.

Place gelatine over a low heat to dissolve, but do not boil. Add to egg yolk mixture and allow to thicken.

Whip cream lightly, reserve 3 tablespoons for decoration, and fold remaining cream into mixture.

Stiffly beat egg whites and gently fold into mixture. A large metal spoon is ideal for this.

Pour into prepared dish and chill until firm.

Remove paper collar from set soufflé. Warm a spatula in very hot water, slip blade between the two thicknesses of greaseproof and run it quickly round the edge. This warms the oil, allowing the paper to peel away easily.

Place soufflé on a sheet of paper or a large plate. Spread reserved cream on top. Using a broad spatula, press hazelnuts on to sides of soufflé—the paper will catch any crumbs that fall and these can be used again. Sprinkle more nuts, in broad lines, on top of cream. Chill. Serves 8-10 generously.

Liqueur Soufflé

Savoury Pancakes

Hungarian Pancakes

Pancakes filled with crab in a paprika cream sauce, coated with brandied mushrooms in cream.

Filling:
60 g (2 oz) butter
1 small onion, finely chopped
1 tablespoon paprika
1 cup Béchamel sauce
125 g (4 oz) small mushrooms, trimmed
   and sliced
1 × 185 g (6½ oz) can of crab, drained
   and flaked
¾ cup cream
salt and freshly ground pepper
¼ cup brandy
8 basic pancakes
30 g (1 oz) grated Parmesan cheese

Filling: Melt half the butter, add the onion and cook slowly for 10 minutes or until soft. Stir in the paprika and cook gently for 2 minutes. Add the Béchamel sauce and continue cooking over a low heat for 5 minutes. Allow mixture to cool slightly.

Sauté the sliced mushrooms in remaining butter and add half of them to the paprika sauce with the crab, half the cream, salt, pepper and a little brandy to taste. Fill the pancakes with this mixture and roll them up and arrange in a buttered oven-proof dish.

Warm remaining brandy, set alight and pour over remaining mushrooms, shake over heat until the flames die out and then add remaining cream. Cook until it thickens slightly, and spoon over pancakes. Sprinkle with cheese and bake in a moderate oven (350°F—170°C) for 10 to 15 minutes until glazed.

Potato Pancakes

This is a Swedish recipe for crunchy, pan-fried potato pancakes which are thin, golden and lacy.

4 medium sized old potatoes
2 tablespoons finely chopped chives
2 teaspoons salt
freshly ground black pepper
30 g (1 oz) butter
2 tablespoons olive oil or other
   vegetable oil

Peel the potatoes and place in a bowl of cold water to prevent them turning black. Taking one potato at a time grate coarsely into a bowl. Do not drain off the potato water which will accumulate in the bowl. Mix the chopped chives, salt and pepper.

Meanwhile heat the butter and oil in a large frying pan and when the butter starts to foam, place small mounds of grated potato mixture into the frying pan and flatten them out with the back of a spoon or spatula so that they are about 8 cm (3 in) in diameter. Lower the heat under the pan and fry the pancakes for 2 to 3 minutes on each side until they are crisp and golden-brown. Drain on crumpled kitchen paper and serve immediately.

Note: When making this recipe there should be no delay between grating the potatoes and frying them. The grated potato turns black if it is allowed to stand.

Dessert Pancakes

Crêpes Suzette

The success of this classic dish named after Mlle Suzette, a star of the Comedie-Francaise, depends on the crêpes being lacy, wafer thin and served piping hot.

Crêpe batter:
1¼ cups plain flour
2 tablespoons caster sugar
pinch salt
3 eggs, beaten
1½ cups milk
2 teaspoons melted butter
1 tablespoon brandy
Sauce:
4 lumps of loaf sugar
1 orange
45 g (1½ oz) butter
extra 30 g (1 oz) butter
juice of 1 orange
few drops lemon juice
½ cup Curacao, Cointreau or
    Grand Marnier
½ cup brandy or cognac

Crêpe batter: Sift the flour with the sugar and salt into a bowl. Make a well in the centre and add the eggs. Using a wooden spoon draw in the flour with ½ cup of the milk. Beat well until the mixture is smooth.

Add the melted butter and whisk in the remaining milk and the brandy. Allow to stand for at least 2 hours before using.

Heat a little butter in an 18 cm (7 in) crêpe pan or shallow frying pan and when it starts to foam, pour in sufficient batter to cover surface of the pan with a thin layer. Rotate the pan quickly to spread the batter as thinly and as evenly as possible. Pour off any excess batter.

Cook the crêpe for about 1 minute on one side until bubbles appear on the surface and then flip it over with a metal spatula and cook another minute. Stack the crêpes flat one on top of the other with greaseproof paper in between each.

Sauce: Rub the loaf sugar on the rind of the orange until well impregnated.

Crush the sugar with 45 g (1½ oz) butter using a fork and mix until creamy.

Place 30 g (1 oz) of butter in a chafing dish or frying pan and add the orange and lemon juice and the liqueur. Bring to the boil. Add the creamed orange butter and stir until dissolved.

Select 10 to 12 crêpes and stack on a plate. Place the crêpes in the sauce one at a time. Fold each crêpe in quarters (like a pocket handkerchief). Sprinkle with a little sugar.

Heat the brandy, set it alight and pour over the crêpes. Serve immediately the flames have died down.

Note: To give you some idea of how fine and lacy these crêpes should be, this batter makes about 30 pancakes but a beginner might make 20 the first time, improving each time. Crêpes freeze well, so any left over may be stored frozen for many months.

Swedish Pancakes

This is a famous Swedish dish customarily served with loganberries or fruit conserves. The pancake is extremely light and tender and we have varied the basic pancake by using a choice of flavourings.

Pancake Batter (makes 2 dozen pancakes)
3 eggs
1 cup milk
1 cup plain flour, sifted
¾ cup cream
90 g (3 oz) unsalted butter, melted
¼ teaspoon salt

Batter: Beat the eggs together with ½ cup of milk for 2 to 3 minutes with a rotary beater or balloon whisk. Add the sifted flour all at the same time and beat until mixture is thick and smooth. Beat in the remaining milk and cream and then stir in melted butter and salt. Cover and allow to stand for at least 2 hours.

Very lightly grease the pancake pan, place it over a high heat and when very hot, lower the heat and drop one tablespoon of batter into each depression. If using a fry pan drop batter into small mounds.

As soon as the batter is poured into the pan sprinkle the surface of each pancake with the desired flavouring or leave plain.

When the pancakes begin to set and bubbles appear on the surface, carefully lift each one and turn it over. Cook for a further 1 to 2 minutes to brown the other side. Serve as soon as possible.

Variations:
Here are some suggested flavourings which are sprinkled on to the batter as soon as it is placed in the pan.
- chopped mixed peel.
- crushed almond macaroons or amaretti.
- chopped toasted almonds.
- dried apricots, soaked.
- grated eating apple, unpeeled.

Apricot Pancakes

Pancake batter
apricot conserve
lemon juice
ground or finely chopped walnuts
sifted icing sugar

Make the pancakes and stack them into a pile with greaseproof paper in between each. Spread each pancake with apricot conserve mixed with a few drops of lemon juice.

Roll them up loosely and arrange in an ovenproof dish. Place in warm oven (200°F—90°C) for 10 minutes. Serve sprinkled with nuts and icing sugar and a bowl of whipped cream.

Variations:
Fill with any one of the following:
- Combine 125 g (4 oz) ricotta or cream cheese with 1 tablespoon of chopped candied peel, the grated rind of an orange and 1 tablespoon of caster sugar. Increase the amount of this filling according to how many pancakes you wish to fill.
- Sweetened stewed apple flavoured with cinnamon—or sweetened stewed peaches, plums or apricots.
- Sweetened chestnut purée flavoured with a little rum.

Fritters

Apple and Banana Fritters

Fritter batter:

1 cup plain flour

pinch salt

$\frac{2}{3}$ cup warm water

2 tablespoons olive oil (or other good
   vegetable oil)

2 eggs whites, stiffly beaten

Filling:

firm ripe bananas

1 lemon

caster sugar

firm sweet apples

oil for deep frying

Batter: Sift the flour with the salt into a bowl. Make a well in the centre, add the water and oil and gradually combine with the flour. Beat with a whisk until mixture is very smooth. Cover and allow to stand for 1 hour. When ready to use, fold in the stiffly beaten egg whites.

Filling: Peel the bananas, slice each into three diagonal pieces. Sprinkle with lemon juice and caster sugar.

Peel and core apples. Cut into rings about 1 cm ($\frac{1}{2}$ in) thick. Sprinkle with caster sugar.

Fill a medium sized saucepan with oil to 10 cm (4 in). Heat oil until very hot. Drain away juices of the fruit, dip each piece in prepared batter and then place in the hot oil until golden on one side. Turn it over and when golden brown on the other side, drain on crumpled kitchen paper and sprinkle with caster sugar. Serve immediately.

These fritters may be served with a bowl of lightly whipped cream.

Shrove Tuesday Fritters

This is a beautiful dish of deep fried pancake strips which are dusted with icing sugar before being served with a bowl of kirsch flavoured Plum Sauce.

Pancake batter

oil for deep frying

sifted icing sugar

Plum sauce:

$\frac{1}{2}$ cup plum jam

$\frac{1}{2}$ cup water

piece of lemon peel, juice of 1 lemon

1 teaspoon arrowroot slaked with 2
   teaspoons water

1 tablespoon kirsh (optional)

Make 8 pancakes (using half the quantity of the basic pancake batter). Stack in a pile. Fold into three and cut into 1 cm ($\frac{1}{2}$ in) strips.

Heat the oil and when very hot put in 1 pancake strip and if the oil sizzles immediately add half the pancake strips and toss with a slotted spoon until golden all over.

Remove from the oil and drain on crumpled kitchen paper. Fry the remaining pancake strips.

Serve piled on to a dish dusted with icing sugar and accompanied by a bowl of plum sauce.

Plum Sauce:

Place the jam, water, lemon peel and juice in a saucepan over a gentle heat and bring slowly to the boil. Thicken with the slaked arrowroot and boil until clear. Strain, flavour with kirsh and serve hot or cold.

beef

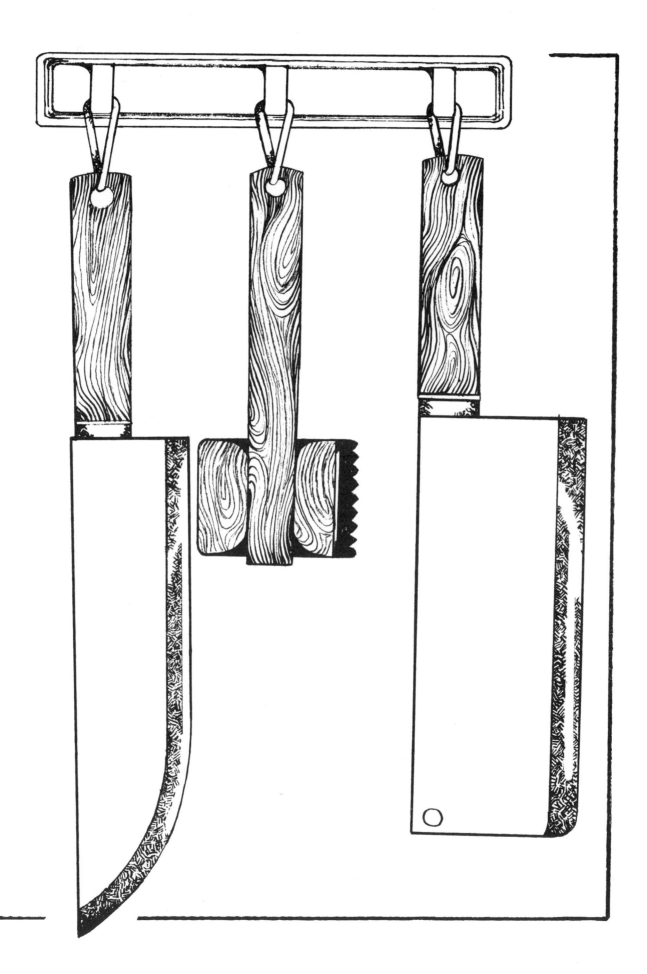

Beef

Roast Beef

Rub over with salt and pepper and put on a rack in a roasting pan. Put in a very hot oven (425°F—200°C) for the first 20 minutes, then reduce heat to moderate (350°F—170°C) for rest of cooking time. Baste meat every half hour with drippings in pan.

Cooking times: For rare beef allow 15 minutes to the pound, for well done, allow 30-35 minutes to the pound.

Buying beef: Good beef has a rich, red colour and fine texture with a reasonable amount of creamy white fat. Beef with a small marbling of fat throughout the lean has best flavour and is moist and tender.

Cuts for Roasting: Sirloin can be roasted on the bone, or boned, rolled and tied.

Fillet, the undercut of the sirloin, is considered the prime cut of beef because it is always tender. Though generally fried or grilled, it is often roasted whole.

Scotch fillet is much cheaper than fillet. This cut from the rib section is also ideal for roasting.

Rump cut from the narrow or corner end is excellent for roasting.

Topside, preferably a corner of topside, is suitable for roasting and often a pocket is cut in the meat and filled with a seasoned stuffing.

Standing rib or rolled rib is an excellent cut for roasting. Two or three ribs can be roasted for a small family.

Silverside (unsalted), particularly when from a young animal, is very good for roasting and is comparatively cheaper.

Bolar blade is another less expensive cut for roasting.

Pan Fried Steak

If your griller is not very efficient, careful pan frying can produce a good steak. Some cuts of meat are better pan fried than grilled. It is essential to have a thick, heavy iron pan. Heat the pan for a few minutes, pour in just enough oil to coat the bottom and, when smoking hot, put in the meat.

Allow 185 to 250 g (6 to 8 oz) of rump, boneless sirloin or a piece of fillet per person, each cut 2.5 cm (1 in) thick. Remove meat from the refrigerator at least 30 minutes before cooking. Slit fat in a few places to prevent the meat from curling.

Season steak with salt and pepper. If the steak has been marinated, dry it thoroughly. Heat a heavy frying pan and add enough oil to cover base. When smoking hot, put in the seasoned steak. Cook for about 1 minute, turn and cook for another minute. Both sides should now be covered with a brown crust. If not, cook a little longer. Lower the heat and continue to cook for 8 to 10 minutes for rump and sirloin (for medium) and 7 to 10 minutes for fillet. Allow an extra minute or two for well done.

Remove the meat to a hot dish and deglaze the pan with $\frac{1}{2}$ cup of stock or wine. Add a nut of butter, swirl it into the sauce and spoon a little over each steak.

● To deglaze is to dissolve the juices caramelised on the bottom of the pan during cooking with a little liquid (stock, wine or vegetable water).

Less tender cuts:

Oyster blade and cross-cut blade (often called barbecue steak) are best marinated before grilling.

Yearling steak does not have the rich flavour of prime beef but the round, fresh silverside and blade steak make excellent cuts for a barbecue.

Grilled Steak

In any country, in any language, a thick, juicy steak is one of man's favourite meals.

Charcoal-grilled steaks are hard to beat, but careful grilling by electricity or gas will give you almost the same result—a crisp crust on the outside and tender juicy meat inside.

The tender, choice cuts of beef such as good quality fillet, rump and sirloin require only to be brushed with butter or oil and then seasoned with freshly ground rock salt and pepper. The cheaper cuts, on the other hand, such as oyster blade and top round, are not so tender, but when marinated also respond well to grilling.

Cuts for grilling:

Fillet steak about 5 cm (2 in) thick—cut from the thicker end of the whole fillet and cooked with a little of their own fat.

Châteaubriand—the most expensive cut for grilling. Cut from the thickest part of the fillet and weighing from 500 g to 1 kg (1 to 2 lb). Trim off all the enveloping skin and fat.

Tournedos—about 2.5 to 3.5 cm (1 to 1½ in) thick. Cut from the thinnest end of the fillet. They have no surrounding fat of their own and should be wrapped with bacon or fresh pork fat.

Porterhouse and T-bone—cut across the sirloin bone containing a piece of the fillet. It should weigh about 1 to 1.5 kg (2 to 3 lb) and is best cooked whole and then cut into portions.

Sirloin—about 2.5 to 3.5 cm (1 to 1½ in) thick. Cut from the sirloin or foreribs without any bone.

Rump—cut 2.5 to 3.5 cm (1 to 1½ in) thick. Best cooked in the piece and then cut into portions.

Grilling Steak

Make sure the griller is preheated. Cut the fat in several places if using rump, sirloin or porterhouse, brush the meat with oil or butter and season with freshly ground salt and pepper on both sides. A little garlic or anchovy rubbed over the steak adds flavour. Place the meat on an oiled rack and sear each side under a very high heat. Turn the heat down and allow the meat to cook through.

Timetable

These times are an indication only. The quality of the beef and the effectiveness of the griller must all be taken into account.

Porterhouse steak: 3.5 cm (1½ in) thick weighing about 750 g (1½ lb)
Medium rare 15 minutes
Medium 20 minutes

Châteaubriand: 5 cm (2 in) thick weighing about 750 g (1½ lb)
Medium rare 15 minutes
Medium 25 minutes

Sirloin: 2.5 to 3.5 cm (1 to 1½ in) thick weighing about 750 g (1½ lb)
Medium rare 15 minutes
Medium 20 minutes

Rump steak: 3.5 cm (1½ in) thick weighing about 750 grams to 1 kg (1½ to 2 lb)
Medium rare 15 to 20 minutes
Medium 20 minutes

Fillet steak: 2.5 cm (1 in) thick
Medium rare 8 to 10 minutes
Medium 10 to 15 minutes

A sign that grilled meat is cooked is when tiny beads of blood appear on the surface. If the meat is firm but springy to the touch, it will be rare. If it feels firm but soft, it needs extra cooking.

- Meat should be brushed frequently with oil or melted butter during grilling to protect the surface and prevent it from scorching and becoming dry.
- Grilled steaks need no sauce, although a rich, delectable bearnaise or a simple flavoured butter is an excellent addition. Grills are versatile and may be served with a tossed green salad, grilled tomatoes, fried onions, creamy mashed or French-fried potatoes, freshly cooked green vegetables such as baby squash, green beans, broccoli, or peas.
- Don't forget mustards, (English, French or German), horseradish and various relishes.

Thick juicy steak grilled to perfection

Steak Diane

2 × 1 cm (½ in) thick pieces of fillet steak
salt
freshly ground pepper
60 g (2 oz) butter
1 garlic clove, crushed
1 tablespoon Worcestershire sauce
2 tablespoons sherry
1 tablespoon brandy
2 tablespoons finely chopped parsley

Trim all the fat from the steak and flatten until 5 mm (¼ in) thick. Season with salt and pepper. Heat the butter in a large pan and when it is foaming add the fillet steaks and sauté for 40 seconds (for underdone) or for 1 minute (medium) on each side. Add the garlic and allow it to cook for 30 seconds and then stir in the Worcestershire sauce. Heat the brandy and sherry until well warmed but not boiling, set alight and pour over the steaks. Shake the pan until the flames die down. Remove the steaks to a heated serving dish, sprinkle with parsley, give the sauce a good stir and pour it sizzling hot over the top.

This recipe serves two. When the steaks are flattened out they are quite large and no more than two can be successfully sautéed at the one time in the average sauté or frying pan.

Grilled Rump Steak with Bordelaise Sauce

Thick Grilled Rump Steak served with one of the great wine sauces of France. The poached beef marrow is cut into dice and added to the sauce but we kept a little aside to garnish the steak.

1 × 5 cm (2 in) piece of rump steak
olive oil
freshly ground black pepper
salt

Preheat the griller. Brush the grill rack with a little oil. Brush the steak with oil and then make a few small cuts through the sinew which lies between the fat and the meat. Season with pepper. Grill for 8 minutes on each side, place on a heated serving dish season with salt cut into thick slices and arrange a slice of beef marrow on each. Spoon over the Bordelaise Sauce.

Bordelaise Sauce

2 teaspoons finely chopped shallots
¼ cup red wine
½ cup brown sauce (page 19)
1 7 cm (3 in) piece of beef marrow in a
    marrow bone
½ teaspoon finely chopped parsley

Put the shallots and wine into a saucepan and cook until reduced to three-quarters of the original volume. Add the brown sauce and cook gently for 10 minutes.

Remove beef marrow from the bone and then poach for 2 minutes. Cut 5 thick slices and then cut the rest into small dice. Add the diced beef marrow to the sauce with the parsley adjust the seasoning and pour over the steak.

Note: When purchasing the marrow bone ask your butcher to split it to enable you to remove the marrow easily.

To make simple sauce for the grilled steak with much the same flavour but not as rich as the Bordelaise, reduce 2 teaspoons of shallots in ¾ cup of wine to half its original quantity, allow to cook gently for a few minutes, remove from the heat, season with pepper, add the chopped beef marrow and any juices which have escaped while grilling the steak (not the fat, of course), the parsley and then swirl in a tablespoon of butter. Serve immediately.

Carpet Bag Steak

It's very likely that this well-known steak took its name from the old-fashioned carpet bag—instead of being crammed with possessions, it's filled with plump oysters! The steak for this dish must be really thick—about 3.5 cm (1½ in) so that a good sized pocket may be cut in it to hold the oysters.

For one serving:
1 piece of fillet steak cut about 3.5 cm (1½ in) thick
6 oysters
salt and freshly ground pepper
3 small pieces of butter

Insert the point of a sharp knife into the middle of steak and cut a pocket about 5 cm (2 in) long.

Season oysters with salt and freshly ground pepper and place into the pocket. Add the small pieces of butter about the size of hazelnuts and secure the pocket with a small metal skewer or wooden toothpicks.

Brush the steak with a little oil and season with freshly ground pepper. Place under a preheated grill and cook for 4 to 5 minutes each side for medium rare. Remove the toothpicks or skewer before serving.

Tournedos Sauté Chasseur

Sauce:
1 tablespoon olive oil
15 g (½ oz) butter
90 g (3 oz) mushrooms with stalks trimmed and cut into fine slices
2 shallots, finely chopped
1 teaspoon plain flour
¾ cup good beef stock
1 teaspoon tomato paste
salt
freshly ground pepper

Tournedos:
6 tournedos cut 2.5 cm (1 in) thick
cut from approximately 750 g (1½ lb) beef fillet
salt and freshly ground pepper
45 g (1½ oz) clarified butter
½ cup white wine
1 teaspoon chopped tarragon
finely chopped parsley

To make sauce: Melt oil and butter in a small sauté or frying pan and add the mushrooms and sauté quickly until just coloured. Add the shallots and sauté for a minute or two. Stir in the flour and allow to cook over a very low heat for 3 to 4 minutes. Stir in the stock, tomato paste and season with salt and pepper. Stir until boiling and then allow the sauce to simmer for 15 minutes.

To prepare Tournedos: Dry the tournedos thoroughly with paper towels and season with salt and pepper. Heat the clarified butter in a large sauté or frying pan and when very hot lay the tournedos in it and sauté for 2 minutes on each side. Place on a heated dish and keep warm. Drain off any excess fat from the pan, add the white wine and deglaze the pan. Boil quickly to reduce the liquid by half and then add the prepared sauce. Bring to the boil once more and stir in the tarragon. Pour the sauce over the tournedos and sprinkle with a little chopped parsley.

● Tournedos are cut from the "eye" or centre of a beef fillet which has been well trimmed. They are smaller than the usual fillet steaks and vary in thickness from 2 cm (¾ in) to 2.5 cm (1 in). Tournedos are usually accompanied by a sauce or garnish which gives the dish its name.

Steak and Kidney Sponge

A steak and kidney pudding with a difference. In this recipe the meat is covered by a light tender sponge which absorbs all the flavours of this wonderfully hearty dish.

Basic steak and kidney

1 kg (2 lb) chuck steak, blade or rump
1 ox kidney or 2 sheep kidneys
1 tablespoon plain flour
1½ teaspoons salt
1 teaspoon freshly ground black pepper
½ teaspoon dried herbs
½ cup water

Remove the gristle from the meat and cut into 2.5 cm (1 in) cubes. Remove the core from the kidney and cut into small pieces. Sprinkle with flour, seasonings and herbs.

Spoon meat into a pyrex basin and add the water. Cover the basin with two thicknesses of greased greaseproof paper or aluminium foil and tie with string. Place the basin in a large saucepan with enough boiling water to reach half-way up the sides. Steam 3½ to 4 hours until the meat is tender. Replace the water as it evaporates in the saucepan with more boiling water. When the meat is cooked correct the seasoning, and keep hot while preparing the sponge topping.

Sponge topping

1 cup self-raising flour, sifted
½ teaspoon salt
2 eggs, separated
1 cup milk
60 g (2 oz) butter, melted

Sift the flour and salt into a basin and make a well in the centre. Beat the egg yolks and stir in the milk. Pour into the flour. Add the melted butter and stir until the mixture is very smooth. Beat the egg whites until very stiff and fold into the mixture.

Spoon the sponge mixture carefully over the steak and kidney so the meat is completely covered. Place the lid on the saucepan and bring the water to a fast boil for about 20 minutes.

- The steak and kidney may also be cooked in a heavy casserole on a low heat on top of the stove or in a moderate oven (350°F—179°C) for 2 hours. Add more water if necessary.

Steak au Poivre

4 steaks (rump or fillet)
1 tablespoon coarsely cracked black pepper
little olive oil
4 teaspoons butter
salt
dash hot pepper sauce, optional
dash Worcestershire sauce
lemon juice
2 tablespoons brandy
chopped parsley
chopped chives

Season both sides of each steak with coarsely cracked pepper. Press into the meat with the heel of the hand. Allow the meat to stand for 30 minutes. Heat a very heavy frying pan and add enough oil to cover base with a thin film. When smoking, put in the steaks and cook until well browned on one side. Turn and cook until golden and crusted on the other side. (For rare, cook steaks on a high heat for a short time and for medium, lower heat to moderate and cook a little longer).

Put 1 teaspoon of butter on each steak and add salt, sauces and lemon juice to taste. Warm brandy; flame and pour over meat. When flames have died, sprinkle the steaks with parsley and chives. Serve immediately. For a creamy sauce, swirl about 2 tablespoons of cream with the pan juices.

Beef Olives Provençal

Beef Olives Provençal

Plump beef rolls filled with a typical Provençal herb and olive mixture baked in a wine-flavoured stock. Ripe sweet tomatoes are added to the sauce just before serving.

4 to 6 slices of round steak cut very thinly, each weighing about 155 g (5 oz) and about 12.5 cm (5 in) in size
2 tablespoons olive oil
2 onions, 2 carrots, 1 stick of celery, cut into dice
¼ cup dry white wine
¾ cup good beef stock
bouquet garni
arrowroot
250 g (8 oz) ripe tomatoes, peeled, seeded and chopped
finely chopped parsley
Stuffing:
30 g (1 oz) butter
1 small onion, finely chopped
185 g (6 oz) minced pork and veal
3 large tablespoons fresh white breadcrumbs
1 tablespoon finely chopped herbs and parsley
1 small egg, beaten
salt, freshly ground pepper
6 green olives, shredded

Flatten out the pieces of steak until very thin.

Stuffing: Heat the butter and add the onion and allow it to soften. Remove from the heat and cool and then combine with the pork and veal mince, breadcrumbs and herbs. Add enough of the egg to moisten the mixture, season with salt and plenty of pepper and add the olives. Mix thoroughly and then spread on the meat slices.

Roll up the beef olives and secure with string or with metal clips.

Heat the oil in a heavy casserole dish, brown the "olives" all over and then remove and keep warm. Place the diced vegetables in the oil and cook until golden brown. Arrange the beef olives on top, add the wine, stock and bouquet garni and season with salt and pepper. Bring the liquid to the boil. Cover the pan tightly, first with a double piece of greaseproof paper and then the lid. Cook in a moderate oven (350°F—170°C) for about 1½ hours or until meat is tender.

Remove the beef olives from the casserole dish, take off the string or metal clips and keep warm. Strain the pan juices. Place back in the pan, bring to the boil and thicken with arrowroot which has been slaked with a little cold water or stock. Add the tomatoes. Simmer for 1 to 2 minutes.

Arrange the beef olives on a mound of Potato Purée and spoon over the sauce. Dust with parsley.

Note: The slices of beef may be cut in half before being filled to make 8 to 12 small beef olives.

Steak Mirabeau

1 × 1.5 kg (3 lb) slice of rump steak
olive oil
freshly ground pepper
Anchovy Butter:
125 g (4 oz) butter
1 tablespoon mashed anchovy fillets
a little milk
a little black pepper
1 teaspoon anchovy essence
Garnish:
about 6 anchovy fillets sliced in half
   lengthways
about 8 stuffed olives, cut in half
finely chopped tarragon leaves (optional)

Preheat the grill to hot. Cut the fat in several places and then brush the rump steak with oil on both sides and season with pepper. Brush the grill rack with oil and place the steak under the grill and sear on both sides. Lower the heat of the grill to medium and continue grilling for 15 to 18 minutes depending on the thickness and the degree of rareness you require.

Place the hot steak on a warm dish, brush with a little anchovy butter and garnish with anchovy fillets which have been cut in half, and stuffed olives. Sprinkle with tarragon leaves if available. Serve the remaining anchovy butter well chilled and cut into slices.

Slice steak into six generous servings.

Anchovy Butter

Cream the butter and add the anchovy fillets which have been soaked in a little milk for 30 minutes, drained and mashed. Mix thoroughly, season with a little black pepper and add 1 teaspoon of anchovy essence to strengthen the flavour and add a delicate pink colour. Form into a roll, wrap in foil and chill. Cut into slices when firm. This butter is also delicious with grilled or baked fish.

Note: If you decide to buy a thick piece of rump steak, it is wise to order it in advance. Ask your butcher for a piece cut about 2.5 cm (1 in) in from the first cut of the rump. This is the perfect cut for a steak cooked in this way and will avoid the sinew in the end cuts of the rump.

Sautéed Steak with Herbs

A selection of the more pungent aromatic herbs added to a pan deglazed with wine makes an excellent sauce for well-aged beef.

1 thick T-bone, rump or fillet steak
½ tablespoon olive oil
30 g (1 oz) butter
salt, freshly ground black pepper
½ cup red or white wine
1 tablespoon freshly chopped mixed
   herbs such as oregano, parsley, chives,
   thyme and tarragon

Trim excess fat off the steak and make small incisions in the fat to prevent the steak from curling. Dry the steak with a paper towel.

Heat the oil and butter in a heavy frying pan and when the butter foam has subsided add the steak and cook for 4 minutes on each side, turning down the heat a little if the meat browns too much. Remove and place on a heated serving dish, seasoning immediately with salt and pepper. Keep warm while making the sauce.

Pour off all but 1 tablespoon of fat from the frying pan. Return the pan to the heat and deglaze with the wine. Allow the wine to boil until it has thickened slightly, add the herbs and pour over the steak. Serve immediately.

Note: If using fillet steak, make sure it is well trimmed of all fat and is cut about 2.5 cm (1 in) thick. The quantity of herb sauce is sufficient for 2 fillet steaks.

Fillet of Beef Wellington

Fillet of beef, flamed in brandy and then spread with pâté and sliced mushrooms is cooked in a puff pastry case. It may be prepared the day before and kept in the refrigerator.

1 × 1.5 kg (3 lb) fillet of beef
salt
freshly ground black pepper
60 g (2 oz) butter
¼ cup brandy
90 g (3 oz) liver pâté
60 g (2 oz) button mushrooms
250 g (8 oz) puff pastry
1 egg, lightly beaten

Trim the beef fillet and season with plenty of salt and pepper. Heat the butter in a large frying pan and sear the fillet over a high heat turning with two spoons until brown on all sides. Warm the brandy, set alight and pour over the beef. Shake the pan until the flames subside. Remove to a dish and allow to cool. Reserve any liquid remaining in the frying pan for the sauce.

Spread the pâté on top of the beef. Slice the mushrooms and cook in a little butter for a few minutes. Arrange them on the pâté.

Roll out puff pastry on lightly floured board to 3 mm (⅛ in) thickness. Trim the edges, place fillet on one side of the pastry. Brush edges with beaten egg. Fold the other half of the pastry over the fillet.

Press the edges of the pastry together and tuck underneath to form a neat parcel. Place on a baking sheet which has been dampened with water.

Cut thin strips of pastry about 5 mm (¼ in) wide. Brush the pastry encasing the fillet with egg and then arrange pastry strips in a lattice fashion about 2.5 cm (1 in) apart. Brush with beaten egg. Bake in a very hot oven (450°F—230°C) for 15 minutes, reduce to moderate (350°F—170°C) and cook for a further 15 to 20 minutes.

If watercress is in season serve the Fillet of Beef Wellington garnished with a few sprigs.

Fresh Silverside Pot Roast

Pot roasting is a most satisfactory method of cooking a piece of fresh silverside which is an extremely lean cut of beef and tends to be rather dry.

2 tablespoons oil
1.5 kg (3 lb) fresh silverside
salt
freshly ground pepper
500 g (1 lb) onions, peeled
500 g (1 lb) carrots, peeled
1 tablespoon butter, 2 teaspoons flour,
    kneaded together

Heat the oil in a heavy casserole and brown the meat on both sides. Remove to a dish and add the onions and carrots and allow them to brown evenly.

Place the browned meat back in the casserole and season well with salt and pepper. Cover with a lid and allow to pot roast over a very low heat for 1½ hours or until the meat is tender. Place the meat on a heated serving dish with the vegetables.

Return the pan to the heat, bring the liquid to the boil and stir in the kneaded butter and cook gently until the sauce thickens. Spoon a little gravy over the meat and serve the remainder separately.

Beef Provençal

Vinaigrette dressing perfumed with basil, tarragon and other freshly picked herbs makes a tomato, zucchini and olive salad warmly aromatic. This salad is delicious with cold roasted fillet of beef or with other cold meats.

1 kg (2 lb) fillet of beef
freshly ground black pepper
1 tablespoon olive oil
30 g (1 oz) butter
¼ cup brandy
500 g (1 lb) tomatoes, peeled
250 g (8 oz) zucchini
60 g (2 oz) black olives
½ cup Green Herb vinaigrette
1 tablespoon mixed freshly chopped herbs such as parsley, basil, oregano and tarragon

Trim the beef leaving a little fat on it. Tie with string to keep it in a good shape during cooking and season with pepper.

Heat the oil in a baking dish and then add the butter. When hot add the beef and brown well all over.

Heat the brandy, set it alight and pour flaming over the beef. Shake the pan until the flames subside. Place in a preheated very hot oven (500°F—260°C) and then turn the heat down immediately to hot (425°F—215°C). Cook for 25 minutes.

While the beef is cooking peel and cut tomatoes in quarters and wash, trim and slice the zucchini into 3.5 cm (1½ in) pieces. Cook for 4 minutes in boiling salted water, drain and refresh until quite cool. Halve the olives and remove the seeds. Combine tomatoes, zucchini and olives together and toss lightly in the Green Herb Vinaigrette.

Remove the beef and allow to cool completely. When cold remove the string and carve into 1 cm (½ in) slices.

Arrange around a serving dish and brush with a little of the Green Herb Vinaigrette to keep meat moist. Spoon the salad into the centre of the dish and sprinkle with finely chopped herbs.

Green Herb Vinaigrette

¾ cup olive oil
¼ cup white or red wine vinegar
1 teaspoon French mustard
1 clove garlic, crushed
salt, freshly ground black pepper
2 tablespoons mixed finely chopped herbs —choose from chives, parsley, basil, oregano and tarragon

Combine all ingredients and mix well.
Note: For a party of 8 to 10 double the amount of beef and salad.

Beef Provençal

Braised Brisket of Beef

Braised fresh brisket of beef is as delicious cold as hot. If you're planning to serve this meat cold don't thicken the meat juices.

2 kg (4 lb) fresh brisket of beef
2 large carrots
1 turnip
3 celery sticks
2 medium white onions
250 g ($\frac{1}{2}$ lb) bacon rashers
salt
freshly ground pepper
$\frac{1}{2}$ cup stock made with beef stock cubes
bouquet garni
1 tablespoon butter
1 tablespoon flour
250 g ($\frac{1}{2}$ lb) tiny white onions, peeled

If the beef is in a long strip, cut in two. Cut the carrots, turnip, celery and the 2 medium onions into small dice. Divide into two portions.

Put a layer of vegetables into a casserole dish just large enough to hold the beef. Lay the beef on top and cover with more vegetables and bacon rashers. Season with salt and pepper.

Pour over the stock and add the bouquet garni. Cover the dish and cook very gently, preferably in a slow oven (300°F—150°C) for $4\frac{1}{2}$ hours or until the meat is tender.

When the meat is cooked pour off $1\frac{1}{2}$ cups of the cooking liquid and skim off the fat.

Make a sauce by melting the butter in a small saucepan adding the flour and then stirring in the $1\frac{1}{2}$ cups of cooking liquid. Allow this to cook gently for 15 minutes. Meanwhile cook the tiny onions in boiling salted water until tender.

Cut the meat into slices, arrange the vegetables and small white onions over it and pour over the sauce. Sprinkle with finely chopped parsley.

Braised Beef Flamande

Braised beef cooked in beer and rich beef stock served on a bed of fried onions and tomatoes.

2 tablespoons oil
1 × 1.25 kg ($2\frac{1}{2}$ lb) piece of topside
$\frac{3}{4}$ celery stalk, coarsely chopped
1 carrot, roughly chopped
1 onion, coarsely chopped
$\frac{1}{2}$ cup beer
$\frac{1}{2}$ cup beef stock
1 tablespoon tomato purée or 1 teaspoon
  tomato paste
bouquet garni
salt
freshly gound pepper
1 tablespoon butter
1 tablespoon olive oil
1 large onion, sliced into rings
500 g (1 lb) tomatoes, peeled
kneaded butter—30 g (1 oz) butter mixed
  with 15 g ($\frac{1}{2}$ oz) flour

Heat the oil in a large heavy casserole pan and brown the meat all over. Remove it to a plate and add the celery, carrot and onion and cook gently until softened.

Place the beef back in the pan and add the beer, beef stock, tomato purée or paste and bouquet garni. Season with salt and freshly ground pepper. Cover tightly and braise for $1\frac{1}{2}$ hours or until the meat is tender.

Just before the meat is cooked, melt the butter and oil in a frying pan and fry the onion rings until they are golden. Slice the tomatoes and add to the onions and allow to warm through.

Remove the cooked meat to a warm dish. Bring the liquid in the pan to the boil and add the kneaded butter gradually. Allow this sauce to cook gently but do not boil until it has thickened.

Place the onion rings and tomato on a heated serving dish, put the meat on top and spoon a little of the sauce over and serve the rest separately.

Pot Roasted Rolled Ribs of Beef

This method of cooking rolled ribs of beef prevents the meat from shrinking and ensures that none of its delicious juices are lost.

4 tablespoons oil
2 tablespoons flour
1 tablespoon mustard
1 × 2.25 kg (4½ lbs) rolled ribs of beef
freshly ground pepper

Heat the oven to hot (425°F—215°C). Heat the oil in a heavy casserole. Combine the flour and mustard and spread over the beef.

When the oil is hot, place the beef in the casserole and brown all over. Cover the casserole dish, place in the oven and cook for 15 minutes. Reduce the oven temperature to moderately low (325°F—160°C) and continue cooking for 1 to 1½ hours basting frequently with the pan juices. Remove the beef to a warm dish and allow to stand for 10 minutes before carving.

Serve with new potatoes which have been boiled until just tender and then added to the casserole after the beef has been taken out. Cook them over a gentle heat until golden which will take about 5 minutes.

Boil some new carrots until tender. Drain, toss in butter and sprinkle with finely chopped parsley.

Arrange the potatoes and carrots around the beef before serving.

Beef Stroganoff

500 g (1 lb) fillet steak, trimmed of all fat
   and sinew
salt
freshly ground black pepper
2 teaspoons plain flour, sifted
1 medium onion, finely sliced
30 g (1 oz) butter
125 g (4 oz) button mushrooms, peeled
   and finely sliced
2 teaspoons tomato paste
¼ cup sour cream

Cut the beef into strips 5 cm (2 in) long and 5 mm (¼ in) wide. Season with salt and pepper and toss in flour. Heat the frying pan, put in half the butter and fry the onion slowly for about 10 minutes until it is just coloured. Add the mushrooms and fry for a few minutes adding more butter if necessary. Remove the onions and mushrooms.

Add the remaining butter and when it is hot add the beef strips and fry briskly for 3-4 minutes.

Return the onion and mushrooms and season with plenty of salt and pepper. Shake over the heat for 1 minute, add the tomato paste and sour cream then cook a few minutes longer until heated through. Serve at once in a ring of boiled rice.

Basmati Rice Ring

2 cups water
1 teaspoon salt
1 slice lemon
1 cup Basmati rice

Bring the water, salt and lemon to a rolling boil in a heavy saucepan. Add the rice slowly so that the water continues to boil. Reduce heat and cook gently for 20-25 minutes covered, until the grains of rice are tender and have no hard centre when pressed between the fingers. Do not lift the lid during the steaming time. Pack the rice tightly into a buttered ring mould or cake tin. Leave for a minute to settle and then turn out on to a hot dish.

Beef Bourguignon

The flavour of the wine sauce is all important in this dish. If possible, use the same wine you will drink with it. Otherwise choose a soft red wine. A piece of beef may be cooked whole using the same method and sauce.

1.5 kg (3 lb) topside steak, in one piece
125 g (4 oz) shoulder bacon
a little beef fat
30 g (1 oz) butter
12 small white onions, peeled
1 onion, finely chopped
1 tablespoon plain flour
1½ cups soft red wine
salt and freshly ground black pepper
1 large sprig thyme
1 bay leaf
1 garlic clove, crushed
250 g (8 oz) button mushrooms, trimmed
30 g (1 oz) butter
triangular croûtons
finely chopped parsley

Cut the steak into 5 cm (2 in) squares and the bacon into strips. Melt the fat and butter in a heavy casserole pan, brown the small onions, place on one side and then brown the beef, remove and keep warm.

Add the onion and bacon and when the onion is soft stir in the flour, cook for 2 minutes and then add the wine. Allow it to bubble for half a minute.

Return meat to the pan, season with salt and pepper, add thyme, bay leaf and garlic. Cover and cook in a slow oven (300°F—150°C) for about 2 hours or until the meat is very tender. Add the browned onions and mushrooms which have been sautéed in butter and cook for a further 10 minutes.

Brush one corner of each croûton with egg white and dip into chopped parsley.

Place the Beef Bourguignon into a heated serving dish and arrange the croûtons around it.

Note: Beef Bourguignon and Coq au Vin are both dishes which originated in wine growing areas. They may be cooked solely in wine or with a little stock added. With litre wines now available at such a reasonable price you can make one of these recipes and have enough wine left over to accompany it.

Steak in Black Bean Sauce

Perhaps the most popular dish on the menu in all Chinese restaurants is this dish with shredded beef pungently flavoured with black beans which are pounded with garlic.

500 g (1 lb) rump steak
½ teaspoon salt
1 egg white
1 tablespoon cornflour
1 tablespoon dried black beans
2 cloves garlic
1 onion
oil for frying
Seasoning:
1 tablespoon Chinese wine or dry sherry
¼ cup water
2 teaspoons soy sauce
2 teaspoons sugar

Shred steak and mix with salt, egg white and cornflour.

Soak beans in cold water to cover for 2 to 3 hours. Drain and rinse well. If using canned beans, rinse under cold running water only.

Drain beans thoroughly and dry in paper towels. Pound to a paste with peeled garlic. Slice onion finely. Combine ingredients for seasonings.

Heat 4 tablespoons oil in a wok or frying pan and cook beef over high heat, turning constantly, until brown. Remove. Add onion to pan and cook until golden, then set aside with the beef.

Add another 1 tablespoon oil to pan and fry bean paste, stirring for 1 minute. Return meat and onion, then add seasonings and mix well. Cook 1 to 2 minutes and serve.

Beef with Bamboo Shoot

A delicious recipe that can be varied using different vegetables.

500 g (1 lb) rump steak
1 teaspoon salt
1 egg white
1 tablespoon cornflour
2 to 3 stalks broccoli, optional
half a canned bamboo shoot
5 to 6 tablespoons oil
1 slice fresh green ginger
1 clove garlic
Seasonings:
1 tablespoon Chinese wine or dry sherry
1 tablespoon soy sauce
1 teaspoon sugar

Pound beef with back of chopper or knife 6 to 8 times. Remove all fat and then slice meat thinly across the grain into strips 5 cm (2 in) long and 5 mm ($\frac{1}{4}$ in) wide. Mix with salt, egg white and cornflour. Beat well with chopsticks or a fork until thoroughly combined.

Wash broccoli well, scrape stalks, then cut into 5 cm (2 in) long strips. Cut bamboo shoot into strips the same size. Combine seasonings in a small bowl.

Heat 2 tablespoons oil in a wok or frying pan, add broccoli and bamboo shoot. Cook, stirring constantly, for 2 minutes. Remove.

Add another 3 tablespoons of oil to wok and add ginger and peeled garlic. When they begin to colour, discard. Add beef and stir constantly over a high heat until meat loses its pink colour.

Return broccoli and bamboo shoot, then pour in the seasonings. Toss well for about 2 minutes and serve.

Beef with Onions: Follow recipe above using 2 finely sliced onions instead of the broccoli and bamboo shoot.

Beef with Carrots: Cut 1 medium carrot into fine shreds and follow recipe for Beef with Bamboo Shoot, omitting the bamboo shoot.

Beef with Peppers: Cut 1 red or green pepper into shreds and use instead of the broccoli and bamboo shoot in the recipe for Beef with Bamboo Shoot.

Oriental Beef (Beef strips and green pepper)

500 g (1 lb) fillet or rump of beef
2 tablespoons soy sauce
2 tablespoons dry sherry
1 teaspoon crushed garlic
1 teaspoon ginger juice
little oil for frying
2 large green peppers, finely shredded

Cut the beef into shreds about 5 cm (2 in) long by 5 mm ($\frac{1}{4}$ in) wide and marinate in a mixture of soy sauce, sherry, garlic and ginger juice for 30 minutes. Heat a little oil in a large frying pan or wok, add the beef and green pepper strips and cook, stirring until the beef is brown and the pepper tender-crisp.

Note: Ginger juice is obtained by grating some peeled root ginger and then squeezing out the juice through a sieve.

Variations

Oriental Beef and Onions: Omit the green peppers. Cut 2 onions into thin shreds and cook gently in oil before adding the beef.

Oriental Beef and Carrots: Prepare as above, but this time use finely shredded carrot as the vegetable.

Oriental Beef and Bean Shoots: Freshly sprouted bean shoots go well in this dish and may be used alone or with any of the above vegetables. Toss in after the beef has been frying for a few minutes.

Top left: Beef Curry (see recipe overleaf)
Top right: Chili Con Carne
Above: Malayan Beef Satays (see recipe overleaf)

Chilli Con Carne

This is a dish which is especially good for an out-doors meal, for a buffet or for serving a crowd. It actually improves with keeping, and if it's made one or two days ahead the spices will penetrate the meat and beans.

Accompany it with golden, sweet-smelling Mexican Corn Bread served warm and fresh from the oven. A marvellous budget meal for 10 people.

2 onions
2 cloves of garlic, crushed with a little salt
4 tablespoons olive oil
1.25 kg (2½ lb) minced steak
1 cup beef stock or beef cubes dissolved in water
1 × 425 g (15 oz) can of tomato purée
3 tablespoons tomato sauce
2 teaspoons salt
1 teaspoon chilli powder
2 teaspoons dried oregano leaves or 1 sprig of fresh oregano
1 teaspoon cummin

Chop the onions and crush the garlic with a little salt. Heat the oil and add the onions, gently cooking them until transparent, add the garlic and fry gently for 1 minute. Remove to a dish and keep warm. Add more oil if necessary and brown the meat over a high heat, stirring constantly.

When all the meat is well browned, add the onions and garlic, stir in the stock, tomato purée, tomato sauce, salt, chilli powder, oregano (if fresh, finely chopped) and cummin. Cover the pan and simmer for 30 minutes. Add the Mexican Beans and simmer for a further 30 minutes until they are tender.

Before serving adjust the seasoning if necessary. Serve with a plate of Corn Bread (page 386).

Mexican Beans

500 g (1 lb) red kidney beans
½ teaspoon ground cummin
1 clove garlic, crushed with a little salt
few parsley stalks
1 onion stuck with a few whole cloves
2 bay leaves
2 teaspoons salt

Soak the beans overnight. Next day drain and place into a large saucepan. Add 6 cups of water and remaining ingredients. Cover and simmer gently for 1½ hours. Remove the onion, bay leaves and parsley stalks. Drain beans and add to the Chilli Con Carne.

Note: 2 × 284 g (10 oz) cans of kidney beans may be substituted—if time is short—for the Mexican Beans. They should be well rinsed in cold water and drained before adding to meat.

Toban-Yaki

500 g (1 lb) rump or fillet steak
2 green peppers
a little oil, preferably sesame
Marinade:
⅓ cup light soy sauce
1 clove garlic, crushed
2 tablespoons sugar
1 tablespoon mirin (sweet sake) or sherry

Cut steak into thin regular-sized pieces, about 8 cm (3 in) square. Remove seeds from peppers and cut each into 4 or 5 pieces, lengthwise. Heat 1 tablespoon oil in frying pan or on a griddle. Dip meat in marinade made by combining all ingredients and add to pan with peppers. Fry, turning, until brown and cooked on both sides, brushing occasionally with marinade—no more than 4 minutes. Serve with side dishes: Toasted sesame seeds mixed with a little crushed rock salt; sauce made with 4 tablespoons tomato sauce and 2 teaspoons Worcestershire sauce.

Note: Meat and peppers can also be grilled. Cook 1-2 minutes each side under a hot, preheated griller, brushing with marinade. Marinade can be used to give flavour to other steaks for dieters—adds flavour without calories. Pork, chicken or fish steaks may also be cooked in the same way.

Beef Curry

The meat for curries should be mature and one of the cheaper cuts which will not break down under the long, slow cooking. In this recipe, no liquid is added. A heavy pan should be used or the curry cooked over an asbestos mat for protection.

2 large onions
5 cm (2 in) fresh ginger
3 to 4 cloves garlic
90 g (3 oz) ghee
3 tablespoons curry powder or curry paste
1 teaspoon turmeric
2 teaspoons black mustard seeds, optional
2 teaspoons salt
1.5 kg (3 lb) blade steak
1 to 2 fresh chillies
3 tomatoes

Finely chop onions, grate ginger and crush garlic. Cook lightly in hot ghee. Add curry powder, mustard seeds, turmeric and salt. Fry gently over low heat 2 to 3 minutes.

Cut steak into 2.5 cm (1 in) cubes, add to curry mixture and fry a few more minutes.

Add finely sliced chillies and sliced tomatoes. Fold lightly together with a large cooking spoon to mix ingredients. Cover pan and simmer very slowly about 2 hours.

Serve with rice and accompaniments. Puris may also be eaten with this beef curry.

Note: If gravy is too thin, when meat is tender remove meat and cook sauce over high heat, uncovered, until reduced. Return meat and gently reheat.

Curried koftas (meatballs)

Koftas:
500 g (1 lb) finely minced steak
1 onion
1 to 2 chillies or 1 green pepper
2 tablespoons chopped fresh coriander or mint
1 to 2 cloves garlic
2 teaspoons salt
1 teaspoon garam masala
$\frac{1}{4}$ teaspoon chilli powder
1 egg
Gravy:
30 g (1 oz) ghee or butter
1 large onion
1 teaspoon chopped green ginger
1 teaspoon turmeric
1 teaspoon salt
$\frac{1}{2}$ teaspoon garam masala
$\frac{1}{2}$ teaspoon chilli powder
250 g (8 oz) tomatoes
1 tablespoon lemon juice

Mix steak with finely chopped onion, chillies, coriander, crushed garlic, salt, garam masala and chilli powder. Knead mixture until stiff and smooth. Roll into walnut-sized balls, dip into well beaten egg and fry slowly in deep hot oil. Leave to drain on absorbent paper while making gravy.

Gravy: In a heavy saucepan heat the ghee and fry finely chopped onion and ginger over medium heat. Add turmeric, salt, garam masala and chilli powder. Allow to sizzle for a few minutes then add peeled and chopped tomatoes, fry, stirring a few minutes. Add lemon juice and koftas. Stir well, cover and simmer 15 to 20 minutes or until the gravy is thick. Serve with rice and accompaniments.

Malayan Beef Satays

No one who has visited Malaysia and Singapore will forget the satay. Satay vendors and their charcoal braziers are part of the charm of the city streets and the smell of grilled meat and hot spices lingers on in the memory. Satays are similar to the popular kebabs of the Middle East, but the spiced meat is threaded on bamboo or wooden skewers rather than metal ones.

1 kg (2 lb) steak, scotch fillet or rump
$\frac{1}{3}$ cup soy sauce
$\frac{1}{3}$ cup peanut oil
2 onions
2 cloves garlic
3 tablespoons toasted sesame seeds
2 teaspoons ground cummin
1 teaspoon lemon juice
salt and pepper

Cut the steak into cubes and put into an earthenware bowl. Combine soy sauce, peanut oil, finely chopped onion, crushed garlic and sesame seeds, pour over meat and leave to marinate for 3 hours. Turn meat from time to time in the marinade. After 3 hours, or longer, drain meat, reserving marinade. Thread 4-5 meat cubes on small bamboo or wooden skewers. Wrap small pieces of aluminium foil around skewer ends to prevent burning. Mix cummin and lemon juice together and brush over meat. Grill satays over the hot coals of a barbecue or under a preheated griller basting with marinade and turning frequently.

Grill satays until tender: 6-8 minutes for rare; 8-10 minutes for medium; 10 12 minutes for well done.

Season with salt and pepper before serving.

Note: Bamboo skewers can be bought in barbecue sections of large department stores.

To toast sesame seeds, sprinkle into a large, heavy frying pan and cook over a medium steady heat for 2-3 minutes or until well browned. Do not use any oil.

A less expensive cut of meat, such as topside, can be used in this recipe—just add $\frac{1}{2}$ cup vinegar to the other marinade ingredients and let stand overnight if possible.

Braised Oxtail

Oxtail has a rich, full, wonderful flavour which actually improves with keeping a day or two.

3 tablespoons oil
1 oxtail, jointed
2 onions, peeled and quartered
2 carrots, peeled and quartered
3 celery sticks (cut in 5 cm (2 in) lengths)
1 tablespoon flour
$2\frac{1}{4}$ cups beef stock (or stock cubes and water)
bouquet garni
salt
freshly ground pepper

Heat the oil and brown the oxtail all over in a heavy casserole dish. Remove and then add the onion, carrot and celery. Brown lightly, then dust with flour. Remove from the heat and pour on the liquid. Place back on the heat and stir until boiling. Place the oxtail pieces on top of the vegetables, add the bouquet garni and season with salt and pepper. Cover the dish and cook in a moderate oven (350°F—170°C) for about $1\frac{1}{2}$ to 2 hours or until the meat is very tender and comes away from the bone easily. Remove the bouquet garni and serve the meat very hot.

Note: If you have the time it is better to cook the oxtail the day before you intend to serve it. The fat will set on top and is easily removed and the flavour will improve.

Moussaka

A dish of Rumanian origin, Moussaka is made in many Mediterranean countries, each with a slight variation. But the main ingredients remain the same—eggplant, minced lamb (or beef) and a custard-like topping which can be a Béchamel sauce, sour cream or yoghurt flavoured with cheese and egg beaten into the mixture to give the characteristic texture.

1 large eggplant
salt
2 tablespoons olive oil
1 large onion, chopped
1 clove garlic, finely chopped
500 g (1 lb) minced lamb or steak
1 teaspoon plain flour
¾ cup beef stock
freshly ground pepper
500 g (1 lb) tomatoes or a 470 g (15 oz)
   can tomatoes
2 to 3 tablespoons grated parmesan cheese
Sauce:
30 g (1 oz) butter
2 tablespoons plain flour
1¼ cups milk
salt and pepper
1½ cups grated cheddar cheese (Red
   Malling is excellent)
2 egg yolks

Cut eggplant into thick slices. Score lightly and place in a dish and sprinkle liberally with salt. Cover with a plate and leave for 2 hours.

Heat 1 tablespoon oil and gently fry onion and garlic until golden. Add the meat. sprinkle with flour and stir for a few minutes, then pour in stock. Season to taste with salt and pepper. Cook gently for a few minutes, stirring constantly. Turn into a greased ovenproof dish.

Peel and slice tomatoes and place on top of meat. If using canned tomatoes, drain before slicing. Drain the eggplant slices, wash well and dry on paper towels.

Heat the remaining oil in the pan in which meat was cooked and fry eggplant slices until golden on both sides. Drain and place on top of the tomato slices.

Pour sauce over eggplant slices in casserole and sprinkle with the parmesan. Bake in a moderately hot oven (375°F—190°C) for about 40 minutes until top is golden.

Sauce: Melt butter in a saucepan, stir in flour and cook over a gentle heat, stirring for 2 minutes. Add the milk and stir until sauce boils and thickens. Season to taste with salt and pepper, then stir in cheddar cheese. Remove from heat and whisk in the lightly beaten egg yolks.

Variations:

Moussaka with Yoghurt Topping: Prepare the Moussaka as described but instead of the sauce, spoon the following mixture over before baking: Beat together 2 eggs and blend in 2 tablespoons plain flour. Whisk in a carton of plain yoghurt.

Moussaka with Sour Cream Topping: Instead of the yoghurt in the above recipe, use 1 carton thick sour cream.

Aberdeen Sausage

250 g (8 oz) bacon, rind removed
500 g (1 lb) topside steak, minced finely
1 cup breadcrumbs
2 teaspoons Worcestershire sauce
1 tablespoon chopped parsley
freshly ground black pepper
1 teaspoon salt
little ground nutmeg
grated rind of ½ lemon
1 egg

Mince the bacon and combine with the steak. Add breadcrumbs, Worcestershire sauce and seasonings and mix well. Moisten with well beaten egg and form into a long roll. Flour well, roll in a scalded floured cloth, tie both ends and plunge into a pan of boiling water. Boil for 2 hours. This sausage may also be steamed in a greased pudding basin. While still hot roll the sausage in extra breadcrumbs and place in a slow oven to dry, about 15 minutes. When cold serve in slices with Horseradish cream sauce or spiced mustard sauce.

Top left: Moussaka
Above: Beef Bourguignon (see recipe on page 144)

Top right: Fillet of Beef Wellington (see recipe on page 139)
Above: Braised Oxtail (see recipe on page 149)

Swedish Meatballs in Cream Sauce

Minced beef, pork and veal are great favourites with the Swedish housewife who moulds them into meat balls, shapes them into patties or into savoury meat loaves. The meat balls are well seasoned, bound with fine white breadcrumbs soaked in cream and milk and fried until golden brown. Often these are served in a creamy sauce with hot boiled rice.

500 g (1 lb) lean minced steak
250 g (½ lb) lean minced pork and veal
1½ cups soft white breadcrumbs
½ cup cream and ½ cup milk
1 onion, finely chopped
30 g (1 oz) butter
1 egg, beaten
1½ teaspoons salt, freshly ground pepper
¼ teaspoon ground ginger, little grated nutmeg
60 g (2 oz) butter
1 tablespoon plain flour
½ cup stock
extra 2 cups cream for sauce

Mix the finely minced meats together. Soak the breadcrumbs in a mixture of cream and milk. Cook the onion in butter until tender but not brown. Combine the meats, breadcrumbs, egg, onion and season with salt, pepper, ginger, and nutmeg. Beat vigorously until very light in texture, chill and form into small balls.

Melt the butter in a large frying pan and lightly brown the meatballs, a few at a time. Remove from the pan and keep warm in a casserole dish in a slow oven (300°F—150°C) while making the sauce.

In the same pan stir in the flour which has been sifted. Cook for 2 minutes stirring all the time. Remove from the heat and add the stock and the cream. Place back on the heat, stir until the sauce comes to the boil, season with salt, pepper and grated nutmeg and cook over a low heat for about 10 minutes until the sauce reduces and thickens, stirring constantly. When ready to serve, pour the cream sauce over the meatballs and scatter with some snipped dill. Serve with boiled rice.

Note: The meatballs may be made and cooked the day before and then reheated in the oven, with the sauce poured over just before serving. For a buffet of 12 people, double the above quantity.

Boiled Rice

Bring 4 cups of water to the boil and sprinkle in 2 cups of long grain rice keeping the water boiling. Stir the rice and then cover tightly and cook over the lowest heat for 17 to 20 minutes. Remove from the heat, uncover to allow the steam to escape and then fluff up with a fork.

Corned Beef

1 large onion
6 whole cloves
1.5 kg (3 lb) corned beef, silverside or rolled brisket
1 tablespoon lemon juice or white vinegar
12 peppercorns
1 blade mace
2 stalks celery
1 bay leaf
bouquet garni
1 carrot
2 tablespoons brown sugar

Halve onion and stud with cloves. Put meat into a large saucepan with all other ingredients and add cold water to cover. Simmer, covered, until tender. Allow 30 minutes per pound (0.5 kg) after it has reached simmering point. Cooking time will vary according to the cut and age of meat. To test, insert a fine metal skewer through thick part of meat and if it comes out easily the meat is cooked. Turn off heat and allow beef to cool in liquid. Chill and serve in thin slices with mustard, pickles or cucumber, spiced mustard sauce or horseradish cream.

Spiced Beef

Beef marinated, pot roasted and cooled in its meat juices makes this delicately spiced summer meat.

2 kg (4 lb) corner of topside fresh
    silverside or bolar blade
2 onions
1 bay leaf
1 teaspoon each ground cinnamon and
    allspice
6 whole cloves
1½ teaspoons salt
1 teaspoon ground black pepper
1 stick celery
1 cup cider vinegar
1 tablespoon oil

Trim any excess fat from beef. Place beef in a china or glass bowl. Slice onions and add to beef with bay leaf, cinnamon, allspice, cloves, salt and pepper. Cut celery and add to bowl. Add vinegar. Place in the refrigerator to marinate overnight or for 12 hours turning the meat occasionally.

Drain beef and reserve marinade. Dry the meat. Heat oil in a heavy fireproof casserole and brown meat on all sides. Heat half the reserved marinade with 1 cup water and pour over meat. Cover and cook in a slow oven (300°F—150°C) for 3 hours or until a fine skewer inserted in the thickest part of the meat comes out easily.

Cool the meat in its liquid, turning meat occasionally. When cold, remove meat to a dish. Strain the pan juices and brush over meat.

● Serve cold in slices with Aiöli or Horseradish Cream Sauce.

A simple salad of finely sliced fennel in a herbed vinaigrette dressing is excellent with this beef.

Calves Liver Sauté

8 slices of calves or lamb liver 5 mm
    (¼ in) thick
salt
freshly ground pepper
60 g (2 oz) plain flour
1 tablespoon olive oil
30 g (1 oz) butter
8 bacon rashers, rind removed
finely chopped parsley
Mustard sauce:
1 tablespoon prepared French mustard
1 tablespoon butter
2 tablespoons stock or white wine

Season the liver with salt and pepper and roll in sifted flour. Shake off excess flour.

Heat the oil, add the butter and when very hot place the prepared liver in the frying pan. Sauté 2 to 3 minutes regulating the heat so that the butter is hot but does not burn. Turn the liver and cook for 1 minute on the other side. Prick the liver with a skewer and if the juices are very pale pink remove to a hot dish.

Toss the bacon in the frying pan until each side is golden and arrange the liver and bacon on a heated serving dish, sprinkle with parsley and cap with mustard sauce.

Mustard Sauce: Combine the mustard with the softened butter. Throw away any fat left in the frying pan. Place it back on the heat and deglaze with stock or white wine stirring all the time. Blend in the mustard butter and then pour it over the liver and bacon.

Pressed Tongue

Pressed Tongue

This dish can be made with either salted or smoked ox tongue. Smoked tongues have a superb flavour and are sold by continental butchers and delicatessens.

1 salted ox tongue
6 whole allspice
6 whole cloves
1 onion, halved
bouquet garni
1 carrot, quartered
1 celery stalk
6 black peppercorns

Wash tongue and curl into a large saucepan. Add cold water to cover and bring slowly to the boil. Skim top, add remaining ingredients and simmer covered for about 3 hours or until a small bone at the root end pulls out easily. Cool the tongue in liquid. Take tongue out of pan, remove bones and trim off root.

Peel off skin. This should come off easily in one piece by pushing the thumbs underneath skin to ease edges.

To press a tongue: Curl the tongue into a 20 cm (7-8 in) cake tin or bowl. Place a plate on top that will just fit inside the tin and put a heavy weight, at least 3 kg (7 lb), on the plate. Chill overnight.

Unmould the tongue onto a serving dish and accompany with Cumberland sauce, spiced mustard sauce or gribiche sauce.

Potted Hough

Most countries have their own cold meat specialities. Many of these are now international and have travelled wherever people have roamed. Bologna, mortadella, salami and frankfurts are known to everyone. But the English and Scots have produced many fine, but perhaps not so well-known, cold meat dishes.

Take Potted Hough, a dish as old as time, and one known to every true Scot. It is a simple dish of chopped meat set in its own good jelly but when served with a little vinegar and hot English mustard it is a dish fit for a prince.

1.5 kg (3 lb) beef shanks, cut into thick slices
2 fresh pig's trotters
6 whole black peppercorns
1 bay leaf
3-4 canned anchovies, mashed
salt and freshly ground black pepper

Put beef shanks, pig's trotters, peppercorns and bayleaf into a large heavy saucepan and cover with cold water, Bring to the boil and skim top. Cover and simmer for 3 hours. Cool and remove meat from the broth. Strain broth. Trim away fat and gristle and remove bones from meat. Chop meat finely.

Return chopped meat to broth. Boil uncovered until reduced for 20 minutes. Add anchovies and season with salt and pepper. Boil a further 5 minutes to blend flavours. Pour into 1 large or 2 small bowls which have first been rinsed with cold water. Cover with plastic wrap or a plate and chill until firm.

Turn out on to serving plate and garnish with cucumber slices.

Accompany the potted hough with vinegar and hot English mustard. Serve with tomatoes, cucumber and a potato salad.
Note: Two veal knuckles, each cut into 3 pieces, may be substituted for the pig's trotters.

veal

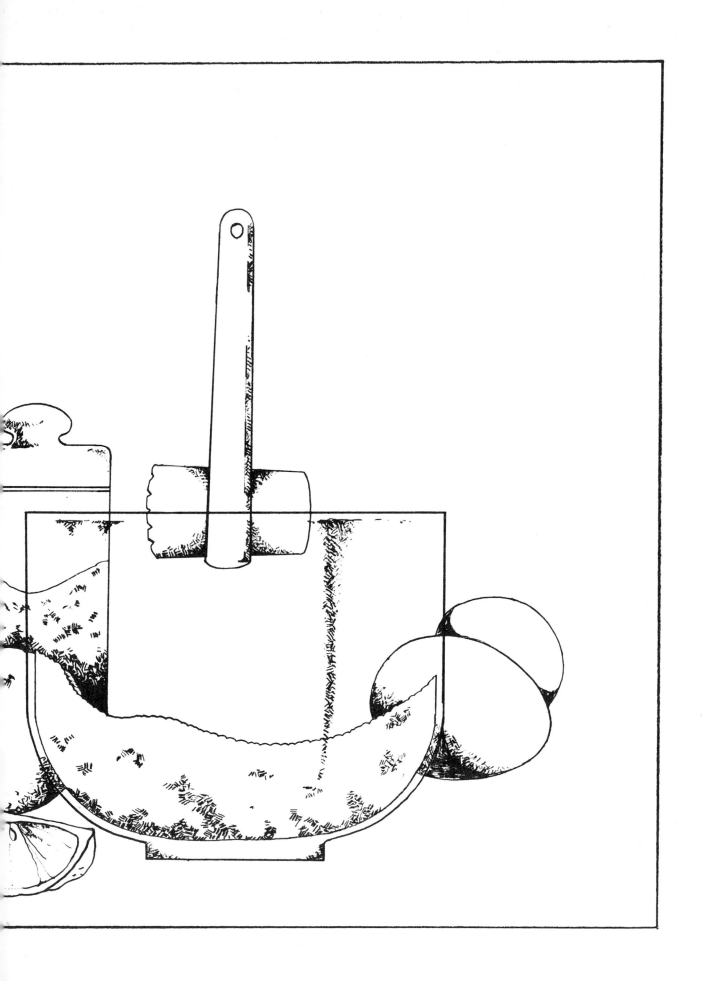

Veal

Roast Veal

To roast veal: As there is little fat on veal, it needs to be basted frequently while cooking. Bacon wrapped around the roast before cooking helps keep meat moist and provides good flavour. Place on a rack in roasting pan and put in a moderately slow oven (325°F—160°C).

Cooking times: Allow 45 minutes for each pound (0.5 kg). Veal should never be underdone.

Buying veal: The flesh should be very pale with just a tinge of pink. There is very little fat which should be white and satiny and the veal should have no unpleasant odour.

Cuts for roasting: Fillet, loin, shoulder (on bone or boned, rolled and tied), **topside.**

Veal Scallopine with Cream

4 small or 2 large veal steaks
seasoned flour
1 small onion, or 4 shallots, finely chopped
125 g (4 oz) small mushrooms
30 g (1 oz) butter
¾ cup white wine
½ cup stock
salt
freshly ground pepper
¼ cup cream
finely chopped parsley

Place the veal steaks between 2 sheets of plastic and gently beat until quite thin. If using large veal steaks cut in half. Lightly dust with a little seasoned flour.

Heat a large sauté pan and add the butter and when it is foaming put in the veal steaks. Sauté briskly 3 minutes each side. Remove to a heated plate and add the onion and whole mushrooms to the pan. Sauté for a few minutes and add the wine.

Allow it to boil and reduce by half then add the stock. Season with salt and pepper. Place the veal back into the pan and when the sauce is boiling, cover the pan and simmer for 6 minutes. Remove from the heat, add 1 tablespoon of buerre manié (1 tablespoon of butter kneaded with 1 teaspoon of flour) shaking the pan to distribute it throughout the sauce.

Place the pan back on the heat, allow the sauce to come to boiling point and add the cream. Adjust the seasoning and simmer for a further minute. Arrange the veal steaks on a heated serving dish, spoon the sauce over them and dust with parsley.

Veal Scallopine with Cream

Wiener Schnitzel

Wiener Schnitzel would be without doubt the most famous dish the Austrians have produced. When perfectly cooked the crust is a warm golden brown and it is possible to slip a knife between the coating and the meat. To enjoy this dish at its best, it should be eaten as soon as it is cooked with a squeeze of lemon juice and chopped hard-boiled egg white and yolk, and a few anchovy fillets.

4 veal steaks cut from the leg
juice of ½ lemon
flour, beaten egg and fine white
  breadcrumbs for coating
60 g (2 oz) butter
2 hard-boiled eggs
4 anchovy fillets
parsley sprigs

Trim or slash any gristle from the veal steaks and beat them out until they are quite thin. Sprinkle with the lemon juice and allow them to whiten. This will take about 5 minutes. Dry with kitchen paper.

Place the flour, beaten egg and breadcrumbs in three separate dishes. Season the flour and coat each steak in flour shaking off any excess, and then holding the steak with two spoons, dip into beaten egg coating it only lightly.

Coat each steak in breadcrumbs gently shaking off any excess.

Melt the butter in a heavy frypan and when it is foaming, add the veal steaks, cooking only two at a time unless there is ample room for more. Cook the schnitzels for 2 minutes on one side until golden brown and then turn on the other side and cook for a further 2 minutes.

Be careful not to disturb the breadcrumb coating. Drain the veal steaks on crumpled kitchen paper and arrange on a heated serving dish. Chop the whites of the hard-boiled eggs and sieve the yolks and sprinkle over each steak. Arrange an anchovy fillet on each.

Serve immediately with lemon wedges or slices and garnish with parsley sprigs.

Saltimbocca Alla Romana

This is a well-known and delicious method of sautéeing veal which originated in Rome.

4 thin veal steaks
4 slices of proscuitto
4 sage leaves
freshly ground pepper
30 g (1 oz) butter
¼ cup dry white wine

Flatten out the slices of veal until they are very thin. Trim if necessary and cut the proscuitto to the same size. Lay a sage leaf on each piece of veal and cover with the proscuitto securing it with a small skewer. Season with pepper.

Heat the butter until it is foaming and then place the veal steaks in the pan and sauté gently until well browned on both sides. Pour in the white wine and when it begins to bubble, cover the pan and simmer for 5 to 6 minutes. Place the meat on a heated dish and pour over the sauce.

Variation:
Thin slices of beef or the lamb minute steaks may be used but they will take longer to cook.

Note: Proscuitto is raw smoked ham which is available in Continental delicatessens throughout Australia.

Saltimbocca Alla Romana

Vitello Tonnato

A summer dish now found all over Italy but which originated in Veneto. The pale, delicately flavoured veal and the creamy tuna sauce make an unusual but most delicious combination.

1 × **1.5 kg (3 lbs) piece of fillet of veal, boned**
2 anchovy fillets, cut into small pieces
1 tablespoon olive oil
⅓ cup dry vermouth
salt and freshly ground pepper
bouquet garni
Sauce:
1 × 170 g (6 oz) tin of tuna
6 anchovy fillets
1 teaspoon capers
2 tablespoons lemon juice
salt, freshly ground black pepper
½ cup mayonnaise
1 large tin of artichoke hearts for garnishing

With a sharp pointed knife make some incisions in the surface of the meat and insert the anchovy pieces. Roll up and tie neatly. Heat the oil in a heavy casserole, preferably one into which the meat fits snugly and brown the meat all over. Pour over the vermouth, season with salt and pepper and add the bouquet garni. Cover the casserole tightly and cook in a moderate oven (350°F—170°C) for 1 to 1¼ hours. Remove from the heat and allow the veal to cool in the liquid, then chill in the refrigerator to make the meat easier to carve.

Sauce: Pound the tuna with the anchovy fillets, capers and lemon juice until smooth. Season with salt and pepper. Stir in the mayonnaise and then place in an electric blender or push through a sieve.

Cut the veal into thick, even slices, spread each slice with the sauce and reshape the joint. Place into the refrigerator until quite firm. Serve surrounded by artichoke hearts which have been well-rinsed and drained and tossed in a well-flavoured vinaigrette dressing.

Alternately, the veal may be cut into thin slices, arranged on a platter, then each covered with the sauce. Serve with lemon wedges and a small dish of capers.

Veal Olives on Skewers

The Italians are very adept at cooking veal and these little Veal "Olives" on Skewers are no exception. It is the interesting combination of the ham, veal, bacon and sage which makes this such an excellent dish.

Veal scallops, cut from the leg of veal
salt, freshly ground pepper
lemon
lean ham
lean bacon
1 onion, peeled and quartered
sage leaves
bread cubes
¼ cup olive oil

Cut the veal into squares about 5 cm (2 in) in size, place between two pieces of plastic wrap and beat until very thin. Season with salt, pepper and lemon juice. On each, lay a piece of ham the same size, roll them up, and around each, place a thin, lean piece of bacon. Thread on to small skewers, alternating each one with a slice of raw onion, a leaf of sage and a small square of stale bread about 2.5 cm (1 in) thick.

Put the skewers into greased ovenproof dish or baking dish and sprinkle with olive oil. Bake in a hot oven (400 °F—200°C) for about 8 minutes, turning them over and basting two or three times. Serve on a bed of rice.

Note: Mint, basil or marjoram may be substituted for the sage if you prefer the flavour, or the meat may be sprinkled with the herb before it is rolled up. The "olives" may also be made with lean pork or lamb.

Veal Cutlets Modena Style

Plump white veal loin cutlets cooked in a style commonly used in Modena, Italy. Just a little marsala is added but its distinctive qualities flavour the sauce and the meat.

6 veal cutlets 2.5 cm (1 in) thick
¼ cup flour
1 egg
pinch of salt
breadcrumbs for coating
125 g (4 oz) butter
1 tablespoon olive oil
1 medium onion, finely chopped
2 tablespoons marsala
½ tablespoon tomato paste
½ cup white stock (chicken or veal)
salt and freshly ground pepper

Trim the cutlets. Fold the tail end inside each cutlet and secure with a small skewer. Beat the egg with a pinch of salt on a plate. Dip the cutlets in flour, then egg and coat with the breadcrumbs.

Heat the butter with the oil in a heavy sauté pan or frying pan. Add the cutlets and brown well on both sides. Add the chopped onion and when it begins to brown pour on the marsala. Cook until it evaporates to 1 tablespoon and stir in the tomato paste with the stock. Season with salt and pepper and continue cooking for 15-20 minutes or until the cutlets are tender when tested with a skewer. Remove small skewers from cutlets. Arrange the cutlets on a heated serving dish and spoon over a little of the pan juices.

● The quick reduction of wine or spirits by boiling removes the alcoholic content and intensifies its flavour.

Veal Scallops in Cream Sauce

Veal, white wine and cream are an excellent combination. The flavour of the sauce can be varied by using a rich sweet white wine or a combination of white wine and vermouth.

4 to 6 veal steaks cut from the leg
30 g (1 oz) butter
1 shallot, finely chopped
125 g (4 oz) white button mushrooms,
  sliced
¾ cup dry white wine
½ cup veal stock
¼ cup cream
2 teaspoons flour blended with 1½
  tablespoons butter
1 teaspoon fresh tarragon finely chopped
  or 1 teaspoon finely chopped parsley

Beat the veal steaks until they are thin. Trim and cut in half. Melt the butter in a sauté or frying pan and when the foam subsides brown the veal on both sides.

Reduce the heat under the pan and add the shallot. When it is soft, add the mushrooms tossing them in the butter for about 3 minutes. Remove and place with the veal.

Pour the wine into the pan, raise the heat and reduce wine by half. Add the stock and cream, bring to the boil and then sprinkle in the buerre manié. Stir until the sauce thickens, add the veal and mushrooms, cover and simmer for 4 to 5 minutes.

Arrange the veal on a serving dish, spoon over the sauce and sprinkle with tarragon or parsley.

Serve with plain steamed potatoes.

Note: This is an example of a wine sauce being made quickly in the pan after sautéeing. The main ingredients are placed back in the sauce for a few minutes to finish cooking and to take up the flavour.

Top: Veal Cutlets Modena (see recipe on page 163)
Above: Ossobucco Milanese

Ossobucco Milanese

4 veal shanks, cut in 8 cm (3 in) pieces
2 tablespoons olive oil
2 tablespoons plain flour
½ teaspoon salt
freshly ground black pepper
1 cup dry white wine
1 tablespoon tomato paste
1 cup water
1 teaspoon chopped parsley
1 clove garlic, chopped finely
1 strip lemon peel
2 anchovy fillets, chopped
3 tablespoons beef stock
30 g (1 oz) butter
Gremolata garnish:
chopped parsley
chopped garlic
chopped lemon rind

Veal shin, cut into segments, is cooked in wine and stock with onions and tomato. It must be cooked gently so as not to disturb the marrow which many find the best part of the dish.

It is usually served bedded on rice, generally the golden Risotto of Milan, and is topped with a mixture of chopped parsley, lemon peel and garlic. This is known as Gremolata.

Heat oil in a large deep pot. Roll the pieces of veal shank in flour and cook until the meat is well browned all over. Season with salt and pepper.

Add the wine, raise the heat under the pan and cook until the wine has evaporated. Add the water and tomato paste, cover the pan tightly and cook over a low heat for 1 hour, adding more water if necessary.

Ten minutes before serving add parsley, garlic, lemon peel and anchovy and cook for 2 minutes longer, turning the bones over once. Remove the strip of lemon peel and arrange the meat on a heated serving dish. Add the stock and butter to the pan gravy, mix it well and then pour over the meat.

Sprinkle with the mixture of parsley, garlic and lemon rind which has been finely chopped together and accompany with Risotto.

lamb

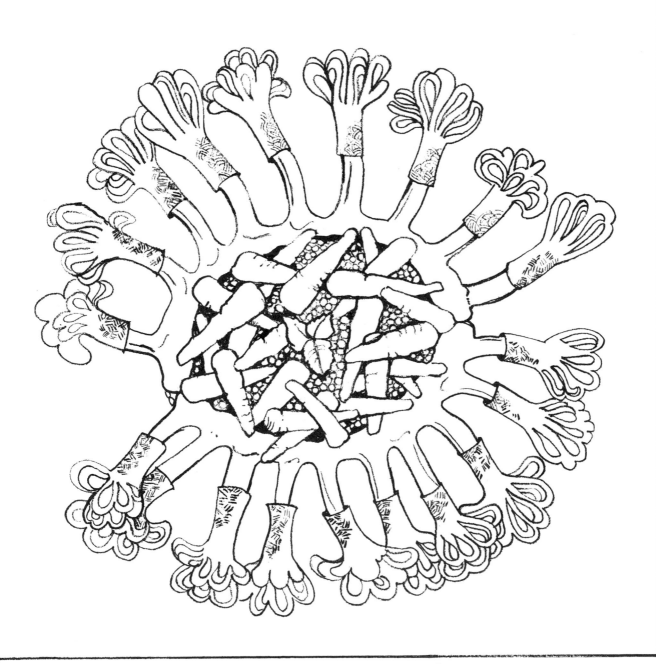

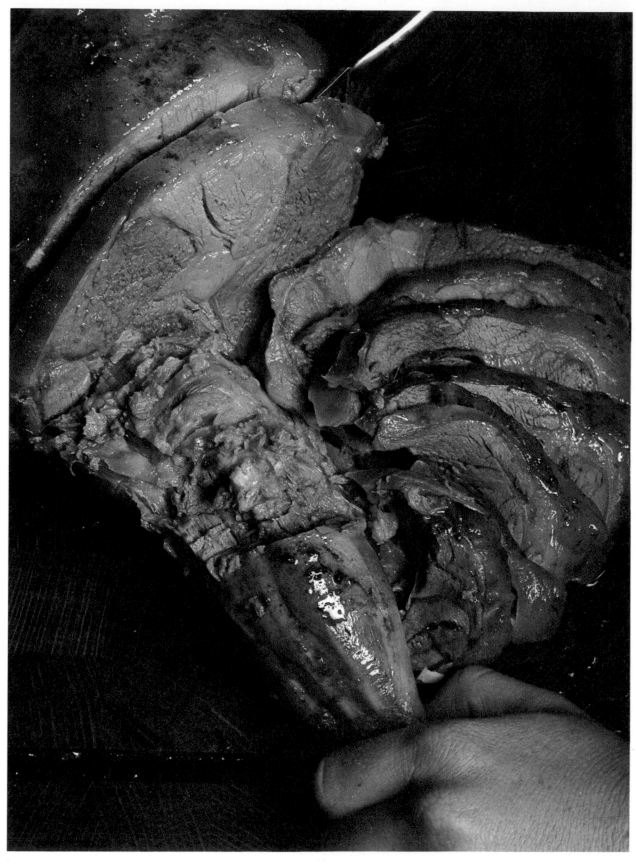

Roast Lamb

Lamb

Roast Lamb

A few slits may be cut under the skin of lamb with a pointed knife and in these slivers of garlic and or a few small sprigs of rosemary may be placed.

Rub meat with salt and pepper and put in roasting pan on a rack. If there is little fat on the lamb, add about 2 tablespoons fat or dripping to pan.

Start the lamb in a very hot oven (425°F—220°C) for the first 20 minutes, then lower heat to moderate (350°F—175°C) for the rest of cooking time.

Cooking times: For well-done lamb allow 30 minutes for each pound (0.5 kg) plus an extra 30 minutes, cooked but still a little pink near the bone allow 20 minutes for each pound (0.5 kg) plus an extra 20 minutes.

Buying Lamb: Choose lamb with a pinkish coloured flesh and an even coating of firm white fat. Very lean lamb is seldom good to eat. The word "lamb" is always stamped on the skin.

Cuts For Roasting: Leg and loin are the prime cuts. Most butchers crack the shank bone of the leg but it looks better and is easier to carve if the bone is left in one piece. Loin may be roasted on the bone, but you can, if you prefer, ask the butcher to bone, roll and tie the loin.

Shoulder and forequarter are both excellent cuts for roasting although there is more fat in proportion to meat than on the leg, making them suitable joints for eating cold. For easier carving these cuts may be boned, rolled and tied before roasting. For added flavour they are often stuffed before being tied.

Rack of lamb is an ideal cut for roasting for a small number of people. It consists of 6-8 cutlets from the ribs. For a crown roast, two racks of lamb are tied together, forming the shape of a crown.

Hogget comes from animals 1-2 years old, the meat having a richer flavour than lamb but still quite tender. Hogget is best cooked well-done so allow 30-35 minutes to the pound (0.5 kg) plus 30 minutes extra.

Mutton is from mature sheep over two years of age. The meat has a deeper colour with a coarse grain. Although not nearly as tender as lamb or hogget, many people prefer the rich flavour and it is less expensive than lamb.

To roast mutton, use a moderate oven (350°F—175°C) and allow 40-45 minutes for each pound (0.5 kg). No fat is needed in the pan. Mutton is best well-cooked. A sliced onion placed on meat before cooking gives it a delicious flavour.

French Roasting: Lamb is ideally suited to roasting French-style, that is, basting the lamb from time to time with stock or water instead of fat. Traditionally the lamb is served with haricot beans. If serving roast vegetables with the lamb, they will need to be cooked in a separate dish.

Prepare lamb in usual way, place on a rack in roasting pan and pour in 1 cup water, 30 g (1 oz) butter and 1 teaspoon salt. Roast in a moderate oven (350°F—175°C) for 17-20 minutes for each pound (0.5 kg). Baste lamb with water in pan every 15 minutes. French roast lamb is always served underdone, with the flesh still bright pink.

For the gravy, add a little water to the pan after meat has been removed. Place pan over a moderate heat and scrape the crustiness on the sides of the pan into juices. Season to taste. Strain and serve with the roast.

Herbed Mustard Leg of Lamb

Mustard flavoured with herbs and spices makes an interesting and aromatic coating for roast lamb.

1 leg of lamb
¼ cup French mustard
2 tablespoons soy sauce
1 clove garlic, crushed
**2 teaspoons finely chopped rosemary or
    thyme**
¼ teaspoon ground ginger
1 tablespoon olive oil

Trim any excess fat from the leg and place on a rack in a baking dish.

Mix remaining ingredients to a paste and spread over the lamb. Allow to stand for at least 2 hours. Place in a hot oven (400°F—200°C) and then immediately turn the temperature down to moderate (350°F—170°C) and cook for 1 to 1½ hours for medium rare. Place on a serving dish and garnish with watercress.

Loin of Lamb Coriander

Give your butcher warning and he will bone the loin for this dish. The coriander seed is the fruit of the coriander plant (better known as Chinese parsley). When ripe it has a sweet orangey aromatic taste and cooked with lamb gives a delicious mild spicy flavour.

1 loin of lamb about 1.5 kg (3 lb)
4-5 garlic cloves
salt
1 tablespoon ground coriander seeds
freshly ground black pepper
30 g (1 oz) butter
¾ cup white wine

Trim meat of any excess fat, remove fillet and bone. Crush the garlic to a fine paste with 1 teaspoon of salt. If coriander seeds are whole, crush with a pestle and mortar or place the seeds between two sheets of paper and crush with a rolling pin.

Mix the garlic and coriander together and spread over the inside of lamb. Roll up and tie at 2.5 cm (1 in) intervals.

Place meat in a baking dish, sprinkle with salt and freshly ground black pepper, add the butter to the dish and pour in the wine. Roast in a moderately hot oven (375°F—190°C) for 1½ hours or until the meat juices are clear.

Remove the meat to a serving platter and keep warm. Allow the meat to stand in a warm place for 10 to 15 minutes "to set" before serving. The juices will be reabsorbed by the meat making carving easier.

Skim fat from pan juices. Mix 1 tablespoon of the fat with 1 tablespoon of flour in a cup. Stir into the pan juices, bring to the boil and simmer for a few minutes. Season with salt and pepper. If the gravy is too thick add a little extra stock or water. Remove the string from the meat and carve into thick slices, serving the gravy separately. Garnish with watercress or Chinese parsley.

Colonial Goose

In the early Australian colonial days, the traditional goose was substituted by a pot roasted leg of lamb filled with a kidney and bacon stuffing—hence the name Colonial Goose.

1 × 1.75 kg (3½ lb) leg of lamb, boned
Stuffing:
2 sheep's kidneys
2 bacon rashers, rind removed
1 medium onion, chopped
nutmeg
salt
freshly ground pepper
1 cup fine breadcrumbs
1 teaspoon rosemary
1 egg
2 tablespoons oil for browning the meat
Glaze:
1 tablespoon honey
2 teaspoons dry mustard

Wipe the meat with a paper towel. Make the stuffing: remove the core of the kidneys and slice thickly. Cut the bacon into thin slices and place in a dry frying pan and when the bacon fat becomes transparent, add the onion. Allow to fry gently for a minute and then add the kidney slices.

Toss together over the heat for a minute or so and then season with nutmeg, salt and pepper. Remove from the heat and stir in the breadcrumbs, rosemary and whole egg. Stuff the cavity where the bones have been taken out, and tie up the leg securely with string.

Heat the oil in a heavy casserole pan and brown the lamb on both sides. Season with salt and pepper. Mix the honey and mustard and spread over the lamb.

Place the lid on the casserole dish and allow to pot roast over a very gentle heat for 1½ hours or until tender. Remove the lamb to a heated serving dish, garnish with parsley sprigs and serve with zucchini and new potatoes.

Crown Roast of Lamb

This is an impressive roast which serves up to 8 people. The centre is filled with a herb flavoured stuffing and then young spring vegetables are arranged on top just before serving.

1 crown roast of lamb consisting of two best ends of neck tied or skewered together
Filling:
2 shallots
15 g ($\frac{1}{2}$ oz) butter
185 g (6 oz) veal mince
1 tablespoon finely chopped parsley, thyme and chives
salt
freshly ground pepper

Ask your butcher in advance to assemble a crown roast or buy two best ends of neck of lamb.

With the outside of the cutlets facing each other firmly skewer or sew each end together and then shape into a circle.

Filling: Chop the shallots and cook in the butter until softened. Mix with the veal mince and herbs and season with salt and pepper. Stir together over the heat for a few minutes. Stand the roast on a baking dish and put the filling in the middle. Roast in a hot oven (400°F—200°C) for about 1$\frac{1}{2}$ hours or until the meat juices run clear when the meat is pierced with a fork. Remove from the oven and allow the meat to stand in a warm place for 10 to 15 minutes while making the gravy. When ready to serve place a cutlet frill on the end of each bone. Arrange some peas and carrots on the filling and duchess potatoes around the roast.

Gravy:
Pour the fat from the baking dish leaving 1 tablespoon. Place the baking dish over a moderate heat, add 1 small finely chopped onion and allow it to brown and then stir in 1 tablespoon of plain flour. When the flour becomes a good brown colour stir in 1 cup of stock or vegetable water. Season to taste. Stir the gravy allowing it to bubble gently for a few minutes. Strain through a sieve and serve piping hot.

To carve: Cut between each two bones into double cutlets.

Roast Lamb Indienne

Deep diamond cuts on the surface of the leg of lamb allow the spicy seasonings to penetrate and flavour the meat. Carve the lamb in thick, but small slices and serve with rich rice pilau and sambols, chutneys or pickles.

1 leg lamb, weighing about 2.5 kg (5 lb)
1$\frac{1}{2}$ tablespoons lemon juice
2 cloves garlic
2.5 cm (1 in) green ginger finely chopped
1 teaspoon soy sauce
3 tablespoons oil
1 teaspoon turmeric
1 teaspoon curry powder or curry paste
2 teaspoon salt, $\frac{1}{4}$ teaspoon pepper
$\frac{1}{2}$ teaspoon garam masala

With a sharp knife, score leg of lamb in diamond pattern in cuts about 5 mm ($\frac{1}{4}$ in) deep.

Combine all other ingredients and rub well into lamb. Cover and allow to stand for 1 hour in refrigerator. Put lamb into shallow roasting pan without rack. Pour 1 cup water into pan and roast in moderate oven (350°F—170°C) for 1$\frac{1}{2}$ hours, basting with pan juices.

Serve on a bed of rice pilau with accompaniments.

Welsh Venison

This loin of lamb will appeal especially to those who enjoy the taste of game. The lamb of course is not strong but the herbs, port and the red currant jelly give the suggestion of venison.

1 loin of lamb, boned and tied
mixed herbs
salt
freshly ground pepper
1 tablespoon each of olive oil and butter
1 large carrot, cut in small dice
2 sticks of celery, cut in small dice
1 onion, peeled and cut into small dice
½ cup stock
bouquet garni
¾ cup port
red currant jelly

Season the lamb with the mixed herbs, salt and pepper. Melt the butter and oil and lightly brown the lamb in a heavy casserole dish. Place on one side and brown the vegetables. Place the lamb back on the bed of vegetables and pour over the stock. Add the bouquet garni, cover and cook very gently on the stove or in a moderate oven for 1½ hours. Remove the lamb and keep warm while you skim the fat off the cooking liquid and reduce it to a thick glaze. Stir in the port and when thoroughly combined glaze the lamb with this sauce. Serve with red currant jelly.

Herbed Racks of Lamb

A rack of lamb is not only the sweetest cut but makes a perfect small roast which is easy to carve.

4 small racks of lamb consisting of 4
**   cutlets each**
Marinade:
¾ cup olive oil
juice of 1 lemon
1 teaspoon salt
freshly ground black pepper
2 garlic cloves, roughly chopped
2 sprigs of rosemary or 1 tablespoon of
**   dried rosemary**

Trim the cutlets (if your butcher has not done so) by cutting away the flesh from the top of the bone and slicing the fat away leaving about 5 cm (2 in) of bone exposed. Score the lamb with shallow diagonal cuts in a lattice fashion.

Combine the first five ingredients for the marinade and pour into a glass, china or enamelled dish large enough to hold the lamb racks. Sprinkle with rosemary. Turn the lamb around in the marinade, cover and allow to stand for at least 2 hours. Turn the racks occasionally so that every part of the meat is impregnated with the flavours.

Place the lamb on a roasting rack in a baking dish. Baste with some of the marinade and roast in a moderately hot oven (375°F—190°C) for 45-50 minutes, basting from time to time with the remaining marinade. When the lamb is cooked the juice will be clear and the scored fat crisp and golden.

Cut each rack in half allowing a double cutlet per portion.
Note: For our photograph we cooked six racks of lamb as these were the first of the spring lamb and were very small.

● A rack of lamb is the best end of neck consisting of 6 to 7 cutlets although this can be cut smaller. The chine bone is cut away and the flap and skin removed. The fat is trimmed away from the top of the cutlets exposing about 5 cm (2 in) of bone.

Top left: Lamb Kebabs (see recipe on page 176)
Top right: Colonial Goose (see recipe on page 170)
Above: Herbed Racks of Lamb

173

Braised Leg of Lamb Provençal

Braised Leg of Lamb with a stuffing flavoured with fresh herbs may be served hot with its wine sauce and colourful vegetable garnish or cold with a green and red pepper salad and a good mayonnaise.

1 small leg of lamb, boned
2 tablespoons olive oil
1 onion, finely chopped
1 carrot, finely chopped
1 celery stick, finely chopped
½ cup white wine
½ cup stock
salt, freshly ground pepper
bouquet garni
Stuffing:
125 g (4 oz) bacon or speck, finely
    chopped
1½ cups fine white breadcrumbs soaked
    in ½ cup of milk
1 garlic clove crushed with a little salt
1 tablespoon chopped fresh herbs—
    thyme, fennel, celery leaves, tarragon,
    parsley
1 egg
salt, freshly ground pepper
Garnish:
2 eggplants
salt
flour for dusting
olive oil
3 green and red peppers
500 g (1 lb) ripe tomatoes, peeled
2 garlic cloves, crushed
sprig of thyme or oregano
salt and freshly ground pepper

Make the stuffing with the bacon, breadcrumbs soaked in milk, crushed garlic, herbs, egg and salt and pepper. Spoon into the cavity in the leg of lamb.

Sew or tie the lamb up securely. Heat the oil in a heavy casserole and brown the lamb all over. Remove and add the onion, carrot and celery and fry until lightly golden. Place the lamb back in the casserole on the bed of vegetables and pour in the wine and stock, season with salt and pepper and add the bouquet garni. Cover tightly and cook over a gentle heat for 1½ hours.

While the lamb is cooking cut the eggplants into thick slices, score and sprinkle with salt. Allow to stand 20 minutes, drain and wash thoroughly. Dry with paper towels. Dust lightly with flour and fry until golden brown in hot oil. Remove and keep warm.

Slice the peppers into rings after removing seeds. Fry in hot oil for a few minutes.

Cut the tomatoes into quarters and fry with the garlic and thyme for a few minutes in oil. Combine the vegetables and toss together. Season with salt and pepper.

Place the lamb on a heated serving dish. Reduce the sauce to thicken it and glaze the lamb. Arrange the vegetables around the lamb and sprinkle with chopped parsley.

Grilled Lamb

There is nothing better in the world than a plump, juicy well-grilled chop. Like beef, if lamb chops are to be tender, they must not be overcooked.

The important thing is to keep the juices inside and to do this the meat should be brushed with a little melted butter or oil, then seared under (or over, depending on the grilling method used) a high heat. When a crust forms on both sides, lower the grill so that it is further away from the heat and continue grilling for about 6 minutes or until cooked.

Cuts suitable for grilling

Short loin chops are cut from the loin section and should be at least 2 cm (¾ in) thick.

Noisettes are boned loin chops, rolled and tied. Your butcher will bone the loin for you. If you wish to try it for yourself, cut down and along the bone with a sharp pointed knife to remove the bone. Trim off the skin, then roll the loin and tie with string at 2.5 to 3 cm (about 1 in) intervals. Cut between string to form noisettes. Alternatively, buy short loin chops at least 2.5 cm (1 in) thick and cut bone out of each, then roll up, winding tail of chop around the inside meat, and tie with string.

Chump chops are lean chops from the chump section between the leg and the loin.

Cutlets come from the rib section. For grilling, ask the butcher not to flatten each cutlet with his chopper.

Leg steaks or chops are not as tender as the other chops and should be marinated. Use cut into thick chunks for kebabs.

Shoulder chops and forequarter chops are from the fore section of the lamb and, like leg chops, are better when marinated.

Best end neck chops have a delicious, sweet flavour when grilled especially when spring lamb is in season (August to December).

Kidneys are particularly suited to grilling.

Lamb's fry can be grilled but must be cooked quickly to prevent toughening.

Grilling Lamb

Preheat griller. Buy chops at least 2 cm (¾ in) thick. Trim the skin away from the chops. Season meat on both sides with freshly ground pepper and rock salt. A pinch of ground or finely chopped fresh herbs such as rosemary, oregano or marjoram or a cut clove of garlic may be rubbed over the meat for extra flavour. Brush the meat with oil or melted butter and place on the greased rack of the griller pan. Grill under a high heat, turning once.

Lamb leg chops and forequarter chops are less tender and will need a moderate heat after they have browned on both sides. Brush these chops with more oil or butter as they grill.

Grilled Lamb's Kidneys

Cut out the core from the kidneys with scissors and remove the skin. Split the kidneys in half, taking care not to sever them completely. Open the kidneys out and run 2 skewers horizontally through them to keep them flat while grilling. Place 2 or 3 kidneys on the skewers.

Season with salt and freshly ground pepper, brush with melted butter or oil and place on the griller rack, cut side uppermost, and cook under a very hot grill for 3 minutes on each side. Remove skewers and serve immediately.

Timetable

Lamb is **never** served rare. It should be a delicate pink when cut.

Short loin chops, chump chops and cutlets 2 cm (¾ in) thick	8 minutes
Noisettes 2.5 cm (1 in) thick	10 minutes
Leg chops and forequarter and shoulder chops 2 cm (¾ in) thick	10 to 12 minutes
Kidneys (halved) under a very hot griller	6 minutes

Serve grilled lamb chops with tiny new potatoes in their jackets, salad, grilled tomatoes and fresh minted peas.

A mixed grill requires only a salad and creamy mashed potatoes.

A flavoured butter is good on grilled lamb but preferably no sauces or gravy of any kind.

Grilled Lamb's Fry

This method of cooking lamb's fry is ideal for people on a slimming or low cholesterol diet.

Remove any thin outside tissue and veins from the lamb's fry and cut into slices about 1 cm ($\frac{1}{2}$ in) thick. Make sure the slices are the same thickness so they cook evenly. Season on both sides with pepper and brush with oil or melted butter. Place on griller rack and cook under a very high heat for 3 or 4 minutes on each side, brushing with a little more butter or oil and sprinkling with salt. Serve with grilled bacon.

Spring Lamb in Egg Sauce

The countryside around Rome abounds in sheep which accounts for the wonderful lamb dishes found in this region. This dish is a delicately flavoured casserole of young lamb cooked in wine. When the meat is cooked, eggs and lemon juice are stirred into the pan juices, making a superb sauce.

**1 × 2 kg (4 lb) shoulder of lamb or 2
  small shoulders, boned and trimmed of
  skin and fat**
4 tablespoons olive oil
30 g (1 oz) butter
1 garlic clove
1 onion, finely chopped
1 tablespoon plain flour
$\frac{1}{3}$ cup dry white wine
1 bay leaf
$1\frac{1}{4}$ cups hot stock or water
salt, freshly ground pepper
2 egg yolks
juice of 1 large lemon
finely chopped parsley

Cut the lamb into 3.5 cm ($1\frac{1}{2}$ in) pieces. Dry the meat thoroughly. Heat the oil and add the butter and, when the foam has subsided, add the garlic clove and saute until golden. Remove. Add the meat and onion and brown all over. Sprinkle with flour and cook over a medium heat for a few minutes, stirring occasionally. Add the wine and bay leaf, raise the heat and cook uncovered until the wine has almost evaporated. Add stock or hot water, season with salt and pepper, cover the pan and cook over a low heat for 1 hour or until the meat is tender. When the meat is cooked there should not be more than a few tablespoons of pan gravy.

Beat the eggs with the lemon juice, pour over the lamb stirring for 1 to 2 minutes until combined and the sauce has set. Remove from the heat immediately. Sprinkle with parsley and serve hot.

Lamb Kebabs

The combination of marjoram and lemon gives lamb a unique and refreshing flavour for these Greek kebabs.

1.5 kg (3 lb) leg of lamb, boned
salt and freshly ground pepper
2 tablespoons lemon juice
**1 tablespoon chopped fresh marjoram or 1
  teaspoon dried marjoram**

Ask the butcher to bone the leg of lamb for you. Remove skin and cut the meat into 2.5 cm (1 in) cubes. Season with salt and pepper and add lemon juice and marjoram. Stir to mix and thread on skewers.

Cook under a pre-heated griller for 8 to 10 minutes, turning until browned and cooked. Serve with a crisp green salad and a lemon wedge.

Sautéed Kidneys in White Wine Sauce

8 lamb's kidneys
1 small onion
125 g (4 oz) white button mushrooms
45 g (1½ oz) butter
1 tablespoon plain flour
¾ cup dry white wine
¼ cup stock
3 tablespoons thick cream
1 teaspoon mustard
salt and freshly ground pepper
freshly chopped parsley

Skin the kidneys, cut in half and remove the core. Chop the onion finely and slice the mushrooms.

Heat the butter and when the foam has subsided, add the kidneys cut side down and sauté for 4 minutes. Remove to a plate and keep warm. Add the mushrooms and onion to the same pan and sauté for a few minutes. Stir in the flour.

Pour in the wine with the stock. Bring to the boil stirring all the time. Place the kidneys back into the sauce, season with salt and pepper and simmer for about 15 minutes. Place kidneys on to a heated serving dish.

Mix the cream with the mustard and swirl into the sauce. Bring to the boil and then pour over kidneys. Sprinkle with finely chopped parsley.

Lancashire Hotpot

A world famous English hotpot with wonderful flavour. Oysters may be added before the dish is placed in the oven for those who enjoy their flavour.

30 g (1 oz) lard
1 kg (2 lb) lamb neck chops
1 onion, sliced
2 tablespoons flour
2 cups stock
salt
freshly ground pepper
1 teaspoon caster sugar
2 sheep's kidneys, skinned and core
   removed
5 mushrooms, peeled
1 kg (2 lb) potatoes
20 oysters, optional

Heat the lard and brown the lamb chops. Place on one side and cook the onion for a few minutes. Sprinkle with the flour and go on cooking until the flour is browned. Pour on the stock and stir to form a gravy. Season with salt, pepper and sugar.

Place the chops in a casserole dish, cover with the kidneys cut in thick slices. Add a layer of thickly sliced mushrooms. Peel and cut the potatoes into thick slices and arrange them in overlapping rings on top of the meat completely covering it.

Strain the gravy over the top, cover with a lid and cook in a moderate oven (350°F—170°C) for about 2 hours. About 20 minutes before the meat is cooked remove the lid to brown the potatoes.

Note: If you wish to add oysters to this dish, arrange them in a layer on top of the mushrooms.

Lamb's Fry in Red Wine Sauce

In Italy, liver is sliced as thinly as bacon and sautéed very quickly. In this recipe, it is garnished with onions and a red wine sauce flavoured with tomato.

¼ cup olive oil
2 large onions, peeled and finely sliced
1 lamb's fry, soaked in milk for 1 hour
   and dried thoroughly
1 teaspoon tomato paste
½ cup dry red wine
salt, freshly ground pepper

Heat the oil in a frying pan, add the onions and fry until they are tender and golden. Remove and keep warm. Using a very sharp knife, slice the lamb's fry as thinly as possible. Raise the heat under the pan and sauté the lamb's fry for 2 minutes, browning it on both sides. Stir in the tomato paste and wine and season with salt and pepper. Lower the heat to medium and cook for a further 3 to 4 minutes, stirring from time to time. Arrange the lamb's fry on a heated serving dish, garnish with the onions and pour over the wine sauce. Serve hot with a crisp green salad.

Noisettes of Lamb with Madeira Sauce

Navarin of Lamb

This is a hearty winter casserole but when young vegetables are substituted for the dried beans and baby lamb is in season this dish becomes appropriately Spring Navarin of Lamb.

750 g (1½ lb) breast of lamb
750 g (1½ lb) shoulder of lamb
4 tablespoons butter
1 tablespoon olive oil
1½ tablespoons plain flour
2 garlic cloves crushed with 2 teaspoons
   salt
3 cups beef stock
1 tablespoon tomato paste
1 bouquet garni
12 small onions
freshly ground black pepper
250 g (½ lb) dried white haricot beans
1 large onion, chopped
1 tablespoon tomato paste
finely chopped parsley

Cut the lamb into 3.5 cm (1½ in) cubes. Heat the butter and oil and brown lamb over a high heat. Drain off the butter and reserve. Sprinkle the meat with the flour. Place the casserole back on the heat and add the garlic. Pour on 2 cups beef stock and the tomato paste diluted in the extra 1 cup stock and add the bouquet garni.

Meanwhile, cook the tiny onions in the reserved butter until golden and then add to the casserole dish. Season with pepper. Cover the dish and simmer the Navarin on the stove or in a moderate oven (350°F—170°C) until the meat is tender —about 1 hour. Allow to cool and then refrigerate overnight.

Soak the haricot beans in water to cover overnight. Next day cook them gently for about 1½ hours with the large onion. Drain.

Remove the fat which has set on top of the Navarin and then remove the bouquet garni. Bring the stew to the boil and add the extra tablespoon of tomato paste and the beans. Cook together for about 10 minutes and then serve dusted with parsley.

Noisettes of Lamb with Madeira Sauce

Noisettes are plump pieces of boned loin rolled up and tied neatly to keep their shape while they are cooking. When cut from baby lamb they are as sweet and tender as meat can be and need only to be sautéed in butter for a few minutes on each side.

1 × 1 kg (2 lb) loin of lamb
2 tablespoons of freshly chopped herbs—
   thyme, tarragon, parsley, marjoram or
   chives
salt, freshly ground black pepper
2 tablespoons olive oil
30 g (1 oz) butter
1 cup Brown Sauce
2 tablespoons Madeira

Remove the heavy chine bone and then cut away the piece of gristle which lies between the fat and the meat. Trim off all the fell (the tough outer skin) if not trimmed already by your butcher. Also cut away the heavy fat or ask your butcher to do it for you.

Spread out the loin and sprinkle inside of meat with herbs, season with salt and pepper and roll up tightly starting from the thick end.

Tie the loin with string at 3.5 cm (1½ in) intervals and then cut in slices exactly half-way between each piece of string.

Heat the oil in a large frying pan, add the butter and when the foam has subsided add the noisettes and sauté for 4 to 5 minutes on each side. Arrange the cooked noisettes on a heated serving dish and snip off the string. Garnish each one with blanched tarragon leaves or parsley sprigs.

Heat the Brown Sauce and then stir in the Madeira. Glaze each noisette with a little sauce and serve the remaining sauce in a sauceboat.

pork

Roast Pork with Crisp Golden Crackling

Pork

Roast Pork

To roast pork: Have the butcher score the skin. Rub coarse salt or cooking salt over skin and put the roast on a rack, skin-side up, in roasting pan. Put in a very hot oven (500°F—260°C) for 30 minutes, until the skin starts to bubble and crisp, then lower heat to moderately slow (325°F—160°C) for rest of cooking. Do not baste pork and don't cover dish otherwise skin will not have crisp crackling.

Cooking times: Pork should always be well-cooked. Allow 30–35 minutes for each pound (0.5 kg) plus an extra 30 minutes.

Buying pork: Look for pale pink flesh that is finely grained with pearly white fat and thin skin.

Cuts for roasting: Leg and loin are the favoured cuts for roasting. A loin of about 5-6 chops is good for a small family. Loin can also be boned and tied.

Hand or shoulder, unsalted, can be cooked on the bone or boned, rolled and tied for a roast.

Shoulder can be boned and rolled also.

Fillet is a very tender cut of pork and is often roasted with a filling of apple and prunes. It needs constant basting unlike other cuts of pork and because there is no skin on a fillet of pork omit the first 30 minutes cooking in a very hot oven.

Spring or belly is used as the outer wrapping for a pork and veal roll.

Cushion, also called foreloin is often roasted.

Loin of Pork Cooked in Milk

This is a most unusual but delicious way of cooking pork. The milk forms a soft golden skin over the top of the meat, keeping the pork succulent.

1 × 1 kg (2 lb) loin of pork, boned and rolled
4 tablespoons olive oil
1 sprig rosemary
1 small garlic clove
salt, freshly ground pepper
2½ cups milk

Heat the oil in a heavy casserole dish into which the pork will fit snugly. Add the rosemary sprig and garlic clove and allow their flavours to penetrate the oil and then add the meat. Brown it all over, turning from time to time and then remove the rosemary and garlic clove. Season with salt and pepper.

Add the milk, bring to the boil and let it bubble over the meat. Lower the heat, cover the dish and allow the meat to cook gently for 30 minutes. Gradually a golden web of skin will form over the top of the meat while the milk is simmering underneath.

Uncover the casserole and cook for a further 30 minutes but do not disturb the golden skin. At this moment scrape the sides of the casserole, stirring all into the milk which will be beginning to thicken. Cook for a further 30 minutes (1½ hours in all) when the milk should be well reduced and the meat encased in a fine crust formed by the milk while it is moist and tender inside. At this stage the meat should be watched very carefully in case the milk evaporates and the meat burns.

Serve the pork cut in medium thick slices. May be served hot or cold.

Crown Roast of Pork

1 crown roast of pork
salt and freshly ground pepper

Onion and Sultana Stuffing:
1 onion, finely chopped
60 g (2 oz) butter
1 cup sultanas
3 cups soft white breadcrumbs
2 teaspoons salt
freshly ground pepper
3 tablespoons chopped parsley
3 tablespoons chopped fresh sage
pinch nutmeg

Place the pork in a roasting pan and cover the tip of each cutlet bone with a small piece of foil to protect it. Season the meat with salt and pepper and spoon the stuffing into the centre of the crown. Roast in a moderately slow oven (325°F—160°C) allowing 40 minutes for each 500 g (1 lb).

When cooked, allow to stand in a warm place to rest for 7 to 10 minutes while making the gravy. Serve surrounded by sweet potatoes and apples and tiny glazed onions piled on top of the stuffing.

Onion and Sultana Stuffing

Cook the onion in the butter until it has softened. Simmer sultanas in water to cover for 5 minutes then drain. Combine the onion, breadcrumbs, sultanas, salt and pepper, parsley, sage and nutmeg.

Gravy:
Pour all but 1 tablespoon of fat from the roasting pan, and then place on top of the stove and stir in 1 tablespoon of plain flour, stirring until brown. Add 2 cups of stock—a good stock may be made in advance from some pork bones—and stir until the gravy boils and is smooth. Simmer the gravy until thickened and then season to taste and strain into a gravy boat.

To carve:
First remove the glazed onions to a warm dish. Cut between each cutlet, removing one at a time and serve with a spoonful of the stuffing.

Spiced Loin of Pork

2.5 kg (5 lb) loin of pork
3 garlic cloves, crushed
2½ teaspoons salt, 1 teaspoon freshly
   ground black pepper
½ teaspoon each dried marjoram, ground
   cummin, powdered saffron
1 tablespoon olive oil
½ cup boiling water
¼ cup grated onion
3 tablespoons finely chopped parsley
½ cup dry white wine
2 tablespoons white wine vinegar
¼ teaspoon chilli powder

Score the pork fat in 5 mm (¼ in) slices and then make diagonal cuts about 2.5 cm (1 in) apart across the loin.

Pound the garlic, salt, pepper, marjoram, cummin and saffron to a paste with oil. Rub into the pork. Wrap in aluminium foil or waxed paper and chill overnight.

Place the pork in a shallow baking dish and roast in a very hot oven (450°F—230°C) for 25 minutes. Reduce the heat to moderate (350°F—170°C) and continue to roast for 2 hours. Transfer the pork to a serving platter and keep warm.

Skim the fat from the baking pan and place the pan over direct heat. Add water, onion, parsley, wine, vinegar and chilli powder and bring to the boil. Deglaze the pan by scraping the meat glaze from the bottom and cook the sauce for 2 minutes. Serve separately in a sauceboat.

Baked Loin of Pork Danish-style

1 loin of pork, boned
12 large prunes
1 cooking apple
1 tspn lemon juice
salt and freshly ground pepper
3 tablespoons olive oil
45 g (1½ oz) butter
1 cup white wine
¾ cup cream
1 tablespoon redcurrant jelly

Remove the skin from the loin of pork and trim away most of the heavy fat.

Place the prunes in cold water and bring to the boil. Remove from the heat and leave the prunes to soak for 30 minutes. Drain, remove the seeds and dry on paper towels. Peel and cube the cooking apple and sprinkle with lemon juice to prevent it discolouring.

Season the inside of the loin with salt and pepper. Mix the apple with the prunes and arrange on the pork. Roll up tightly and tie at 3.5 cm (1½ in) intervals.

Preheat the oven to moderate (350°F—170°C). Heat the oil in a large baking dish and then add the butter. Brown the loin all over, turning it with the help of two spoons. Remove all the fat from pan, add the wine and when it is bubbling stir in the cream. Bring to a gentle simmer on the stove, cover the pan and place in the oven and bake for 1½ to 2 hours, 35 minutes per 500 g (1 lb), basting occasionally. When cooked, remove the loin from the pan and keep warm.

Skim the fat from the pan juices and bring the liquid to the boil on top of the stove. When the liquid has reduced to 1 cup, stir in the redcurrant jelly, correct the seasoning and stir over a low heat until the sauce is smooth. Pour into a sauceboat.

Grilled Pork

Pork should **always** be served well-done. Grilling is a quick method of cooking and pork should be grilled under a moderate heat and basted frequently with oil or melted butter to prevent the meat from drying out.

A carefully grilled pork chop served with a pan fried apple sauce is a delicious change to the daily menu.

Cuts for Grilling:

Pork loin chops are the best cut for grilling. They should be cut from 2 cm (¾ in) thick.
Leg or chump chops can be grilled but are better pan fried or braised.

Grilling Pork

Preheat the griller. Select chops that are about 2 cm (1 in) thick. If the chops are cut too thin the meat will cook quickly, becoming tough and dry. Use a sharp knife to cut through the skin and fat around the chops at 1 cm (½ in) intervals (to prevent the chops curling while they are grilling). Season with freshly ground pepper, rock salt and brush with oil or melted butter. Place on a greased griller rack and cook under a moderate heat, brushing the chops about every 2 minutes with more oil or melted butter to keep them moist. Turn them a few times while grilling. Pork chops may be served with apple slices (lightly fried in butter until golden) or with apple sauce. A little horseradish mixed with the apple sauce is a more unusual but excellent accompaniment. Pickled red cabbage and sauerkraut are also good.

Pork loin chops 2 cm (¾ in) thick   14 minutes.
Pork leg or chump chops 2 cm (¾ in) thick 14 to 16 minutes.

Pork is cooked when the thickest part of the meat, pierced with a fine skewer, releases clear juices. If any pink juice appears the meat needs more cooking.

Tourtière

The Tourtière is a French-Canadian pork pie which is traditionally served on Christmas eve after midnight mass.

The early settlers in Quebec who invented this dish had very little meat except a few precious pigs and the game they shot. Consequently, the Tourtière was often made with a combination of venison, hare, wild duck or partridge as well as the pork, and the pie crust made with lard.

Nowadays, this pie is generally made with lean minced pork only but there are many variations and it is difficult to find two Quebec housewives who make it the same way. Sometimes minced garlic is added, sometimes celery salt, sometimes cooked mashed potatoes are mixed in and sometimes beef is minced with the pork.

Our version is uncomplicated but the flavour is exceptionally good. The Tourtière may be frozen unbaked for many weeks which makes it ideal for today's active host or hostess.

Filling:
500 g (1 lb) pork mince
1 teaspoon salt
1 egg yolk
1 tablespoon chopped herbs
1 tablespoon brandy
freshly ground pepper
1 tablespoon butter
Pastry:
375 g (12 oz) packet of commercial
   puff pastry
1 egg yolk, lightly beaten

Filling: Combine the pork mince, salt, egg yolk, herbs, brandy and pepper and allow to marinate for 1 hour. Heat the butter and brown the pork mince mixture over a high heat. Turn on to a plate and allow to cool.

Pastry: Divide the pastry in half. Roll out one half to a 20 cm (8 in) circle. Glaze the edge of one half with egg yolk and place it on a greased baking sheet. Mound the cool pork mince on the pastry leaving a good 1 cm (½ in) edge all around.

Roll out remaining pastry to a 25 cm (10 in) circle. Decorate with the back of a knife. Cover the meat with it and press the edges together firmly. Glaze with egg yolk.

Bake the Tourtière in a hot oven (425°F—220°C) for 10 minutes. Reduce the heat to moderate (350°F—180°C) and bake for a further 35 minutes. Serve hot or cold. Serves 6.

Stuffed Baked Ham

Tinned leg ham stuffed with dried fruits, pistachio nuts and spices is baked in the oven until the outside is caramelised.

4 dates, seeded
4 prunes, stoned
2 tablespoons raisins
4 tablespoons port
1 × 1 kg (2 lb) tinned Plumrose leg ham
½ cup fresh breadcrumbs
¼ cup shelled pistachio nuts
2 tablespoons brown sugar
1 pinch each nutmeg, cinnamon
   and cloves
¼ cup sherry

Roughly chop the dates and prunes and place them in a bowl with the raisins. Pour over half the port and stand for 15 minutes. Add the breadcrumbs, pistachio nuts, brown sugar, spices and the remaining port.

Using a trussing needle or the end of a wooden spoon carefully make deep incisions in the ham.

Force the mixture into the cavities.

Press the remaining mixture over the ham. Place in a small baking dish or ovenproof dish, pour over the sherry and bake in a moderate oven (375°F—190°C) for 1 hour. Serve hot in fairly thick slices. May also be served cold.

Top: Tourtière
Above: Stuffed Baked Ham

187

Pork Chops Mexico

Thick, oven-baked pork chops flavoured in the Mexican style with green peppers, rice and tomato.

4 thick pork loin chops
1 large onion, thinly sliced
4 tablespoons long grain rice
2 green peppers, diced
1 × 454 g (16 oz) can Rosella tomato
** soup diluted with 1 can of water**
salt
freshly ground pepper

Place the pork chops closely together in a casserole and cover with sliced onion. Put 1 tablespoon of uncooked rice on top of each chop and then scatter with diced pepper. Pour over the diluted soup and season with salt and pepper. Cover and bake in a moderate oven (350°F—170°C) for 1¼ to 1½ hours.

Baked Glazed Ham

For open house entertaining, or in fact for any large buffet meal, nothing is easier to serve than a baked ham. It makes a splendid centrepiece on the table, feeds 20 to 25 people, is simple to carve and is just as enjoyable cold as hot.

7 kg (14 lb) mild cured leg of ham
Glaze:
1½ cups brown sugar
2 teaspoons dry mustard
¾ cup clear honey
whole cloves
½ cup orange juice

Cut a scallop pattern around the thick end of the ham shank.

With a sharp knife ease the skin away from the fat and then carefully ease the skin away with the fingers.

Turn the ham over and carefully ease away the skin which should come off in one piece. Place the ham, fat side uppermost, on a rack in a roasting pan containing about 3.5 cm (1½ in) of water. Cover the baking dish with aluminium foil making it as airtight as possible and bake in a moderately slow oven (325°F—160°C) for 2½ hours. Remove from the oven, pour off the liquid in the baking dish and score the fat with 5 mm (¼ in) deep diagonal cuts first one way, then the opposite way to form a diamond pattern.

Mix the sugar, mustard and honey together and using a brush or a spatula spread half the misture over the ham. Stud each diamond with a clove. Mix the remaining glaze with the orange juice. Replace the ham in a hot oven (400°F—200°C) for a further 30 to 40 minutes, basting it every 10 minutes with the remaining glaze. Serve hot or cold.
Note: If your oven is small, it may be necessary to ask your butcher to cut the shank off the ham.

Pickled Pork

1 hand of pickled pork weighing
** 1.5 kg (3 lb)**
1 onion stuck with 4 cloves
12 peppercorns
1 bay leaf
few celery stalks

Place pork into a large saucepan and add enough water to cover. Add all remaining ingredients and bring to the boil. Cover the saucepan and simmer gently until cooked. Allow approximately 35 minutes for each pound (0.5 kg). A skewer inserted into the thickest part of the pork comes out easily when the pork is cooked. Cool in the liquid. Remove and place in the refrigerator. Serve with apple and horseradish sauce.

Pork and Veal Fricadelles

These pork and veal rissoles are particularly good with mint-flavoured tomato sauce and a beetroot relish.

½ cup fine white breadcrumbs
½ cup milk
30 g (1 oz) butter
1 medium onion, finely chopped
500 g (1 lb) veal and pork mince
1 egg
pinch of nutmeg
½ teaspoon salt
black pepper
flour seasoned with salt and pepper
30 g (1 oz) butter
2 tablespoons olive oil

Soak the breadcrumbs in milk. Melt the butter in a heavy frypan and cook the onion gently until it is transparent. Mix the pork and veal mince, onion, breadcrumbs and egg together and season with nutmeg, salt and plenty of black pepper.

Shape into rissoles about 5 cm (2 in) in diameter. Dust with seasoned flour.

Heat the butter and oil in a large frypan and brown the fricadelles for 2 minutes on each side. Transfer them to a roasting pan and cook in a moderate oven (350°F—170°C) for 30 minutes.

Sweet and Sour Pork

Crisp-cooked pork is combined with a sweet and sour sauce for this favourite dish. It is important to serve the pork immediately it is combined with the sauce.

500 g (1 lb) pork fillet
2 teaspoons Chinese wine or dry sherry
1 tablespoon soy sauce
1 tablespoon plain flour
2 tablespoons cornflour
oil for deep frying
1 quantity sweet and sour sauce

Prepare sauce first and keep hot while preparing pork.

Cut pork into 2.5 cm (1 in) cubes and mix with wine, soy sauce and both flours. Stir to coat cubes evenly with mixture.

Heat oil in a wok or pan, add pork and cook until golden, separating pieces with a chopstick or fork. Drain.

Reheat oil and when very hot, return pork and remove almost immediately. Pour hot sauce over and serve.

Sweet and Sour Sauce

2 green peppers
1 onion
1 cooked carrot
1 bamboo shoot
2 slices canned pineapple, optional
3 tablespoons oil
3 tablespoons sugar
1 tablespoon soy sauce
1 tablespoon Chinese wine or dry sherry
1 tablespoon white vinegar
2 tablespoons tomato sauce
2 tablespoons cornflour blended with
  ½ cup water

Cut all vegetables and pineapple into 1 cm (½ in) squares. Heat oil and sauté the vegetables until tender but not coloured.

Add the pineapple, sugar, soy sauce, wine, vinegar and tomato sauce. Bring to the boil, then stir in cornflour mixture and continue stirring until sauce boils and thickens. Use for pork and fried fish.

Pork Vindaloo

Vindaloo, or Bindaloo as some prefer, was first made in India by Portuguese settlers. Use pork loin or part of the leg and, for authentic flavour, use mustard oil which is available from David Jones.

1 kg (2 lb) pork
¼ cup tamarind pulp
¾ cup mustard oil or vegetable oil
12 whole peppercorns, 2 to 3 bay leaves
Marinade:
3 large cloves garlic, crushed
1 tablespoon ground ginger, 1 tablespoon ground chilli
1 tablespoon curry powder or Vindaloo curry paste
½ teaspoon ground cloves, ½ teaspoon cardamom
1 teaspoon cinnamon, ½ teaspoon salt
½ cup malt vinegar

Combine all the ingredients for the marinade in a bowl. Cut the pork into large cubes and add to the marinade. Leave for 18 to 24 hours.

Pour 1¼ cups boiling water over tamarind pulp and cool. When cold, push through a sieve and reserve the liquid. Heat the oil in a heavy pan, add the meat, marinade, peppercorns, bay leaves and tamarind juice.

Cover and simmer gently 2 hours or until meat is tender. Serve with plain boiled rice of pilau, or serve with puris.

- Some spices, particularly turmeric, will colour everything they touch. Thin plastic gloves, the kind you can get easily from the chemist, will protect hands. This will allow you to rub the mixed spices well into the scored flesh.

Barbecued Pork

Barbecued pork can be bought from Chinese food stores, but it is easy to cook and a recipe any learner could master. Serve the pork warm or cold in thin slices as an hors d'oeuvre, or slice it and add to soups or cut into dice for fried rice.

750 g (1½ lb) pork fillet
Marinade:
2 tablespoons soy sauce
2 tablespoons hoisin sauce
1 tablespoon Chinese wine or dry sherry
2 tablespoons oil
1 tablespoon honey
2 tablespoons sugar
1 teaspoon salt
¼ teaspoon 5-spice powder

Place the pork in a glass or earthenware dish and pour on the marinade ingredients which have been mixed together. Leave to marinate for 2 hours, turning meat occasionally. (In hot weather, cover with plastic wrap and marinate in the refrigerator.)

Lift pork out of marinade, allowing the mixture to drain off and then place on a rack in a shallow roasting pan. Pour about 2.5 cm (1 in) water into pan and put into a hot oven (400°F—200°C) for 10 minutes.

Reduce oven temperature to moderately slow (325°F—160°C) and cook for a further 35 minutes, or until cooked. Brush pork with the marinade every 10 minutes.

Serve warm or cold, cut in slices as an hors d'oeuvre with plum sauce, hot Chinese mustard or soy sauce for dipping.

The cooking time for the pork fillets depends on their thickness. Test pork with a fine skewer, when it comes out easily, the pork is cooked. The safest way is to cut the fillet in half and if the centre is pink, brush over with marinade and return to oven.

Top left: Cold Parsleyed Ham (see recipe overleaf)
Bottom left: Barbecued Pork

Top right: Pork Vindaloo
Bottom right: Loin of Pork Cooked in Milk (see recipe on page 183)

191

Barbecued Pork Chops

Pork chops are cut into pieces and marinated, then baked in a spicy mixture for this pungent dish.

1 kg (2 lb) pork loin chops
2 teaspoons Chinese wine or dry sherry
½ teaspoon salt
2 teaspoons soy sauce
2.5 cm (1 in) piece fresh green ginger
2 shallots
1 tablespoon hoisin sauce
pinch 5-spice powder
Garnish:
1 large onion, sliced
2 tablespoons oil
shallots curls

Remove skin from chops but leave fat on. Cut out bone, then cut each chop into 4 pieces.

Put into a bowl with wine, salt, soy sauce, the finely chopped ginger, chopped shallots, hoisin sauce and spice. Turn chops in mixture, then cover and marinate for 30 minutes.

Put the chops and marinade into a baking dish, in one layer, and bake in a moderate oven (350°F—170°C) for 45 minutes, turning once.

For the garnish, fry onion in oil until tender but not coloured. Drain and place on serving plate. Top with the pork chops and then shallot curls which are made by cutting green tops of shallots into fine shreds.

Jellied Hock

The whole pig's hock is a very good buy—you have the meaty hocks for one dish and the trotters for another and they can both be cooked in the same pot. The hock and pig's trotter contains natural gelatine and makes an excellent jellied meat which may be served for lunch or is ideal for a picnic.

Jellied meats look more attractive when they are set in interesting shapes. Set in a ring mould, the centre can be filled with a tempting crisp salad just before it is placed on the table. It doesn't take much time to decorate a jellied meat and it really does make a difference to its appearance. A thin layer of jelly is set in the bottom of the mould and then different ingredients are arranged in a pattern on top and coated with another layer of jellied stock. This is allowed to set before the chopped meat and remaining stock is added.

8 pork hocks
1 onion, peeled
2 carrots, scraped
a large bouquet garni containing a
**   generous amount of parsley and a**
**   strip of lemon peel**
a good teaspoon salt
peppercorns
To decorate:
black olives
parsley leaves, salad burnet leaves or
**   leaves of another herb**
lemon peel cut into fine strips
lettuce
peeled tomatoes
chopped parsley

Place the hocks in a heavy pan with cold water to cover with the onion, carrots, bouquet garni, salt and peppercorns. Bring to the boil, cover the pot tightly and simmer for 1¾ hours or until the hocks are tender. Remove the hocks from their liquid and strain it. Season liquid if necessary. Remove meat from the hocks and chop it roughly.

Rinse out a mould with iced water and pour a thin layer of the cooking liquid which has cooled, into the bottom. Chill in the refrigerator until set and then arrange some black olives which have been cut in half and stoned, some parsley leaves or leaves of another herb and some fine strips of lemon peel in a decorative pattern on this jellied base. Coat with a little more stock and chill until firm. Fill the mould with the chopped meat and pour on the remaining stock. Set in the refrigerator and when firm, turn out onto a chilled plate. Accompany with a crisp green salad tossed with a couple of ripe tomatoes cut into quarters and some black olives. Scatter the salad with some chopped parsley.

Offer some English mustard, vinegar and a bowl of pickles. This is an English custom and they really go very well with meats and brawns.

Crumbed Pigs' Trotters with Rémoulade Sauce

Pigs' trotters are considered a great delicacy in France where they may be bought freshly cooked and crumbed from the local delicatessen. Sometimes they are boned and stuffed with chopped pork or sausage meat and studded with truffles. The trotters are then brushed with butter and grilled or baked. It is most important when serving crumbed pigs' trotters that they be sizzling hot and placed on hot plates.

8 pigs' trotters
1 onion, peeled
2 carrots, scraped
a large bouquet garni containing a
    generous amount of parsley and a
    strip of lemon peel
salt
peppercorns
plain flour seasoned with salt and pepper
1 egg, lightly beaten
fine white breadcrumbs
60 g (2 oz) butter, melted
Rémoulade sauce:
2 cups mayonnaise
½ cup gherkins, finely chopped
2 tablespoons capers, finely chopped
1 tablespoon prepared mustard
1 tablespoon of mixed chopped parsley
    and tarragon (if available)

Place the pigs' trotters in a heavy pan with cold water to cover with the onion, carrots, bouquet garni, salt and peppercorns. Bring to the boil, cover the pot tightly and simmer for $1\frac{3}{4}$ hours or until tender. Remove from the liquid which may be strained and used for a soup or a jellied meat.

When the trotters are cool split each in half with a sharp knife.

Lightly flour them with the seasoned flour and then dip into the beaten egg with the aid of two spoons and coat in breadcrumbs.

Lay the crumbed trotters in a large ovenproof dish in one layer, spoon over the melted butter and bake in a moderate oven (350°F—170°C) for about 15 minutes or until the breadcrumb coating is crispy and golden. Serve hot on hot plates with a bowl of rémoulade sauce.

Note: The crumbed trotters may also be grilled until the breadcrumb coating is crisp.

Another method of serving the trotters is to split them and while still warm, arrange in a large ovenproof dish, brush with about 90 g (3 oz) melted butter. Sprinkle with 90 g (3 oz) of breadcrumbs pressed well down and bake as above.

Rémoulade Sauce

To 2 cups of mayonnaise add the finely chopped gherkins and capers. Stir in the mustard and chopped parsley and tarragon and turn into a bowl.

Cold Parsleyed Ham

1 × 1 kg (2 lb) cooked ham
1¼ cups of well-flavoured chicken or
    veal stock, or use soup cubes
½ cup dry white wine
freshly ground black pepper and nutmeg
1 cup finely chopped parsley
2 tablespoons gelatine
1 to 2 tablespoons tarragon vinegar

Cut the ham into 2.5 cm (1 in) cubes. Simmer gently in the stock and white wine flavoured with pepper and nutmeg, for 5 minutes. Drain, reserving the liquid. Put the ham into a bowl which has been rinsed out with water and lightly dusted with a little finely chopped parsley.

Soften the gelatine in a little water and then stir into the hot liquid. When it has dissolved, add the remaining parsley and tarragon vinegar. Allow to cool and when syrupy pour over the diced ham. Place in the refrigerator to set for 4 hours and then unmould.

poultry
and game

Chicken

Roast Chicken

1 × 1.5 kg (3 lb) chicken
salt, pepper
60 g (2 oz) butter
few tarragon or parsley stalks
3 strips orange rind (optional)

Put a little salt and pepper, 30 g (1 oz) butter, tarragon or parsley stalks and strips of orange rind inside chicken. Truss, fold wing tips back, run string over wings and cross over back. Turn chicken over and tie legs. Rub bird all over with remaining butter and put on its side in roasting pan. Place in a hot oven (400°F—200°C) for 10 minutes, turn chicken on other side. Reduce temperature to moderately hot (375°F—190°C) and continue to cook, turning and basting every 15 minutes. Cook about 1 to 1½ hours or until chicken is tender, turning it on its back for the last 15 minutes until the breast is golden brown.

To test, run a fine skewer into thigh joint of chicken. If juice is pink, the bird is not quite cooked. When cooked, juice should be clear and colourless. Place chicken on heated platter and garnish with watercress. Serve with gravy or cream gravy.

Gravy: Pour off all but 2 tablespoons of juice from the pan. Add 1 scant tablespoon flour and stir well until lightly browned. Add remaining chicken stock or stock and water to make 1½ cups, stir until thickened. Season with salt and pepper.

Cream Gravy: Pour off all but 2 tablespoons of juice, stir in 1 scant tablespoon plain flour. Stir well until lightly browned, add ¾ cup chicken stock and 155 mls (¼ pint) cream. Cook gently and scrape the brown off the bottom of the pan to flavour the gravy. Strain if necessary.

Bread Sauce: Put 315 mls (½ pint) milk, 1 onion, 1 bay leaf and 6 peppercorns in small saucepan, simmer gently for 30 minutes. Strain. To milk, add 250 mls (1 cup) soft, white breadcrumbs and ½ teaspoon salt. Simmer gently until a creamy consistency. Finish with a little butter or cream.

Roast Chicken: Weight and Temperature Chart

Ready to Cook Weight	Serves	Cooking Time
Size 5: 500 g (1 lb)	1 or 2	30 minutes
Size 6: 600 g (1 lb 3 oz)	2	40 minutes
Size 10: 1 kg (2 lb)	2 or 3	50 minutes
Size 14: 1.4 kg (3 lb) (approx)	4	1 hour
Size 16: 1.6 kg (3 lb 2 oz)	4	1 hour 10 minutes
Size 19: 1.9 kg (4 lb) (approx)	4 or 5	1 hour 20 minutes
Size 21: 2.1 kg (4 lb) (approx)	5 or 6	1 hour 30 minutes
Size 24: 2.4 kg (5 lb) (approx)	6 or 8	1 hour 40 minutes

Oven temperature: Set the oven at hot (400°F—200°C). After the first 10 minutes cooking time, turn the oven down to moderately hot (375°F—190°C).

Grilled Sesame Chicken Breasts

1 tablespoon oil
¼ cup soy sauce
¼ cup dry white wine
1 teaspoon dried tarragon
1 teaspoon dry mustard
4 boned chicken breasts
sesame seeds to coat

Combine oil, soy sauce, wine, tarragon and mustard. Marinate the chicken breasts in this mixture for 2 to 3 hours.

Preheat grill. Brush grill rack with a little oil and grill the chicken breasts slowly for about 4 minutes each side, basting with a little of the marinade from time to time. Grilling over hot charcoal takes approximately the same cooking time.

Remove the breasts from the heat, brush with the marinade and roll each breast in sesame seeds. Place under the grill once more to brown the sesame seeds. Accompany with green beans flavoured with nutmeg or a good squeeze of lemon juice or alternatively with a tossed Watercress Salad.

Note: These chicken breasts may also be cooked at 400°F (200°C) for about 15 minutes and basted from time to time.

Roast Tarragon Chicken

This method of cooking chicken is much beloved by the French. The frequent basting gives the whole chicken a crisp golden skin and ensures that the meat is tender, juicy and well flavoured with butter. The distinctive flavour of tarragon combines beautifully with the delicate white meat and provides the basis for the full flavoured gravy made from the pan juices.

2 × 1.25 kg (2½ lb) chickens
125 g (4 oz) butter
1 tablespoon dried tarragon
salt and freshly ground pepper
½ cup water

Remove giblets and necks from inside of chickens.

Soften butter and cream together with tarragon, salt and pepper. Place a walnut-sized piece of tarragon butter in each chicken. Truss chickens.

Spread remaining butter over breasts and legs. Place chickens in a roasting pan with breasts uppermost.

Cover breasts with a sheet of buttered greaseproof paper to prevent them drying out. Add giblets and necks to pan and pour in water. Put in oven (400°F—200°C) for 10 minutes. Remove paper.

Turn chickens and baste them with the liquid in the pan. Return to oven and reduce temperature (375°F—190°C) and continue to cook turning and basting every 15 minutes, adding more water if necessary. There should be just enough water to keep the juice in the pan from scorching. Cook 45 minutes to 1 hour or until chickens are tender, turning the birds on their backs for the last 10 minutes to brown the breasts. When chickens are cooked, remove trussing string and cut birds in half.

Arrange chicken halves on a heated serving dish. Keep warm while preparing gravy.

Gravy: Pour juices from pan into a small container. Skim fat from top and return 2 tablespoons to pan, placing pan over direct heat. Add 1 scant tablespoon plain flour and stir well until lightly browned. Stir in skimmed chicken juices and enough water to make 1 cup. Stir until thickened. Season with salt and freshly ground pepper and strain. For creamy gravy add 3 tablespoons cream.

Devilled Grilled Poussins

Tender baby chickens, split in half and coated in a spicy mixture with a bite to it, are gently grilled and garnished with sprigs of watercress or green shallots.

2 × 500 g (1 lb) chickens
60 g (2 oz) butter
2 tablespoons tomato chutney
1 tablespoon Worcestershire sauce
1 tablespoon soy sauce
1 tablespoon fruit chutney
dash of Tabasco
Dry Devil Mixture:
1 desertspoon salt
1 desertspoon sugar
1 teaspoon ground pepper
1 teaspoon ground ginger
1 teaspoon mustard
$\frac{1}{2}$ teaspoon curry powder

Split the chickens in half and cut away the back and rib bones. Mix the ingredients for the devilled mixture and rub into the surface of the birds. Allow to stand for at least 1 hour. Melt the butter in a small saucepan, brush the chickens with butter and grill slowly for about 10 minutes until brown and crisp. Remove the rack from the grill pan and place the birds in the pan.

Mix the chutney, Worcestershire sauce, fruit sauce, soy sauce and Tabasco together with the remaining butter. Heat it gently in a saucepan and then spoon over the chicken. Continue cooking slowly for 20 minutes under the grill, basting the chicken frequently with the sauce.

Arrange the chicken in a serving dish. Dilute the sauce in the pan with a little stock or potato water and spoon over the top. Garnish with watercress or green shallots.

Note: In Eastern countries where hot spicy dishes are served, they often offer green or raw onion to enhance the flavour.

Green shallots
To curl: Trim shallots of their tougher green leaves, shred the ends of the stem and drop into iced water so that the stem curls.

Sauté of Chicken Chasseur

1 × 1.5 kg (3 lb) chicken
30 g (1 oz) butter
$\frac{1}{2}$ cup finely chopped shallots
500 g (1 lb) ripe tomatoes
$\frac{1}{2}$ clove garlic, crushed
salt and pepper to taste
1 teaspoon fresh basil, finely chopped or
  $\frac{1}{2}$ teaspoon dried
$\frac{1}{2}$ cup white wine
$\frac{1}{2}$ cup chicken stock
250 g ($\frac{1}{2}$ lb) button mushrooms, sliced
  thinly
15 g ($\frac{1}{2}$ oz) butter

Joint chicken. Peel tomatoes. Remove seeds by holding peeled tomato over a sieve and squeezing gently. Reserve strained juice of tomato.

Melt butter in a sauté pan and add chicken pieces, skin side down. Cook over a medium heat for about 20 minutes until the chicken is golden brown on both sides. Give the pan a good shake from time to time to prevent the chicken sticking. Remove from pan and keep warm.

Add shallots and cook for 1 minute. Chop the peeled tomatoes and add with garlic, seasonings and herbs. Cover and cook for 5 minutes. Pour in the wine and stock. Boil rapidly for a few minutes to reduce the liquid, then add chicken pieces. Cook covered for 15 minutes or until the chicken is tender. Fry the mushrooms separately in the butter and keep warm, then add just before serving.

Sprinkle the dish with freshly chopped parsley. Serve with buttered noodles and a fresh green vegetable.

Basic Chicken Sauté

1.2 kg (2 lbs 10 oz) chicken cut into
   serving pieces
60 g (2 oz) butter
1 tablespoon oil
salt and pepper to season
1 teaspoon chopped parsley (optional)
extra butter

Dry chicken pieces thoroughly (they will not brown if they are moist). In a heavy sauté pan or frying pan heat butter and oil. When the foam has subsided, add the chicken pieces, skin side down in one layer. Sauté for 2 to 3 minutes and when chicken is golden, turn and sauté other side.

As chicken browns, remove to a warm plate and add more pieces to the pan until all are browned. Season with salt, pepper and add the parsley. Replace the leg and thigh joints in the pan, adding a little more butter if necessary and cook slowly for 8 to 9 minutes. Add the breast and wing joints. Cover and continue cooking for about 15 minutes, turning and basting several times during cooking.

To test: Pierce the thickest part of the drumstick with a fine skewer. The juice should be clear, not pink.

Variations:

In all the following variations, use the Chicken Sauté recipe (above) as a base.

Chicken Sauté Bercy

When the chicken is cooked, place it on a serving dish and keep warm. In the pan in which the chicken was cooked, brown 1 tablespoon of chopped shallots, pour in $\frac{1}{2}$ cup white wine and reduce it by half, then add a squeeze of lemon juice and 125 g (4 oz) finely chopped mushrooms. Cook for 5 minutes, swirl in 1 tablespoon of butter and pour the sauce over the chicken. Sprinkle with chopped parsley.

Chicken Sauté with Mushrooms in Cream Sauce

Sauté chicken. When nearly cooked add 1 cup of sliced mushrooms. Cover the pan and cook until tender. Arrange on a heated serving dish, spooning mushrooms around the chicken. Deglaze the pan with a little sherry. Stir in $\frac{1}{4}$ cup of cream. Bring to the boil; stirring all the time and pour over the chicken.

Hungarian Style

When the bird is brown all over, add 1 small onion, finely chopped. When onion begins to brown, sprinkle the chicken with $\frac{1}{2}$ teaspoon of paprika. Cook for a further 2 minutes then add $\frac{1}{4}$ cup of white wine and 3 tomatoes (peeled, seeded and chopped). Continue cooking until chicken is tender. Just before serving stir in 2 tablespoons of cream. Bring to boil. Arrange the chicken on a heated serving dish and pour over the sauce.

Chicken Sauté in Cream Sauce

Sauté the chicken as above. Remove to a warm dish. Stir $\frac{1}{4}$ cup of cream into the pan. Add $\frac{1}{4}$ cup of chicken stock and simmer for a minute. Correct seasoning and then stir in 1 tablespoon of butter. Pour over the chicken.

Chicken Sauté Normandy

Sauté chicken until half cooked. Place the pieces in a casserole with 375 g ($\frac{3}{4}$ lb) of sliced and peeled apples. Add $\frac{1}{4}$ cup of brandy and bring to the boil. Allow to boil 1 minute, then cover the casserole and cook until it is tender.

Chicken Sauté in Red Wine Sauce

1 × No 14 (3 lb) chicken
salt
freshly ground pepper
2 tablespoons clarified butter
2 shallots, finely chopped
½ tablespoon plain flour
1 cup red wine
1 large onion, peeled
finely chopped parsley

Cut the chicken into pieces, dry thoroughly with paper towel and season with salt and pepper. Heat the butter in a sauté or large frying pan and arrange the chicken pieces in it, skin side down. Sauté over a medium heat until golden brown on one side.

Turn the chicken over to the other side. Partly cover the pan with a lid and continue cooking for about 15–20 minutes. Remove the breast and wings and keep warm.

Continue cooking the remaining pieces for 10 minutes or until the juice runs clear when the chicken is pierced with a fork. Place with the breast and wing pieces and keep warm. Add the chopped shallots and the flour to the butter in the pan.

Add the wine and stir until it comes to the boil. Boil for a few minutes stirring in all the brown juices in the pan. Adjust the seasoning.

Return the chicken to the pan and allow it to simmer for 5 minutes to heat through.

While the chicken is heating through, cut the onion into rings and fry in butter until golden and crisp.

Arrange the onion rings on the cooked chicken and sprinkle with chopped parsley. Serve sauté potatoes as an accompaniment.

Chicken Sauté with White Wine and Mushrooms

1 × No. 14 (3 lb) chicken
2 tablespoons olive oil
8 small onions or shallots, peeled
4 slices ham, chopped
2 bay leaves
pinch dried thyme or small sprig fresh
    thyme
salt
freshly ground pepper
125 g (4 oz) fresh small mushrooms
2 tablespoons finely chopped parsley
½ cup dry white wine
½ cup chicken stock

Cut the chicken into serving pieces and dry thoroughly with paper towels. Place the chicken into the pan skin side down and sauté on both sides until golden brown in the hot oil. Remove and brown the onions.

Return the chicken to the pan with the remaining ingredients. When the liquid comes to the boil, lower the heat, partly cover the pan and simmer for 30 minutes or until the chicken is tender.

Place the chicken on a heated serving dish, adjust the seasoning in the sauce, swirl in a knob of butter and then pour over the chicken. Sprinkle with freshly chopped parsley.

Chicken Sauté in Red Wine Sauce

Chicken Provençal

Provence—region of sunshine, robust flavours, exuberance and good food. Tomatoes and garlic together are the basic flavourings of any dish cooked "à la Provençale", such as this chicken cooked "en cocotte". It is served in the local manner with a saffron tinted pilaf.

1 × No 14, 1.4 kg (3 lb) chicken
2 tablespoons olive oil
4 small white onions, quartered
3 tomatoes, halved
2 cloves garlic, peeled
sprig of parsley
1 bay leaf
sprig thyme
1 cup dry white wine
1 cup water
salt and freshly ground pepper

Remove the neck and any giblets from the chicken, season the cavity with salt and pepper and truss. Heat the oil in a large, flameproof casserole in which the chicken will fit comfortably and fry over a medium heat until golden all over. Remove to a dish and keep warm. Add the onions and fry until just starting to colour. Replace chicken, breast side up, and add the tomatoes, garlic, herbs (tied together), white wine and water. Season with salt and pepper. Cover the casserole and cook over a low heat or in a moderate oven (350°F—170°C) for 1 to 1¼ hours.

When cooked, remove chicken to a heated serving dish, arrange the vegetables around it and keep warm. Place the casserole over a high heat and boil the liquid until reduced to half its original quantity.

Serve chicken with saffron pilaf (page 267) with a little of the sauce spooned over.

Chicken Grilled with Mustard

2 × 500 g (1 lb) or 1 × 1.4 kg chicken
125 g (4 oz) butter
1 tablespoon oil
¼ cup French mustard
3 tablespoons chopped shallots
¼ teaspoon thyme
pepper and salt to taste
2 cups breadcrumbs
pinch of cayenne pepper

Split the chickens or joint them into good-sized pieces. Heat the grill, melt the butter, add the oil to it and brush over the chicken on the grill pan, (with the skin side upper-most). Grill for 10 minutes on each side, basting frequently. Blend the mustard with the chopped shallots, thyme nd seasonings, slowly blending in half the melted butter and oil, drop by drop, to make it thick.

Spread chicken with this mixture, and then roll the pieces in breadcrumbs. Return chicken to the grill, baste with the mustard mixture and after 10 minutes turn and baste again. Continue grilling for another 10 minutes until golden and tender.

Grilled Lemon Chickens

2 × 500 g (1 lb) chickens
60 g (2 oz) butter
rind of 1 lemon, cut into thin strips
salt and freshly ground white pepper
Sauce:
2 tablespoons butter
2 tablespoons flour
1 cup chicken stock
salt and freshly ground white pepper
2 tablespoons cream
few drops of lemon juice

Split the chickens in half and cut away back and rib bones. Arrange them skin side uppermost on the rack of a grilling pan. Melt butter, add lemon rind and simmer gently for a few minutes. Brush chickens with lemon butter and grill slowly for about 30 minutes, turning from time to time and basting frequently with lemon butter.

Sauce: Melt butter and add flour. Cook until straw-coloured. Remove from heat and stir in chicken stock. Return sauce to the heat and stir until thickened. Allow to simmer for 10 minutes (to cook out the flour). Season with salt and pepper, to taste, and stir in the cream and lemon juice.

Arrange chickens on a serving dish and serve the sauce separately.

Chicken Newburg

A creamy chicken dish such as this is good for buffet eating. It may be eaten just with a fork and needs no other accompaniments other than some boiled rice. If obtainable, Basmati rice with its excellent flavour, would be our choice.

60 g (2 oz) butter
½ cup sliced mushrooms
10 cooked chicken breasts
¼ cup dry sherry
salt and freshly ground white pepper
½ cup milk
½ cup cream
3 egg yolks
paprika

Heat the butter in a large saucepan and cook the mushrooms in it until softened. With a sharp knife slice the chicken breasts in half diagonally.

Add chicken to the mushrooms with half the sherry. Season with salt and pepper, cover and simmer gently for two minutes.

Combine the milk with the cream and add to the chicken and mushrooms and allow to heat, very gently. Beat the remaining sherry with the egg yolks, add a little of the hot sauce and combine.

Pour the egg yolk mixture into the hot sauce and heat gently until thickened. Correct the seasoning and serve sprinkled with a little paprika and accompanied with a dish of hot boiled rice.

Grilled Chicken Polonaise

2 × 500 g (1 lb) or 1 × 1.4 kg chicken
125 g (4 oz) butter, melted
fresh breadcrumbs for coating
2 tablespoons chopped parsley
2 hard-boiled eggs, chopped
pepper and salt to taste

Split chickens in half. Heat the grill and when quite hot place the chickens on the grill pan, skin side uppermost. Brush with half of the melted butter and grill for 10 minutes before turning and basting again. Cook for a further 25 to 30 minutes, basting and turning frequently.

When the chicken is cooked, coat with the breadcrumbs which have been mixed with remaining ingredients. Brush again with the melted butter and return to the grill, turning when necessary to crisp the breadcrumb mixture. Serve with boiled rice.

Steamed Chicken in Cream Sauce

1 × 2 kg (4 lb) boiling fowl
1 lemon
2 carrots, scraped
3 leeks or 2 onions, peeled
1 stick celery, chopped
salt and pepper to taste
185 g (6 oz) button mushrooms
1 teaspoon lemon juice
Sauce:
1 tablespoon butter
1 tablespoon flour
375 ml (1½ cups) stock from chicken
2 egg yolks
2-3 tablespoons cream

Rub skin of bird with cut lemon. Truss and put into large pan with prepared carrots, leeks or onions, celery, salt and pepper. Add hot water just to cover. Cover tightly and barely simmer until tender (about 2 to 3 hours). Simmer mushroom caps for 5 minutes in a little salted water and the lemon juice.

When tender, drain chicken, remove skin and cut into joints.

Arrange joints on dish and keep warm. Make sauce by melting butter and flour, stirring for 2 minutes. Add stock, whisk until boiling and simmer 10 minutes then remove from heat. Blend egg yolks and cream together and whisk into the sauce little by little. Reheat gently, but do not boil. Coat chicken with sauce and garnish with drained mushrooms.

Coq au Vin

Coq au Vin

Coq au Vin is a robust Burgundian dish made with chicken (or a cockerel) cooked gently in a soft red wine with tiny onions and bacon cubes. Traditionally, the wine used is a young red burgundy. Sometimes a little of the older, fuller wine which is intended to be drunk with the dish is added near the end of cooking to give depth of flavour.

1 × No 14 (3 lb) chicken or cockerel

2 cups red wine

2 bay leaves

sprig of thyme

1 clove garlic, crushed

250 g (8 oz) button mushrooms, wiped
  and stalks trimmed

125 g (4 oz) speck or shoulder bacon cut
  in one piece

30 g (1 oz) butter

2 tablespoons olive oil

12 small onions, peeled

$\frac{1}{4}$ cup brandy

extra bouquet garni

1 garlic clove, peeled

salt and freshly ground pepper

3 thick slices of bread

oil for frying

1$\frac{1}{2}$ tablespoons butter

2 teaspoons plain flour

finely chopped parsley

Chicken Stock:

chicken giblets

1 onion, peeled and cut in half

1 carrot, cut in large pieces

bouquet garni

2 cups water

salt

Cut the chicken into portions. Make a chicken stock by placing the chicken giblets into a saucepan with the onion, carrot, bouquet garni. Cover with 2 cups of water and add a pinch of salt. Bring to the boil and simmer for 1 hour. Strain. Remove any fat from the surface and adjust the seasoning.

Place the red wine in a saucepan with the bay leaves, thyme, crushed garlic clove and $\frac{2}{3}$ cup of chicken stock. Allow to boil vigorously until reduced by half. Just before the reduction is complete add the mushrooms. When reduced, remove from the heat and take out the mushrooms with a slotted spoon.

Strain the wine and place on one side.

Cut the speck or shoulder bacon into 1 cm ($\frac{1}{2}$ in) dice. Heat the butter with the oil, add the speck and when the fat starts to run add the onions and fry until both are golden brown. Season the chicken pieces, which have been well dried with paper towels, and place in the pan skin side down. When the skin is golden turn the pieces over and let them cook for another minute. Heat the brandy in a ladle or small saucepan, set alight and pour flaming over the chicken. Shake the pan over the heat until the flames die, then add the bouquet garni and garlic clove. Season with salt and freshly ground pepper.

Add the strained wine. Bring to the boil. Lower the heat, cover the pan tightly and let the Coq au Vin simmer for 40 minutes. Add the mushrooms and cook for 5 more minutes.

Meanwhile, remove the crusts from the bread, cut each slice into four triangles and fry in hot oil which is about 2.5 cm (1 in) deep. When golden remove and keep warm in the oven.

Transfer the chicken, mushrooms, onions and diced speck to a heated serving dish. Mix the butter and flour together and break into small pieces. Drop these into the sauce in the pan and stir over a low heat until the sauce thickens and comes just to the boil. Spoon this sauce over and around the chicken. Sprinkle with chopped parsley and arrange the triangles of fried bread around the edge of the dish.

Note: This is a dish where the flavour of the wine is most important. Although it is not necessary to use an expensive wine, it should be a red wine with softness and good flavour such as Lindemans Bin 50 burgundy.

Poule au Pot

1 × 1.75 kg (3½ lb) chicken
15 g (½ oz) butter
Stuffing:
250 g (½ lb) pork (neck or belly) finely
    chopped
2 tablespoons herbs (parsley, chives,
    tarragon, lemon thyme), finely chopped
1 egg
salt and freshly ground white pepper
Braising Vegetables:
1 celery stalk, sliced finely
1 carrot, sliced finely
1 turnip, sliced finely
1 onion, sliced finely
2 cups chicken stock or water
1 bouquet garni (bunch of fresh herbs)
Cream Sauce:
15 g (½ oz) butter
15 g (½ oz) flour
1 cup chicken liquid, skimmed of all fat
2 egg yolks
1 cup cream
salt and freshly ground white pepper

Mix the finely chopped pork, herbs and egg together. Season with salt and pepper.

Stuff chicken with seasoned pork mixture. Tie the chicken legs together.

Melt the butter in a large casserole in which the chicken will fit comfortably and put in the chicken on its side. Brown all over. Remove the browned chicken and keep warm.

Add the sliced vegetables to the pan and fry until golden. Place chicken on top of vegetables, pour over the stock, add bouquet garni and season with salt and pepper. Cook covered for 2½ to 3 hours, or until juice from the chicken runs clear when tested with a skewer. Strain off liquid and skim the fat. Measure 1 cup.

Sauce: Melt the butter in a saucepan and add flour. Cook until this combination (the roux) turns straw-coloured. Remove pan from heat and gradually add the stock, stirring all the time. Return to the heat, stirring until the sauce comes to the boil and thickens. Mix the egg yolks with the cream in a bowl and slowly pour the sauce onto this mixture, whisking as you pour. Return mixture to the saucepan and heat until bubbling gently. A squeeze of lemon juice may be added.

Serve the chicken with a little sauce spooned over it. Serve remaining sauce in a sauceboat. Accompany the bird with boiled potatoes and carrots sprinkled with freshly chopped parsley.

Combination Chow Mein

250 g (8 oz) chicken breast
124 g (4 oz) each raw prawns and
    barbecued pork
1 teaspoon Chinese wine or dry sherry
1 teaspoon cornflour
1 small red pepper
6 dried mushrooms
3 tablespoons oil
fried noodles for serving
Seasoning:
2 teaspoons Chinese wine or dry sherry
1½ teaspoons salt
½ teaspoon sugar
few drops sesame oil

Remove bone and skin from chicken and shred flesh. Shell prawns, halve if large and shred pork. Put all three into a bowl with wine and cornflour and mix thoroughly.

Shred pepper. Soak mushrooms in warm water for 20 minutes, drain and squeeze dry. Cut into shreds and discard stalks. Mix ingredients for seasonings.

Heat 1 tablespoon oil in a wok or frying pan and fry pepper and mushrooms for 2 minutes. Remove. Add remaining oil to wok and add chicken mixture, turning ingredients until chicken turns white and prawns are pink.

Add mushrooms and pepper, then seasoning, toss all together for 1 minute and then serve immediately over noodles.

Chicken with 40 cloves of garlic

Season one No 16 (3½ lb) chicken inside and out with salt and freshly ground pepper and place a small bouquet of herbs (parsley, thyme, sprig of rosemary and tarragon) inside it. Pour ¾ cup of olive oil into an ovenproof pot just large enough to hold the chicken and add 40 unpeeled garlic cloves. Place a bunch of fresh herbs (rosemary, thyme, sage, bayleaf, parsley and celery) on top of the garlic. Gently warm the oil and then turn the chicken in the oil which is already lightly perfumed with the garlic and herbs. Cover the pot and seal it with a flour and water paste. Bake in a moderate oven (350°F—170°C) for 1½ hours. Break the pastry seal and clean the pot. Take the chicken to the table and lift the lid and let your guests enjoy the fine aroma. The chicken will be golden, tender and flavoured with the garlic and herbs. Accompany with thick slices of crusty bread.

Chicken Kiev

For this classic Russian dish from Kiev, boned and flattened chicken breasts are wrapped around chilled fingers of butter, then coated in breadcrumbs and fried. They should be served as soon as they are golden brown and crisp. When cooked, the chicken will release a jet of golden butter when pierced with a fork.

This dish requires care and attention when cooking. The oil must be hot enough to brown the chicken breast but not so that it will colour before the exact time is up. Try it out once or twice and you will find with practice you will be able to cook perfect Chicken Kiev.

1 whole chicken breast with wing tips
attached—cut from a large chicken
30 g (1 oz) butter
salt and freshly ground black pepper
2 tablespoons finely chopped chives
plain flour
1 egg, lightly beaten
1 cup soft white breadcrumbs which
have been rubbed through a sieve
oil for deep frying

Halve the chicken breast. Using a sharp pointed knife remove all the bones from the breast, leaving the wing joint attached. Peel away the skin. Place the chicken breast between two pieces of waxed paper or plastic wrap and pound until thin with a mallet, the flat side of a heavy knife or the end of an empty champagne bottle. Take care not to split the flesh. Remove the paper.

Cut the butter into two pieces and roll each into a cork shape. Chill. Place the butter at the base of each chicken breast diagonally in line with the wing bone. Sprinkle with salt, pepper and chives. Fold the chicken flesh over the butter, then roll up towards the bone, folding the sides in as you go so that the butter is completely enclosed in the chicken. The flesh will adhere without skewers.

Coat each breast lightly with flour, brush with egg and roll in breadcrumbs. Refrigerate for at least 2 hours.

Heat the oil in a large saucepan (you will need enough oil to cover the chicken breasts). Cut a piece of bread and place it in the hot oil. If it rises to the surface immediately the oil will have reached the correct temperature for frying the chicken. Gently lower the chicken into the hot oil and fry for 4½ to 5 minutes. If the chicken starts to brown too quickly, lower the heat. When golden brown remove from the oil and drain on absorbent kitchen paper. Serve immediately with Potato Straws (page 210).

Note: Sometimes the chicken breast is sold with the wing joint removed. If this is so, proceed with the recipe ignoring the missing joint.

Top : Poached Chicken Breasts
Below : Chicken and Mushroom Pie (see recipe on page 213)

Poached Chicken Breasts

To prepare the basic cold poached chicken breast: Place chicken into hot water to cover, with 1 sliced carrot, 1 sliced onion, 1 small stick of celery, a small bouquet garni and pinch of salt. Cover the pan tightly and allow the chicken breast to cook gently on the lowest heat for 15 minutes or until tender.

Remove from the heat, allow the chicken breast to cook in its liquid. Place chicken in a dish. Strain the cool chicken stock over the breasts. Keep in the refrigerator until ready to use.

Here's how you can vary the poached chicken breast:

For one serving:

- Make a salad dressing of 2 tablespoons light sour cream blended with $\frac{1}{4}$ teaspoon prepared mustard, salt and freshly ground pepper.

    Slice half a chicken breast into shreds and place in a salad bowl with a quarter of a green pepper which has been cut into shreds, 4 walnut halves and 1 small apple peeled and cut into dice. Toss together in the cream dressing and chill before serving. Serve on a crisp lettuce leaf.

- Make the same dressing as above. Halve the chicken breast and arrange it with some peeled, seeded grapes (a small bunch) or $\frac{1}{4}$ cup of canned grapes, on a chilled plate. Spoon over sour cream dressing and dust lightly with paprika.

- Remove the seeds from half a cucumber and cut the flesh into 2.5 cm (1 in) pieces. Combine with one sliced half chicken breast with sour cream dressing to which 1 teaspoon grated green ginger has been added. Sprinkle with finely chopped parsley before serving.

- Combine 1 cup finely shredded cabbage with 1 orange peeled and cut into segments and one half chicken breast sliced. Toss with sour cream dressing and serve chilled. Garnish with fine shreds of blanched orange peel.

- Combine one sliced half chicken breast with one bouquet of watercress sprigs and 2 tablespoons bean sprouts. Season with salt and freshly ground pepper, squeezed lemon and 1 teaspoon olive oil. Top together and serve chilled on crisp lettuce leaves. Arrange a few cherry tomatoes on the side. Serves one.

Tarragon Chicken in a Pot

1 × 1.5 kg (3 lb) chicken
90 g (3 oz) butter
$\frac{1}{2}$ garlic clove
$\frac{1}{2}$ teaspoon salt
$1\frac{1}{2}$ teaspoons dried tarragon
$\frac{1}{2}$ teaspoon freshly ground black pepper

Place the clay pot and lid in very hot water and leave for 2 hours. The water must completely cover the pot.

Trim chicken and wipe dry with paper towels. Soften the butter. Crush the garlic with salt and mix the butter, garlic, tarragon and pepper. Divide the mixture in two. Put half inside the chicken and tie legs together. Rub remaining butter mixture over the breast and legs.

Remove pot from water and put in the chicken, breast-side up. Cover and cook in a hot oven (400 to 450°F—200 to 230°C) for $1\frac{1}{2}$ hours.

Chicken in Jelly

1 boiling fowl
1 lemon
1 onion, peeled and cut in half
1 carrot, cut into chunks
water
bouquet garni
salt
10 peppercorns
1 tablespoon gelatine

Wash the boiling fowl and dry inside and out with paper towels. Pare the rind from the lemon and insert under the skin of the fowl. Place into a large pot with the onion and carrot. Add water to cover the bouquet garni, salt and some peppercorns. Bring to the boil, cover pan tightly and simmer for $2\frac{1}{2}$ hours or until tender. Remove from the pan and allow chicken to cool. Remove flesh and place into a terrine or bowl which has been rinsed out with water. Skim surface of stock and strain. Heat gently. Dissolve gelatine in a little cold water and then add to 2 cups of the chicken stock. Allow to cool and when syrupy pour over the chicken. Place in the refrigerator and allow to set. Unmould.

Chicken in a Basket

4 × 500 g (1 lb) spring chickens
60 g (2 oz) butter
salt, freshly ground black pepper

Smear chickens with the butter and season the birds' cavities with salt and pepper. Set in a roasting pan and cook in a moderately hot oven (375°F—190°C) for 30 minutes or until the juice runs clear when a skewer is placed into the thickest part of the leg. Arrange paper napkins in small baskets. Place spring chicken in each and scatter with the Potato Straws and Fried Bananas. Alternatively, serve on hot plates or platters.

Potato Straws

6 large potatoes
oil for deep frying
salt

Peel the potatoes and cut into straws about the size of a matchstick. Place in a bowl of iced water for about 30 minutes. Drain and dry well in a tea towel. Heat the oil in a large saucepan until it just begins to smoke (when the oil reaches the right temperature, a piece of bread dropped in it will brown very quickly). Place the dried potatoes in a basket and lower them into the hot oil or just drop them in and scoop them up with a draining spoon. Fry until tender but not browned.

Remove potato straws from the oil and drain on crumpled kitchen paper. Just before serving, reheat oil, return chips and fry until golden and crisp. Drain well on crumpled kitchen paper, to ensure the straws drain properly. Sprinkle with salt and serve immediately.

Fried Bananas

8 bananas
60 g (2 oz) butter

Split the peeled bananas in two lengthwise and then halve across. Melt the butter and, when beginning to froth, place the bananas in the pan. Cook the bananas until golden and tender. Keep warm until ready to serve.

Plain Pilau with Fried Onion Rings

90 g (3 oz) butter or ghee
1 onion, finely chopped
2 cups long grain rice
1 teaspoon salt
3½ cups boiling stock
½ cup oil
2 onions, sliced

Melt butter in a heavy saucepan, add finely chopped onion and cook gently until transparent. Add rice and cook for 5 minutes, stirring continually until each grain of rice is coated with butter.

Add salt and half of the boiling stock, bring to the boil, cover then reduce heat and simmer gently for 20 minutes adding more stock as it is absorbed or until rice is tender and the liquid is absorbed.

Meanwhile heat oil in small saucepan and fry onions until golden and just starting to crisp. Care must be taken so that the onions do not burn yet are well cooked and golden. Do not have the heat too high. Drain on crumpled kitchen paper and scatter over the pilau at the last moment.

Chicken in a basket

Chicken with Peppers

The tender breast meat of chicken is particularly suited to the stir-frying method of cooking which is quick, ensuring the meat stays moist and tender.

500 g (1 lb) chicken breasts
1 egg white
1 tablespoon Chinese wine or dry sherry
1 tablespoon cornflour
½ teaspoon salt
1 small green pepper and 1 small red pepper
4 tablespoons oil
slice of fresh green ginger
1 clove garlic
few drops sesame oil
Seasonings:
1 tablespoon Chinese wine or dry sherry
1 teaspoon sugar
2 teaspoons Soy Sauce
1 teaspoon cornflour
3 tablespoons chicken stock or water

Remove skin and bones from chicken breasts and cut flesh into 1 cm (½ in) cubes. Put into a bowl with egg white, wine, cornflour and salt. Stir with chopsticks or a fork until well mixed.

Halve peppers, cut out stem and remove seeds and membrane. Cut the peppers the same size as chicken. Mix all ingredients for seasonings in a small bowl.

Heat 3 tablespoons of oil in a wok or frying pan and add ginger and peeled garlic. Discard when they begin to colour. Add a few drops of sesame oil to the hot oil, then add chicken and stir over a high heat until it begins to colour. Remove to a plate.

Add remaining oil to pan and fry peppers for 2 minutes. Return chicken, stir well and then add the seasonings. Stir until mixture boils. Serve immediately with boiled rice.

Arroz con Pollo

Arroz con Pollo is a chicken and rice dish found all over Spain. The rice is cooked with chicken and chicken stock and then various colourful ingredients added not long before the dish is ready for serving, giving it a most attractive appearance.

1 × 2 kg (4 lb) chicken
2 tablespoons olive oil
15 g (½ oz) butter
1 onion, finely chopped
1 cup rice
2 cups chicken stock
salt, freshly ground pepper
1 green pepper, blanched and shredded
1 canned pimento cap, shredded
2 mushrooms, sliced and browned in 15 g (½ oz) butter
3 tomatoes, peeled and chopped
2 chicken livers
15 g (½ oz) butter
1 bay leaf

Cut the chicken into pieces and dry thoroughly with a kitchen towel. Heat the oil, add the butter and when the butter has melted add the chicken pieces a few at a time browning them well all over. Place on one side and keep warm.

Add the onion to the same pan and cook slowly until golden then stir in the rice and coat it in the oil and butter. Return the chicken pieces to the pan and add the bay leaf. Season with salt and pepper. Pour on the chicken stock, bring to the boil and then lower the heat, cover the pan and simmer for 30 minutes.

During this time sauté the chicken livers in hot butter until golden brown. Remove from the pan and chop them. Add the green pepper, pimento, mushrooms, tomatoes and chicken livers, cover the pan once more and cook for a further 10 minutes or until the chicken is tender.

Chicken and Mushroom Pie

1 × No 16 boiling chicken
Chicken stock:
1 carrot, chopped
1 medium onion, chopped
2 sticks celery, chopped
1 bouquet garni
water to cover
Pie Filling:
salt
freshly ground pepper
125 g (4 oz) button mushrooms
125 g (4 oz) bacon rashers with rind
    removed
1 medium onion, finely chopped
1 tablespoon parsley, finely chopped
1 × 339 g (12 oz) packet commercial
    puff pastry
1 egg
pinch of salt

Cut the chicken into pieces, remove the skin and carefully cut the flesh from the bones. Cut the chicken into strips. Place the chicken bones and skin in a saucepan with the chopped carrot, onion, celery and bouquet garni. Cover with water, bring to the boil and then simmer the chicken stock for 1½ to 2 hours. Strain the stock and measure 1 cup. Season the chicken pieces with salt and pepper. Cut the mushrooms into quarters and the bacon into 1 cm (½ in) pieces. Arrange the chicken, mushrooms, bacon, onion and parsley in layers in a 4–4½ cup pie dish. Fill up the dish with the chicken stock.

Roll out the pastry thinly and cut a 2.5 cm (1 in) strip to fit the rim of the pie dish. Dampen the rim with a little water and press the pastry strip on to it. Brush this strip with water and lay the remaining pastry over the pie dish using the rolling pin. Trim off any excess pastry and reserve for decorating.

With blunt edge of knife or tips of fingers mark around the edge, then with the back of the knife "knock up" the edge. In this way the edge of the pastry is slightly raised and will begin to flake readily when cooking. Make a hole in the centre of pie to release the steam.

Cut the remaining pastry into diamonds about 8 cm (3 in) long and with the back of the knife mark to represent the veins of a leaf. Lightly beat the egg with a pinch of salt and brush over the pie. Arrange the leaves on the pie and brush lightly with egg. Place the pie dish on a baking sheet and place in a hot oven (400°F—200°C) for 30 to 40 minutes. Lower oven temperature to moderate (350°F—170°C) and cook another hour.

Chicken Curry

2 medium onions
1 clove garlic
2.5 cm (1 in) green ginger
60 g (2 oz) ghee
1 tablespoon curry powder or curry paste
2 large tomatoes
2 teaspoons paprika
2 whole cloves
8 cm (3 in) stick cinnamon
2 cups coconut milk
2 teaspoons salt
2 green peppers
1 × 1.5 kg (3 lb) chicken
2 tablespoons cream or sour cream
1 tablespoon fresh mint

Finely chop onions, crush garlic and grate ginger. Cook gently in hot ghee until beginning to turn golden. Add curry powder or curry paste and cook 3 to 4 minutes. Add peeled, seeded and diced tomatoes, paprika, cloves, cinnamon, coconut milk, salt and seeded, shredded green peppers.

Simmer covered about 15 minutes, then add chicken cut into serving pieces and simmer 30 to 40 minutes until chicken is tender. Add cream and chopped fresh mint. Heat through and serve.

Serve with rice and accompaniments. Serves 4 to 6.

Goose

Roast Goose with Apple and Prune Stuffing

For centuries, roast goose has been served traditionally throughout Europe and England at Christmas time. Each country has its own favourite stuffing; apple and prune for the Danes, sage and onion for the English, and a truffle or two for the French.

Goose was also traditionally served on Michaelmas Day (29th September.) Legend has it that Good Queen Bess, who was particularly partial to goose, was indulging her fondness when she was brought the news of the Spanish Armada's defeat. To celebrate, she decreed that roast goose should be served on this day each year in commemoration of this great event.

1 × 3 kg (6 lb) goose
4 large cooking apples
salt and freshly ground pepper
12 large prunes, stoned
rind of 1 lemon
2 tablespoons plus 2 teaspoons plain
    flour
¼ cup brandy
1 cup stock made with the giblets

Remove any excess fat from the inside of the goose and wipe the inside of the cavity and outside skin with a damp towel. Using kitchen scissors remove the oil sac from the parson's nose. This has a strong taste and if not removed can flavour the flesh of the bird.

Peel, core and roughly chop two of the cooking apples, season with salt and pepper and mix with the prunes and lemon rind. Spoon this stuffing into cavity.

Place a whole apple in the body cavity to give the goose a good shape and then truss it.

Lightly dust the goose with 2 tablespoons of flour and place in a lightly oiled roasting pan. Sear the goose over a high heat. Heat the brandy, set alight and flame the bird. This adds flavour and at the same time sears off the tiny pin feathers.

Place in a hot oven (400°F—200°C) for 15 to 20 minutes, then cover the pan, reduce the oven temperature to moderate (350°F—170°C) and continue to cook for 2¼ hours.

When the goose is cooked take it out of the oven and place on a serving platter or a carving board and remove the trussing string. Keep warm.

To make the gravy: Skim 2 tablespoons of the fat from the pan juices into a cup and discard any extra fat. Blend the fat to a smooth paste with the remaining 2 teaspoons of flour. Place the roasting pan on to a gentle heat and add the remaining apple which has been peeled, cored and chopped very finely. Cook gently for 2 to 3 minutes until the apple is soft. Add the hot stock made from the giblets and then blend in the paste of flour and goose fat and bring to the boil, stirring and scraping all the pan juices. Simmer for another 2 to 3 minutes. Serve gravy separately in a sauceboat.

Surround the roast goose with poached apple halves stuffed with prunes.

Poached Apples Stuffed with Prunes

4 medium-sized Granny Smith apples
8 large dessert prunes, stones removed

Cut the apples in two, remove core and any pips. Place a prune in the centre of each apple half. Place apples on a lightly buttered ovenproof dish and cover the bottom of the dish with a little water. Cover dish with lid or foil and poach gently in a moderate oven (350°F—170°C) for 10 minutes.

Note: If the oven space is at a premium this dish may be cooked over a gentle heat in a flameproof dish.

Rabbit

Sautéed Rabbit in Red Wine Sauce

Hare was originally used in this robust dish with its red wine sauce. We used rabbit as it is easier to come by. Serve it with plain boiled potatoes followed by a fresh green salad.

2 rabbits, jointed
flour for dusting
1 tablespoon olive oil
30 g (1 oz) butter
125 g (4 oz) bacon cut into small strips
¾ cup red wine
1 clove garlic, crushed
3 tablespoons thick tomato purée
salt and freshly ground pepper
freshly chopped parsley

Dust the rabbit pieces with a little seasoned flour. Heat the oil and add the butter and when melted and the foam has subsided, brown the rabbit all over. Remove the rabbit as you brown it to a warm plate.

Sauté the bacon for 2 minutes until lightly browned. Add the wine, raise the heat and allow to reduce a little. Stir in the garlic and tomato purée and season with salt and pepper. Return the rabbit to the pan, cover tightly and simmer for 1 hour or until the rabbit is tender. Adjust the seasoning if necessary and serve sprinkled with chopped parsley.

Saleux Rabbit

One of the best ways to cook rabbit is to casserole it. It absorbs the flavours of the bacon, wine, garlic and herbs cooked with it and is served with its own delicious sauce.

1 rabbit
60 g (2 oz) flour
salt and freshly ground pepper
30 g (1 oz) butter mixed with 2
    tablespoons olive oil
10 small white onions, peeled
90 g (3 oz) bacon, diced
1 cup dry white wine or dry cider
½ cup water
1 tablespoon tomato purée
1 sprig thyme
1 bayleaf
1 garlic clove, crushed
2 tablespoons snipped chives
500 g (1 lb) small mushrooms
extra butter and oil

Cut the rabbit into 6 pieces. Lightly coat in flour seasoned with salt and pepper. Heat the butter and oil and fry the rabbit pieces until golden brown. Place on one side and keep warm. Add the tiny onions to the pan with the bacon and fry until the onions are coloured. Place the rabbit back into the pan and add the wine and then the water which has been mixed with the tomato purée. Add the thyme, bayleaf, garlic and chives. Season with a little extra pepper. Cover the pan and simmer for about 1 hour or until the rabbit is tender.

Just before the rabbit is cooked, toss the mushrooms in hot butter and oil for a few minutes and then add to the rabbit.

Remove the thyme and bayleaf. Place the rabbit pieces with the vegetables on a heated serving dish, pour the sauce over and sprinkle with finely chopped parsley.

Drunken Rabbit

Rabbit braised in beer is a dish for those who enjoy the robust flavour of game.

1 rabbit
salt
freshly ground black pepper
1 large onion, sliced finely
1 large carrot, diced
125 g (4 oz) streaky bacon, chopped
30 g (1 oz) butter
2 tablespoons olive oil
1 cup beer
2 teaspoons sugar
bouquet garni
1 teaspoon French mustard
1 teaspoon arrowroot mixed with 2
  tablespoons water (optional)
finely chopped parsley

Soak the rabbit in cold salted water to cover for 1 hour. Dry it well and cut into joints. Season with salt and pepper.

Heat the butter and oil in a heavy pot and brown the rabbit all over. Remove to a dish. Add the onion, carrot and bacon and place the lid on the pot. Allow the vegetables to sweat for about 7 minutes.

Place the rabbit on the bed of vegetables and bacon, season with salt and pepper and pour over the beer. Add the sugar, bouquet garni and mustard.

Bring the liquid to the boil, cover the pot and allow to simmer on a very low heat for $1\frac{1}{2}$ hours or until the rabbit is tender. When the rabbit is cooked, skim any fat from the surface. If necessary, thicken the sauce with arrowroot mixed with a little water. Sprinkle with finely chopped parsley before serving.

Lapin Moutarde

Lapin Moutarde (or rabbit with French mustard) is a casserole with the flavour of bacon and mustard. Gentle cooking and a subtle combination of flavours make it a delicately delicious dish.

1 rabbit
2 teaspoons vinegar
1 tablespoon plain flour
1 tablespoon olive oil
30 g (1 oz) butter
4-6 onions, peeled
125 g (4 oz) streaky bacon, diced
3 cups of stock or water with chicken
  cubes
salt and pepper
2 tablespoons French mustard
bouquet garni (bunch of fresh herbs)
$\frac{1}{2}$ cup cream
2 teaspoons parsley, finely chopped

Joint the rabbit and soak overnight in salted water to cover, with the vinegar added. Drain and dry the rabbit thoroughly, then coat with the flour. Heat the oil and butter in a fireproof casserole or heavy saucepan, add the onions, cut into quarters, and cook for 3 minutes. Remove. Add the rabbit and bacon and cook until golden brown. Pour in stock, add salt, freshly ground pepper, mustard and bouquet garni. Return onions. Bring slowly to the boil and simmer, covered, for $1\frac{1}{2}$ hours or until tender. If the sauce is too thin, remove the rabbit to a heated serving dish and then boil the sauce rapidly until slightly thickened. Add the cream and chopped parsley. Correct the seasoning. Pour the sauce over the rabbit and serve with boiled new potatoes or creamy mashed potatoes.

Rabbit with Prunes

Cut one rabbit into joints and marinate in the following mixture for 24 hours.

2 tablespoons vinegar
6 tablespoons olive oil
1 sprig thyme
1 bay leaf
1 sprig parsley
1 clove garlic, crushed
1 carrot, sliced
1 onion, sliced
salt and freshly ground black pepper to
    taste

Drain rabbit and pat dry with a paper towel. Dust lightly with flour. In a heavy flameproof casserole or saucepan cook gently in a little butter until lightly coloured. Pour over the marinade and cook for 15 minutes. Add ½ cup of prunes (which have been stoned), cover the pan and cook gently over a low heat until tender—about 1½ hours.

About 1 tablespoon of gooseberry jelly or jam may be added just before serving.

Duck

Roast Duckling

The duck is a very festive bird and ideal for a special occasion. Its meat is rich in flavour and combines superbly with fruits such as oranges, cherries, apricots and apples. Wines and brandies, either of fruit or grape origin, as well as olives, herbs and spices will also complement the bird's flavour.

2 × 1.5 kg (3 lb) ducklings
salt
freshly ground black pepper
brandy
½ onion, sliced
½ peeled apple, sliced
few celery leaves
1 clove garlic
1 cup white wine
Gravy:
1 cup duck stock
3 tablespoons port
1 tablespoon butter

Cut off necks and remove excess fat from the ducklings. Wipe with a damp cloth inside and out and rub the birds' cavities with brandy. Season with salt and pepper and stuff with the onion, apple and celery leaves. Rub the outside of the ducklings with a cut clove of garlic and season with salt and pepper. Place breast side up on a rack in a roasting pan and cook in a moderate oven (375°F—190°C) for 30 minutes. Remove ducklings and skim excess fat from the pan. Add the white wine and place the birds back on the rack to roast for a further 35 minutes or until tender, basting with the pan juices from time to time.

Remove ducklings and keep warm. Tilt the roasting pan and spoon out all but 1 tablespoon of fat. Add 1 cup of duck stock and boil rapidly, scraping up coagulated roasting juices, until liquid is reduced at least by half. Correct seasoning. Add 3 tablespoons of port and simmer a minute to evaporate the alcohol. Remove from heat and, just before serving, swirl the butter into the sauce and strain into a sauceboat.

To serve the duck, remove trussing strings and seasonings from the cavity. Place on a heated serving dish and spoon over a little gravy.

- If the duck is very fat, prick the skin with a fork. After 15 minutes roasting, pour off any excess fat from the pan and then continue cooking.

Braised Duckling with Marsala Sauce

Braised Duckling with Marsala Sauce

While most people like to roast duck for its crisp skin, we consider braising a duck gives the best flavour. The marsala gives the sauce a rich caramel flavour which is quite excellent.

1 × 2.25 kg (4½ lb) duck
salt and freshly ground black pepper
1 strip pared orange rind
15 g (½ oz) butter
1 celery stalk, finely sliced
1 turnip, onion and carrot, finely sliced
1 cup chicken stock
½ cup marsala
1 tablespoon arrowroot slaked with 2
    tablespoons marsala

Remove the excess fat from the duck and season the cavity with salt and pepper. Place a piece of pared orange rind inside the duck. Truss it and dry thoroughly with kitchen paper.

Melt the butter in a large heavy casserole or deep roasting pan with a lid and when the foam has subsided, place in the duck breast side down. Brown the duck lightly all over and then remove it and keep warm. Pour off the fat leaving about 1 tablespoon in the pan. Add the sliced celery, turnip, onion and carrot, season with salt and pepper and cook until lightly coloured. Place the duck on top of the bed of vegetables and pour in the chicken stock. Bring to the boil and cover the casserole. Place in a moderate oven (350°F—170°C) and cook for 1½ hours or until the duck is tender. Remove from the oven, cut away the string and place on a heated serving platter and keep warm.

Strain the liquid in which the duck was cooked into a saucepan and spoon off any excess fat. Add the marsala and the arrowroot and stir until the sauce has come to a simmer and has thickened slightly.

Remove from the heat and spoon a little sauce over the duck to glaze it. Serve remaining sauce in a sauce boat. Accompany with baked jacket potatoes and sautéed whole tomatoes.

Duckling with Glazed Turnips

1 × 2.5 kg (5 lb) duckling
30 g (1 oz) butter
1 carrot, chopped
1 celery stalk, chopped
1 onion, chopped
1 cup dry white wine
bouquet garni
salt and freshly ground black pepper
1 kg (2 lb) small white turnips
1 kg (2 lb) small white onions
2 tablespoons sugar
60 g (2 oz) butter
1 cup water

Wipe the duckling with a damp cloth and truss it. Melt the butter in an oval casserole to fit the duckling and, when hot, place the duckling in on its side to brown. Brown all over then remove and keep warm. Throw out excess fat from the casserole, leaving about 1 tablespoon. Add the carrot, celery and onion and cook until golden and softened. Place duckling on the bed of vegetables, add the wine and the bouquet garni, season with salt and pepper. Cover casserole and cook in a moderately hot oven (375°F—190 °C) for 1½ hours.

Quarter the peeled turnips and peel the onions. Place in a heavy saucepan with the sugar, butter and water. Cover and cook until just tender. Remove lid and allow the liquid to evaporate until a thick syrup remains and the vegetables are glazed.

Remove the cooked duck to a serving dish, cut off the trussing string and keep warm. Strain liquid in the pan and skim off fat. Thicken the pan juices with a little cornflour mixed with water and pour into a gravy boat. Surround duckling with glazed turnips and onions.

Duck à l'Orange

This is the best loved of all duck dishes. The duck is roasted and then served with an orange sauce. The sauce varies from restaurant to restaurant. Our recipe includes port as well as cointreau which makes a particularly delicious sauce. The best oranges for this classic dish are Seville. These are difficult to come by but if available, substitute them for sweet oranges.

1 × 2.5 kg (4½ lb) duck
salt and freshly ground pepper
rind of 1 orange
Sauce:
3 tablespoons sugar
¼ cup vinegar
1 cup duck stock
1 tablespoon arrowroot slaked with 2
   tablespoons port
1 orange
½ cup port
2 tablespoons cointreau liqueur
salt, freshly ground pepper
15 g (½ oz) butter

Remove all the excess fat from the inside of the duck and place the pared rind of one of the oranges into the cavity. Season with salt and pepper and truss the duck. Wipe the duck with paper towels and place breast side up in a roasting pan. Bake in a hot oven (425°F—215°C) for 15 minutes until the duck has browned lightly and released some of its fat. Remove the duck and pour off the excess fat. Lower the temperature to moderately hot (375°F—190°C) and place the duck back to roast for an hour.

During this time boil the sugar and vinegar over a high heat until it forms a thick syrup. Remove from the heat and gradually stir in the duck stock. When smooth place back on the heat and bring to the boil. Gradually add the arrowroot mixture and the orange rind which has been cut into shreds. Simmer the sauce for about 4 minutes or until the sauce is clear and thickened.

When the duck is cooked, remove the trussing string and place it on a serving dish and keep warm.

Remove all the fat from the baking dish leaving all the juices in the bottom. Place on the heat and stir in the port, scraping up all the pan juices and allow to reduce to half. Strain into the prepared sauce base and bring to a gentle simmer, then stir in the cointreau. Adjust the seasoning and when ready to serve, remove the sauce from the heat and swirl in the butter. Spoon a little of the sauce over the duck to give it an attractive glaze and serve the rest in a sauceboat.

Note: The flesh of the oranges may be cut into segments and added to the sauce at the last moment for extra orange flavour.

Duck Stock:
Heat a little oil in a saucepan and brown the neck and giblets of the duck. Pour off all the fat and add 2 cups of water, a bouquet garni and allow to simmer for an hour. Strain before using.

Turkey

Roast Turkey

An Englishman would feel cheated if his roast Christmas turkey wasn't flavoured with two stuffings: pork and veal forcemeat in the crop, and chestnut stuffing in the body cavity. We have reproduced this English classic and French-roasted it. This method of cooking is especially good if the turkey is to be served cold.

1 × 6 kg (12 lb) No 55 turkey
1 quantity pork and veal forcemeat
1 quantity prune, chestnut and celery
   stuffing
60 g (2 oz) butter
salt and freshly ground pepper
2 cups stock made from the giblets
Gravy:
2 tablespoons plain flour
30 g (1 oz) butter
3 cups extra turkey giblet stock
1 turkey liver or 3 chicken livers

Wipe the cavity of the turkey with a damp kitchen cloth and place the pork and veal stuffing lightly into the neck or crop being careful not to pack it too tightly.

Press the outside of the breast to give it a good shape and bring the skin over the back and secure it with small skewers.

Spoon the prune, chestnut and celery stuffing into the body of the turkey.

Tuck the wings under the turkey to give the bird a neat shape.

Tuck the turkey flap under the wings to hold it.

Insert small skewers around the opening and lace together with fine string. Fasten the legs close to the body by tying ends of drumsticks together. Wipe well with a damp kitchen towel.

Soften the butter and spread all over the turkey, making sure that the breast and legs are well covered. Season with salt and pepper. Place on a rack in a roasting pan and pour over the stock.

Cover baking dish tightly with aluminium foil and roast the turkey in a moderate oven (350°F—170°C) for about $3\frac{1}{2}$ to 4 hours or until the turkey is tender, basting it every 25 minutes. Remove the foil for the last half-hour of cooking, to allow the turkey to brown.

Test the turkey to see if it is cooked by piercing the thickest part of the thigh and drumstick with a fine skewer. If ready, the juice should run clear.

Remove to a heated serving platter and allow the turkey to rest in a warm place for 15 minutes while you make the gravy and serve the vegetables. This resting period gives the flesh time to set and makes carving easier. The best place for this is the warming drawer. On top of the steaming pudding is good for this purpose too.

Cooking time for turkey
Weight unstuffed at 350°F—170°C
(For a *stuffed* bird allow an additional 30 to 40 minutes.)
A 3 to 4 kg (6 to 8 lb) bird will take 3 to $3\frac{1}{2}$ hours and will serve 8 to 10 people.
A 4 to 6 kg (8 to 12 lb) bird will take $3\frac{1}{2}$ to 4 hours and serves 10 to 14 people.
A 6 to 8 kg (12 to 16 lb) bird will take 4 to 6 hours and serves 14 to 16 people.

Turkey Stock

Gently simmer the turkey giblets with 1 halved onion, 1 bayleaf and 1 good stick of celery in 7 cups of water until reduced to 5 cups. Strain.

Pork and Veal Forcemeat

750 g (¾ lb) pork and veal mince
1½ cups fresh breadcrumbs
1 tablespoon chopped herbs, parsley,
    thyme, sage
1 to 2 onions, finely chopped
60 g (2 oz) fatty bacon, finely chopped
    (2 rashers)
½ beaten egg
grated rind of ½ lemon
salt and freshly ground pepper

Mix all the ingredients together, season with salt and pepper and pound with a pestle or the end of a rolling pin to make a smooth forcemeat.

Note: Double these quantities if stuffing a 5 kg (10 lb) turkey with this mixture only.

Prune, Chestnut and Celery Stuffing

12 large dessert prunes
½ cup red wine mixed with ½ cup water
30 g (1 oz) butter
1½ cups finely chopped celery
1 large onion, finely chopped
250 g (8 oz) dried chestnuts or 1 × 290 g
    (10 oz) can of whole chestnuts
1 tablespoon herbs finely chopped—
    parsley, thyme, sage,
grated rind of ½ a lemon
salt and freshly ground pepper
½ beaten egg

Soak the prunes in the wine and water overnight and next day, simmer gently in this liquid until tender. Drain and reserve the juice. Stone and cut each in quarters.

Melt the butter in a large pan and cook the celery and onion very gently until softened.

Soak the dried chestnuts in water overnight and next day cook in this liquid for 20 to 25 minutes or until tender. (If using canned chestnuts, drain only.)

Mix all the ingredients together, season with salt and pepper and bind mixture with a beaten egg adding a little of the prune juice if necessary.

Turkey Gravy

Skim about 2 tablespoons of fat from the pan juices and blend with the flour to a smooth paste. Pour off excess turkey drippings, leaving about 3 tablespoons. Place the roasting pan on the heat, stir in the butter and flour and allow to brown lightly. Stir in the 3 cups of stock scraping up all the crusty pan residue and bring to the boil. Simmer for 2 minutes. Strain.

Fry the turkey liver separately in a little butter until browned all over, but still a pale rosy pink inside—about 2 minutes—remove from heat, cut into dice and add to the strained gravy just before serving. Adjust the seasoning if necessary and skim any excess fat from the top. Be sure to serve the gravy piping hot.

Carving the Turkey

First make sure your carving knife is razor sharp.
- Remove the trussing string and poultry pins and place the bird on a carving board.
- Place the knife between the thigh and the body of the bird and cut through the skin to the joint. Separate the leg from the bird by pressing the leg outward with the knife and bending the leg back with the fork.
- Separate the thigh and drumstick and slice off dark meat.
- Disjoint the wing and separate from the body in the same manner.
- Insert the fork through the ribs above the backbone. Make a cut above the wing joint through to the carcass.
- Slice downward with straight, even strokes, beginning half-way up to the breast. When the knife reaches the incision above the wing bone, the slice will fall free. Continue slicing breast by beginning at a higher point each time until the crest of the bone is reached. Slice stuffing in neck of turkey.
- It is a good idea to serve on each plate, a large slice of white meat with a slice of neck stuffing, and another of dark meat. Don't forget the stuffing in the cavity—place a spoonful by the side of the meat.

Turkey in Aspic

For those who prefer a cold Christmas dinner, we include a recipe for turkey served in a wine flavoured aspic.

Braise the turkey if it is small, or if large French-roast it. When cool, cover and keep in the refrigerator until ready to carve it.

Carve turkey breast into thin slices, taking a little of the neck stuffing with each slice, or carve the stuffing separately.

Pour a layer of cool aspic (recipe below) on to a chilled serving plate and place in the refrigerator to set. Arrange the slices of turkey breast on the aspic bed, overlapping each slice.

Brush turkey with aspic. Place in the refrigerator to set and then brush once more and chill as before. Arrange crisp bouquets of watercress dipped in vinaigrette dressing at each end of the dish before serving.

Aspic Jelly

2 cups chicken stock
30 g (1 oz) gelatine
$\frac{1}{4}$ cup dry white wine
1 egg white

Make the stock, strain and cool in the refrigerator. Remove any fat which has set on the surface and turn into a large saucepan. Soften the gelatine in the wine. Whisk the egg white to a light froth, add to the pan, set on a gentle heat and whisk backwards—from left to right. When just hot, add the gelatine mixture and continue to whisk as before until the liquid reaches boiling point. Remove the whisk and allow the contents to boil up. Draw carefully aside and leave to settle for 4 to 5 minutes. Repeat this process twice more without stirring, bringing the liquid rapidly to the boil each time. After the third time and when the liquid has been left to settle, pour the contents through a cloth which has been scalded and wrung out well. This process should be repeated once more for a crystal clear aspic.

Note: The aspic may be prepared well in advance and stored in the refrigerator. Before using, melt over a low heat and allow to cool.

Note:
- The best way to thaw a frozen turkey is in the refrigerator. This will take 2 to 3 days. Thawing may be hastened if the giblets are removed as soon as the cavity is partially thawed.
- Before the turkey is stuffed, the inside of the bird must be well wiped with a paper towel or a damp cloth.
- Remember to order your turkey well in advance and if buying a very large bird, first make sure your oven is large enough to hold it.
- Stuff the crop of the turkey first, fold over the skin of the neck and secure it with a poultry pin and then stuff the interior cavity. Never overstuff the turkey. The stuffing expands during cooking and can cause the skin to burst.
- A well stuffed turkey not only has a beautiful shape but goes further than a hollow one.
- The advantage of French-roasting a turkey is it keeps the flesh succulent and tender and makes the accompanying gravy rich and full of the flavour of the bird. French-roasting is especially good if the turkey is to be served cold.
- An indication the turkey is cooked is when the meat shrinks away from the knuckle end of the drumstick.
- If the turkey legs are slightly undercooked don't worry, they will be all the better for a reheated dish the next day. *Never* hurry the cooking of a bird at a high heat, as the outside skin will scorch before the heat has penetrated the interior.

Braised Turkey with Chestnut Stuffing

We have found braising the best method of cooking a small turkey. It keeps the meat very succulent and the pan juices form the basis of a well-flavoured gravy.

1 × 3 kg (6 lb) turkey
2 × 290 g (10 oz) cans of whole chestnuts
1 turkey liver or 3 chicken livers
2 tablespoons chopped parsley
salt and freshly ground pepper
1 egg
375 g ($\frac{3}{4}$ lb) chipolata sausages
125 g (4 oz) butter
1 onion, 1 carrot, 1 celery stalk, roughly chopped
1 cup giblet stock (page 221)
1 tablespoon plain flour

Remove the giblets from the turkey and make the stock (page 221). Wipe the cavity of the turkey with a damp cloth. Make the stuffing for the turkey crop by mashing half a can of chestnuts with a fork or pureeing them in an electric blender. Chop the liver and add to the pureed chestnuts with the chopped parsley, salt, pepper and egg. Stuff the crop of the turkey lightly.

Fry the chipolata sausages in 30 g (1 oz) butter until golden and mix with the remaining whole chestnuts. Season generously with salt and freshly ground pepper. Spoon this filling into the body cavity of the turkey.

Pull skin over opening and secure with poultry pins and string.

Fasten the legs close to the body by tying ends of drumsticks together. Wipe the bird dry with a kitchen towel.

Melt the remaining butter in a large baking dish with a lid or a casserole dish in which the turkey will fit comfortably, and when the foam has subsided, brown the turkey gently all over, turning frequently. Take out and keep warm. Add the chopped onion, carrot and celery, cover and allow to sweat for 5 minutes. Place the turkey on to the bed of vegetables. Season with salt and pepper, pour over stock, cover the pan and braise in a moderate oven (350°F—170°C) basting frequently, for 3 hours or until the turkey is tender. For the last 15 minutes cook the bird uncovered to brown the skin. When cooked, keep the bird warm.

Strain the liquid and discard the vegetables. Skim the fat, reserving about 2 tablespoons to blend with the flour and then return this to the liquid in the pan. Bring to the boil and simmer for 2 to 3 minutes. Adjust the seasoning and then pour into a sauceboat.

Green Beans and Water Chestnuts

1 kg (2 lb) green beans
$\frac{1}{2}$ cup sliced water chestnuts
60 g (2 oz) butter
salt and freshly ground pepper

Wash the beans and top and tail them. Cook in boiling salted water for 10 to 15 minutes, depending on how young the beans are. Drain and refresh under cold water.

Place back in the saucepan with the butter and the sliced water chestnuts and toss over a moderate heat until warmed through. Season with salt and pepper.
Note: Water chestnuts are available in cans from most delicatessens. When drained, any remaining may be covered with cold water and stored in the refrigerator. Change the water each week if storing them for any length of time.

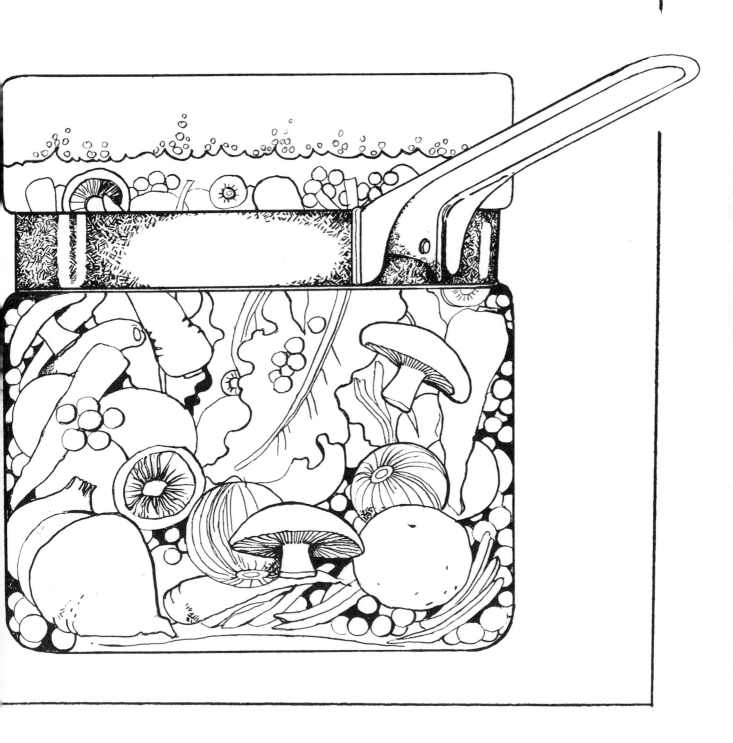

Vegetables

Those versatile vegetables

Spring comes at different times in Australia. It's early in the North and late in the South but when it comes, the display of fresh young vegetables is hard to resist.

When vegetables are at their peak, they are best cooked and served in the simplest way. Just boiled or steamed with a herb sprig added for flavour—mint for peas and new potatoes, oregano for zucchini, lemon thyme for button marrows and mushrooms and savory with beans.

The best accompaniment for these beautiful young vegetables is fresh butter. Just toss them in a little butter and give them a grinding of fresh pepper. But, if you're on a low cholesterol diet or if you're a weight-watcher try a squeeze of lemon juice instead.

Cooking vegetables, like soup, is a test of the cook's ability and ingenuity. The watchword is "undercook" rather than "overcook". Young vegetables need very little cooking. When still slightly crunchy they should be drained and refreshed under cold water to preserve their texture and fine colour.

There's an old rule that's still about and makes sense (though like all rules, there are exceptions):
Vegetables that grow under the ground should be placed in cold water and cooked in a covered saucepan and vegetables that grow above the ground should be cooked uncovered in boiling water.

Green Beans

When very young, green beans need only to be topped and tailed. Cook them whole or slice diagonally. Older beans will need the strings removed before cooking. The "stringless" bean is delicious and requires to be topped and tailed only.

Beans go well with garlic or finely sliced onion and look very fresh scattered with finely chopped parsley. A good grating of nutmeg is delicious too. Combine small whole beans with new potatoes for a beautiful vegetable dish.

Beans with Maître d'Hôtel Butter

500 g (1 lb) green beans
Maître d'Hôtel Butter:
60 g (2 oz) butter
1 tablespoon finely chopped parsley
squeeze of lemon juice

Top, tail and string the beans. Cook them whole in boiling salted water for 10 minutes. Drain and refresh under cold water. Place back in the saucepan over a low heat and allow to heat through. Arrange on a heated serving dish, season with freshly ground pepper and a slice of maître d'Hotel Butter. Serve the remaining butter cut into slices on a small dish.

Maître d'Hôtel Butter
Beat the butter until very creamy. Add the parsley and lemon juice. Spread the butter in a mound on a piece of aluminium foil.

Roll the butter in the foil to form a log shape about 2 cm (1 in) thick. Chill and serve sliced in rounds.

Green Beans and Butter Beans

500 g (1 lb) beans
salt
30 g (1 oz) butter
freshly ground pepper
freshly chopped parsley

Wash the beans and top and tail them. Bring two cups of water to the boil and add salt and beans. Cook for 10 to 15 minutes depending on the age of the beans. Drain and refresh under cold water.

Return them to the pan with the butter and shake the beans over a low heat until the butter is melted and the beans have warmed through. Season with freshly ground pepper. Scatter with parsley and serve hot.

Note: If you wish to serve the beans cold, boil as above and refresh them and then toss while warm in vinaigrette dressing and chill before serving.

Butter Beans

These beans resemble green beans but are pale butter yellow in colour. They are prepared in the same way as green beans but take less time to cook. They make an extremely good salad on their own or combined with green and purple beans.

Broad Beans

When really young, broad beans are eaten pod and all but the larger broad beans should be slipped out of their pods before cooking. Flavour them with fresh herbs, crushed garlic or with some finely chopped crisp bacon.

Broad Beans with Poulette Sauce

Broad beans, carrots and other vegetables served in a Poulette Sauce make a delicious vegetable entrée. This sauce is also good with brains, sweetbreads, boiled veal and chicken.

3 cups broad beans (shelled)
pinch salt
1 cup Velouté sauce (see page 18)
juice of ½ lemon
1 tablespoon finely chopped parsley

Place the beans into boiling salted water and cook for 5 to 10 minutes, according to their age. Drain, refresh under cold running water and remove the jacket of each bean.

Return to the saucepan with 1 tablespoon of the Velouté Sauce and warm them through. Place in a heated vegetable dish. Heat the remaining sauce with the lemon juice and chopped parsley and then spoon some of this sauce over the beans. Serve remaining sauce separately in a sauceboat.

Note: Frozen broad beans are available all the year round and are excellent.

Broccoli

Fresh broccoli should always be a bright green colour with compact heads and without any yellow buds. Soak head down in plenty of cold water with a little vinegar and trim off the tough stalk ends.

Stand the stalks of broccoli upright in a deep saucepan in about 2.5 cm (1 in) of boiling salted water. Cook for about 12 minutes until the stalks are just tender. Drain. Refresh under cold water and place on the heat with some melted butter. Serve hot.

Broccoli with Garlic Butter

1 bunch of broccoli or frozen broccoli
Garlic Butter:
1 clove of garlic, crushed with a pinch of
  salt
60 g (2 oz) butter
freshly ground pepper

Trim off the tough stalk ends. Soak broccoli head down in plenty of cold water with a little vinegar added. Drain and stand the broccoli upright in a deep saucepan in about 2.5 cm (1 in) of boiling salted water. Cook for about 12 minutes or until the stalks are tender. Drain and refresh under cold water. If using frozen broccoli cook according to package instructions. Make the Garlic Butter by mixing the crushed garlic with the butter which has been well creamed. Season with freshly ground pepper.

Reheat the Broccoli with Garlic Butter.

Cabbage

Cabbages should be tightly furled with a firm heart. This is the most delicious part. When preparing a cabbage first remove any discoloured outside leaves. These may be washed and used in the stockpot or in vegetable soups. Shred the rest of the cabbage or cut into wedges. Blanch in boiling salted water and then cook in butter for a few minutes. Season with salt and pepper.

Cabbage Wedges

Cut a cabbage into 6 or 8 wedges discarding any discoloured outside leaves. Place into a saucepan of boiling salted water. Lower the heat and simmer for 15 minutes. Drain and toss in a little melted butter. A teaspoon of caraway seeds may be added with the butter.

Buttered Cabbage

1 small cabbage or half a large one
60 g (2 oz) melted butter
salt and freshly ground pepper

Remove any discoloured outer leaves on the cabbage. Quarter the cabbage and remove the core. With the pointed end of the cabbage quarter placed down on a board to hold the cabbage leaves firmly, cut the leaves into shreds. Blanch in boiling salted water for two minutes and drain well.

Melt the butter in a good-sized saucepan, add the drained cabbage and cook for 8 to 10 minutes or until tender. Season with salt and pepper.

Braised Red Cabbage

60 g (2 oz) butter
½ red cabbage, shredded
1 tablespoon vinegar
2 apples, peeled and cut into thick slices
1 tablespoon sugar
salt
freshly ground pepper

Place the butter into a thick saucepan. Add the shredded cabbage and the vinegar, apples and sugar. Season with salt and pepper. Cover the saucepan and cook for 20 minutes. Serve hot or cold.

Carrots

Carrots are an indispensable flavouring for soups, stocks, sauces and casseroles. Young carrots picked when very tiny are a great treat. They should be cooked whole and just glazed with butter and sugar. Older carrots are also delicious cooked this way.

Vichy Carrots

**500 g (1 lb) small carrots or if large carrots
  cut in thick slices**
¼ cup water
30 g (1 oz) butter
1 tablespoon sugar
freshly ground pepper

Wash and scrape carrots with a small vegetable knife. Put into a heavy pan with the water, butter and sugar. Cover the pan and cook gently for about 20 minutes, taking the lid off for the last 10 minutes to allow the liquid to reduce and the carrots to become glazed. Season with freshly ground pepper.

Carrot Purée

Peel and cut carrots into large pieces. Place in cold salted water and cook for 30 minutes or until soft enough to mash.

Drain and push them through a coarse sieve. Mix with an equal amount of mashed potato, a good lump of butter, salt, freshly ground pepper with a good grating of nutmeg.

Eggplant

The eggplant is a deep purple-black fruit with white flesh. It is usually cut into slices and fried in olive oil (very often with some garlic).

Sometimes it is cut in half lengthways, stuffed and baked or dipped in batter and fried in deep fat. Eggplant is an essential ingredient of many of the Mediterranean vegetable dishes.

Before it is cooked, whether it is cut in slices or halves, the flesh is always sprinkled with salt which in the period of 20 to 30 minutes brings out its indigestible and bitter juices. The pieces are then drained, washed well and dried.

Fried Eggplant

1 large eggplant
salt
flour for coating
olive oil for frying
freshly ground pepper
2 cloves garlic crushed (optional)

Cut the eggplant into 1 cm (½ in) slices. Sprinkle with plenty of salt and allow to stand for at least 30 minutes. Drain off the liquid, wash the eggplant slices thoroughly and dry on paper towels.

Lightly flour slices. Add sufficient oil to just cover the base of a frying pan and fry the eggplant until golden-brown on both sides. Season with some freshly ground pepper and salt and arrange overlapping on a heated serving dish.

Note: If using garlic add to the hot oil just before the eggplant slices.

Top left: Green Peas—French Style (see recipe on page 236)
Centre left: Mushrooms Nicoise (see recipe on page 235)
Above left: Garlic Fried Sliced Peppers (see recipe on page 239)

Top right: Gratin Dauphinois (see recipe on page 242)
Above right: Curried Cauliflower (see recipe on page 248)

233

Stuffed Eggplant

2 medium eggplants
salt
olive oil
Filling:
2 tablespoons olive oil
1 small onion, chopped finely
750 g (1½ lb) minced lamb
1 teaspoon salt
1 teaspoon Tabasco
2 teaspoons tomato paste
2 tablespoons finely chopped mint
1½ cups cooked rice

Cut the eggplants in half lengthways. Make criss-cross incisions in the flesh. Sprinkle with salt and leave to drain for 30 minutes. Wash well and dry. Scoop out some of the inside flesh leaving about 1 cm (½ in) thickness and dice and set aside. Brush the eggplant halves with olive oil.

Filling:
Heat the oil and fry the onion gently until softened, add the scooped out eggplant and continue frying for 1 minute. Add the minced lamb and when lightly browned, season with salt and Tabasco. Stir in the tomato paste, mint and rice.

Correct the seasoning and stuff each eggplant half. Cover with oiled paper. Place on a baking sheet and cook in a moderate oven (350°F—170°C) for 30 minutes or until the eggplant is tender. Serve hot or cold.

Kohlrabi

Kohlrabi is a swelling of the stem of a plant which grows above the ground and is not, as is commonly thought, one of the root vegetables. It may be prepared in the same manner as turnips. Its flavour is rather like that of a turnip though it is more delicate.

Glazed Kohlrabi

2 kohlrabi
2 tablespoons sugar
60 g (2 oz) butter
1 cup water

Peel the kohlrabi and cut into thick slices or wedge-shaped pieces. Place in a heavy saucepan with the sugar, butter and water. Cover and cook until tender—about 20 minutes. Remove the lid and allow the liquid to evaporate until a thick syrup remains and the kohlrabi is glazed.

Kohlrabi Country-style

2 kohlrabi, peeled and cut into thick slices
1 tablespoon butter
1 tablespoon olive oil
1 onion, finely sliced
125 g (4 oz) shoulder ham, cubed
freshly ground pepper
½ cup dry white wine
½ cup stock

Heat the butter and oil and fry the onion until golden. Add the ham cubes and the slices of kohlrabi. Season with pepper. Add the wine and stock and cook gently until the kohlrabi is tender.

Mushrooms (Grilled)

250 g ($\frac{1}{2}$ lb) mushrooms
30 g (1 oz) butter
salt
freshly ground pepper

If you are using field mushrooms peel them and trim their stalks. For small cultivated mushrooms trim the stalks only, and wipe with a damp cloth. Heat the griller and place the mushrooms stalk end down on the grilling pan.

Brush the caps with melted butter. Grill for 2 minutes and turn them over. Brush with the remaining butter and sprinkle with a little salt. Return to the griller and continue cooking for another 2 minutes. Season with freshly ground pepper.

Mushrooms Nicoise

500 g (1 lb) mushrooms
1 lemon
salt and pepper
3 tablespoons olive oil
30 g (1 oz) butter
2 to 3 tomatoes
2 teaspoons each chopped parsley and
    tarragon (or 1 tablespoon parsley)
8 black olives, stoned

Wash mushrooms and trim stems. Put into a bowl and squeeze the juice of the lemon over. Season with salt and pepper.

Heat 2 tablespoons oil in a shallow fireproof pan or frying pan, add the butter and when melted add mushrooms and cook over a gentle heat, without browning, until tender, about 5 minutes.

Place dish in a hot oven (400°F—200°C) for 7 to 8 minutes. If using a frying pan keep the mushrooms over a gentle heat.

Peel, seed and chop tomatoes finely. Heat remaining tablespoon of oil and cook the tomatoes in this with salt and pepper and herbs until thoroughly heated. Stir in olives and spoon over the mushrooms.

Crumbed Mushroom Caps

Wipe mushroom caps with a damp cloth and brush with oil. Mix 1 tablespoon of finely chopped parsley with $\frac{1}{2}$ cup fine dry breadcrumbs and half a small crushed garlic clove. Roll the mushroom caps in this mixture, season with salt and pepper and grill 5 minutes on each side, brushing with more oil if necessary.

Note: When using mushrooms for kebabs, drop the mushrooms into boiling water for 1 minute and drain. They will now thread on the skewers without splitting.

Braised Chinese Mushrooms

This is one Chinese dish that can be cooked in advance. Serve the mushrooms hot as an accompaniment to a meat or seafood dish, or cold, cut into quarters or slices for hors d'oeuvres.

125 g (4 oz) dried mushrooms
1 tablespoon sugar
1 tablespoon Soy Sauce
1 teaspoon sesame oil
$\frac{3}{4}$ cup chicken stock
3 tablespoons peanut oil

Soak mushrooms in warm water for 20 minutes, then drain and squeeze out excess water. Cut off stems and discard.

Mix sugar, Soy Sauce, sesame oil and stock. Heat oil in a wok or frying pan and cook mushrooms, turning constantly, for several minutes. Add stock mixture.

Cover and simmer for 25 minutes, turning occasionally.

Peas

These are delicious sweet vegetables. And when flavoured with a little mint and fresh butter they are a superlative dish on their own and make the perfect partner for baby carrots and small button mushrooms.

If peas are to be shelled and kept for a time, wrap them in a damp towel or cover with their pods so they don't lose moisture. When cooking peas, a few young pea pods are often added for flavour. The water remaining in the saucepan after the peas have been cooked can be added to stock or used instead of water to make a gravy.

When buying peas remember you lose more than half their weight with shellings so you will need about 1 kg (2 lbs) for 4 healthy servings.

Green Peas

1 kg (2 lb) peas
2 cups water
pinch salt
1 sprig of mint
1 teaspoon sugar
30 g (1 oz) butter

Shell the peas. Bring the water to the boil, add a pinch of salt and add the peas with the mint and sugar. Cook for 10 minutes, drain well, refresh under cold water and return to the pan with the butter. Shake the peas over a low heat until the butter has completely melted.

Peas with Mushrooms

Prepare the peas as above. Slice 125 g (4 oz) mushrooms thickly. Toss in hot butter until lightly browned, season with salt and pepper and combine with the peas.

Green Peas (French-style)

This is the way in which petits pois, the tiny pea adored by the French, is cooked. The clever French housewife saves the tougher outside lettuce leaves for dishes such as this, as she knows they have all the flavour. Even frozen peas respond to this treatment.

1 kg (2 lb) fresh peas
6 lettuce leaves
12 spring onions
60 g (2 oz) butter
1 teaspoon sugar
salt to taste
3 tablespoons water
2 parsley sprigs
2 sprigs of chervil (or pinch of dried
   chervil)

Shred the lettuce finely. Shell the peas and peel the onions.

To a large saucepan add half the lettuce, onions, peas, sugar, salt, water, butter, parsley and chervil and then remaining lettuce. Cover the pan and cook over a gentle heat for 15-20 minutes until the peas and onions are quite tender. Shake the pan from time to time during cooking. Remove the parsley and chervil, adjust the seasoning and toss the ingredients in the pan to mix them.

Note: 500 g (1 lb) of frozen peas may be substituted for fresh ones.

Peas with Mushrooms

Braised Snow Peas

500 g (1 lb) snow peas
2 tablespoons oil
½ teaspoon salt
2 tablespoons stock or water
½ teaspoon sugar
2 teaspoons Soy Sauce

Wash peas, string and remove tops. Heat oil in a wok or frying pan, add peas and toss for 30 seconds, without browning. Add remaining ingredients, stir to coat peas, then cook further 1 minute. The peas should be tender, but still crisp. Serve immediately.

Spring Onions

Spring onions can be grown easily from seeds. This is a wonderful vegetable to have on hand fresh for slicing and adding flavour to other vegetables and for salads. They are also good served piping hot glazed with butter and sugar.

Glazed Onions

250 g (8 oz) spring onions or baby onions
30 g (1 oz) butter
1 teaspoon sugar
salt
freshly ground pepper

Peel the onions. If using spring onions trim off the stalks. Place in a saucepan of cold water. Bring to the boil and simmer for 5 minutes. Drain well. Place into a pan with the butter, sugar and season with salt and pepper. Cover the pan and cook gently for about 10 minutes until tender and well-glazed. Shake the pan frequently during this time to prevent the onions from sticking.
Note: When cooking small onions to add to a casserole omit the butter and sugar and cook them for 20 minutes in the water. Drain.

Braised Onions

½ cup stock
500 g (1 lb) small onions, peeled
30 g (1 oz) butter
salt and pepper

Bring the stock to the boil, add the onions and butter. Cover and cook gently for 10 minutes. Remove the lid and cook for a further 5 minutes to reduce the liquid. Season with salt and pepper.

Peppers

Peppers are also known as capsicum, bell pepper and pimento. They are the highly decorative and delicious fruit of a small plant and are available throughout the year. They may be coloured green, red or yellow or a combination of these colours. They are often stuffed with rice, fish or savoury meat and baked, fried in olive oil or combined with other vegetables in dishes with a Mediterranean flavour.

Before they are cooked or added to savoury dishes split them in two lengthways, cut away the pithy veins and remove the seeds. Cut into pieces or strips. Blanch in boiling salted water for 2 minutes and then proceed as the recipe indicates.

Garlic Fried Sliced Peppers

3 red peppers
2 green peppers
3 tablespoons olive oil
3 cloves garlic, crushed
salt
freshly ground pepper

Cut the peppers in half lengthways. Remove the seeds and pithy veins. Drop into boiling salted water for 2 minutes. Drain thoroughly and slice into strips. Dry on a paper towel. Heat the olive oil. Add the garlic and fry gently but do not allow it to colour. Add the peppers and sauté for 10 minutes.

Sicilian Stuffed Peppers

Stuffed peppers are found everywhere in the countries around the Mediterranean. This particular recipe with its filling of eggplant, tomato and olives comes from Sicily.

1 medium eggplant
salt
olive oil for frying
4 to 6 green or red peppers or a mixture
    of both
1 cup fresh tomato sauce (page 22)
12 green olives, stoned
2 tablespoons drained capers
salt and pepper

Dice eggplant and sprinkle with salt. Cover with a plate and leave for 1 hour. Wash well and dry thoroughly. Heat 2.5 cm (1 in) of oil in a frying pan and fry eggplant until golden. Drain.

Remove the core carefully from each pepper with a small sharp knife. Rinse the peppers under cold water to make sure no seeds remain. Drain and then drop into a pan of boiling water for 1 minute, drain and refresh under cold water.

Combine the tomato sauce with the eggplant, olives and capers. Season with salt and freshly ground pepper. Fill each pepper, place in an ovenproof dish in which they will stand up nicely and sprinkle with a little olive oil. Bake in a moderate oven (350°F—170°C) for about 1 hour, basting from time to time with the pan juices.

Serve piping hot or cold.

Potatoes

Potatoes are the best loved vegetable and a very valuable food. Wash them, peel them and place in cold salted water. Cover and cook them until they are easily pierced with a fork—about 20 to 30 minutes depending on the size. Drain and place back in a covered saucepan on a very low heat to dry them out. Add some butter or finely chopped parsley or serve as they are.

Creamy Mashed Potatoes

6 medium potatoes, peeled
salt
30 g (1 oz) butter
$\frac{1}{2}$-1 cup milk
freshly ground white pepper

Place the potatoes into saucepan and cover with cold, lightly salted water. Cook covered until the potatoes are easily pierced with a fork—about 20 minutes. Drain thoroughly, then shake the pan over the heat for a few minutes until potatoes are quite dry. Mash or put through a potato ricer or a coarse sieve.

Beat with a wooden spoon until very smooth. Scald the milk. Add the butter to the potatoes and gradually beat in the hot milk until the potatoes are light and fluffy. Season with salt and pepper.

Game Chips

New Potatoes

These are a vegetable dear to young and old. They are best eaten in the fingers with melted butter. Some people like to dip them into salt first and others like them tossed in butter and flavoured with fresh herbs.

500 g (1 lb) small new potatoes
2 cups water
pinch salt
sprig of mint
30 g (1 oz) butter
finely chopped mint or parsley

Wash and scrape the potatoes. Bring the water to the boil and add the potatoes with the salt and mint. Cook for 15 to 20 minutes according to the size.

When tender drain and return to the pan with the butter and toss until the butter is melted and each potato glistening. Sprinkle with finely chopped mint or parsley or a combination of both and serve hot.

Note: New potatoes are an exception to the rule and are placed into boiling salted water. Older potatoes, like other root vegetables, are placed into cold water.

Fried Potatoes or Chips

4 large even-sized potatoes
oil for deep frying
salt

Peel the potatoes and cut into 5 cm (2 inch) lengths, 1 cm ($\frac{1}{2}$ in) wide. Wash them and soak in ice-cold water. Dry thoroughly with paper towels.

Heat some oil in a deep heavy pan and when a thin blue haze rises from the surface (or a bread cube turns brown in less than 1 minute), lower the potatoes into it in a frying basket. This is not strictly necessary but makes it much easier. Cook until soft but not brown. Lift out.

Increase the temperature of the oil to very hot. Gently lower the potatoes into the hot oil. They will immediately become brown and crisp. Drain on crumpled absorbent paper. Sprinkle with salt and serve immediately.

Game Chips

Wafer thin potato chips are often served at Christmas with the Roast Turkey. Also good with pheasant.

1 kg (2 lb) old potatoes
oil or lard for deep frying
salt

Peel the potatoes, shape into cylinders so that each slice will be approximately the same diameter. Slice very finely with a sharp knife or with a mandolin. Soak the slices in cold water to remove the surface starch and dry thoroughly.

Heat the oil or lard to a temperature of 400°F—200°C and lower the potato slices gently into this. Keep them moving about so that they do not stick together. After a minute or two, the slices will begin to come back to the surface which will indicate that they are nearly cooked. At this stage they must be carefully watched as they turn colour very quickly. When golden and crisp, remove gently from the oil, drain on crumpled kitchen paper, sprinkle with salt and serve on a folded napkin.

Gratin Dauphinois

The mountain province of Dauphine in France produces excellent potatoes which are used in their "gratins". Cheese does not play any part in the genuine Gratin Dauphinois but we particularly enjoy the flavour of cheese when this dish is served with a baked ham.

1 kg (2 lb) potatoes
1 garlic clove, crushed
salt and freshly ground pepper
freshly grated nutmeg
125 g (4 oz) grated cheese (gruyère or
    emmenthaler)
1 cup cream
30 g (1 oz) butter

Peel and slice the potatoes very thinly. The slices should be as thin as a twenty cent piece.

With a piece of greaseproof paper rub the garlic around the inside of an ovenproof dish and butter it well.

Arrange the potato slices in concentric circles seasoning each with salt, pepper and nutmeg and sprinkling with grated cheese. Pour the cream over the layers, scatter the butter which has been cut into small pieces over the top and sprinkle with the remaining cheese. Bake in a moderate oven (350°F—170°C) for 1 hour or until the potatoes are tender and the top golden and crisp.

Brandied Sweet Potatoes

6 medium sweet potatoes
⅔ cup firmly packed brown sugar
¼ cup water
2 tablespoons butter
¼ cup seedless raisins
¼ cup brandy

Wash the sweet potatoes but do not peel. If the potatoes are very large, cut into smaller pieces. Boil in salted water to cover until barely soft—about 15 minutes. Drain, cool and peel. Arrange the slices in a greased shallow ovenproof dish. Place the brown sugar, water, butter and raisins in a saucepan and bring to the boil. Add the brandy and pour over the potatoes. Bake in a moderate oven (350°F—170°C) uncovered for 30 minutes, basting from time to time with the syrup in the dish.

Scalloped Potatoes

With so many ways to cook potatoes, how can anyone serve them only boiled, mashed or baked? In this tasty dish, the potatoes are sliced thinly, layered in a dish with butter, salt and freshly ground pepper, covered with milk, flavoured with nutmeg and topped with slices of gruyère cheese. This is a variation of the popular French dish, Gratin Dauphinois.

1 kg (2 lb) old potatoes
1 garlic clove
90 g (3 oz) butter
1 cup milk
freshly grated nutmeg
salt and freshly ground white pepper
60 g (2 oz) gruyère cheese

Peel potatoes, slice thinly into rounds and dry thoroughly in a cloth. Rub a shallow ovenproof dish with a cut clove of garlic and smear with 30 g (1 oz) of butter. Carefully arrange the potato slices in layers in the dish, seasoning each layer with salt and freshly ground pepper. Scald the milk and add a little freshly grated nutmeg. Season with salt and pepper. Cut the cheese into thin slices and arrange on top of potatoes.

Carefully pour over the milk and add the rest of the butter cut into small pieces. Bake in a moderate oven (350°F—170°C) for 40 to 45 minutes or until tender and golden. Cut in wedges and serve from the dish.

Top: Brussels Sprouts with Chestnuts (see recipe on page 247)
Above: Sicilian Stuffed Peppers (see recipe on page 239)

Potatoes en Papillote

New potatoes seasoned with butter and mint are cooked sealed in paper to capture the wonderful natural flavours.

750 g (1½ lb) small new potatoes
2 mint leaves, finely chopped or
   1 teaspoon dried chervil
60 g (2 oz) butter
salt

Scrape the potatoes. Cut a fair-size piece of greaseproof paper into a heart shape. Place the potatoes on one side of the paper with the butter and chopped mint or chervil, season with salt.

Fold the other side of the paper over and seal the edges completely.

Place on a baking sheet and cook in a moderate oven (375°F—190°C) for about 35 minutes. Take to the table in the bag.

Baked Stuffed Potatoes

4 old potatoes
60 g (2 oz) butter
4 rashers fried bacon
60 g (2 oz) cheese, grated
salt
freshly ground pepper

Scrub and dry the potatoes and bake in a hot oven (400°F—200°C) for 1 hour or until soft when pricked with a skewer.

Remove the potatoes, cut a cross in the top, scoop out the soft centre and place in a bowl. Mash lightly with a fork. Add the butter, the bacon which has been cut into small pieces and the cheese. Season with salt and pepper. Pile the mixture back into the potato skins and place back into the oven for about 10 minutes to heat through.

Variations:

Replace the bacon and cheese with:
- ¼ cup crumbled blue cheese, ¼ cup sour cream and 4 chopped shallots which have been sautéed in a little butter. Sprinkle tops with paprika.
- ½ cup freshly chopped mixed herbs. A spoonful of grated cheese is optional.
- 1 cup finely chopped celery and sprinkle potatoes with snipped chives.
- 2 tablespoons of finely chopped herbs and ½ cup red salmon.
- 2 tablespoons finely chopped chives and ¼ cup sour cream.
- 1 diced green pepper which has been cooked in oil for 10 minutes.
- 1 large onion, finely sliced, which has been fried in butter for 5 minutes or until golden brown.
- 60 g (2 oz) cream cheese mixed with 2 tablespoons of grated parmesan cheese. Sprinkle the tops of potatoes with parmesan and brown under grill.
- 1 tablespoon tomato paste. Sprinkle tops with breadcrumbs and butter and brown under grill.
- ½ cup sieved cooked spinach and nutmeg and sprinkle tops with grated cheese. Brown under grill.

Note: A beaten egg may be added to the mashed hot potatoes. This makes a rich dish that is a snack meal in itself.

Sugar-browned Potatoes

These caramelised potatoes are a great favourite in Denmark and are particularly good with ham and pork.

24 small new potatoes
125 g (4 oz) caster sugar
125 g (4 oz) clarified butter

Boil the potatoes in their jackets for 10 to 15 minutes or until just cooked. Let them cool a little, then peel them if skins are not a good colour.

Melt the sugar in a heavy frying pan over a low heat. Continue to cook the sugar slowly until it becomes a light brown caramel, stirring to prevent the sugar from burning. Stir in the melted butter and add as many potatoes as possible without crowding the pan. Shake the pan from time to time until the potatoes are coated with the caramel. Remove from the heat and serve as soon as possible.

Duchess Potatoes

Puréed potatoes rich with egg and butter which may be piped into small mounds or on to borders of seafood and meat dishes.

1 kg (2 lb) old potatoes
salt
freshly ground pepper
nutmeg
60 g (2 oz) butter
2 whole eggs

Peel the potatoes, wash them and cook them whole in salted water until they are easily pierced with a fork. Drain and place them back on a gentle heat, covered to dry.

Rub them through a sieve. Season with salt, pepper and a little nutmeg, then beat in the butter which has been cut into small pieces. When the purée is light and fluffy beat in the lightly beaten eggs.

Pipe into small mounds on to a greased baking sheet.

Brush with a little egg yolk and bake in a very hot oven (450°F—230°C) until lightly browned.

Noisette Potatoes

Potatoes cut into tiny balls the size of hazelnut, sautéed in butter till golden brown.

1 kg (2 lb) old potatoes
60 g (2 oz) clarified butter
salt

Peel the potatoes and place into a bowl of cold water to prevent discolouring. Cut into tiny balls with a melon baller —the smaller the better. Place in the bowl of water until ready to use.

Melt the butter and when hot, dry the potatoes thoroughly and place them in pan. Sauté until golden brown and tender— about 10 minutes. Season with salt before serving.

Leeks Vinaigrette

Leeks Vinaigrette

6 young leeks
Vinaigrette dressing:
3 tablespoons olive oil
1 tablespoon wine vinegar
1 garlic clove crushed with ½ teaspoon salt
freshly ground pepper
½ teaspoon French mustard
1 tablespoon finely chopped herbs
   (parsley, chives, tarragon, oregano)

Slit the leeks right down one side and wash thoroughly under cold running water to remove any grit. Trim the root ends and remove any coarse outer leaves. Place in boiling salted water and allow to simmer for 8 minutes or until tender but not breaking up. Drain and refresh under running cold water. Place in a serving dish.

Make the dressing by combining the oil, vinegar, garlic crushed with salt, pepper and mustard. Stir in the chopped herbs and spoon the dressing over the leeks. Allow them to marinate for at least 2 hours before serving. Serve chilled.

● Many vegetables may be served in this way. They are cooked for about 5-8 minutes and then steeped in the vinaigrette.

Variations:
● 500 g (1 lb) small onions.
● 500 g (1 lb) French beans. Top and tail, and if very small cook whole.
● Cauliflower. Break a small head into pieces and cook.
● Carrots. Cut into small sticks or if very small leave whole.
● Celery. Cut into small sticks and cook for 5 minutes.
● Button mushrooms. Wipe with cloth dipped in lemon juice and water and place into boiling water for 5 minutes before steeping in the vinaigrette dressing.

Brussels Sprouts with Chestnuts

1 kg (2 lb) brussels sprouts or 580 g
   (2 packets) frozen sprouts
250 g (8 oz) whole canned chestnuts
1 cup chicken stock
1 stick celery
1 teaspoon sugar
1 tablespoon butter
freshly ground pepper

Blanch fresh or frozen sprouts in boiling salted water for 7 minutes. Drain.

In a saucepan, place the sprouts and the drained whole chestnuts, stock, piece of celery, and sugar. Bring to the boil and simmer for 10 minutes. Remove the celery, drain the brussels sprouts and chestnuts and then toss them over a gentle heat with the butter. Season with freshly ground pepper.

Red Cabbage with Allspice

1 large onion, thinly sliced
1 medium head of red cabbage, shredded
60 g (2 oz) butter
1 cup red wine
1 teaspoon brown sugar
¼ teaspoon ground allspice
salt and freshly ground black pepper

Melt the butter in a large saucepan and sauté the onion until it is golden. Stir in the cabbage. Add the wine, brown sugar, allspice and season with salt and pepper. Cover and cook over a moderate heat until tender but still slightly crisp. Serve with pork.

Cauliflower

Cauliflower should be very white with firm compact flowerets. Before cooking, remove the leaves and heavy stalk and soak head downwards in cold water with a little lemon juice for a few minutes. This helps to keep it white.

Make a crosswise cut in the stalk end and put the cauliflower downwards into boiling salted water. Cook uncovered for about 12 minutes or until you can pierce the stalk easily. Drain.

Refresh under cold water and then reheat with butter, a little lemon juice and season with freshly ground black pepper. Cauliflower broken into flowerets is cooked in the same way until just tender.

Curried Cauliflower

1 kg (2 lb) cauliflower
45 g (1½ oz) ghee or butter
2.5 cm (1 in) green ginger
1 onion
½ teaspoon turmeric
1 teaspoon curry powder or curry paste
1 teaspoon paprika
2 teaspoons salt
pinch chilli powder (optional)
1 teaspoon garam masala

Break cauliflower into sprigs and cut into 1 cm (½ in) thick pieces, taking care to keep some of the stalk with the flower. Wash and drain. In a deep frying pan, heat ghee and fry chopped ginger and onion. Add turmeric, curry powder and paprika. Put in slices of cauliflower and allow to sizzle for 5 to 10 minutes. Add salt and chilli powder, if used. Keep covered on low heat until tender, turning frequently with a spatula (*not* a spoon) to avoid crushing. Remove lid and allow any liquid to evaporate. Add garam masala 5 minutes before taking off heat. This curry goes well with rice and curried meat dishes.

Other vegetables may be cooked in much the same way as this cauliflower recipe:
- Substitute zucchini cut into thick slices for cauliflower, then proceed with recipe.
- Top and tail beans, cook in boiling, salted water for 5 minutes, drain, then proceed with recipe.
- Chokoes—peel, cut into 6 pieces, cook in boiling salted water for 5 minutes, drain, then follow cauliflower recipe above.

Grilled Tomatoes

If the tomatoes are large, cut in halves. Cut a thin slice from the top of each, season with salt and freshly ground black pepper and brush with oil. Place under a preheated griller and cook (rounded side up first) for 2 minutes. Turn and cook a further 2 to 3 minutes or until brown and tender when tested with the point of a sharp knife.

A little sugar may be sprinkled on the cut surface after the tomatoes have been turned.

Sautéed Tomatoes

6 ripe, red medium tomatoes
30 g (1 oz) butter
salt and freshly ground pepper
freshly chopped parsley

Peel the tomatoes. Melt the butter in a sauté or large frying pan with a lid and add the tomatoes. Season with salt and pepper and cover. Cook very gently for 4 to 5 minutes or until the tomatoes are just soft but have not lost their shape. Sprinkle with chopped parsley and serve immediately.

Tomatoes in Sour Cream

6 firm tomatoes
1 onion, finely chopped
salt and freshly ground black pepper
60 g (2 oz) butter
1 cup sour cream

Cut the tomatoes into thick slices and season with salt and pepper. Melt the butter in a frying pan and fry the onion until it is golden. Add the tomato slices and cook over a low heat for 5 minutes. Stir in the sour cream and cook for about 3 minutes, or until the cream is heated through. Do not allow it to boil. Serve with grilled steak or lamb chops.

Tomatoes Provençale

2 medium tomatoes
salt
freshly ground pepper
$\frac{1}{4}$ cup soft breadcrumbs
2 teaspoons melted butter
1 garlic clove, crushed

Halve the tomatoes, season with salt and pepper. Mix the breadcrumbs with the butter and garlic, season with salt and pepper. Spoon on to the tomato halves and grill under a moderate heat until the crumbs have browned and the tomatoes heated through or bake in a moderately hot oven (375°F—190°C) for 15 minutes.

Zucchini

1$\frac{1}{2}$ lb (750 g) zucchini
salt
30 g (1 oz) butter or 2 tablespoons olive
　oil
freshly ground black pepper

Top and tail the zucchini and slice them diagonally. Blanch in boiling salted water, drain and return to the saucepan with the hot butter or oil. Continue cooking gently until the zucchini are tender, about 5 minutes. Season with the freshly ground pepper and serve.

Baked Zucchini with Mozzarella

In Naples, many of the pizzas and vegetable dishes combine the colours of the Italian flag: The red tomatoes, the white mozzarella cheese and the green of zucchini or basil. This vegetable dish, or one extremely like it, can be found in nearly every Neapolitan restaurant.

750 g (1$\frac{1}{2}$ lb) zucchini
salt
olive oil
2 teaspoons tomato paste
$\frac{1}{2}$ small onion, finely chopped
250 g ($\frac{1}{2}$ lb) ripe tomatoes, peeled,
　seeded and chopped
2 sprigs of basil, finely chopped
125 g (4 oz) mozzarella cheese, sliced
　thinly
2 anchovy fillets, cut into quarters
　lengthwise
freshly ground black pepper

Trim the zucchini and cut into thin slices. Sprinkle with salt and leave to drain for 30 minutes. Wash and dry thoroughly with paper towels. Heat some olive oil and fry the zucchini until lightly golden. Drain on paper towels.

Dilute the tomato paste with a little warm water. Heat 1 tablespoon of olive oil, add the onion, and when it softens add the tomatoes, tomato paste and basil. Cook over a fairly high heat for about 8 to 10 minutes.

Brush an ovenproof dish with oil, cover the bottom with zucchini, spread with the tomato, then cover with the mozzarella cheese. Arrange the anchovies on top in a pattern and season with pepper. Bake in a moderate oven (350°F—170°C) for about 30 minutes or until the cheese has melted and begun to brown.

Zucchini with Tomatoes

500 g (1 lb) small zucchini
1 tablespoon olive oil
1 large garlic clove, crushed
500 g (1 lb) tomatoes, peeled and seeded
salt
freshly ground pepper
sprig of oregano

Slice the ends of the zucchini and wash well. Leave them whole if tiny, otherwise cut into 2.5 cm (1 in) diagonal slices. Dry thoroughly. Heat the olive oil and add the garlic. Fry gently for about 30 seconds and then add the zucchini and toss in the oil.

Chop the tomatoes roughly and combine with the zucchini. Season with salt and pepper and add the oregano. Cook covered for about 10 minutes over a very gentle heat. Remove the oregano sprig before serving and sprinkle with finely chopped parsley.

Silverbeet

Silverbeet may be cooked in any of the ways used for spinach. The leaves are separated from the heavy stalk and washed well in several changes of water. The stalks themselves make a delicious vegetable when cooked separately.

Buttered Silverbeet

1 bunch silverbeet
salt
freshly ground pepper
60 g (2 oz) butter
nutmeg
sprig of rosemary, optional

Trim off the heavy stalk and put aside. Wash the leaves thoroughly in cold running water or soak them in several changes of water. Pack in a saucepan as they are. The water remaining on the leaves is quite sufficient. Season with salt and pepper. A small rosemary sprig added at this stage gives a delicious flavour. Add a nut of butter and cover the saucepan with a lid.

Place over a moderately high heat and cook about 8 minutes shaking the pan from time to time. Drain well. Chop the spinach. Heat the remaining butter in the saucepan and toss the spinach in it until heated through. Adjust seasoning and add a pinch of nutmeg.

Creamed Spinach

1 bunch spinach OR 1 packet frozen
   spinach
salt
freshly ground pepper
30 g (1 oz) butter
$\frac{1}{4}$ cup cream
pinch of ground nutmeg

Remove the stalks. Wash the spinach thoroughly and pack it into a saucepan. There will be sufficient water remaining on the leaves in which to cook it. Season with salt and pepper. Cover with a tight fitting lid and cook gently for about 10 minutes, shaking the pan from time to time. Drain. Press out all the moisture and pass through a sieve.

If using frozen spinach, allow it to thaw and press out all the moisture. Omit the preliminary cooking.

Heat the butter until it just starts to turn a light brown. Stir in the spinach. Increase the heat and cook until all the surplus moisture has evaporated. Add the cream and season with pepper and nutmeg.

Top: Cabbage Pirog (see recipe overleaf)
Above: Zucchini with Tomatoes

Cabbage Pirog

This could be described as a large Piroshki. It has the same light, soft bread dough on the outside and a delicious filling inside. There are a variety of fillings used. In our version, cabbage, chopped hard-boiled eggs and speck are the main ingredients.

½ small cabbage
125 g (4 oz) speck or bacon pieces
2 hard-boiled eggs
1 teaspoon sugar
salt, freshly ground pepper
basic yeast dough
milk
1 egg, beaten

Remove the hard core from the cabbage and chop finely. Place in a colander and pour boiling water over to blanch. Place immediately under cold running water and then dry well with kitchen paper.

Cut the speck into small dice and place in the frying pan over a medium heat. Cook for 2 to 3 minutes until it starts to colour. Add the cabbage and toss with the speck and fry for 10 minutes, stirring from time to time to prevent the cabbage sticking. Remove from the heat and combine with the roughly chopped hard-boiled eggs, sugar, salt and pepper.

Place the risen dough on a floured board, knead lightly and quickly and divide in half. Place one half on a greased baking tray. Press out gently to form a 1 cm (½ in) circle. Spread the filling evenly over the dough to within 1 cm (½ in) of the edge. Brush edge with milk. Press out remaining dough to a circle of the same size and cover the filling. Pinch edges of dough together. Cover with a damp cloth and leave in a warm place for 15 minutes to prove.

Brush top with beaten egg. Bake in a hot oven (400°F—200°C) for about 30 minutes or until the pirog is golden brown. Before removing the pirog from the oven, tap the crust with your knuckles. It will sound hollow when it is cooked. Accompany with a bowl of sour cream.

Basic Yeast Dough:

30 g (1 oz) compressed yeast
1 tablespoon sugar
3 cups plain flour
1¼ cups milk
125 g (4 oz) butter
2 teaspoons salt
1 egg yolk

Stir the yeast and half the sugar in a small bowl until dissolved. Sprinkle with 1 teaspoon of the measured sifted flour and leave in a warm place. Gently heat the milk, butter, salt and remaining sugar until lukewarm, stirring occasionally.

Sift the remaining flour into a large warm bowl and make a well in the centre. Pour in the lukewarm milk mixture, add the yeast and lightly beaten egg yolk. Stir with a wooden spoon, gradually incorporating the flour.

Beat the dough vigorously with your hand until it becomes smooth and elastic. This process will take about 3 minutes. Sprinkle a little extra flour over the top, cover with a damp cloth or some plastic wrap and leave in a warm place for about 1 hour until it has doubled in bulk.

Braised Celery

1 head of celery
60 g (2 oz) butter
½ cup light veal or chicken stock
salt and freshly ground pepper

Remove string fibres from celery stalks and cut into 5 cm (2 in) lengths. Blanch celery by plunging into boiling, salted water for a few minutes. Drain well. Place celery, butter and stock into a saucepan and season with salt and pepper. Cover with 2 sheets of damp greaseproof paper and the saucepan lid. Allow to braise for 15 minutes. Remove lid and paper and reduce liquid until celery is glazed.

Brunoise Garnish

1 carrot, scraped
1 stick celery
1 medium onion, peeled
1 shallot, trimmed
30 g (1 oz) butter
3 tablespoons consommé

Cut the carrot, celery, onion, and shallot (including the green leaves) into fine dice. In a small saucepan melt the butter, add the vegetables and consommé. Cover with a round of waxed paper with a small hole in the centre and cover the pan. Braise the vegetables on a very gentle heat for about 15 minutes or until very tender. Drain and add to hot consomme just before serving.

Note: A good canned beef consommé may be substituted. Just flavour with dry sherry and add the Brunoise Garnish.

Ratatouille

This combination of colourful vegetables cooked in olive oil is excellent with grills. Ratatouille can also be served hot or cold as a first course, as a filling for omelets or with pan-fried fish.

2 medium eggplants
4 onions, finely sliced
4 tomatoes, peeled and sliced
2 green peppers, cut into strips
3 garlic cloves, peeled and finely chopped
4 zucchini, sliced (optional)
½ cup olive oil
salt and freshly ground black pepper
125 g (4 oz) black olives
chopped parsley to garnish

Cut unpeeled eggplants into 2 cm (¾ in) slices. With a sharp knife score each slice in a criss-cross pattern 5 mm (¼ in) deep on each side. Sprinkle with salt and allow to stand covered for 1 hour. Drain and rinse under cold water and dry on paper towels.

Arrange the vegetable in a medium size pan in layers. First the onion and garlic, then the green pepper, eggplant slices, zucchini and lastly the tomato slices. Season each layer with salt and black pepper. Pour oil over the vegetables. Cover and simmer for 40 minutes. Serve hot or cold, garnished with black olives and finely chopped parsley.

Mixed Vegetable Curry

Vegetables have unusual flavour prepared in this way. They should be tender and crisp when cooked.

½ cup oil
½ teaspoon mustard seed
6 to 8 curry leaves
1 teaspoon turmeric
2 cloves garlic, crushed
2.5 cm (1 in) piece green ginger, grated
   finely
pinch chilli powder (optional)
3 carrots, cut into strips
250 g (8 oz) green beans, strung and cut
   diagonally into 2.5 cm (1 in) pieces
½ small cabbage, shredded
salt to taste

Heat oil, fry mustard seed and curry leaves for a minute or two. Add turmeric, garlic, ginger and chilli powder and fry until golden. Turn in carrots and beans and fry over medium heat, stirring for 8 to 10 minutes until vegetables are half-cooked and still crisp. Add cabbage and fry for further 5 minutes. Add salt to taste, cover and simmer 2 to 3 minutes. Serve at once.

rice
and pasta

Pasta

Egg Pasta

2 cups plain flour
2 large eggs
cold water

Sift the flour into a bowl, make a well in the centre and add the eggs. Stir with a knife adding a little cold water (about 3 tablespoons) and form into a firm dough with the hands. Turn out on to a floured board and knead, turning and pushing out with the heel of the hand. Knead for about 15 minutes until the dough is smooth and elastic. The dough will be stiff at first but will become more pliable as you knead. Shape into a ball, dust with a little flour and wrap in plastic wrap. Place in the refrigerator and allow to stand for at least 30 minutes.

Roll out the dough on a slightly floured surface until it is paper thin. Sprinkle the board with a little more flour occasionally to prevent the pasta sticking to it. Cut into the desired shapes. The pasta may be left for 30 minutes before cooking. Just sprinkle a towel with a little flour and lay the pasta on it.

● Egg pasta may be used to make any of the following:

Tagliatelle (ribbon noodles)
Roll the pasta dough to an oblong shape. Starting from the shorter side, roll up dough, then cut across into 10 mm ($\frac{1}{2}$ in.) strips. Unravel each strip and spread on a lightly floured tea towel until required. Drop into boiling salted water for about 5 minutes or until the pasta is tender. Drain and serve with a sauce or with butter and grated parmesan cheese.

Tagliolini
Roll up dough as above but cut into thin 5 mm ($\frac{1}{4}$ in) strips. Serve similarly or in soup.

Lasagne
Cut into oblongs about 8 × 10 cm (3 × 4 in) and follow directions for Green Lasagne (see page 263).

Ravioli
Divide pasta into two sheets—place teaspoons of the desired filling 5 cm (2 in) apart in regular lines on one sheet of pasta. Brush between moulds of filling with water then cover with the other pasta sheet. Press firmly between mounds, sealing the two sheets of dough together and cut into squares with a pastry wheel. Cook in boiling salted water for 15 minutes. Drain, toss in butter and grated parmesan cheese or in Ragu sauce (page 263).

Lasagne (see recipe on page 262)

257

How to Cook Noodles

Drop bundles of noodles in a large pan of boiling, salted water with 1 teaspoon oil added. When the bundles begin to soften, separate with a chopstick or fork. Take care not to overcrowd pan.

When tender, drain the noodles in a colander and rinse under running water. Drain again, then lay on a tray covered with absorbent paper. Sprinkle lightly with about 1 tablespoon oil to prevent sticking.

Cook the noodles in one of the following ways:

Crisp-Fried Noodles

Heat 1 cup oil in a wok or frying pan and fry handfuls of noodles separately, turning once or twice until brown on both sides. Drain and repeat with more noodles. Use for Chow Mein dishes.

Soft-Fried Noodles

Heat 2 tablespoons oil and fry noodles until heated through, turning constantly in the wok. Serve with Chow Mein or other braised meat or vegetable dishes.

Green Pasta

**1 × 315 g (10 oz) packet frozen chopped
spinach
2½ cups plain flour
1 egg
cold water or extra plain flour**

Put the spinach in a saucepan and stir over a low heat until melted. Turn into a fine sieve and press with a spoon to extract all the liquid. When cool enough to handle, squeeze the spinach with the hand to extract as much of the remaining liquid as possible. Sift the flour into a bowl or on to a pastry board and make a well in the centre.

Put the egg and spinach in the well in the flour. Combine the egg and spinach and then using a palette knife gradually incorporate the flour. It may be necessary to add a little cold water—or more flour—to make a firm dough.

Scrape the board clean using a palette knife to prevent flecks of flour in the green dough.

Knead dough on a floured board until smooth which will take about 15 minutes. Lightly dust with flour and wrap in clear plastic. Chill in the refrigerator for at least 20 minutes.

Halve the dough. Roll out on a floured board until paper thin. Cut into strips for green noodles.

Cut into rectangles 8 × 10 cm (3 × 4 in) for Green Lasagne. Spread out on to a lightly floured tea towel until ready for use.
- A simple way to cut pasta into noodles is to fold the pasta into three lengthwise and then to cut across into strips of the desired width. Unfold and use as desired.

Green Buttered Noodles

**1 quantity of homemade green pasta
cut into 1 cm (½ in) strips OR 250 g
(8 oz) packed green noodles
60 g (2 oz) butter
grated Parmesan cheese**

Add salt and 1 tablespoon olive oil to a large pan of rapidly boiling water and drop in the noodles. Stir the pasta after it is added to separate each strand and then allow it to boil until tender—about 10 minutes for homemade pasta, 15 minutes for bought. Drain in a colander. Place the noodles back in the pan with the butter and toss until each strand is glistening. Pile into a warm serving dish and grate parmesan cheese over the top.

Polenta Ring with Chicken Livers

(Anello di Polenta con fegatini)

Golden polenta, set into a ring which is filled with sautéed chicken livers and mushrooms in a wine sauce.

Polenta ring:
6 cups of water
2 teaspoons salt
1½ cups polenta
Filling:
3 slices lean bacon, diced
30 g (1 oz) butter
500 g (1 lb) chicken livers
250 g (8 oz) mushrooms, sliced
salt and freshly ground pepper
3 small sage leaves
¼ cup dry white wine

Polenta Ring

Bring the water to the boil with the salt and gradually add the polenta, stirring constantly with a wooden spoon to keep it smooth. Cook over a moderate heat stirring frequently for about 30 minutes or until the polenta comes away cleanly from the sides of the pan. Turn into a greased ring tin and keep warm in a larger pan of hot water while preparing the chicken livers.

Chicken Liver Filling

Place the bacon into a frying pan and sauté until crisp. Add the butter, chicken livers and mushrooms and sauté over a medium flame just long enough to brown the livers, about 2 minutes. Season with salt and pepper and add sage and wine. When the wine starts to boil, lower the flame and cook for 2 to 3 minutes. Remove the sage leaves.

Ease the polenta away from the edge of the tin and then turn on to a serving dish.

Fill the ring with the mushrooms and livers and then spoon the sauce over them.

Polenta Baked in Tomato Sauce with Parmesan Cheese

1 quantity of basic polenta
1 cup tomato sauce (page 22)
freshly grated parmesan cheese

Turn the cooked polenta into a greased baking tray and, when cool, cut into 5 cm (2 in) squares. Place in a lightly greased, shallow ovenproof dish, spoon over the tomato sauce and sprinkle generously with parmesan cheese. Bake in a moderately hot oven (375°F—190°C) for 30 to 40 minutes or until a golden brown.

Polenta Casserole

1 quantity of thick polenta
500 g (1 lb) mushrooms, sliced
30 g (1 oz) butter
3 cups cooked chicken, diced
1 quantity tomato sauce
½ cup grated parmesan cheese

Spread polenta in a buttered casserole dish. Sauté the mushrooms in the butter for 3 minutes and scatter over the polenta with the chicken. Coat with the sauce and sprinkle with the parmesan cheese. Bake in a moderate oven (350°F—170°C) for 45 minutes. Serves 6.

Canneloni

Basic Thick Polenta

6 cups water
2 teaspoons salt
1½ cups of fine polenta

Bring the water to the boil with the salt and gradually add the polenta, stirring constantly with a wooden spoon to keep it smooth. Cook over a moderate heat, stirring frequently for about 50 minutes, or until the polenta comes away cleanly from the sides of the pan. This produces a thick polenta, suitable for baked, grilled or fried dishes. Use as required.

At this stage, the polenta may be turned into a greased baking tray, left to cool, then cut into squares, or turned into a greased ring tin, then turned out to be filled with chicken livers and mushrooms (see recipe page 259) or it can be turned into a greased cake tin, cut into squares, then served warm with freshly grated parmesan.

Rich Baked Polenta

1 quantity of basic thick polenta
125 g (4 oz) Gruyère or Emmenthal cheese
freshly ground black pepper
45 g (1½ oz) butter

Turn the boiled polenta into a deep buttered cake tin and leave until quite cold. Turn out on to a board and cut into 5 mm (¼ in) slices. Place a layer of polenta in a buttered ovenproof dish, cover with some thin slices of cheese and season with black pepper. Repeat these layers until the ingredients are used up, ending with a layer of polenta. Cut the butter into small pieces and scatter over the top. Bake in a hot oven (400°F—200°C) until well-browned.

Note: In Italy, a butter cheese called Fontina is used in this dish. When unavailable, Swiss Gruyère is the closest substitute.

● When a recipe calls for thin slices of polenta, allow the boiled polenta to cool completely, then slice with a fine stainless steel wire or a thick piece of thread.

Canneloni

6 packaged canneloni tubes
Filling:
4 fresh Italian pork sausages
2 cups ricotta cheese
5 tablespoons grated parmesan cheese
1 beaten egg
salt
freshly ground pepper
90 g (3 oz) butter
grated parmesan cheese
1 cup chicken stock

Cook the canneloni tubes in plenty of salted boiling water for 12 minutes. Drain in a colander.

Make the filling by pricking the sausages with a fork and simmering them in a little water for 20 minutes or until the water has evaporated. Brown the sausages on all sides in their own fat. Remove the sausage skin and mince or chop finely. Add ricotta and parmesan cheese, combine with the beaten egg and season with salt and pepper. Cool the stuffing and fill into a piping bag without a tube. Pipe into the canneloni tubes, or spoon in, forcing mixture in from one end.

Arrange the canneloni side by side in a well-buttered ovenproof dish. Put pieces of butter on top and then sprinkle generously with parmesan cheese and pour the chicken stock over the canneloni. Cook in a moderate oven (350°F—170°C) for 15 minutes until well-heated through and the butter, cheese and stock have formed a rich sauce.

Lasagne

Lasagne is an excellent choice for a large party dish. It can be made easily in large quantities and it doesn't hurt it to stand in a low oven for some time. Usually the filling is a combination of meat and sauce and cream sauce with parmesan cheese. This variation is rather more unusual with a filling of tiny meatballs, tomato sauce and three types of cheese which form a golden creamy covering.

750 g (1½ lbs) minced topside of beef

salt and freshly ground pepper

4 tablespoons olive oil

500 g (1 lb) packet lasagne

3 cups Tomato Sauce

500 g (1 lb) ricotta or cottage cheese

500 g (1 lb) mozzarella cheese

1 cup grated Parmesan cheese

Season the meat with salt and pepper. Shape into balls a little larger than a marble. Heat the olive oil in a frying pan and brown the meatballs in three portions, so that the oil keeps hot and free from moisture. Then place all the meatballs back in the pan and allow them to cook gently for 5 minutes.

Bring a large pot of water to the boil, add salt and place the lasagne pasta in the boiling water gently easing it around the pot as it softens. Boil for 12 minutes or until tender. Drain and refresh in cold water. Leave in cold water until ready to use.

Butter a large baking dish or ovenproof casserole and spoon one-third of the tomato sauce into it. Arrange half of the lasagne pasta on top and then spoonfuls of ricotta cheese. Slice the mozzarella cheese and arrange in a layer and sprinkle with one-third of the parmesan cheese.

Spoon over another third of the tomato sauce and then add the meatballs, one-third of the cheese and the remaining lasagne pasta. Coat with remaining tomato sauce and then add remaining cheeses, ending with a layer of parmesan cheese. Bake in a moderate oven (350°F—170°C) for about 45 minutes or until the top is golden.

Note: If preferred instead of shaping the minced meat into meatballs it can just be browned, seasoned and cooked for 5 minutes and then arranged in a layer as indicated in the recipe.

Tomato Sauce

Heat 3 tablespoons of olive oil in a saucepan, add ½ stalk chopped celery, 1 finely-chopped onion and 1 crushed garlic clove and brown lightly. Add 500 g (1 lb) ripe tomatoes or a 470 g (15 oz) can of tomatoes, ½ cup tomato purée and 1 tablespoon of tomato paste. Season with salt and freshly-ground black pepper adding a bayleaf and bouquet of herbs at the same time. Cook gently for 45 minutes. Remove the bayleaf and bouquet garni and rub through a fine sieve.

Green Lasagne

1 quantity of homemade green pasta OR
250 g (8 oz) commercial green lasagne
1 quantity Ragu Sauce
1 quantity Béchamel Sauce
grated Parmesan cheese

If making fresh green pasta prepare dough. Divide in half and roll each half out thinly to a rectangle, 40 × 45 cm (16 × 18 in). Trim edges and cut dough into oblongs 8 × 10 cm (3 × 4 in). Add salt to a large pan of rapidly boiling water and drop in the pasta oblongs one at a time. Cook in at least 2 lots. Boil the pasta until tender, about 10 minutes for home-made pasta, 15 minutes for bought. Turn into a colander, rinse with cold water and place pasta on a clean cloth so they are not touching.

Prepare Ragu sauce and Béchamel sauce.

Butter a large deep ovenproof dish and spoon some of the Ragu sauce on the bottom, then a layer of Béchamel, then a layer of green lasagne. Commence again with Ragu then Béchamel and green lasagne until the dish is filled, ending with a layer of Ragu sauce and Béchamel sauce. Sprinkle generously with grated parmesan cheese. Bake in a moderate oven (350°F—170°C) for 40 minutes or until the cheese has melted and the top golden.

Ragu Sauce (Bolognese)

185 g (6 oz) bacon, both fat and lean
1 tablespoon butter
2 onions, finely chopped
2 carrots, finely chopped
1 stick celery, finely chopped
500 g (1 lb) minced beef
250 g (8 oz) chicken livers, chopped
2 tablespoons tomato paste
1 cup white wine
salt
freshly ground pepper
nutmeg
2 cups beef stock

Cut the bacon into very small pieces and brown gently in the butter. Add the onion, carrot and celery and stir them into the butter. Allow them to fry gently until lightly browned. Add the minced beef and stir until it browns. Add the chicken livers and cook for about 2 minutes. Stir in the tomato paste and the white wine. Allow the wine to come to the boil and reduce a little. Season with salt, pepper and nutmeg and pour on the beef stock. Cover the pan and simmer gently for 40 minutes.

Béchamel Sauce

60 g (2 oz) butter
3 tablespoons flour
1 bay leaf
$2\frac{1}{4}$ cups milk
salt
freshly ground pepper
nutmeg

Melt the butter and stir in the flour to form a roux. When thoroughly combined remove from the heat, add the bay leaf and the milk by degrees stirring it until a smooth sauce is obtained. Place back on the heat and season with salt, pepper and nutmeg. Bring to the boil and allow to cook for 5 minutes.

● Lasagne may be varied. It may be made with egg pasta, home made or bought in packets. Bought lasagne is packaged either in sheets or ribbons which are at least 2.5 cm (1 in) wide and sometimes have frilled edges.

Mozzarella cheese cut into slices may be layered between the meat and the sauce. Also a beaten egg is sometimes added to the topping of Béchamel sauce. Just fold the egg into the remaining sauce and spread over the top before baking.

Spaghetti

Spaghetti, like all pasta, should be cooked in lots of boiling salted water. Allow at least 12 cups of water for 250 g (8 oz) of pasta, and 2 teaspoons of salt. A tablespoon of olive oil added to the water helps the pasta to stay separated.

To cook spaghetti:
Have the pot filled with boiling water. Hold the spaghetti at one end and place in the boiling water curling it around as it softens until the whole strands are submerged. Stir to prevent the pasta sticking together and add 1 tablespoon of olive oil. Cook in the boiling water until tender but still firm to the touch (about 12 minutes). Remove the pot from the heat, pour in about 2 cups of iced water to stop the spaghetti cooking and drain in a colander. Place the spaghetti back into the pan on the heat and add 4 tablespoons of butter or olive oil. Toss the spaghetti until each strand is coated in butter or olive oil. Season with freshly ground pepper. Serve with a bowl of grated parmesan cheese.

Variations:
- Crush 1 garlic clove and add to the butter or oil before mixing into the spaghetti.
- Crush 2 anchovy fillets and 1 teaspoon capers and mix into the butter or oil, toss lightly into spaghetti.
- Spoon 2 tablespoons of Ragu sauce over the spaghetti and toss.
- Combine 2 tablespoons of finely chopped herbs (parsley, oregano and chives) and add to the butter or oil, toss into spaghetti.

Rice

The Chinese, Arabs, Greeks, Italians, Indians, Spaniards, Turks and Persians all have their own marvellous rice dishes. Bowls of pure white rice with each grain separate; crispy fried rice; pilafs hiding fruits, spiced lamb and other delights; risottos—delicate with saffron; spicy pilafs flavoured with green ginger, cinnamon and cardamoms; paellas rich with seafood.

The rice grain may be short, medium or long. For rice fanciers there is a variety of rice for each purpose:
- The Australian long grain rice is good for boiled rice and pilafs.
- The short grain is an all-purpose rice and especially good for slowly cooked rice puddings.
- The long grain Indian Basmati has a special flavour and is excellent for pilafs.
- The plump Italian rice is the best for risottos. This type of rice will absorb a large quantity of liquid.

Boiled Rice

12 cups water
3 teaspoons salt
2 slices lemon
1½ cups rice

Bring water, salt and lemon slices to the boil in a large saucepan. Add the rice slowly so that the water continues to boil. Boil for 12 to 15 minutes uncovered until the grains are tender and have no hard centre when pressed between the fingers. It is important to keep the water boiling rapidly during the entire cooking period.

Drain at once through a colander. The rice may need cold water poured through to separate the grains and wash out any clinging excess starch. Make small holes in the rice with the handle of a wooden spoon to allow the steam to escape. Makes 4 to 4½ cups of rice.

Variations:
Into the hot rice stir one or more of the following with a knob of butter:
- Finely chopped onion cooked in a little butter.
- Cooked sliced mushrooms.
- Snipped chives.
- Cooked red or green pepper.

Spaghetti with Ragu Sauce

Steamed Rice

The old 2 to 1 method of cooking rice results in well defined grains which have absorbed the liquid but which are never sticky or lumpy (2 cups water to 1 rice).

Bring the water to the boil and add the salt. Sprinkle in the rice but do not allow the water to stop boiling. Stir the rice and then cover with a well fitting lid and turn the heat down as low as possible. (If necessary use an asbestos mat.) Cook very gently for 17 to 20 minutes. Remove from the heat, uncover for a few minutes to allow the steam to escape and fluff up with a fork.

Variations:
- Stock cubes dissolved in the water or stock may be substituted for water.
- A strip of lemon peel may be added.
- Add a bayleaf and sprig of thyme.
- A knob of butter added to the water.

Indian Ghee Rice

The easiest way to cook rice, and the one that guarantees success, is the absorption method. The rice is first fried in ghee, then simmered in stock and spices until all the liquid has evaporated, the rice tender, but each grain still separate.

60 g (2 oz) ghee or butter
1 onion
1 teaspoon turmeric
2 cups rice
3½ cups stock or water and stock cubes
8 peppercorns
2 whole cloves
4 bruised cardamom pods
2 teaspoons salt
1 stick cinnamon
1 cup cooked peas

Heat ghee in a heavy saucepan with lid. Finely slice onion and add half to pan. Fry gently until a good golden brown. Make sure they are well cooked, but do not allow to burn. This frying takes quite a while. Add turmeric and cook stirring for 1 minute. Add rice and fry 5–10 minutes, stirring constantly, until it is golden. Add boiling stock, or stock cubes dissolved in boiling water, with spices, salt and remaining sliced onion. Bring to boil stirring from time to time. When boiling, turn heat down very low, cover pan tightly and cook gently 20–25 minutes. Turn heat off and keep covered until ready to serve.

A few minutes before serving, uncover pan to allow steam to escape. Fluff rice up with a fork, remove whole spices and garnish with peas.

Note: To get the best flavour onions must be allowed to cook gently for a long time.

Do not stir rice once it has come to the boil.

Rice Pilau

Butter is used in every pilau recipe and usually twice the weight of liquid to rice. The seasonings may vary from a few cardamom pods, a stick of cinnamon to sweet plump raisins and almonds.

90 g (3 oz) butter
1 small onion
2 cups long grain rice
3½ cups boiling stock
1 teaspoon salt
½ cup sultanas or raisins
½ cup halved almonds, toasted

In a heavy saucepan or pot melt butter and sauté finely chopped onion until transparent. Add rice and cook stirring until golden. Add stock and salt and simmer over gentle heat, covered, for approximately 20 minutes or until rice is tender. If the pan is not a heavy one place an asbestos mat under it, this helps distribute the gentle heat over the base of the pan. Add sultanas, return the lid and allow the fruit to plump.

Add the almonds and lightly fork the pilau into a heated serving bowl. Serve immediately.

Saffron Pilaf

Pilaf is a method of cooking rice which originated in the Middle East. It may be served plain, perfumed and coloured with saffron or garnished with fruit and nuts.

60 g (2 oz) ghee
1 small onion, finely chopped
2 cups long grain rice (preferably basmati)
salt
freshly ground pepper
4 cups chicken stock
½ teaspoon saffron
125 g (4 oz) unsalted cashews
60 g (2 oz) ghee
125 g (4 oz) raisins

Melt the ghee in a heavy saucepan and add the onion. Allow to cook gently in the ghee until soft and golden. Stir in the rice and season with salt and pepper. Heat the stock with the saffron and pour on to the rice. Stir the rice and allow it to come to the boil. Cover the saucepan tightly and lower the heat. Cook the rice gently for about 18 to 20 minutes or until all the liquid is absorbed and the rice tender. Remove the lid and allow the rice to cook for a few minutes to release the steam.

Fry the cashews in the ghee for a few minutes until they are golden. Add the raisins and cook for 2 more minutes.

Spoon the pilaf on to a hot serving dish. Fork it up and then scatter the raisins and cashews over the top.

● Basmati rice is a very fine long grain Indian rice. It is available from some grocery stores and from delicatessens and health food stores. It has a special flavour all of its own and is an excellent rice for savoury pilafs.

Fried Rice

On a Chinese menu fried rice is served as a separate course, not as an accompaniment to other dishes. The ingredients added to the rice can be varied to suit your own taste or whatever you have on hand.

6 dried mushrooms
3 eggs
salt to taste
6 tablespoons oil
5 to 6 shallots, chopped
¾ cup diced barbecued pork or ham
6 cups cold cooked rice
1 cup cooked peas
Seasonings:
¼ cup chicken stock or water
1 tablespoon Chinese wine or dry sherry
2 teaspoons Soy sauce

Soak mushrooms in bowl of warm water to cover for 20 minutes. Beat eggs with pinch salt. Heat 2 tablespoons oil in a wok or large frying pan and fry eggs in a flat pancake, turn and cook other side. Remove and cut into shreds.

Drain mushrooms, squeeze dry and cut into small squares, discarding the tough stems. Mix seasoning ingredients together.

Heat remaining oil in wok and fry shallots, pork and mushrooms for 2 minutes, stirring all the time.

Add the rice and cook, turning constantly so no rice sticks to pan and burns, until thoroughly heated.

Stir through the egg shreds and peas, then sprinkle with seasonings and mix well. Serve immediately.

● The secret in making Fried Rice is to boil the rice the day before frying. This way the rice dries out completely and every grain separates as you cook it.
● Stock mixture added just before serving the rice gives a little moistness.

Paëlla

Paella need not be a luxury dish. It may be made with any ingredients you have on hand as long as you have the basic olive oil, onions, garlic and rice.

A paella is really simple to make:
- pieces of pork or chicken are fried until golden and placed aside till later
- onions and garlic are fried to give the basic flavour
- the rice is stirred in and spices, tomatoes or peppers added
- the stock is added, the rice seasoned and the browned meat added to cook through
- the rice is now allowed to cook and absorb the liquid
- when the rice is almost tender, arrange the other ingredients decoratively on top. Cover and steam for about 10 minutes to heat them through and, olé—a paella.

These last-minute ingredients may include olives, peas, cubes of ham or spicy sausages, seafood, tinned artichoke hearts or small whole mushrooms first fried for a few minutes.

The better your imagination—the better your paella.

$\frac{1}{4}$ cup olive oil

500 g (1 lb) pork loin chops, trimmed of excess fat

1 onion, chopped

1 clove garlic, chopped

1 teaspoon saffron

2$\frac{1}{2}$ cups long grain rice

2 tomatoes, peeled

5 cups chicken stock

salt

freshly ground pepper

250 g ($\frac{1}{2}$ lb) large prawns

1 jar pickled mussels OR

500 g (1 lb) fresh mussels in their shells

1 squid, cleaned with the skin removed

6 scallops, bearded

1 red or green pepper

Heat the oil in the paella pan or in a large frying pan and when hot add the pork chops. Cook for about 10 minutes on each side. Remove the chops from the pan and keep warm. Add the onion and garlic to the pan with the saffron and when the onions are lightly coloured add the rice. Mix with the onion and fry for a further 5 minutes. Chop the tomatoes and add to the rice with the stock. Season with salt and pepper. Spread the rice to the edge of the pan. Cut the pork chops into small pieces, removing the bone and add to the rice and continue cooking. Shell the prawns, leaving the tails intact.

Drain the mussels and slice the squid into rings. Remove the beard from the scallops and cut the pepper into shreds. When most of the liquid has been absorbed into the rice add these ingredients arranging them decoratively. Cook over a moderate heat for a further 10 minutes adding more stock if necessary.

Note: If using fresh mussels scrub them well. Discard any with open shells.

Rissoto

30 g (1 oz) butter

1 medium onion, sliced

185 g (6 oz) short grain rice or Italian rice

60 g (2 oz) mushrooms, sliced (optional)

2$\frac{1}{2}$ cups chicken stock

1 cup white wine

1 clove garlic crushed with $\frac{1}{2}$ teaspoon salt

pinch of saffron soaked in a little warm water for 20 minutes

OR 1 packet powdered saffron

freshly ground pepper

1 bay leaf

30 g (1 oz) freshly grated parmesan cheese

30 g (1 oz) butter

Melt the butter in a heavy saucepan, add the onion and when it is soft but not coloured stir in the rice. Cook for a few minutes then add the mushrooms and cook quickly for a minute or two, stirring constantly.

Add 2 cups of the stock, $\frac{1}{2}$ cup wine, the garlic, saffron, pepper and bay leaf. Simmer until the rice is soft but not mushy and the consistency resembles that of thick cream. Add more stock and wine from time to time as the rice absorbs it, stirring it occasionally and keeping it gently simmering.

When rice is cooked remove from the heat, take out the bay leaf and adjust the seasoning. Sprinkle the top with grated parmesan cheese. add the remaining butter, cover the pan and leave for 4–5 minutes. Stir lightly with a fork and turn out onto a hot dish.

Pizza

Pizza

1 cup lukewarm water
30 g (1 oz) compressed yeast
3 tablespoons olive oil
3 cups plain flour
1½ teaspoons salt
freshly ground pepper

Measure water into a large bowl. Crumble the yeast into water and stir until smooth. Stir in the olive oil. Sift the flour with the salt over the yeast mixture and season with pepper. Blend with a spoon. Turn the dough on to a lightly floured surface and knead gently until smooth and elastic.

Place in a large greased bowl, turn the dough to grease it all over. Cover with tea towel and leave in a warm place for about 2 hours or until doubled in bulk.

Turn out on to a lightly floured board and knead 4 to 5 times. Divide mixture into two. Roll out each portion about 5 mm (¼ in) thick to a 30 cm (12 in) circle. Place on to a greased baking sheet, cover and allow to rise in a warm place for about 15 minutes, place the filling on top and bake in a hot oven (400°F—200°C) for 18 to 20 minutes until the crust is golden and crisp around the edge. Serve immediately.

Note: Pizza dough can be prepared, allowed to rise until doubled in bulk and then refrigerated overnight. The next day the dough has only to be knocked down and rolled out and then allowed to rise before filling and baking.

The pizza dough may also be rolled out, placed on the baking sheet, allowed to rise and filled and stored in the refrigerator for 2 to 3 hours before cooking. Brush the dough with olive oil to prevent a crust from forming.

Basic Tomato Filling:

This filling is used as a base for nearly all pizzas. If fresh tomatoes are used, select good flavoured red tomatoes. If not available use drained tinned whole tomatoes.

750 g (1½ lbs) red tomatoes
2 garlic cloves, crushed
1 tablespoon brown sugar
2 tablespoons tomato paste

Peel and slice the tomatoes. Put into a saucepan with the garlic, brown sugar and tomato paste. Allow to simmer gently for 30 to 40 minutes, stirring occasionally. Cool.

Ham and Mushroom Pizza

2 basic pizzas rolled out on baking sheets
4 tablespoons olive oil
½ cup grated parmesan cheese
1 quantity of basic tomato filling
125 g (4 oz) ham, cut into strips
6 to 8 mushrooms, sliced finely
salt, freshly ground pepper

Brush the pizza dough with half the olive oil and sprinkle with half of the parmesan cheese. Spoon the tomato filling over each and then add the ham and the mushrooms, seasoning with salt and pepper. Sprinkle with the remaining olive oil and parmesan cheese and bake in a hot oven (400°F—200°C) for 18 to 20 minutes until the crust is golden and cooked.

salads

Potato, beetroot and green salad, all marvellously appetising.

Salads

Mayonnaise

2 egg yolks
$\frac{1}{2}$ teaspoon salt
pinch white pepper
$\frac{1}{2}$ teaspoon dry mustard
2 teaspoons vinegar
1 cup olive oil

Mayonnaise is easiest to make when all ingredients are at room temperature. In cold weather, warm the bowl in hot water to take the chill off the egg yolks. Warm the oil over hot water if it is cold. Wrap a damp cloth around base of bowl to keep it steady while you are making sauce. Place egg yolks, seasonings and 1 teaspoon vinegar in bowl and beat with a wire whisk to combine. As soon as they are thick, they are ready to take in the oil.

Beating steadily, begin to add oil drop by drop from a teaspoon. In these intial stages, oil must be added very slowly to egg so that it will not curdle. Continue to slowly drop in oil until $\frac{1}{4}$ cup has been added. Now as mixture thickens, oil can be increased to a steady thin stream, but you must keep beating constantly. Stop now and then to check oil is well blended. When all oil is added, beat in remaining vinegar.

If mayonnaise should show signs of separating, add a small spoonful of boiling water and beat well before adding any more oil.

Garlic Mayonnaise or Aïoli: For crudites, boiled meats, fish and vegetables.
Crush 2 to 3 cloves garlic to a paste with salt in a bowl. Add egg-yolks and seasoning and mix until thick. Add oil as for basic recipe. Do not add too much vinegar.

Sauce Tartare: For fried fish.
Add 2 teaspoons chopped capers, 1 tablespoon chopped gherkins, chopped whites of 2 hard-boiled eggs, 2 teaspoons chopped fresh herbs, and seasoning to taste to 1 cup mayonnaise.
A little cream may be added to lighten consistency.

Mayonnaise Verde or Green Herb Mayonnaise: For cold fish, eggs.
1 to 2 tablespoons finely chopped fresh green herbs are stirred into 1 cup mayonnaise with a little cream. Use a combination of parsley, chives, (mainly) with watercress and spinach.

Green Salad

Use fresh, unblemished salad greens. Wash and dry thoroughly, using a wire salad basket or clean tea towel to shake off all water. Break greens with fingers into bite-size pieces. Chill well in a plastic bag, or a bowl covered with plastic food wrap. Put salad greens in bowl just before serving and toss with French dressing until every leaf is glistening.

Use any combination of green leaf vegetables—lettuce, escarole, chicory, endive, watercress, young spinach, romaine lettuce, young nasturtium leaves. Quartered tomatoes, chopped shallots or other salad vegetables are sometimes added to green salad. It is then called a mixed salad.

Vinaigrette

The basic oil and vinegar dressing of France is a mixture of good olive oil, wine vinegar, salt and freshly ground black pepper. Mustard, if you like it, and fresh herbs in season are added to suit the food the vinaigrette is going to dress. Garlic is favoured in the south of France and features in the more robust salads.

The usual proportion of oil to vinegar is three parts to one, but this can be varied to suit your own taste. Some salads call for a dressing where the oil is only lightly spiked with vinegar. If you find the one in three proportion too oily, add salt rather than increase the vinegar to cut the oiliness.

A squeeze of lemon juice is sometimes added to vinaigrette. Cider vinegar, red wine and any of the flavoured vinegars such as tarragon or herb are excellent.

Be sure the salad greens are perfectly dry so that the dressing will adhere to the leaves.

2 tablespoons good vinegar
$\frac{1}{4}$ teaspoon salt
$\frac{1}{2}$ teaspoon dry mustard
freshly ground black pepper
6 tablespoons olive oil

Put vinegar into a small bowl with mustard. Mix well with a fork or birch whisk and slowly add oil. If the dressing tastes sharp add more oil or 1 teaspoon of castor sugar. If the dressing is too oily for your taste, add more salt as this "cuts" the oiliness.

Garlic: There are several ways to add garlic to your dressing. If you like a pungent dressing, crush 1 to 2 cloves of garlic to a paste with salt, add vinegar and other seasonings and then the oil. You can also chop garlic and add to the finished dressing for a more rustic salad. For a more delicate flavour bruise the peeled garlic and steep in the vinegar for 1 to 2 hours. The vinegar brings out the more delicate flavour of the garlic, while oil brings out the stronger flavour.

Fresh herb: When adding herbs it is best to sprinkle half of the freshly chopped herbs over the salad, adding the remaining herbs to the dressing. Tarragon, basil, chives and parsley add their own distinctive flavour. They may be used separately or in combination. One or two spoons of chopped herbs is sufficient.

Provençal Salad

750 g (1$\frac{1}{2}$ lbs) ripe firm tomatoes, cut into quarters
10 black olives
half a small fennel stem, finely sliced
salt, freshly ground black pepper
3 tablespoons vinaigrette dressing flavoured with a clove of garlic
finely chopped herbs (parsley, basil, tarragon, oregano or chives)

Combine the tomatoes, olives and finely sliced fennel in a salad bowl. Place in the refrigerator to chill slightly. Season with salt and pepper and toss in the dressing. Sprinkle generously with finely chopped herbs.

Provençal Salad

Sour Cream Sauce

½ cup sour cream
2 teaspoons bottled horseradish
1 tablespoon finely chopped shallots or
onion
½ teaspoon salt
squeeze lemon juice
½ teaspoon capers

Stir ingredients well until mixed. Serve with cold meats or fish or spoon over beetroot, sliced cucumber or artichokes.

Lettuce and Celery Salad

1 lettuce
2 celery stalks, sliced
salt and freshly ground pepper
2 tablespoons olive oil
1 tablespoon lemon juice
4 tablespoons cream

Discard the outer leaves of the lettuce. Wash the heart and tear into small pieces. Mix the lettuce and celery in a salad bowl. Season with salt and pepper and dress with the olive oil and lemon juice. Toss lightly and then spoon over the cream.

Cucumber Salad

2 cucumbers, peeled
2 tablespoons salt
4 tablespoons vinaigrette dressing
2 tablespoons snipped chives

Cut the cucumbers into quarters lengthwise and scoop out the seeds. Cut into 5 cm (2 inch) lengths and place in a colander. Sprinkle with the salt and leave to stand for 30 minutes to drain. Rinse the cucumber under cold water to remove any excess salt. Drain and dry.

Place in a salad bowl, toss in the Vinaigrette Dressing and sprinkle with chives. Serve as soon as possible.

Mixed Green Salad with Chapons

Chapons are slices of French bread (flavoured liberally with garlic, a good olive oil and salt and pepper) which are tossed with a salad of mixed greens to add a distinct garlic flavour. Much better than merely smearing the serving bowl with garlic!

selection of salad vegetables: lettuce,
curly endive, spinach, shallots, parsley,
watercress and green pepper
1 cucumber
6 slices French bread
2 cloves garlic
olive oil
salt and pepper

Wash, dry and chill salad greens. Tear into bite-sized pieces. Peel cucumber leaving a little green colour on the flesh. Cut in half lengthwise and scoop out seeds with a spoon. Cut into 5 cm (2 in) lengths. Crush garlic, put in a small bowl with a few tablespoons of olive oil and a good grinding of black pepper. Mix well. Brush on slices of French bread. Add to bowl with salad greens and just before serving toss with a little vinaigrette dressing.

Watercress Salad

Fresh sprigs of dark green leaves well-flavoured with a mustard dressing provide colour and texture.

1 bunch of watercress
French Dressing:
3 tablespoons olive oil
1 tablespoon wine vinegar
½ teaspoon dry mustard
freshly ground black pepper
salt

Trim the coarse stalks and divide the watercress into small bunches. Place head down into cold water to make crisp.
Dressing:
Combine the olive oil with the wine vinegar, mustard and season with salt and black pepper. Drain the watercress well and place in a bowl with the dressing. Toss and serve.

Potato Salad

1 kg (2 lb) potatoes
vinaigrette dressing
snipped chives

If using tiny new potatoes scrape the skins with a small sharp knife, plunge them into boiling salted water, and cook until tender. If using large potatoes cover with cold salted water, boil until tender and when cooked, peel off the skin. Cut into large dice. The potatoes should be moistened with vinaigrette while still warm. To serve, pile into a bowl and garnish with the snipped chives.

Creamy Potato Salad

Prepare potatoes according to recipe. Just before serving toss in ½ cup mayonnaise and sprinkle with chives.

Florentine Salad

¼ cup olive oil
1 tablespoon wine vinegar
½ teaspoon mustard
2 anchovy fillets, finely chopped
½ heart of lettuce
½ heart of curly endive
½ a fennel bulb sliced finely
2 radishes, trimmed and thinly sliced
freshly ground black pepper
salt
1 radish, finely sliced for garnishing

Mix the oil with the vinegar, mustard and anchovy fillets until thoroughly blended.

Tear the lettuce and curly endive into pieces, toss with the sliced fennel and radishes. Chill. When ready to serve, season the salad with freshly ground pepper and a little salt (but remember the anchovies are salty) and toss with the dressing. Garnish with thinly sliced radish. Excellent with cold chicken, ham or veal.

Three Bean Salad

1 cup dried red kidney beans
1 cup dried haricot beans
250 g ($\frac{1}{2}$ lb) green beans
4 cups chicken stock
2 bay leaves
2 sprigs parsley
1 onion
2 whole cloves
12 peppercorns
2 teaspoons salt
vinaigrette dressing
chopped parsley

Soak beans separately overnight in water to cover. Next day drain and put in separate saucepans. Put 2 cups stock (or water and chicken stock cubes), 1 bay leaf, a parsley sprig, $\frac{1}{2}$ onion, 1 clove, 6 peppercorns and teaspoon salt in each pan and bring to boil. Simmer until beans are tender, about $1\frac{1}{4}$ hours for kidney beans and $1\frac{1}{2}$ hours for haricot beans. Drain and chill, removing seasonings. Top, tail and string green beans and cut in halves. Cook in boiling salted water until barely tender, about 10 minutes, then drain and rinse under cold water. Drain well. Toss in vinaigrette dressing while still warm. Chill. Combine all beans in a large serving bowl. Toss with additional vinaigrette dressing and sprinkle with chopped parsley.

Mixed Slaw

$\frac{1}{4}$ red cabbage
$\frac{1}{4}$ white cabbage
$\frac{1}{2}$ bunch radish
vinaigrette dressing
parsley

Shred red cabbage finely with a stainless steel knife. Bring a large saucepan full of water to the boil, add red cabbage and stir vigorously for 1 minute, then drain immediately into a colander. Rinse cabbage under cold water to set colour and cool. Leave aside to drain.

Finely shred white cabbage, slice washed radishes. Pat red cabbage with a cloth to dry. Put in a large salad bowl with white cabbage and diced radishes. Toss well with $\frac{1}{2}$ cup vinaigrette dressing. Sprinkle salad with finely chopped parsley and garnish with a radish rose.

Creamy Mixed Slaw: Prepare as above but add $\frac{1}{2}$ cup sour cream or mayonnaise just before serving.

Sour Cream Coleslaw

$\frac{1}{2}$ medium cabbage
$\frac{1}{2}$ cup mayonnaise
2 tablespoons chopped celery
dash tabasco
$\frac{1}{2}$ cup sour cream
$\frac{1}{2}$ red pepper, thinly sliced
$\frac{1}{2}$ green pepper, thinly sliced
2 tablespoons shallots, finely chopped

Shred cabbage finely with a stainless steel knife. Put in a large salad bowl. Combine remaining ingredients, pour over cabbage, toss and chill well before serving.

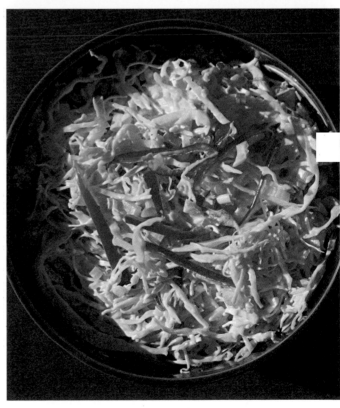

Top left: Mixed Green Salad with Chapons (see recipe on page 276)
Bottom left: Three Bean Salad

Top right: Mixed Slaw
Bottom right: Sour Cream Coleslaw

Dressed Beetroot

2 bunches beetroot
vinaigrette dressing
chopped parsley

Trim leafy tops off 2 bunches of beetroot. Wash the beetroot and bake in a moderate oven (350°F—175°C) for 1½ hours or until tender and the skin slips away easily. Use rubber gloves to prevent beetroot staining your hands. When beetroot is cold, slice thinly and arrange in a salad bowl, moisten with a little vinaigrette dressing, toss in and sprinkle with chopped parsley.

We used a serrated knife to cut the beetroot in a decorative pattern.

Tomato, Orange and Pickled Walnut Salad

An imaginative salad which originated at one of London's best-known clubs.

500 g (1 lb) ripe red tomatoes of medium size
2 oranges
2 pickled walnuts
Dressing:
2 tablespoons olive oil
1 tablespoon pickled walnut juice
1 teaspoon French mustard
salt and freshly ground pepper

Peel the tomatoes and cut into quarters. Peel the oranges and cut into segments. Slice the pickled walnuts. Arrange in a salad bowl.
Dressing: Combine oil, pickled walnut juice and mustard and season with salt and pepper. Stir well and mix with the salad.
To prepare orange segments:
Using a small sharp-pointed vegetable knife, peel the orange over a plate—to catch the juice—removing all the white pith.

Free each segment by cutting it close to the membrane on each side and lift out. Flick out any pips.

Mushroom Salad

One of the nicest ways of serving very young mushrooms is in a raw mushroom salad. In restaurants in Italy, these salads are made at the table—your waiter slicing and dressing them to perfection before your eyes.

2 tablespoons vinegar
salt and pepper
¼ teaspoon dry mustard
1 clove garlic
½ cup olive oil
1 tablespoon sour cream
250 g (8 oz) button mushrooms
250 g (8 oz) Gruyère or Emmenthaler cheese
250 g (8 oz) leg ham cut 5 mm (¼ in.) thick

Mix vinegar with salt, pepper and mustard. Bruise the garlic and add to the vinegar. Add oil and beat with a fork until thoroughly combined. Stir in sour cream.

Slice mushrooms thinly, and cut cheese and ham into matchstick strips. Remove garlic from the dressing, just before pouring over the mushrooms, ham and cheese. Toss salad and pile into a serving dish. This makes a good hors d'oeuvre or light meal.

Bean Sprout Salad

Combine 1 cup bean sprouts with other fresh salad greens such as watercress, Chinese cabbage, cucumber, blanched zucchini and lettuce. Place these vegetables in the refrigerator to make them crisp before serving them tossed in a light vinaigrette dressing (2 parts oil to 1 part vinegar). Scatter with freshly chopped herbs. For an oriental flavour, season the vinaigrette dressing with a little soy sauce.

● Combine a small handful of bean sprouts with the omelet mixture before adding to the pan.
● Add bean sprouts to any clear soup or vegetable soup just before serving.
● Vegetable dishes—stir fry in 1 tablespoon of oil for 1 minute, 2 celery stalks shredded and 250 g ($\frac{1}{2}$ lb) bean sprouts. Add salt, 1 teaspoon soy sauce and 2 tablespoons of stock. Heat through and cook covered 2 to 3 minutes over a medium heat.

Variations:
● Add 4 dried mushrooms previously soaked for 30 minutes, squeezed dry and cut into shreds to the celery and bean sprouts and proceed as above.
● Stir fry celery and bean sprouts and add 1 finely chopped slice of fresh ginger root to the seasonings.
● Add a sliced green pepper to the celery and bean sprouts and add a little finely chopped green ginger to the seasonings.

Pepper and Cheese Salad

3 peppers (preferably yellow but red or green will do)
125 g (4 oz) Gruyère cheese (if Fontina is not available)
30 g (1 oz) black olives, seeded
$\frac{1}{4}$ cup vinaigrette dressing
$\frac{1}{2}$ teaspoon mustard
1 tablespoon cream

Cut the peppers in half, discarding the core and seeds. Grill them under a high heat until the skins blacken and blister. When cool enough to handle, pull off the thin outer skin and cut the flesh into long, even strips.

Cut the cheese into dice and mix in a salad bowl with the pepper strips and olives which have been cut in half. Combine the vinaigrette dressing with $\frac{1}{2}$ teaspoon mustard and 1 tablespoon of cream and toss with the salad. Chill for at least 1 hour before serving.

Salad of Fennel and Cucumber

The Italians love the fresh, aniseed flavour of the Florence fennel bulb and use it generously in their salads or cook it and serve it as a hot vegetable.

1 cucumber
1 fennel bulb, cut into thin strips
3 radishes, trimmed and finely sliced
1 tablespoon finely chopped mint
salt and freshly ground pepper
$\frac{1}{4}$ cup of vinaigrette dressing to which 1 crushed garlic clove has been added
2 hard-boiled eggs
freshly chopped herbs, basil, parsley, oregano, tarragon

Cut an unpeeled cucumber into thin slices and combine with the fennel, radishes and mint. Season with salt and pepper. Chill and then toss with the vinaigrette dressing. Garnish with the hard-boiled eggs cut into quarters and scatter some finely chopped herbs over the salad.

Sicilian Tomato Salad

6 large firm but ripe tomatoes
125 g (4 oz) mushrooms
125 g (4 oz) dill pickles or Italian pickles
1 dozen olives, stoned
1 tablespoon capers
1 cup cooked white haricot beans
salt, freshly ground pepper
1 cup mayonnaise

Peel the tomatoes and cut into quarters. Cut the mushrooms and pickles into thick slices and the olives in halves, or if large, into quarters. Place the tomatoes, mushrooms, pickles and olives into a bowl with the capers and beans. Season with salt and pepper and chill. Just before serving mix gently with the mayonnaise.

Orange Salad

Fresh sweet orange segments or slices, dusted with caster sugar and a light sprinkling of finely chopped mint make a refreshing first course, or a side salad for cold ham, tongue or pork.

Another delicious salad combines orange segments and Belgian endive leaves. Both are well-chilled and then dressed with a vinaigrette dressing to which a good dash of sugar has been added. Equally good with cold or hot ham, tongue, pork or duck.

Japanese Salad

A delightfully unusual salad to serve with prawns, crayfish or chicken.

Combine equal amounts of ripe pineapple, orange and tomato which have been cut into dice, sprinkle with lemon juice and arrange in a bowl. Spoon over some sour cream which has been mixed with a little chilled water or milk to make it thinner and chill before serving. Serve each portion in a crisp lettuce leaf.

Avocado Provençale

2 avocados
vinaigrette dressing
1 green pepper
8 black olives
crisp lettuce leaves
finely chopped parsley

Cut avocados in half, then remove skins and seeds and slice flesh lengthwise. Sprinkle with about 4 tablespoons of vinaigrette dressing. Slice green pepper in thin strips. Drop into boiling water for 1-2 minutes. Drain and rinse under cold water. Add drained pepper to avocado. Add halved stoned olives. Roll ingredients gently with dressing to coat then, arrange attractively on lettuce leaves. Garnish with parsley.

Belgian Endive Salad

Belgian endive makes an attractive salad with its elongated white leaves and pleasant sharp tang. Endive is at its best served simply with a seasoned dressing or with one other ingredient equally distinctive in flavour such as pickled walnuts, orange or beetroot.

endive
lemon juice
olive oil
salt and pepper

Discard outer leaves of endive. Break off the crisp leaves or cut through into 2.5 cm (1 in) lengths. Squeeze just a little lemon juice over to prevent discolouration, season with good olive oil, salt and pepper and roll gently until all leaves are glistening.

Belgian Endive is only available from May until August.

Waldorf Salad

The success of this salad depends on the flavour of the walnuts which should be freshly cracked and the sweet-tart flavour of unpeeled new season Jonathans. It is a salad which may be served as a first course or as a luncheon dish. Always chill well.

375 g (12 oz) chicken breasts
3 medium sized Jonathan apples
juice of 1 lemon
6 young crisp celery stalks
30 g (1 oz) walnut halves
1 cup mayonnaise
1 small lettuce heart

Dice the chicken breasts which have been poached in water to cover with a sliced carrot, onion and celery stalk, a bouquet garni and a little salt for 15 minutes or until tender. Core and dice the apples and sprinkle with lemon juice. Slice the celery and add to a bowl with the chicken, apple and walnut halves. Toss with well seasoned mayonnaise and chill. Serve piled up on crisp lettuce leaves.

Note: If the mayonnaise is very thick, it may be lightened with a tablespoon or two of lightly whipped cream.

Avocado and Tomato Salad

4 medium tomatoes
4 shallots or 2 very small white onions
2 avocados
vinaigrette dressing
chopped parsley
½ small red pepper
choice lettuce leaves

Drop tomatoes one at a time into boiling water for just 8 seconds and lift out and rinse under very cold water. This quick blanching loosens the skin to make peeling easier. Quarter peeled tomatoes, remove seeds and cut quarters into chunky pieces. Finely slice white part of shallots or finely chop the onions. Halve avocados, remove skin and cut flesh into large dice. Put in bowl and toss with about 3 tablespoons vinaigrette dressing. Add tomato and shallot. Cut pepper into small dice. To serve, line individual serving plates with small crisp lettuce leaves. Arrange avocado mixture on lettuce, sprinkle with parsley and finely diced pepper.

Sicilian Bean Salad

The Italians have had a great love of beans ever since they were introduced into Italy by the Duke of Florence in the 15th century. In this salad, haricot beans are combined with all the typical flavours of the sunny Mediterranean.

1 cup dried haricot beans
salt
125 g (4 oz) button mushrooms
½ cup vinaigrette dressing
2 teaspoons drained capers
¼ cup pitted black olives
3 tablespoons mayonnaise
freshly ground pepper
2 firm, ripe tomatoes
chopped parsley

Soak beans in water to cover for 3 hours. Drain, cover with fresh cold water, add a good pinch of salt and cook over a low heat for about 1 hour or until tender. Cool and then drain.

Wash mushrooms, trim stems and slice. Put into a bowl with the vinaigrette. Combine beans, capers and olives and gently fold in the mushrooms with the dressing. Add mayonnaise and salt and pepper to taste.

Quarter tomatoes and add to the salad with a good spoonful of chopped parsley.

desserts

Strawberries

A famous writer once said that only birds and children know what strawberries really taste like—and there's much truth in that statement. They both have sharp eyes for the things they like, and that's the very reason the ripest sweetest strawberries disappear from the garden before you've had a chance to taste even one.

Strawberries, once called strayberries because they propagate themselves by runners, were known to epicures in Roman times. Today's varieties are no doubt much changed but let us be thankful for those experiments which have given us a berry not only beautiful in shape and colour but delicately perfumed and refreshing.

Nothing compares with the flavour and fragrance of ripe strawberries. They have enough natural sweetness not to need sugar but this is really a matter of choice. They are wonderful on their own but take to other ingredients extremely kindly—with cream, sprinkled with red wine or orange juice, with fresh cream cheese and, oddly enough freshly ground black pepper.

Strawberries Romanoff

8 pieces of lump sugar
2 oranges
2 punnets of strawberries
6 tablespoons curacao
Cream Chantilly:
1 cup cream
sugar to taste
vanilla essence to flavour

Rub lumps of sugar over the skins of oranges until they are well impregnated with the flavour of the fruit. Crush the sugar. Wash and hull strawberries. Macerate them in curacao and sugar in a covered container in the refrigerator until serving time.

Arrange them in a bowl in a pyramid shape. Put the Cream Chantilly into a piping bag with a rose piping tube and decorate the strawberries.

Cream Chantilly: Whip the chilled cream with sugar to taste until firm. Fold in vanilla essence to taste. Serves 6.

Venetian Strawberries

2 punnets of strawberries, hulled
4 tablespoons caster sugar
freshly ground black pepper
1 cup demi-sec chamgagne

Wash the strawberries and drain them and place in a bowl. Sprinkle with sugar and allow to stand for 10 minutes. Grind some fresh black pepper over them and then pour over champagne. Stir carefully to combine the flavours. Believe it or not, the pepper enhances the strawberries' delicate flavour.

Strawberries in the Snow

2 cups of strawberries, hulled
2 tablespoons of kirsch (optional)
$\frac{1}{2}$ cup caster sugar
4 egg whites
1 cup cream

Slice the strawberries and sprinkle with 1 tablespoon of sugar and kirsch. Allow to macerate for 15 minutes.

Beat the egg whites stiffly and then continue to beat adding remaining sugar. Whip the cream stiffly. Fold the egg whites into the cream and then gently and carefully mix with the macerated strawberries. Spoon into a large bowl or individual dishes and serve chilled.

Note: A few whole ripe strawberries may be used for decoration.

Strawberries in the Snow

Strawberries in Wine with Sponge Fingers

2 punnets strawberries

caster sugar

6 tablespoons fortified wine (muscat,
  port, marsala, madeira)

Sponge Fingers

3 eggs, separated

vanilla

5 tablespoons sugar

¼ cup plain flour

1 tablespoon caster sugar

Wash, drain and hull strawberries. Arrange in individual glass dishes or in a serving bowl.

Sprinkle heavily with sugar and sprinkle over wine. Chill in refrigerator for several hours. Serve chilled, accompanied by a crisp biscuit such as sponge fingers.

Line 2 baking trays with greased greaseproof paper and dust with sifted flour. Mark trays with guide lines 8 cm (3 in) apart to ensure biscuits are all the same length. Set oven at moderately hot (375°F—190°C).

Beat egg yolks and vanilla with sugar until thick and lemon-coloured. Sift flour and fold gently into egg yolk mixture. Beat egg whites with salt until stiff but not dry and fold in caster sugar. Quickly but gently fold egg whites into egg yolk mixture.

Fill mixture into a piping bag fitted with a plain tube and pipe finger-lengths onto prepared trays, leaving room for spreading. Dust with caster sugar and bake in a moderately hot oven for 20 minutes. Remove from tray and cool on wire rack. Store in an airtight container.

Note: Sponge fingers, like true sponges, contain no fat.

Always use a metal spoon when folding beaten egg whites or flour into a cake mixture. The clean sharp edge allows the mixture to combine without overfolding.

When folding in stiffly beaten egg whites, make sure not to overwork them as they will lose their bulk.

If there's no time to make sponge fingers go to a good delicatessen and select one of the many Italian-type crisp biscuits like Savoy fingers, amaretti, etc.

Strawberries Sarah Bernhardt

2 punnets of strawberries, hulled

3 tablespoons caster sugar

⅓ cup cointreau

vanilla ice cream

2 slices glacé pineapple, finely sliced

Cream:

1 cup cream

sugar to taste

1 tablespoon cointreau

Place strawberries into a bowl. Sprinkle with caster sugar and cointreau and chill for a few hours, covered.

Place a scoop of vanilla ice cream into 6 individual dishes, sprinkle with slices of glacé pineapple and spoon over the strawberries, reserving six for decoration. Mask the dessert with whipped sweetened cream which has been flavoured with cointreau. Decorate with a whole strawberry.

Strawberries Wilhemine

Macerate some fine large strawberries with kirsch, caster sugar and orange juice. Serve with sweetened whipped cream flavoured with vanilla.

Apples

Apples are with us all the year round. We start off with little Christmas apples and then we have crisp Jonathons with their wonderful flavour and red Delicious, firm and juicy. Golden Delicious appear a little later, and of course the Granny Smith, green, juicy and firm, but used more for cooking than eating.

Apple desserts are universally popular be it apple pie or an apple strudel. Apples flavoured discreetly with cinnamon, lemon rind or cloves make a wonderful compote, and when they are cooked in butter, their aroma is nothing short of bliss.

Apple sauce has a particular sweet-tartness which suits richer meats admirably. Apples go well with celery for salads to accompany chicken or ham.

Apples Brûleés

Buttery puréed apples served cold under a golden toffee glaze.

1.5 kg (3 lb) cooking apples, peeled and cored

30 g (1 oz) butter

60 g (2 oz) sugar

60 g (2 oz) caster sugar for glaze

Slice the apples and place them in a heavy saucepan with the butter and sugar. Cover with a piece of dampened greaseproof paper. Place a close-fitting lid on top and cook the apples gently until soft. Put through a sieve or purée in a blender. Pour the apple purée into an ovenproof mould which will fit under the griller.

Sprinkle the caster sugar over the apples in an even layer and place under a very hot griller until the sugar has completely caramelised. Remove from the heat and leave to cool for at least two hours.

Apple Strudel

Making the pastry for an Austrian Apple Strudel is a delicate operation. This version is simplified by using commercial puff pastry. The filling is still delicious spiced apple, crisp breadcrumbs and nuts. To enjoy this wonderful pastry at its best, serve it warm with lightly whipped cream or vanilla ice cream.

1 × 375 g (12 oz) packet commercial puff pastry

1 cup fine white breadcrumbs

125 g (4 oz) unsalted butter

4 large cooking apples, peeled, cored and cut into thin slices

2 tablespoons vanilla

2 tablespoons brown sugar

grated rind of 1 lemon

$\frac{1}{4}$ cup ground walnuts

$\frac{1}{2}$ cup raisins and currants mixed

2 teaspoons cinnamon

1 tablespoon allspice

60 g (2 oz) melted butter

icing sugar to dust

lightly whipped cream or vanilla ice cream

Macerate the apple slices in the vanilla and brown sugar for 30 minutes. Drain them and mix with grated lemon rind, nuts, raisins, currants, cinnamon and allspice. Roll out pastry very thinly into a rectangle approximately 50 cm × 75 cm (20 in × 30 in). Place on a tea towel.

Fry the breadcrumbs in the butter until crisp and scatter over one end of pastry. Arrange fruit on top of breadcrumbs.

Fold in edges of pastry. Brush folds with melted butter and roll up like a Swiss Roll.

Roll Strudel very carefully from the cloth on to a well greased baking tray. Brush with melted butter and bake in moderately hot oven (375°F—190°C) for about 45 minutes, brushing with butter every 10 minutes. Allow to cool a little on a wire rack, dust with icing sugar and serve warm with lightly whipped cream or vanilla ice cream.

Apple Charlotte

1 loaf sliced white bread

2 eggs, beaten

2 cups soft white breadcrumbs

Filling:

5 large cooking apples, peeled
    and cored

60 g (2 oz) butter

2 tablespoons caster sugar

pinch cinnamon

½ teaspoon grated lemon rind

3-4 tablespoons apricot jam

Grease a 3½-cup charlotte mould or soufflé dish.

Remove the crusts from the bread and cut each slice into 2 strips. Dip these in the beaten egg and then into the breadcrumbs and arrange around the sides of the mould overlapping them slightly.

Line the base of the mould with bread slices or, if you wish for a more decorative finish when turned out, cut a few bread slices into heart shapes. Set aside sufficient bread slices for the top of the mould.

Filling: Slice the apples. Melt the butter in a saucepan, add the apples, sugar, cinnamon and lemon rind. Cook over a high heat stirring continuously. When the apples are thick and reduced to a purée stir in the jam.

Spoon into the prepared mould and top with the reserved bread slices which have been dipped in beaten egg and breadcrumbs. Bake in a moderate oven (350°F—170°C) for 35 to 40 minutes. Allow the Apple Charlotte to remain in the mould for a few minutes before turning it out on to a warmed dish.

Serve with lightly whipped cream.

Apple Dapple Pudding

½ cup self-raising flour

½ cup sugar

1 teaspoon cinnamon

¾ cup water

1 egg, slightly beaten

1 teaspoon almond essence

1 tablespoon lemon juice

4 cups sliced cooking apples

½ cup slivered almonds

½ cup raisins

Topping:

½ cup self-raising flour

¼ cup firmly packed brown sugar

1 teaspoon cinnamon

¼ teaspoon salt

1 teaspoon grated lemond rind

60 g (2 oz) butter

Sift the flour, sugar and cinnamon together. Combine the water, egg, lemon juice and almond essence. Add the sliced apples, almonds and raisins. Mix in the flour, sugar and cinnamon.

Turn into a well-greased 20 cm × 20 cm × 5 cm (8 in × 8 in × 2 in) ovenproof dish. Sprinkle topping over this filling and bake in a moderate oven (350°F—170°C) for about 1 hour.

Serve warm with cream or a good egg custard.

Topping:

Combine the flour, brown sugar, cinnamon, salt and grated lemon rind. Cut the butter into small pieces and mix into the dry ingredients with the fingertips until the mixture resembles coarse breadcrumbs.

Flamed Apples

Whole apples poached in a cinnamon syrup are piled up into a pyramid, brought to the table and flamed with rum.

2 cups water
1 cup sugar
2.5 cm (1 in) stick of cinnamon
8 small cooking apples, Granny Smith
   or Golden Delicious
few drops of red food colouring
extra sugar
$\frac{1}{4}$ cup rum

Bring the water, sugar and cinnamon stick to the boil to make a syrup. Peel and core the apples and place them in the syrup. Cover the pan and poach them until they are tender—about 10 minutes. While they are cooking spoon some of the syrup over them from time to time. Be careful not to overcook them. They should be firm to the touch but tender.

With a slotted spoon remove the apples from the syrup. Arrange them in a pyramid on a serving dish. Mix the red food colouring with a little of the syrup and paint a pale pink blush on the apples.

Boil the syrup until it is quite thick. Pour over the apples and sprinkle with a little extra sugar. Heat the rum but do not allow it to boil. Take the apples to the table, set alight the hot rum and pour it flaming over them.

Apple Pie

1 quantity rich shortcrust pastry
   (see page 355)
7 apples
$\frac{3}{4}$ cup sugar
1 tablespoon plain flour
1 teaspoon ground cinnamon
pinch grated nutmeg
pinch salt
30 g (1 oz) butter
egg white, slightly beaten
extra sugar
whipped cream for serving

Cut off a third of the pastry and reserve for the top of the pie. Roll out the rest of pastry on a lightly floured surface and line a greased 23 cm (9 in) pie plate. Peel and core apples and slice thinly. Combine sugar, flour, spices and salt, mix with the apples slices. Spoon into the pastry case and dot with butter. Roll remaining pastry to cover pie.

Trim edges, crimping the pastry as you go. Brush with slightly beaten egg white to glaze. With a pointed knife make steam vents and sprinkle lightly with sugar. Bake in a hot oven (400°F—200°C) for 1 to $1\frac{1}{4}$ hours. Reduce the heat if the pastry begins to darken. Serve with whipped cream.

Rhubarb and Apple Pie

The sweet and tart flavour of apple and rhubarb make a delicious filling for a fruit pie:

250 g (8 oz) rich shortcrust pastry
   (see page 355)
500 g (1 lb) Granny Smith apples, peeled
1 bunch rhubarb, cut into 3.5 cm
   ($1\frac{1}{2}$ in) lengths
grated rind of 1 orange
3 tablespoons sugar
1 tablespoon caster sugar for pie crust

Slice the apples. Mix with the rhubarb, orange rind and sugar. Fill pie dish.

Roll out pastry. Cut off a 1 cm ($\frac{1}{2}$ in) strip and press around the rim of a 25 cm (10 in) pie dish. Brush with a little water. Lift the remaining pastry with the rolling pin and lay over the dish.

Trim off excess pastry.

Seal pastry by pressing around the edge with the back of a knife and then press around with the thumb making a decorative edge. Sprinkle with caster sugar. Cook in a moderately hot oven (375°F—190°C) for 30 minutes. Serve piping hot.

Danish Apple Cake

Apple Sponge

1 cup sugar
1½ cups water
piece lemon rind
6 large cooking apples, peeled and
   thickly sliced
Sponge mixture:
60 g (2 oz) butter
½ cup caster sugar
grated rind of ½ lemon
2 eggs
1 cup self raising flour
pinch salt
⅔ cup milk

Blend the sugar, water and lemon rind to make a syrup. Boil for 5 minutes and then add the apple slices and allow them to poach over a gentle heat until tender. Drain off excess syrup and place into a round ovenproof dish.

Make the sponge by creaming the butter, caster sugar and lemon rind. Beat in the eggs one at a time and when thoroughly incorporated fold in the flour which has been sifted with salt, alternately with the milk.

Spoon the sponge mixture over the apples and bake in a moderate oven (350°F—170°C) for 40 minutes or until the sponge is well risen and delicately brown.

Danish Apple Cake

This is a lovely dessert cake made from very simple ingredients. It is found with slight variations from town to town throughout Denmark. Sometimes this dessert is completely coated with whipped cream and is known as Veiled Country Lassie.

1.5 kg (3 lb) cooking apples
½ cup water
1 cup sugar
60 g (2 oz) butter
4 cups fine breadcrumbs (white, brown
   or rye)
1 teaspoon cinnamon
3 tablespoons redcurrant jelly
½ cup cream, whipped

Peel and slice the apples and place in a saucepan with the water and the sugar, reserving 2 tablespoons for the breadcrumbs. Cook until the apples turn to a thick purée.

Melt the butter in a heavy pan, add the breadcrumbs, the remaining sugar and cinnamon and combine so that all the breadcrumbs are coated in the butter and sugar.

Grease a 20 cm (8 in) springform tin and spoon one-third of the buttered breadcrumbs in the bottom. Cover with half the apple purée.

Spread 1 tablespoon of the redcurrant jelly over the apple purée and then repeat the layers of breadcrumbs and apple purée spread with redcurrant jelly ending with a layer of breadcrumbs. Bake in a moderate oven (350°F—170°C) for 45 minutes. Remove the cake from the oven and cool. Place in the refrigerator for a few hours, or preferably overnight. Unmould and decorate with whipped cream and the remaining redcurrant jelly.

Pears Almina

The pears are poached in an orange flavoured syrup and served chilled with orange custard.

Syrup:
1 cup sugar
2 cups water
4 pears
1 small orange
Custard:
3 egg yolks
3 tablespoons caster sugar
1 tablespoon arrowroot
grated rind and juice of orange
1 cup milk, scalded

Syrup: Dissolve the sugar in the water, bring to the boil and then lower the heat and simmer gently for 5 minutes.

Peel and halve the pears and remove the stalk and core with a teaspoon. Place the pears in the syrup with a strip of orange rind and poach them gently until they look transparent. Allow them to cool in the syrup.

Custard: Cream the egg yolks with the sugar, arrowroot and grated rind of half the orange. When the mixture is thick and light in colour combine with the scalded milk, stirring all the time. Pour back into the saucepan and stir on a low heat until the custard comes to the boil and thickens. Strain, cover with plastic wrap or dampened greaseproof paper and allow to cool. Chill in the refrigerator until ready to use.

Cut the remaining orange rind into needle shreds and blanch for 1 minute in boiling water. Drain, refresh and dry thoroughly on a paper towel.

When ready to serve, place drained pear halves in individual dishes, add the strained juice of half the orange to the chilled custard, coat the pears and sprinkle with a little blanched orange rind.

Poached Pears in Red Wine

6 small pears
½ cup water
½ cup red wine
½ cup sugar
strip of lemon rind
small stick of cinnamon
1 level teaspoon arrowroot (optional)

Using this French method of cooking pears, they are equally good ripe or stone-hard. When tender, you will find they have become impregnated with flavoured wine syrup and are stained a beautiful mahogany colour.

Peel the pears, but do not remove stalks. Dissolve sugar in the water and wine. Add lemon rind and cinnamon stick. Bring to the boil for 1 minute. Place pears into an ovenproof dish, into which they will just fit, and pour over the wine syrup. To hold them in position while they cook, cut a disc of greaseproof paper the size of the dish and make a small hole for each pear stalk.

Cover the pan and poach the pears in a moderate oven (350°F—170°C) until tender, about 1 hour. If pears are very firm, they may take about 2 hours. Remove, and strain the syrup. Reduce if necessary to make 1 cup. (The syrup may be thickened with arrowroot mixed with a little water. Add to the syrup, stir until boiling and cook until quite clear).

Arrange pears in a serving dish and carefully pour over wine sauce. They are served cold and may be accompanied by a bowl of whipped cream.

Note: Extra sugar may be sprinkled over the pears before cooking.

The Winemakers' Pears

4 cooking apples, peeled
1 tablespoon butter
1¼ cups sugar
2 small pieces cinnamon bark
2 tablespoons walnuts, roughly chopped
1 cup red wine
1 strip of lemon peel
6 pears
a little rum—about 2 tablespoons

Cut apples into quarters and then chop very finely. Place in a saucepan with butter and ¼ cup of sugar and 1 piece of cinnamon bark and cook gently until the apples are soft. Remove from the heat, take out cinnamon stick and stir in the walnuts.

Combine the wine, remaining cup of sugar, lemon rind and other piece of cinnamon stick. Stir over the heat until the sugar dissolves and then boil gently for 5 minutes. Peel the pears, leaving them whole with their stalks on and cook them in this wine syrup until transparent. Place the apple sauce into a dish and place the pears on top. Cook the syrup until it has reduced to half its original quantity and spoon over the pears. Just before serving, heat the rum, pour it over the dish, take to the table and set alight.

Pears with Sabayon Sauce

Poached pears coated with a creamy sweet wine sauce and decorated with toasted flaked almonds.

4 pears, peeled with their stalks left on
1 cup sugar
2 cups water
vanilla bean
Sabayon Sauce:
4 egg yolks
½ cup sweet white wine
⅓ cup caster sugar
1 tablespoon Cointreau, Grand Marnier or Curacao
30 g (1 oz) flaked almonds browned in a moderate oven

Make a syrup of the sugar, water and vanilla bean and boil for 5 minutes. Poach the pears in this syrup until tender. Allow the pears to cool in the syrup.

Place the egg yolks, sugar, white wine and liqueur in the top of a double boiler over simmering water. Beat vigorously with a rotary beater until the mixture becomes thick and creamy. Do not allow the water underneath to boil or the mixture will curdle.

Drain the pears. Place in serving dishes. Coat with the sabayon sauce and sprinkle with flaked almonds.
Note: Sabayon sauce may be served alone in long glasses or over a spoonful of ice cream. It is also good with hot winter puddings.

Ginger Glazed Pears

These pears look marvellous with their deep golden glaze. For appearances sake, select pears of uniform size with long stalks.

1½ cups sugar
2.5 cm (1 in) piece of peeled green ginger
2 cups water
6 small pears

Place the sugar, ginger and water into a saucepan, stir until sugar dissolves and then bring to boil. Lower the heat and boil gently for 10 minutes. Add the pears which have been peeled and rubbed with lemon juice and poach until golden and transparent. This will take about 20 minutes depending on the size of the pears. Place the pears into a shallow dish, boil syrup until it has the consistency of honey, cool a little and then spoon over pears. Serve well chilled by themselves or with ice cream or chilled pouring cream.
Note: A strip of lemon peel may be substituted for the ginger and the syrup may be made with white wine instead of water.

Fresh Orange Jelly

125 g (4 oz) lump sugar
4 medium sized oranges
1 cup water
1 packet of gelatine
1 lemon
little red colouring

Rub the sugar lumps over the oranges until they have rubbed off all the outer peel and are steeped with the aromatic oils. Take care not to get down to the bitter white pith. Place the sugar and water into a saucepan, stir over a low heat until the sugar has dissolved. Soften the gelatine in a little water and then stir into the hot syrup.

When it has dissolved, remove from the heat and cool a little. Add the strained orange and lemon juice to make up to $2\frac{1}{4}$ cups of liquid. Add the merest suspicion of red food colouring just to heighten the colour. Pour into chilled glasses, or a mould which has been rinsed out with chilled water, and set. **Note:** Strawberries or those tiny green sultana grapes set in this Fresh Orange Jelly make a particularly beautiful dessert. If it is set in a mould, unmould on to a dish and surround with a simple fruit salad made of orange segments and strawberries, lightly sweetened and perfumed with kirsch or cointreau.

Orange Slices in Spiced Red Wine

The dessert is exceptionally good—a pleasant surprise for those who believe wine and citrus fruit don't mix.

$\frac{3}{4}$ cup sugar
1 cup water
1 cup dry red wine
2 cloves
1 × 7 cm (3 in) stick of cinnamon
2 lemon slices
8 oranges

Dissolve the sugar in the water and add the wine. Add the cloves, cinnamon and lemon slices. Bring to the boil and cook until the mixture is thick and syrupy. Allow to cool a little.

Peel oranges and remove all the white pith. Cut into 1 cm ($\frac{1}{2}$ in) slices. Place in a bowl and pour over warm spiced wine. Chill. Serve alone or with a jug of pouring cream.
Note: In many countries where fruit grows in abundance it is a happy coincidence that the grape also grows. It is natural that fruit is often cooked gently in the wine. Pears in red wine or white wine and also peaches, plums and even dried fruits like prunes benefit from this treatment.

Fruit and Nut Compote

A wonderful combination of plump dried fruits, apple and almonds. This fruit salad may be made days in advance and stored in the refrigerator. If you wish, a little rum or brandy may be added.

250 g ($\frac{1}{2}$ lb) large prunes
250 g ($\frac{1}{2}$ lb) dried figs
250 g ($\frac{1}{2}$ lb) dried apricots
sugar
30 g (1 oz) raisins
2 medium Granny Smith apples, peeled
30 g (1 oz) blanched almonds, cut
  into slivers

Soak prunes overnight in a little cold tea. Soak the figs and apricots in cold water to cover. Cook the fruit with their juice and a little sugar until soft and plump. Remove the fruit with a slotted spoon and boil the juice to reduce it. Pour over the fruit. Soak raisins 30 minutes to plump them. Peel and slice the apples. Cook them with 2 tablespoons each of sugar and water until soft but not broken up. Cool.

Mix the fruits together. Spoon into a serving dish and scatter the almonds over the top. Serve chilled with thick cream.
Note: This may be made with dried fruit bought in a mixed pack.

Fruit and Nut Compote

Peaches

This luscious fruit is supposed to have originated in Persia, although it is well known that the Chinese have cultivated them for thousands of years. There are two specific types—the clingstones and the freestones. Both may be either golden-fleshed or delicate white.

Peaches have a fine balance of sweet and sour which makes them a joy to eat raw, with the bloom still on them, and perfect for cooking. They are delicious with wine, mixed in a fruit salad, simply stuffed or as a filling in tarts.

There are authorities who say the only way to pick a peach is to stroke it off the tree with a fond and delicate hand, using a delicate rotary movement. Perhaps this is taking sensuality too far!

Baked Stuffed Peaches

4 large peaches
1½ tablespoons caster sugar
1 egg yolk
1 tablespoon creamed butter
6 amaretti biscuits, crushed

Alternative filling:
60 g (2 oz) ground almonds
⅓ cup sifted icing sugar
3 tablespoons Ricotta cheese
2 tablespoons finely-chopped ginger

Skin and halve the peaches and remove stones. Crack a couple of the stones and remove the kernels. Chop them finely and reserve for stuffing.

Mix together the sugar, egg yolk, butter and crushed amaretti biscuits. Add the finely chopped kernels.

Scoop a little flesh from the peach making the hollow larger and add this to the stuffing. Stuff the peaches and bake them in a buttered ovenproof dish for about 30 minutes at 350°F—170°C). Serve hot with pouring cream.

Alternative filling:
Combine together with the scooped out peach flesh and stuff into peach hollows. Bake as indicated.

Peach and Plum Compote

A dessert of fresh soft summer stone fruit in a light liqueur-flavoured syrup is the perfect finish for a meal.

1 small orange
1 cup sugar
1 cup water
1 tablespoon lemon juice
Cointreau
4 large ripe peaches
4 large ripe plums

Using a potato peeler, thinly pare the rind from the orange, then with a small sharp knife cut rind in long fine strips. Put sugar and water in a heavy saucepan and stir over low heat until sugar dissolves. Bring to boil, add orange rind strips and boil for 5 minutes. Set aside to cool. Pour boiling water over fruit and allow to stand for about 3 minutes, then drain, remove skin and place whole in a glass serving bowl. Add lemon juice and approximately 2 tablespoons. Cointreau to cooled syrup before pouring over fruit. Cover bowl with food wrap and chill.

Note: If you do not have Cointreau, another orange-based liqueur such as Grand Marnier can be used.

Do not be tempted to add too much liqueur to the syrup. While a little can complement, too much can overpower the natural fragrance and flavour.

Boiling water is poured over the fruit to loosen skins and make fruit easier to peel. The standing time of 3 minutes will vary. Really ripe fruit may require less time.

Tumbling Peaches

Choose one fine ripe peach per person, prick it all over with a fork, place into wide-necked, long-stemmed glass and fill up with chilled champagne, rose or sweet white wine. Eat the peach and then enjoy the peach flavoured wine.

Peaches in Wine

Peel and slice some ripe peaches into long-stemmed wine glasses. Sprinkle with a little caster sugar and fill up with red or white wine. Best of all leave out the sugar and fill up with an old, luscious, sweet white wine. Chill for an hour. Serve with cigarettes russe or other thin crisp sweet biscuits.

Cherries

Cherries are a beautiful summer fruit which reach their peak around Christmas time. Dark and juicy and sweetly scented, they can be held by their stalk and bitten off one by one or they can be stoned, cut in half and mixed with a fruit salad, colouring it a deep pink. They are luscious stewed with a piece of cinnamon bark or lemon peel and a little brandy stirred in while still warm.

Brandied Cherries

Brandied Cherries are a great treat and so simple to do! Try not to open them for at least 3 months.

185 g (6 oz) sugar
1 cup water
1 strip lemon peel
1.5 kg (3 lb) dark cherries, stoned
brandy

Make a syrup with the sugar and water and lemon peel. Bring slowly to the boil, stirring until the sugar has dissolved and then boil for 10 minutes. Add the stoned cherries and cook gently for 5 minutes.

Pack into warm sterilized jars, half-fill with brandy and top up with syrup. Seal jars straight away. Store in a dark cool place for at least 1 month.

Note: A few cloves, a piece of vanilla pod or a small cinnamon stick may be placed in the jar with the cherries.

Rancin

This is a family pudding originating in Alsace. It is made with black cherries when they are at their peak and are juicy and sweet.

Put a layer of very thinly sliced bread and butter in an ovenproof dish. A pyrex pie plate would do very well. Fill nearly to the top with black cherries which have been cooked for a few minutes with plenty of sugar. Do not add any of the syrup. Cover with a second layer of bread and butter and sprinkle with sugar. Bake in a hot oven (400°F—200°C) until the top is golden and crisp. Dust with caster sugar or icing sugar before serving and offer a jug of cream.

Note: This is delicious made with thin slices of bun loaf, brioche or other rich yeast bread.

Brandied Cherries in Wine

Half-fill a wine glass with some brandied cherries and some of their liquor. Fill up with chilled red wine. Serve with a crisp, macaroon-type biscuit.

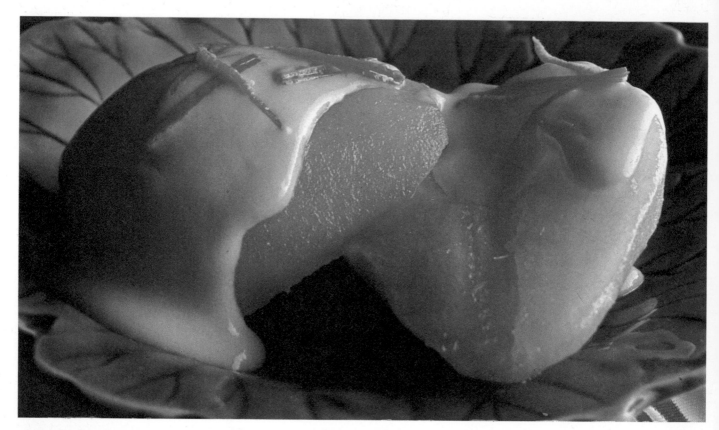

Top : Pears Almina (see recipe on page 294)
Above : Pineapple in Kirsch

Pineapples

A ripe pineapple should be sweet with a lingering perfume. They say if a leaf can be pulled out easily the fruit is ripe but smell is a good test too.

The sweet-acid flavour of pineapple with just a sprinkling of kirsch is perfect at the end of a rich meal. This simple and lovely dish is a particular favourite with the French. Pineapple mixed with grapefruit and finely chopped mint is excellent for brunch, lunch or as a first course for dinner. Grilled or baked with a sugar glaze it is a good accompaniment for ham and pork. Pineapple is, however, at its best fresh and ripe.

Pineapple in Kirsch

This is one of the best-known and loved French desserts. Kirsch and pineapple make a perfect combination and are delightful at the end of a rich meal.

2 ripe pineapples

a little sugar (depending on the sweetness of the pineapple)

4 tablespoons kirsch

Peel the pineapple. Cut into quarters and then cut each quarter in half, removing the core from each wedge. Arrange on a dish, sprinkle with sugar if necessary and then with kirsch. Chill before serving.

Note: If kirsch is not available, use port, marsala or a light muscat. The flavour, though entirely different, is still superb.

To peel a fresh pineapple:

Using a small sharp serrated stainless steel knife top and tail the pineapple. Holding the pineapple firmly with the left hand, cut downwards between the eyes at an angle of 45°.

Remove the strips of skin between the eyes. When all the skin has been removed cut the pineapple into wedges. This method of peeling a pineapple not only eliminates waste but gives the surface a most attractive appearance.

Summer Fruits in Wine

Chilled fruit compotes are one of the simplest and loveliest desserts. Nicest of all are combinations of summer stone fruits. One could make this compote of peaches and plums for their colour alone with hardly a thought to their warmly spiced wine syrup.

1 cup sugar

1 cup red or white wine (or water)

1 piece of cinnamon bark

4 large golden peaches

4 large blood plums

Put sugar, wine and cinnamon bark in a heavy saucepan and stir over a low heat until sugar dissolves. Bring to boil and then boil for 5 minutes.

Pour boiling water over the peaches and allow to stand for 3 minutes. Drain and remove the skins. Carefully lower the fruit into the syrup, return to heat and cook gently for 5 to 6 minutes. Remove plum skins if so desired. Spoon fruit into a glass bowl and pour over the hot syrup, cover and allow to cool. Chill in refrigerator.

Serve with a crisp biscuit and offer pouring cream, though this is not strictly necessary.

Note: A little cointreau may be added to the fruits while they are still warm.

Lemons

Lemons are the most indispensible fruit in the kitchen. Their fresh acid juice enhances the flavour of many dishes. Just think of a fried or grilled fish without lemon to squeeze over it!

Lemon juice is added to many fruits and also to some vegetables to bring out their particular flavour. It replaces vinegar in salad dressings and also in mayonnaise and is used as an astringent corrective as well as a flavouring for rich foods and meats.

Its peel with its highly aromatic oils, flavours cakes, ice creams, custards, soufflés, batters, marinades and meat dishes. It's almost as if the lemon, as a seasoning, comes second only to salt.

Lemons and other acid fruits should be cut with a stainless steel knife, as their acid eats into carbon steel, staining it badly.

Lemon Fluff

The lightest of desserts with the clean, sharp taste of lemon which is so very refreshing.

4 lemons
4 eggs, separated
6 tablespoons caster sugar
1 tablespoon gelatine

Grate the rind of the lemon taking care not to include any of the bitter white pith. Squeeze the juice and strain.

Beat egg yolks with the sugar until thick and pale, then stir in the lemon juice. Dissolve the gelatine in a little warm water and then add to the lemon mixture. Leave in a cool place until it is just starting to thicken and then fold in stiffly beaten egg whites. Spoon into individual dishes or into one large one and set in refrigerator. Serve with pouring cream.

The dessert may be decorated with some chopped peel or sliced strawberries.

Lemon Delicious Pudding

45 g (1½ oz) butter
½ cup sugar
4 tablespoons self raising flour, sifted
grated rind 1 lemon
juice of 1 lemon
2 eggs, separated
1¼ cups milk

Butter a 4-cup pyrex or other ovenproof pudding dish.

Cream the butter with the sugar and fold in the sifted flour with the lemon rind and juice. Beat the egg yolks with the milk and add slowly to the butter and sugar mixture. When thoroughly combined beat the egg whites until they stand in stiff peaks and then fold into mixture. Pour into greased dish and bake in a moderate (350°F—170°C) oven for 30 to 40 minutes.

Variations:
● Substitute half lemon and orange rind for the whole lemon rind or half lemon and orange juice.
● Add 3 passionfruit to the mixture.

Melon with Port

The port (or you could substitute marsala or a rich old sherry) permeates the flesh of the melon, giving it a rich, cool flavour. This fabulous dish may be used for a first course or as a dessert after spiced food.

Choose a ripe rockmelon, cut off a neat cap from the stalk end and with a slender spoon, remove the seeds. Pour in a quarter of a cup of the chosen wine. Cover with the "lid". Chill for at least 2 hours before cutting it into wedges and serving.

Alternatively, the flesh can be scooped out with a melon baller and piled back into the melon with the wine. Strawberries may also be combined with the melon balls. Two varieties of melon may be used.

Chinese Gooseberries

Chinese gooseberries grow best in the Yangtse basin in China and in New Zealand. In New Zealand they grow wild in abundance. Yet when they are flown to us they become something of a luxury.

This little fruit is very compact. It has its own built-in napkin and only needs to have a thin slice cut from the top and can then be held in the fingers and the flesh eaten with a teaspoon—no messy fingers, just the sheer delight of its superb flavour, something between grapes and bananas.

The flesh of the Chinese gooseberry is a cool, delicate green with beautiful dark markings which can be seen to advantage when the fruit is peeled and cut into slices.

Chinese gooseberries are delicious served in the following ways:
- Mixed with strawberries and chilled and, if one can go so far when thinking thin, perfumed with a little kirsch.
- In slices on their own sprinkled with lemon or lime juice.
- As a garnish for cold ham, peeled prawns and, surprisingly enough, with grilled fish.
- Mashed to a purée, stirred into skim milk yoghurt with halved strawberries for a lovely refreshing lunchtime treat.
- Served with ricotta or cottage cheese.

If the fruit is too firm, the ripening process may be speeded up by storing them in a closed polythene bag with an apple or a banana at room temperature. Chill the Chinese gooseberries, when ripened, before serving.

Bananas Caribbean

Bananas, brown sugar and rum are a most wonderful flavour combination—the smell when they come to the table surpasses all description.

6 medium bananas
¼ cup brown sugar
½ cup orange juice
grated rind 1 orange
¼ teaspoon cinnamon and nutmeg
½ cup sherry
30 g (1 oz) butter
4 tablespoons rum
vanilla ice cream or ½ cup cream, whipped

Peel the bananas and place in a flat buttered baking dish. Combine the brown sugar with the orange juice, rind, bananas, spices and sherry. Heat and then pour over the bananas. Cut the butter into small pieces and scatter over the top. Bake the bananas for 10 to 15 minutes in a moderately hot oven (375°F—190°C), basting from time to time.

When the bananas are tender, remove and place on serving dish. Pour over heated rum and set alight. Spoon the sauce over the bananas until flames die down. Serve with vanilla ice cream or whipped cream.

Meringues Chantilly with Apricot Sauce

Perfect little crisp meringues sandwiched together with Chantilly Cream accompanied by Apricot Sauce.

Meringues:
3 egg whites
⅛ teaspoon cream of tartar
1 cup caster sugar
caster sugar for dusting
Chantilly Cream:
1 cup cream
1 teaspoon caster sugar
vanilla
Apricot Sauce:
250 g (8 oz) dried apricots
½ cup sugar
1 stick cinnamon

Meringues: Beat the egg whites with the cream of tartar until they stand in stiff peaks. Add 2 tablespoons of the caster sugar and continue to beat for a further 2 minutes. Fold in the remaining sugar all at once with a metal spoon.

Using a rose piping tube, pipe small meringues on to a baking sheet which has been lined with greased greaseproof paper. Sprinkle the meringues with a little caster sugar and bake in a very slow oven (250°F—120°C) for 1½ hours or until the meringues are completely dry.

Make a small hole in the bottom of each meringue while they are warm and then cool them on a cake rack. When completely cold pipe Chantilly Cream into each meringue and join them together in pairs.

Pile up on a serving dish and serve with a jug of Apricot Sauce.

Chantilly Cream: Whip the cream with the sugar and vanilla until it is stiff. Chill.

Apricot Sauce: Soak the apricots for several hours in water to cover. Bring to the boil with the cinnamon stick and simmer until soft. Remove the cinnamon stick. Rub through a sieve and add the sugar. Return to the heat and cook until the sugar has dissolved. A little more water may be added if the sauce is too thick. Allow to cool before serving with the Meringues Chantilly.

Note: Instead of piping the meringues on to the baking sheet they may be shaped with two spoons.

Heavenly Hash

1 small can mandarin segments
1 bottle red maraschino cherries
1 small can pineapple pieces
1 small packet white marshmallows
1 small packet pink marshmallows
1¼ cups light sour cream
pinch ground cardamom
¼ teaspoon ground ginger
1 teaspoon grated orange rind
1 tablespoon cointreau, optional

Drain fruit, halve marshmallows. Toss carefully together in a large bowl. Whip sour cream with remaining ingredients.

Fold cream mixture through fruit and marshmallows. Chill until serving time—about 1-2 hours.

Note: If sour cream is unavilable use fresh sweet cream and add 1 tablespoon lemon juice to fruit mixture.

Maraschino cherries with stems are imported and sold under the Durkee label and are available at specialty delicatessens.

Mango Mousse

Mangoes are the most heavily perfumed of all tropical fruit. They have a soft golden-pink flesh which is ideal for creamy desserts and ice creams. We have added orange juice and rum to flavour this refreshing mango mousse.

1 envelope (1 tablespoon) gelatine
½ cup water
470 g (15 oz) can crushed mango pulp
** or 2 cups fresh mango pulp**
½ cup orange juice
2 tablespoons rum
2 egg whites
2 tablespoons sugar
½ cup cream

Sprinkle gelatine over water and leave for 5 minutes to soften. Dissolve over a low heat but do not allow to boil. Combine mango pulp, orange juice and rum in a bowl, stir in dissolved gelatine and chill until it is on the point of setting. Beat the egg whites until stiff peaks form then add the sugar gradually, beating until thick and glossy.

In a separate well-chilled bowl, whip chilled cream until soft peaks form. Fold the cream into the mango mixture and then fold in the egg whites.

Turn into a serving bowl and chill. Decorate with whipped cream and orange or mandarin segments.

- When chilled cream is beaten in a bowl over ice, the cream whips up more quickly and is less likely to curdle. Egg whites should be whisked until stiff peaks form before gradually adding sugar or the mixture will lose its bulk.

Chocolate and Orange Mousse

This subtle orange flavour of cointreau gives this version of chocolate mousse originality. Serve it plain with a thin biscuit like a cigarette russe or decorate it with whipped cream, shaved chocolate and slivers of orange rind.

185 g (6 oz) dark chocolate
¼ cup water
1 tablespoon caster sugar
15 g (½ oz) butter
2 tablespoons Cointreau or 1 tablespoon
** grated orange rind**
3 egg yolks
3 egg whites, stiffly beaten

Melt the chocolate with the water and sugar in a small saucepan over a gentle heat stirring until it is creamy. Let it cool a little and then stir in the butter cut into small pieces and the cointreau or orange rind. When thoroughly combined stir in the egg yolks which have been lightly beaten. Cool then fold in the stiffly beaten egg whites. Fill 8 to 12 (depending on size) small mousse pots or demi-tasse coffee cups. Chill for at least 3 hours before serving. Serve plain or decorated with whipped cream, shaved chocolate or orange rind.

Apricot Mousse

Australian dried apricots are in a class of their own. They can be found in shops and markets all over the world wherever good foods are sold.

500 g (1 lb) dried apricots
½ cup sugar
¾ cup cream
½ teaspoon vanilla
cream to decorate

Simmer apricots in water to cover for 25 minutes. Stir in the sugar and cook for 5 minutes longer. Push through a sieve or purée in an electric blender. Cool. Whip the cream and add the vanilla. Fold in the puréed apricots.

Put the mousse into small pots or other small dessert dishes. Decorate with whipped cream and sprinkle with toasted slivered almonds and chill thoroughly.

Top: *Apricot Mousse*
Above: *Mango Mousse*

Prune Mousse

This is an exception to the rule that a mousse must contain egg yolks and cream. The thick consistency of the seived prunes gives a mousse-like texture which does not need the enrichment of egg yolks.

500 g (1 lb) large dessert prunes
water
rind and juice of 1 orange and 1 lemon
1 tablespoon port
1 envelope of gelatine
2 egg whites, stiffly beaten
½ cup caster sugar
½ cup cream, whipped

Stone the prunes and cook in water to barely cover, until tender. Sieve them and measure the purée. If there is not 1½ cups add a little water to make up this amount. Add the lemon and orange rind to the purée, the lemon and orange juice and the port. Reserve a little orange juice and soak the gelatine until soft and then place over a gentle heat until dissolved. Stir into the purée and place mixture into the refrigerator until it starts to thicken.

Add the sugar gradually to the stiffly beaten egg whites whisking until it forms a stiff meringue.

Fold the meringue into the prune mixture.

Spoon mousse into individual glass dishes or into a lightly oiled mould. Place in the refrigerator for at least 1 hour. Decorate with a little whipped cream.

Peach Sherbet

4 ripe peaches or 470 g (15 oz) can
    unsweetened peaches or apricots
1½ cups buttermilk
½ teaspoon liquid sweetener
¼ cup lemon juice
finely grated rind of 1 lemon
pinch salt

Turn refrigerator to highest setting. If using fresh peaches, peel and stone. If using canned fruit, drain well. Mash fruit with a fork, adding lemon juice and rind. Add buttermilk and salt, sweeten with liquid sweetener, then pour into an ice-cube tray and place in freezing compartment.

When mixture is frozen almost solid, turn into a bowl and whip until very light. Return to tray and freeze until set. Spoon sherbet into serving glasses and decorate, if liked, with sliced fruit. Serves 6.

Italian Coffee Ice Cream

With ice creams as with most things the Italians don't go half way. Only the best ingredients will do. The result is superb. Smooth, creamy with a delicate flavour of coffee which is only possible when the coffee beans have been steeped in the ice cream mixture.

6 egg yolks
½ cup caster sugar
2 cups cream
1½ cups coffee beans

Beat the yolks with the caster sugar until light and pale in colour. Scald the cream with the coffee beans and pour on to the yolks and sugar, stirring until combined.

Pour back into the saucepan and stir over a low heat until the mixture thickens and coats the back of a spoon. Allow the mixture to cool leaving the beans in the custard. Strain into a chilled ice cream tray, cover with foil or plastic wrap and freeze.

When the ice cream is starting to set around the edges transfer it to a chilled bowl and beat with a rotary or electric beater until smooth. Pour back into the ice cream tray, cover once more and freeze until almost firm, then give the ice cream a second beating. Return to tray, cover and freeze until firm.

May be served with strawberries which have been macerated in rum and a little lightly whipped cream or with a small crisp amaretti biscuit.

Watermelon Ice

Nothing seems as cool as a melon on a hot sticky day.

Think back to those chilled slices of watermelon enjoyed with gusto over the kitchen sink and think of melons, hollowed out and filled with melon balls of green, gold and pink. Well, we have come across something even cooler— Watermelon Ice. This makes a great summer party sweet. Pile it up into a clear glass dish and decorate with a fresh sprig of mint.

4 cups diced watermelon without seeds
½ cup sugar
strained juice of 1 lemon
mint to decorate

Place the watermelon in a blender and blend at medium speed for 30 seconds or crush with a potato masher and push through a coarse sieve.

Combine the sugar and lemon juice and stir well. Add to watermelon purée. Pour into chilled ice cream trays and freeze until firm. Remove, turn into a bowl and beat until smooth. Return to ice cream trays, cover with foil and freeze till firm. Spoon into glass serving dishes and decorate with mint sprig.

Pawpaw Sorbet

Pawpaw has an exceptional flavour, only evident when really ripe. Then it needs only lemon juice. The fruit also makes an excellent sorbet, which is particularly good after curries or highly spiced foods.

1 ripe pawpaw
1 to 3 tablespoons lemon juice
1 egg white
2 tablespoons caster sugar

Peel pawpaw, cut in halves and remove seeds. Chop the flesh roughly and put into a blender a few pieces at a time, or rub through a sieve. Blend at high speed for 1 or 2 minutes until you have a smooth purée. Combine with the lemon juice and pour into a chilled ice cream tray. Freeze until it just starts to set around the edges of the tray.

Whisk the egg white stiffly and then beat in sugar gradually. Place the pawpaw into a chilled bowl and beat until smooth. Fold in the meringue and pour once again into the freezer tray, cover with foil and freeze until firm.

Serve by itself or with whole strawberries.

Mango Sorbet

A cool fruit sorbet may be served as a dessert or to refresh the palate in between rich courses.

1 × 625 g (20 oz) can of mangoes
1 teaspoon gelatine
juice of half a medium lemon
2 teaspoons rum
1 egg white

Place 2 tablespoons of the mango juice in a small saucepan and sieve the fruit with the remaining juice to make a purée. Dissolve the gelatine in the mango juice over a low heat and stir into the purée with the lemon juice and rum.

Turn the freezer to maximum temperature. Place the sorbet in an ice cream tray, cover with foil and freeze until mushy. Remove the sorbet to a bowl and beat with a rotary beater until smooth but not melted. Fold in the stiffly beaten egg white. Turn the freezer temperature to normal and freeze the sorbet till firm.

Allow the sorbet to stand at room temperature for a few minutes before serving.

Mango Sorbet (see recipe on page 309)

Italian Coffee Ice Cream (see recipe on page 308)

Lemon Sorbet

185 g (6 oz) cube sugar
6 lemons
2½ cups water
1 egg white

Rub sugar cubes over rind of two lemons until cubes are impregnated with lemon oils. Place in saucepan with water and stir over low heat until sugar dissolves. Bring to boil and boil 6 minutes. Cool.

Slice tops off remaining 4 lemons and scoop out the pulp carefully. Strain pulp to extract all the juice. Wash lemon shells and lids and set aside.

Add lemon juice to cold sugar syrup, pour into cold freezer trays and freeze until soft and mushy.

Turn semi-frozen ice into a chilled bowl and beat with a rotary beater until smooth, but not melted. Have egg white stiffly beaten and fold quickly into ice. Return to tray, cover with foil and replace in freezer for at least 1 hour or until firm.

To serve: Pile sorbet into chilled lemon shells or well-chilled glass dishes. Accompany by a chocolate savoy finger, cigarette russe or some other sweet, crisp biscuit.

Note: An equally refreshing sorbet may be made by substituting 3 large oranges with the juice of half a lemon or an equal quantity of orange and lemon juice. Grapefruit mixed with a little lemon juice is also wonderful.

- After beating the semi-frozen sorbet it may be piled into the prepared lemon shells and frozen. When the time comes for serving, the lemons will be attractively white and frosty.

  The true citrus flavour, the one that greets your nose when you sniff the ripe fruit, is best obtained from the oils in the rind. To capture this full flavour in your cooking, rub sugar cubes over the rind until they are completely impregnated with the coloured, perfumed zest, then dissolve them in water and make a syrup.

Zabaglione

This most famous of all Italian desserts is a familiar sight in restaurants and cafes all over Italy—at any time of the day or night—for it is a sweet and a restorative all in one. Taste this rich, mellow marsala-flavoured custard and you will understand why the Italians claim it can do miracles.

6 egg yolks
6 tablespoons caster sugar
6 half egg shells of marsala
1 half egg shell of brandy

Place the egg yolks and sugar in the top of a double boiler. Stand it over very hot water and whisk with a rotary beater until the mixture is thick, pale and smooth.

Add the marsala and brandy and continue whisking briskly.

When the mixture is very thick and a little dropped from the beaters will form a ribbon, remove from the heat and pour into warmed glasses. Accompany with sponge fingers.

Note: Zabaglione may be flavoured with vanilla, grated orange and lemon rind or an appropriate liqueur. It can also be transformed into a delicious ice cream by folding 1 cup of whipped cream into the above quantity of cool Zabaglione. Freeze until firm in a tray covered by a plastic film.

Ricotta Cheese with Sugar and Rum

Ricotta cheese is a creamy cheese made from buttermilk—much used for desserts in Italy. These desserts are quick to make and quite delicious.

500 g (1 lb) ricotta cheese
2 tablespoons sour cream
125 g (4 oz) caster sugar
4 egg yolks
6 tablespoons rum
2 egg whites
4 amaretti biscuits

Beat the ricotta cheese with the sour cream and then mix in the sugar. Add the egg yolks one at a time, beating until the mixture is light and creamy. Add the rum and fold in stiffly beaten egg whites. Spoon the mixture into individual glasses and chill for several hours. Serve each with an amaretti biscuit. **Note:** Amaretti—small, crisp, Italian almond biscuits—may be purchased at most continental delicatessens.

Ricotta Cheese Dessert Tuscan Style

500 g (1 lb) ricotta cheese
2 tablespoons sour cream
60 g (2 oz) ground almonds
125 g (4 oz) caster sugar
grated rind of 1 lemon
4 egg yolks
90 g (3 oz) chopped candied peel
30 g (1 oz) dark chocolate, roughly
    chopped
extra candied peel and dark chocolate
    for decoration

Beat the ricotta cheese with the sour cream and then add the almonds, caster sugar and lemon rind. When thoroughly combined, beat in the egg yolks and then fold in the candied peel and chocolate. Spoon into individual dishes and chill for a couple of hours before serving. Decorate with a few pieces of candied peel and some shaved chocolate and offer an amaretti or crisp wafer biscuit.

Monte Bianco

Sweetened chestnut purée, piped through a paper cone so it falls into a light spidery mound and topped with rum-flavoured whipped cream, makes an Italian pastry cook's impression of Monte Bianco, the highest peak in the Alps.

    This dessert should be prepared as near to serving time as possible to achieve the best effect.

$\frac{1}{4}$ cup sugar
$\frac{1}{3}$ cup milk
1 × 440 g ($15\frac{1}{2}$ oz) can chestnut purée
1 cup cream
1 tablespoon rum
grated chocolate for decorating

Dissolve the sugar in the milk over a gentle heat. Add the chestnut purée and stir until the mixture is smooth. Take off the heat, cool, and chill the mixture until it thickens. Whip the cream and fold half into the mixture. Flavour with the rum.

    Make a greaseproof funnel, fill with the chestnut cream and pipe loosely on to individual serving plates into 6 cone shapes, or use a star pipe and swirl into mountain shape. Spoon the remaining cream over each one and sprinkle with the grated chocolate.

Strawberry Pavlova

There is no need to explain this dessert so dear to the hearts of Australians and New Zealanders. We have presented it in three different ways, piled into a fluted china flan dish, moulded in a springform tin with a regular shape, or shaped into a dome on a baking sheet.

6 egg whites
2 cups caster sugar
1½ teaspoons vinegar
1½ teaspoons vanilla essence
1 punnet of strawberries OR
½ cup passionfruit pulp
1 tablespoon kirsch (optional)
icing sugar
1 cup cream, whipped

Note: If using a gas range set the oven at hot (450°F—230°F) immediately you start to beat the egg whites.

Beat egg whites until they stand in stiff peaks. Add sugar gradually, 1 tablespoon at a time, beating at high speed if using an electric mixer.

When all the sugar has been thoroughly incorporated and a stiff glossy meringue has formed, fold in the vinegar and vanilla essence.

Grease some aluminium foil and cover a baking sheet. Heap the Pavlova mixture on to the foil. Mould up the sides with a spatula and make a slight depression on top. **OR** pile the mixture into a 20 cm (8 in) greased springform tin and lightly smooth the top **OR** pile the mixture into a greased 20 cm (8 in) china flan dish.

If using a gas range turn the heat to the lowest temperature just before putting the Pavlova in to cook for 1½ hours.

If using an electric oven cook the Pavlova at a low temperature (300°F—150°C) for 45 minutes and then turn off heat and leave for 1 hour.

When cooked, remove from the oven and cool completely. Slice strawberries, sweeten with a little icing sugar if necessary and sprinkle with the kirsch.

Pile cream on to Pavlova and decorate with sliced macerated (or whole) strawberries.

Above top: Pavlova prepared in three different ways—in a
Springform Tin (foreground) in a China Flan Case (left)
and on a Foil-lined Baking Sheet (right)

Above left: Strawberry Pavlova
Above right: Passionfruit Pavlova

Hazelnut Meringue

Meringues are one of the loveliest confections ever dreamed up by a pastry chef. Their invention is attributed to a Swiss pastry cook and in no time they became a favourite with the French Court. Queen Marie-Antoinette, according to Larousse, made them with her own fair hands at the Trianon.

4 egg whites

1 cup caster sugar

3 drops vanilla essence

½ teaspoon vinegar

1 cup ground hazelnuts browned in the oven for 5 minutes

1 cup cream, whipped

1 punnet strawberries, hulled

sifted icing sugar

Grease and flour two 20 cm (8 in) sandwich tins and line the bottom with a disc of greased paper.

Whisk the egg whites until they stand in stiff peaks, then gradually whisk in the caster sugar, a tablespoon at a time and continue beating until the mixture is very stiff and is standing in peaks. Whisk in the vanilla essence and vinegar and then fold in the nuts with a metal spoon. Divide the mixture between the two prepared tins and bake in a moderately hot oven (375°F—190°C) for 35 to 40 minutes. Turn out on to wire cake racks to cool.

When cool, fill with whipped cream and whole strawberries and dust the top with icing sugar.

Note: Always fill meringues at least three hours before serving to prevent them splintering when cut into portions.

Trifle

The English Trifle as we know it today is the old-fashioned tipsy cake made with a whole sponge cake soaked with sherry mixed with brandy, sometimes with a layer of red fruit jam, and garnished with almonds and surrounded by custard.

We still use the old-fashioned sponge soaked with a good sweet sherry but we omit the jam and substitute slices of fresh pineapple, cover these with a good egg custard and decorate with whipped cream, cherries and angelica. To be sure, the sponge may be bought, the custard made from custard powder and the pineapple canned but really to do justice to this lovely dessert make your own cake and custard and use a fresh ripe pineapple.

1 × basic English sponge cake (see page 349) made day before

½ cup oloroso or amorosa sherry

1 small ripe pineapple

1 cup egg custard

1 cup cream, whipped

5 glacé cherries, cut in half

angelica, washed in warm water to remove sugar coating

Cut the sponge into 3.5 cm (1½ in) pieces. Arrange in a bowl. Sprinkle with sherry and allow to stand while making the custard (see recipe below).

Peel the pineapple, cut into slices, remove the core and cut each slice in half. Arrange on the soaked sponge cake. Make the egg custard and allow to cool. Spoon over pineapple. Decorate with whipped cream, glacé cherries and pieces of angelica which have been cut into small diamond shapes. Chill in the refrigerator for at least 2 hours before serving.

Note: If possible, make a trifle a few days ahead of time to allow it to mature.

English egg custard: Scald 1 cup of milk with a piece of vanilla bean. Beat 2 egg yolks with 2 tablespoons of caster sugar until light in colour. Beat in 1 teaspoon cornflour. Remove the vanilla bean and stir in the scalded milk. Return to the heat and stir until the custard comes to the boil and thickens. Cover the surface with a piece of plastic wrap and allow to cool.

Rhubarb Fool

A fool is a traditional English dessert which derives its name from being "something foolish"—a mere trifle. This delicious dessert is composed of a thick fruit purée into which chilled vanilla custard and thick cream are swirled giving the purée a marbled appearance.

1 bunch rhubarb, trimmed of its leaves
4 cooking apples
1 cup cream, lightly whipped
Syrup:
¾ cup sugar
1 cup water
Vanilla Custard:
½ cup milk
1 vanilla bean
2 egg yolks
1 teaspoon arrowroot
3 tablespoons caster sugar

Cut the rhubarb into 3 cm (1¼ in) lengths. Peel and slice the apples. Dissolve the sugar in the water and bring to the boil. Boil the syrup for 5 minutes. Add the rhubarb and apple and poach until soft. Remove from the syrup and reserve a few pieces of rhubarb for decoration. Rub the remaining rhubarb and apple through a sieve and leave the purée to cool. Chill in the refrigerator. Stir the custard into the fruit purée and gently fold in the cream, leaving the fool slightly marbled. Spoon into individual glass dishes and decorate with a few pieces of rhubarb. Chill until ready to serve. Accompany with sponge fingers.

Vanilla Custard: Scald the milk with the vanilla bean. Remove from the heat, cover and allow to infuse for 2 to 3 minutes. Remove the vanilla bean. With a wooden spoon cream the egg yolks with the arrowroot and sugar until thick and light and then stir in the flavoured milk. Return to the saucepan and stir over a gentle heat until the mixture coats the back of the spoon. Strain into a bowl and allow to cool. Chill in the refrigerator.

Chocolate Truffles

Very rich, very moreish and very, very French. Shaped to resemble the little "black diamond" the French worship so highly. In the hot weather these are rather inclined to soften, so once they are made they should be stored in a box in the refrigerator. The wooden boxes made by a well-known chocolate manufacturer are ideal.

1 tablespoon instant coffee
3 tablespoons boiling water
250 g (8 oz) dark chocolate
125 g (4 oz) unsalted butter
3 tablespoons brandy or rum
cocoa

Combine the instant coffee, boiling water and chocolate in the top of a double boiler over hot water. Heat until the chocolate has dissolved and then remove from the heat.

Cut the butter into small pieces and beat in to the chocolate mixture gradually, a piece at a time, until all the butter is thoroughly incorporated. Beat in the brandy or rum and chill for at least 4 hours or until firm.

Break off pieces of the chilled mixture and roll into small balls. Place in a dish containing a generous quantity of sifted cocoa and shake until the truffles are thoroughly coated.

Place truffles in paper cups, arrange in a box or in an airtight tin and store in a cool place.

This quantity will make about 18 truffles.

Note: The mixture may be made well ahead of time, wrapped and stored in the refrigerator.

Variations:
- Roll chocolate truffle mixture around a small piece of glacé ginger or glacé orange peel.
- Roughly chop some walnuts and stir into the mixture before chilling.

Profiteroles filled with Praline Cream

Profiteroles filled with Praline Cream

Toffee-coated choux pastries filled with whipped cream flavoured with praline.

Choux pastry:
¾ cup water
90 g (3 oz) butter
1 cup plain flour, sifted
3 whole eggs
Toffee coating:
¾ cup caster sugar
Praline:
30 g (1 oz) sugar
30 g (1 oz) almonds, shelled
½ cup cream, whipped

Choux pastry:
Place the water and butter in a saucepan over a gentle heat and when the butter has melted bring the water to the boil. Remove from the heat and add the flour all at once. Beat until smooth, place back on a gentle heat and beat until the mixture leaves the sides of the saucepan.

Turn mixture on to a plate to cool.

Whisk the eggs together lightly and then add by degrees to the cooled mixture beating thoroughly after each addition. When all the eggs have been added the finished choux pastry should be smooth and shiny and hold its shape.

Using a piping bag with a 1 cm (½ in) piping tube pipe small mounds (or drop in heaped teaspoonfuls) on to a greased baking tray. Choux pastry is best baked in an oven with a rising temperature so place the choux in a moderately hot oven (375°F—190°C) and then raise the heat to 400°F (200°C) and bake for 25 to 30 minutes until each profiterole is quite firm to the touch and the centre well dried out. If necessary make a small hole in the side and scoop out any soft centre. Place on a cake rack to cool.

Toffee: Place the sugar in a small heavy pan and cook slowly to a rich brown colour. Remove from the heat and dip each Profiterole to coat the top and then allow the toffee to set hard.

Split each toffee coated Profiterole and fill with whipped cream flavoured with 2 tablespoons of praline powder. Serve piled up on a serving dish.

Praline: Place the sugar in a small frying pan and set over a low heat until the sugar melts and turns a pale golden brown. Stir in the almonds with a metal spoon and continue cooking until the sugar turns golden brown.

Turn the praline immediately on to an oiled plate or baking tray.

When hard, crush to a powder in a mouli grater or with a rolling pin or empty champagne bottle. Store in an airtight container until ready to use.

Note: This recipe makes about a dozen Profiteroles.

Nesselrode Pudding

This pudding was originally a very rich frozen dessert containing candied fruits, chestnuts and liqueurs and was invented by the chef to the Russian statesman, Count Nesselrode, who had a love for lavish living.

Our version is equally delightful but less complicated and not frozen. Set in an attractive bowl, smooth, light and creamy, it looks very festive with its decoration of rum-soaked cherries and grated chocolate.

3 egg yolks
¾ cup sugar
1½ cups cream
1 tablespoon gelatine softened in a
**   little cold water**
½ cup canned crushed pineapple
½ cup raisins
2 tablespoons diced glacé cherries
**   soaked in 2 tablespoons rum**
¼ cup finely chopped dark chocolate
1 cup whipped cream
extra glacé cherries soaked in a little rum
extra dark chocolate

Combine the egg yolks with the sugar in the top of a double boiler, and then gradually stir in the cream, softened gelatine and the crushed pineapple. Stir over simmering water until the custard has thickened slightly. Pour into a chilled ice cream tray and place in the freezer until the mixture is firm.

Spoon this frozen mixture into a bowl and beat with an electric beater or rotary whisk until smooth and creamy.

Fold in raisins, cherries, chocolate and whipped cream.

Pour into a glass bowl and place into the refrigerator to set.

Serve decorated with rum-soaked glacé cherries and grated chocolate.

Note: We made two of these desserts to serve 16 to 20 people.

Pineapple Upside Down Pudding

This is a highly decorative American dessert cake which is served hot with an egg custard, ice cream or a sweet sauce.

Caramel:
75 g (2½ oz) butter
⅓ cup firmly packed brown sugar
Cake mixture:
1½ cups self raising flour
½ teaspoon salt
60 g (2 oz) butter
¾ cup caster sugar
1 egg, well whisked
½ cup milk
Decoration:
3 slices of canned pineapple
6 cherries
6 walnut halves

Lightly grease and line the base of a 20 cm (8 in) cake tin with sloping sides.

Make the caramel by creaming the butter and brown sugar together. Spread this mixture over the bottom and sides of the prepared tin. Slice pineapple through to make 6 thin slices and arrange on the caramel and decorate with the glace cherries and walnut halves.

Sift the flour and salt three times and place on one side. Cream the butter and sugar and beat in the well-whisked egg. When this mixture is light and fluffy stir in the flour alternately with the milk.

Spoon the cake mixture over the fruit and bake the pudding in a moderate oven (350°F—170°C) for 50 to 60 minutes.

Invert the pudding onto a serving plate immediately it is taken from the oven. Leave for a few minutes for the caramel mixture to run down over it and then remove the tin. Serve hot with custard, ice cream, hard sauce or whipped cream.

Note: Fruit of your own choice may be substituted for the pineapple. The important thing is that the pudding looks decorative when turned out.

Pineapple Upside Down Pudding

Rice Pudding

4 tablespoons rice
3½ cups milk
4 tablespoons sugar
nutmeg to flavour
15 g (½ oz) butter
1 vanilla bean

Butter a deep oven dish and add all the ingredients, stir together. Bake in a moderate oven (350°F—170°C) until the rice is quite soft and the milk thickened and creamy. If necessary add a little more milk to keep the mixture creamy. The top will have a thin golden crust and the centre will be creamy. Serve with pouring cream and stewed fruit.

Variations:
- Omit the vanilla bean and add a bay leaf OR 2 bruised cardamom pods.
- Omit vanilla bean adding 2 tablespoons of raisins and ½ cinnamon stick.
- Substitute a strip of orange or lemon peel for the vanilla bean.
- Infuse 60 g (2 oz) roughly ground coffee beans in the milk for 1 hour and strain before using.
- Add 2 tablespoons candied fruits mixed with a little rose-water.

Steamed Syrup Pudding

1 cup self raising flour
pinch salt
90 g (3 oz) butter
½ cup caster sugar
1 teaspoon vanilla
2 eggs
4 tablespoons milk
2 tablespoons each honey and
   golden syrup
lemon juice

Sift the flour and salt. Beat the butter until creamy and then add the sugar and vanilla and beat until light. Beat in the eggs one at a time and then fold in the milk alternately with the flour. Spoon into a 4-cup pudding basin which has been thoroughly greased. Cover with two thicknesses of pleated greased greaseproof paper, tie firmly with string and place the basin in a large saucepan of boiling water. Cover pan tightly and steam for 1½ hours.

Remove pudding from the saucepan and allow to stand for a few minutes before turning it on to a serving dish. Combine the honey and golden syrup and heat in a small saucepan. Add lemon juice to taste, pour a little over the pudding and serve the remaining sauce in a jug.

Steamed Date Pudding

125 g (4 oz) butter
½ cup brown sugar, firmly packed
1 teaspoon vanilla essence
2 eggs, lightly beaten
½ cup chopped dates
1¼ cups self raising flour
pinch salt
4 tablespoons milk

Cream the butter and gradually beat in the sugar and the vanilla essence. When the sugar is thoroughly incorporated, gradually mix in the beaten eggs. Add the dates. Sift the flour with the salt and using a metal spoon fold it into the creamed mixture alternately with the milk.

Spoon into a well-greased pudding basin, cover with double thickness of pleated buttered greaseproof paper and tie firmly with string.

Steam briskly for 2 hours. Add extra boiling water when necessary. When cooked remove paper and string and turn out onto a heated plate.

Rich Christmas Pudding

This is a richer version of a Christmas pudding steamed in a basin rather than a pudding cloth. This pudding improves with a month's keeping and is particularly good served with a Brandied Butter, a custard sauce or a sabayon sauce.

250 g (8 oz) raisins
60 g (2 oz) candied peel
250 g (8 oz) currants
250 g (8 oz) sultanas
3 tablespoons overproof rum or brandy
250 g (8 oz) butter
250 g (8 oz) brown sugar
grated rind of 1 orange and 1 lemon
4 eggs
60 g (2 oz) blanched almonds
1 cup plain flour
$\frac{1}{2}$ teaspoon each salt, mixed spice, nutmeg,
    ginger, cinnamon and bicarbonate
    of soda
125 g (4 oz) soft breadcrumbs

The day before, chop the raisins and candied peel. Mix with the currants, sultanas, sprinkle with rum and leave overnight.

The next day, cream the butter and add the sugar gradually with the fruit rinds. Add the eggs which have been lightly beaten, a little at a time to prevent the mixture from curdling, then stir in the fruit and blanched chopped nuts alternately with sifted dry ingredients and breadcrumbs.

Put into a large well-buttered pudding basin lined with a circle of greased greaseproof paper cut to fit the base. Cover with another circle of greased greaseproof paper (to fit the top of the pudding basin) then with a pudding cloth which has been scalded, wrung out and floured lightly. Tie firmly with string.

Steam covered in a saucepan with boiling water to come half-way up the sides of the pudding basin for 6 hours. Add more boiling water if necessary. Remove from the water and when cold cover with fresh greaseproof paper and tie up once more.

On Christmas Day put the pudding into a saucepan of boiling water as described above and steam for $2\frac{1}{2}$ hours.

Turn the hot pudding on to a heated serving plate. Warm a little rum or brandy in a soup ladle or small saucepan, set alight and pour over the pudding at the table. Serve immediately.

Cumberland Rum Butter

The combination of a chilled hard sauce flavoured with the spirit of your choice and a piping hot rich fruit pudding is particularly enticing. These flavoured butters may be made at the same time as the pudding and stored successfully in the refrigerator.

250 g (8 oz) unsalted butter
125 g (4 oz) brown sugar
1 teaspoon grated lemon rind
$\frac{1}{2}$ teaspoon lemon juice
freshly grated nutmeg
2 tablespoons overproof rum

Cream the butter until soft and white. This may take a little time but it's well worth the effort. Beat in the sugar gradually until the mixture is light and fluffy, then beat in the lemon rind, juice and nutmeg. Lastly, add the rum a little at a time, beating constantly so the mixture does not curdle. Pack the rum butter into a container with a firm fitting lid, first covering the top with plastic wrap or foil. Store in the refrigerator until Christmas Day.

Malakoff Torte

Malakoff Torte

A rich, luscious torte made of layers of ladyfingers dipped in rum syrup and almond coffee butter cream.

18 sponge fingers
1 cup water
1 cup rum
2 tablespoons sugar
coffee cream
1½ cups cream
vanilla
hazelnuts to decorate
Coffee cream:
280 g (9 oz) butter
90 g (3 oz) sugar
4½ tablespoons ground almonds
1½ tablespoons strong black coffee
5 tablespoons cream

Grease a 25 cm (10 in) spring form tin and line the base with greased greaseproof paper (this step is optional). Split sponge fingers in half diagonally. Combine water, rum and 1 tablespoon of sugar in a shallow dish. Dip the sponge finger halves in this mixture quickly to prevent them from becoming soggy and arrange one layer around the base of the tin.

Spread with half of the coffee cream. Repeat the layers ending in a layer of sponge fingers. Place in the refrigerator for at least 3 hours, or preferably overnight.

Turn out on to a serving plate and decorate with toasted hazelnuts.

Whip the cream with the remaining sugar and flavour with vanilla essence. Serve separately.

The torte may also be decorated with piped cream and hazelnuts.

Coffee cream:
Beat the butter until soft and creamy and then add the sugar, gradually beating until soft and fluffy. Fold in the almonds and then stir in the coffee and cream gradually until the mixture is smooth and light.

Note: Make the strong black coffee by combining 3 teaspoons of instant coffee powder with 1½ tablespoons of boiling water.

Yorkshire Pudding

1 cup plain flour
½ teaspoon salt
1 egg
1 cup milk

Sift flour and salt into a bowl. Make a well in the centre, add egg and milk. Beat mixture in centre of bowl with a balloon whisk, gradually incorporate the flour until batter is smooth. Allow to stand about 1 hour.

Spoon 2 to 3 tablespoons hot dripping from around roast beef into a smaller baking dish (a cake tin or enamel dish is ideal) and heat until smoking. Pour in batter and bake for 30-40 minutes in a hot oven (400°F—200°C) until puffed and golden. Cook the pudding in the hottest part of the oven, usually near the top, while beef finishes roasting.

The batter for Yorkshire Pudding can be prepared in a blender. Simply put all the ingredients into blender container and blend until smooth. Put container into refrigerator to rest for about 30 minutes, then blend again before pouring into the pan of smoking fat. The pudding will be very light and puffy.

Summer Pudding

250 g (8 oz) apples
500 g (1 lb) raspberries or blackcurrants
250 g (8 oz) sugar
stale white bread, sliced, with the crusts cut off

This is a delicious pudding made with berry fruits. You only need fruit, sugar and stale bread. A bowl of whipped cream adds the finishing touch.

The stale bread mops up the fruit juices which are poured over it and transforms into a really delightful fruit pudding.

Peel, core and slice apples. Place in a pan with the raspberries or blackcurrants and sugar. Heat gently until sugar dissolves and juices run from the fruit.

Butter the inside of a pudding dish and line with slices of bread. Overlap the bread slightly to prevent juices escaping.

Fill with the fruit and cover with bread slices. Butter the bottom of a small plate that will fit into the top of the basin. Place it on top of the pudding and press down with a 2 kg (4 lb) weight. Refrigerate overnight.

Turn out on to a dish and serve with a bowl of whipped cream.

Frozen or canned raspberries or blackcurrants, which have been drained, may be substituted for fresh fruit.

Pekin Pudding

A light steamed pudding flavoured with orange and decorated with chopped glacé ginger.

2 tablespoons glacé ginger, chopped
125 g (4 oz) butter
grated rind of 1 orange
½ cup caster sugar
1 cup self raising flour, sifted
2 eggs, separated
juice of 1 orange

Grease a 5-cup pudding basin and decorate with 1 tablespoon of the chopped ginger.

Cream the butter with the orange rind and then gradually beat in the sugar. When the mixture is light and fluffy beat in 1 tablespoon of the flour and then the egg yolks, one at a time.

Fold in the sifted flour alternately with the orange juice and the remaining ginger and then fold in the stiffly beaten egg whites.

Pour into the prepared pudding basin, cover first with buttered greaseproof paper and then with a piece of aluminium foil. Tie securely and place into a large saucepan with enough boiling water to come halfway up the sides of the basin.

Cover the saucepan and steam the pudding for 1½ to 2 hours. Watch the level of the water and top it up from time to time.

Turn the pudding out on to a warmed plate and serve with an egg custard to which a tablespoon of ginger syrup or finely chopped glacé ginger has been added.

Boiled Plum Pudding

Everyone has their favourite recipe for plum pudding. This is a very old one we coaxed a great aunt to part with. It is not as heavy as the usual pudding and has no spices, but develops a marvellous flavour after two weeks maturation. So easy and quick to prepare too!

155 g (5 oz) raisins, roughly chopped
125 g (4 oz) dates, roughly chopped
155 g (5 oz) sultanas
125 g (4 oz) currants
90 g (3 oz) mixed peel
¼ cup brandy
4 cups self-raising flour
1 teaspoon salt
250 g (8 oz) suet, grated
1 cup caster sugar
½ cup treacle
1½ cups water

Soak the fruit in the brandy overnight.

Sift the flour and salt into a large mixing bowl. Grate the suet and add to the bowl.

Rub the grated suet into the flour until it resembles breadcrumbs. Stir in the sugar, fruit and then the treacle mixed with the water. Mix thoroughly to a firm batter.

Put a large pudding cloth in boiling water, remove (using rubber gloves) and wring out well. Sprinkle with sifted flour and shake off any excess.

Turn pudding mixture into the centre of the cloth and gather the cloth firmly around the pudding. Secure the cloth firmly with string.

Tie the ends of the pudding cloth around a wooden spoon and rest the wooden spoon on the edges of the boiler preventing the pudding touching the bottom of the pot. Cook in boiling water to cover and place a lid over the top. Steam for 1 hour and by this time the pudding will have taken shape and the wooden spoon may be removed. Steam for a further 2½ hours.

Hang the pudding for at least 2 weeks to mature in a dark, dry place.

On Christmas Day, steam the pudding for a further 1 to 1½ hours. Turn on to a heated platter, heat some brandy, set alight and pour flaming over the pudding, taking it immediately to the table.

Serve with vanilla ice cream, Brandied Butter or just whipped cream.

Brandied Butter

250 g (8 oz) unsalted butter
125 g (4 oz) icing sugar
1 teaspoon grated orange rind
½ teaspoon Grand Marnier or orange juice
2 tablespoons brandy

Cream the butter until soft and white, then beat in the icing sugar. When creamy, beat in the orange rind and Grand Marnier or orange juice. Lastly, add the brandy drop by drop beating all the time so the mixture doesn't curdle (a liqueur brandy is the best if you have it).

This butter may be made on the same day as the pudding. Pack it into a bowl with a lid, first covering it with aluminium foil and store in the refrigerator. Remove it from the refrigerator well beforehand on Christmas Day, spoon it into a bowl and fluff up with a fork.

Savarin

Savarin

Most of the credit for this wonderful rum-soaked yeast cake should go to King Stanislas Leczinski, the father-in-law of King Louis XV. His recipe contained raisins and was named Baba after Ali Baba of A Thousand and One Nights. In the mid 1800's a clever pastry cook changed the shape, omitted the raisins, renamed the cake Brillat-Savarin and introduced it to the Parisians. Everyone went wild over it.

The Savarin is usually flavoured with rum but sometimes cherry brandy or kirsch is used and the centre filled with cherries soaked in the same liqueur. Other times the Savarin is glazed and decorated with glacé fruits.

500 g (1 lb) plain flour
½ teaspoon salt
30 g (1 oz) compressed yeast
1½ tablespoons sugar
1 cup warm milk
4 eggs (60 g size)
250 g (8 oz) softened butter
Syrup:
2 cups water
500 g (1 lb) sugar
2.5 cm (1 in) vanilla bean
6 tablespoons rum
2 cups of fruit (mixture of pineapple, strawberries, cherries, orange slices, apricots or any other fruits in season)

Sift the flour and salt into a large warmed bowl. Cream the yeast with the sugar and tepid milk in a small bowl. Make a well in the centre of the flour and add the yeast mixture.

Sprinkle a little of the flour from the sides over the top, cover with a cloth and leave in a warm place for 15 minutes. Beat the eggs. Cream the butter.

Add the eggs and softened butter to the yeast mixture beating it in vigorously with the hand until the dough is smooth and elastic. Cover with a cloth and allow it to double in bulk in a warm place. This will take about 30 minutes.

Grease two 23 cm (9 in) savarin moulds or ring tins. Divide the mixture in two and put into prepared tins. Allow them to stand in a warm place until the mixture rises to the top of the tins. Bake in a hot oven (400°F—200°C) for about 20 minutes.

Remove the savarins from the oven, place on a cake rack and while still hot spoon over the rum syrup. When all the syrup has been absorbed allow the savarins to cool. Place on a serving dish and fill the centre with the fruit (the fruit is optional, it is delicious with or without). Accompany with a bowl of whipped cream.

Syrup: Combine the water, sugar and vanilla bean in a saucepan. Stir over the heat until the sugar dissolves. Bring to the boil and boil for 10 minutes. Stir in the rum.

Note: Plain and fluted savarin moulds are available from the kitchen shops of large department stores and specialty kitchen shops which stock Cuisine International cooking utensils. The moulds we used came from The Village Store, 298 Darling Street, Balmain, NSW.

● Savarins may be cooked and frozen. Do not pour the syrup over before freezing. Allow them to thaw the night before you serve them.

cakes and pastries

Rich Fruit Cake

Cakes and Sponges

Rich Fruit Cake

This beautiful Rich Fruit Cake may be used as a Christmas cake, the base of a wedding cake or just for good eating. It should be made at least 2 weeks before being used and will keep up to 4 months.

375 g (12 oz) raisins
375 g (12 oz) sultanas
125 g (4 oz) mixed peel
125 g (4 oz) glacé cherries
125 g (4 oz) dates (stoned)
3 tablespoons rum
3 tablespoons sherry
Cake Mixture:
250 g (8 oz) butter
1 cup brown sugar
grated rind of 1 lemon
1 tablespoon golden syrup
2 tablespoons marmalade
5 large eggs
2 cups plain flour
1 teaspoon mixed spice
1 teaspoon cinnamon
$\frac{1}{4}$ teaspoon salt
125 g (4 oz) blanched almonds, chopped
extra almonds
extra rum

Prepare fruit. Chop the raisins and place into a bowl with the sultanas and finely chopped peel. Cut the cherries and dates into small pieces and add to the other fruit. Sprinkle with rum and sherry, cover and leave overnight.

Grease a 20 cm (8 in) round or square cake tin and line it with 2 thicknesses each of brown and buttered greaseproof paper.

Beat the butter until soft and creamy then beat in the brown sugar and lemon rind. When the mixture is creamy and light in colour add the golden syrup and marmalade. Beat well. Add the eggs one at a time, beating after each addition. Add 1 tablespoon of flour with the last egg. Sift the remaining flour. spices and salt together and stir into the creamed mixture alternately with the fruit and chopped almonds.

Spoon the mixture into the prepared tin. Arrange the extra almonds in a pattern around the top. Bake in a slow oven (300°F—150°C) for about 4 hours or until cooked. Remove the cake from the oven and immediately sprinkle with about 1 tablespoon of extra rum. Remove the cake from the tin leaving the paper on the cake. Wrap the cake in a tea towel and allow it to cool. Store in an airtight tin or wrap in foil or plastic wrap.

Date and Orange Cake

2 cups self-raising flour
125 g (4 oz) butter
$\frac{1}{2}$ cup caster sugar
grated rind of 1 orange
1 egg
$\frac{3}{4}$ cup milk and water, mixed together
185 g (6 oz) chopped dates
90 g (3 oz) chopped candied peel

Sift the flour into a bowl, rub in the butter and stir in the sugar with a palette knife and then the grated orange rind. Make a well in the centre, add the egg and gradually beat in the milk and water mixture. When the mixture is smooth, stir in the dates and candied peel.

Turn into a deep greased 18 cm × 9 cm × 9 cm (7 in × 3$\frac{1}{2}$ in × 3$\frac{1}{2}$ in) loaf tin and bake for 1 hour 20 minutes in a moderate oven (350°F—170°C) or until a skewer inserted in the middle comes out cleanly. Turn on to a wire rack to cool.

Orange Cake

A basic butter cake flavoured with orange rind and juice. It has a fine texture and keeps well. Serve it plain, dusted with caster sugar or iced with an orange icing and decorated with finely shredded blanched orange rind.

250 g (8 oz) softened butter
rind of 1 large orange
250 g (8 oz) caster sugar
4 × 60 g eggs
250 g (8 oz) self raising flour
pinch salt
juice of 1 large orange

Grease and lightly flour a large loaf tin (5-cup size) and line the base with greased paper.

Cream the butter with the orange rind until very smooth. Gradually add the sugar, beating well in between each addition until it is thoroughly incorporated and the mixture light and fluffy.

Beat the eggs until blended and gradually pour into the butter and sugar mixture beating thoroughly to prevent the eggs from curdling the mixture.

Sift the flour with the salt. Using a metal spoon fold in the flour alternatively with the orange juice. Turn the mixture into the prepared tin and bake in a moderate oven (350°F—170°C) for 45 minutes or until the cake is cooked when tested. Remove from the tin and cool on a cake rack.

- This cake is made on the old principle of 4 eggs, and their weight in butter, sugar and flour, but for ease we have converted these ingredients into precise weights. It is a good idea to weigh your ingredients by this method, particularly if you are using farm eggs of different sizes.

Orange Icing

30 g (1 oz) butter
1 tablespoon grated orange rind
1 tablespoon orange juice
2 cups sifted icing sugar

Cream the butter with the orange rind and stir in the orange juice. Gradually add the sifted icing sugar beating until smooth.

Walnut Loaf

A nut loaf or tea bread is essential to the variety of cakes and biscuits on the afternoon tea table. Ours is flavoured with walnuts and lemon rind.

45 g (1½ oz) butter
½ cup sugar
grated rind of 1 lemon
1 egg, beaten
½ cup milk
1½ cups of self-raising flour
salt
½ cup walnuts, roughly chopped

Grease and line a nut loaf tin with a sheet of paper. Cream the butter with the sugar and beat in the grated lemon rind. Sift the flour with the salt. Beat in the egg and when thoroughly combined fold in the flour alternately with the milk. Add the walnuts. Spoon the mixture into the prepared tin and bake in a moderate oven (350°F—170°C) for 1 hour. Turn out onto a cake rack to cool.

This nut loaf is best made the day before it is to be eaten.

Madeira Cake

This rich orange and lemon flavoured butter cake, very popular in Victorian England, was often served with a glass of Madeira.

250 g (8 oz) butter
1 cup caster sugar
finely grated rind of 1 lemon and 1 orange
$\frac{1}{2}$ teaspoon ground cinnamon
5 eggs
1$\frac{1}{2}$ cups plain flour
$\frac{1}{2}$ cup self raising flour
$\frac{1}{2}$ teaspoon salt
1 tablespoon milk
1 tablespoon mixed peel or 1 slice glacé
  orange cut into small dice

Grease a deep 20 cm (8 inch) round cake tin and line the whole tin with buttered greaseproof paper.

Cream the butter with the sugar, rind and cinnamon. When pale and creamy, add the eggs one at a time beating well after each addition.

Sift the flours with the salt. Fold half the flour into the basic mixture and when thoroughly incorporated, mix in the milk. Fold in the remaining flour. Turn into the prepared tin and bake in a moderately slow oven (325°F—160°C) for 45 minutes. Open the oven door and sprinkle the top of the cake with the peel or diced glace orange. Bake for a further 40 to 45 minutes or until the cake has shrunk away from the sides of the tin and is cooked when tested. Remove the cake from the tin and cool on a rack.

Linzer Torte

In Vienna they say that "a torte is a round cake but not every round cake is a torte"!

Linzer Torte, named after the town of Linz on the Danube, is made by capable cooks all over Austria. It's usual to fill it with raspberry jam but as always creative cooks use their own initiative. If raspberry jam is not available and there is a store of strawberry or glossy plum jam on the shelves they use that to fill the torte.

Linzer Torte is distinguished by its unique spiced almond pastry and its covering of pastry lattice strips. It may be served plain or dusted with sifted icing sugar.

1 cup plain flour
$\frac{1}{4}$ cup caster sugar
2 teaspoons cocoa
$\frac{1}{2}$ teaspoon ground cinnamon
pinch ground cloves
$\frac{1}{2}$ teaspoon baking powder
pinch salt
125 g (4 oz) ground almonds
125 g (4 oz) butter
milk or kirsch
1$\frac{1}{2}$ cups of jam, raspberry, strawberry
  or plum
1 egg, lightly beaten for glazing
sifted icing sugar (optional)

Sift the plain flour, sugar, cocoa, cinnamon, cloves, baking powder and salt into a mixing bowl. Add the ground almonds. Rub in the butter which has been cut into small pieces, and mix lightly with the fingertips to a dry dough, adding milk or kirsch if necessary. Wrap the dough in a piece of alfoil and chill in the refrigerator for at least 30 minutes.

Divide the dough and roll out two-thirds and press on to the base of a 20 cm (8 in) greased spring-form tin. Spread the jam on top. Roll out remaining pastry, cut into 1 cm ($\frac{1}{2}$ in) wide strips and arrange in lattice fashion on top using the last one as an edging around the cake. Press down lightly and chill for 30 minutes. Remove the torte from the refrigerator, brush with beaten egg and bake in a moderately hot oven (375°F—190°C) for 35 to 40 minutes. Allow to cool in the tin. Dust with icing sugar if preferred. Serve with whipped cream.

Top: *Gingerbread*
Above: *Austrian Coffee Cake*

Austrian Coffee Cake

This Austrian coffee cake is one of the magnificent cakes which you may find in an Austrian coffee house. It is equally delicious served as a dessert—of course with whipped cream—or with coffee. Bake it the day before to allow the coffee and rum syrup to flavour and moisten the cake.

185 g (6 oz) butter
¾ cup caster sugar
3 eggs, slightly beaten
1½ cups self-raising flour
pinch of salt
1-2 tablespoons milk

Grease a 6½ cup cake mould. Sprinkle with fine, dry breadcrumbs. Set oven temperature at moderate.

Beat the butter until it is soft, add the sugar a little at a time and continue beating until light and fluffy. Gradually pour in the eggs, beating thoroughly after each addition. Fold in the sifted flour and salt alternatively with enough milk to make a dropping consistency.

Pour into the mould and bake in a moderate oven (350°F—170°C) for 40 to 45 minutes, or until a skewer inserted in the centre comes out clean. Leave to cool in the mould for a few minutes. Turn out on to a cake rack. When cold, replace the cake in the mould. Slowly pour coffee syrup over the cake. Refrigerate and remove from mould just before serving. It can be served as a dessert, masked with whipped cream.

Coffee Syrup

1¼ cups of strong black coffee
⅓ cup sugar
⅔ cup water
2 tablespoons rum

Put the coffee into a jug. Heat the sugar and water in a saucepan and allow to boil for two minutes. Add to the coffee and allow to cool. Flavour with the rum.

Gingerbread

Rich, spicy Gingerbread is always a great favourite. This is rather a special version filled with raisins and chopped ginger. It is best made several days before it is to be eaten. It may be served plain or with a tart lemon icing.

185 g (6 oz) butter
1 tablespoon ground ginger
2 teaspoons cinnamon
½ teaspoon allspice
1 cup brown sugar
1 cup golden syrup
1 large egg
3 cups plain flour
1 cup milk　　　　　 ⎫ dissolved together
1 teaspoon carb soda ⎰ over a gentle heat
1 cup of raisins and preserved ginger
　　mixed together

Grease a large loaf pan (8-cup size) and line the base with buttered greaseproof paper.

Cream the butter with the ginger, cinnamon and allspice until very soft. Gradually add the sugar, beating until smooth. Add the golden syrup and mix in well. Lightly beat the egg and add gradually, beating until it is thoroughly incorporated. Sift the flour and fold into the basic mixture alternatively with the milk. Chop the raisins and ginger and fold in.

Turn into the prepared tin and bake in a moderate oven (350°F—170°C) for 1 hour 20 minutes or until a skewer or straw inserted in the centre comes out clean. Remove from the tin and cool on a cake rack.

Chocolate Sandwich Cake

A light, fine-textured chocolate cake with the special flavour of raspberry jam.

2 tablespoons cocoa
boiling water
2 tablespoons raspberry jam
125 g (4 oz) butter
¾ cup sugar
1 teaspoon vanilla
2 large eggs
2 cups self raising flour, sifted
extra raspberry jam for filling

Brush 2 × 18 cm (7 in) sandwich tins with melted butter and line the base with buttered greaseproof paper.

Sift the cocoa and mix with boiling water to smooth thin paste. Add the jam and mix in sufficient boiling water to make ¾ of a cup. Allow to cool.

Cream the butter until soft. Beat in the sugar gradually and flavour with vanilla. Add the lightly beaten eggs little by little mixing well after each addition. If using an electric mixer, add the unbeaten eggs one at a time beating well after each.

Fold in the sifted flour alternately with the cocoa and jam mixture. Spread evenly into two tins and bake in a moderate oven (350°F—170°C) for 25 to 30 minutes until the cake springs back when lightly touched with the finger. Turn out on to cake racks to cool.

Fill with raspberry jam and glaze with chocolate icing.

Chocolate Glacé Icing

90 g (3 oz) dark block chocolate
4 tablespoons water
1¾ cups icing sugar
½ teaspoon oil
2 to 3 drops vanilla essence

Cut the chocolate into small pieces and place in a small basin with the water over a saucepan of hot water and allow it to melt slowly. As soon as it is melted remove from the heat. Overheating will cause the chocolate to become granular. Allow to cool slightly. Beat in the icing sugar a spoonful at a time. Add the oil and vanilla and warm over a low heat to enable it to spread easily.

Banana Bread

Teacakes are very quick and easy to make, less sweet than most cakes, and beautifully firm and moist—a perfect background to lots of creamy butter. This one is decorated with chopped walnuts and is delicious eaten with butter and honey.

60 g (2 oz) butter
½ cup caster sugar
2 large or 3 small bananas
1 egg
2 cups self-raising flour
½ teaspoon salt
3 tablespoons yoghurt
30 g (1 oz) walnuts, roughly chopped

Cream butter and beat in the sugar gradually until the mixture is light.

Mash the bananas to a pulp and combine with the egg and add gradually to the creamed mixture, beating thoroughly.

Sift the flour with the salt and add alternately with the yoghurt.

Pour into a deep greased 18 cm × 9 cm × 9 cm (7 in × 3½ in × 3½ in) loaf tin, sprinkle with walnuts and bake for 1 hour in a moderate oven (350°F—170°C). Cool on a wire rack.

Top left: Banana Bread
Bottom left: Victoria Sponge (see recipe on page 351)

Top right: Chocolate Almond Cake (see recipe overleaf)
Bottom right: Chocolate Sandwich Cake

Chocolate Almond Cake

This is a special rich continental-style chocolate cake to serve with coffee or as a dessert. It is moist in the centre and has a light crisp crust on top. Unfilled it will keep in an airtight tin or sealed plastic bag for at least a week.

125 g (4 oz) chocolate
2 tablespoons rum
125 g (4 oz) butter
125 g (4 oz) caster sugar
3 egg yolks
4 tablespoons ground almonds
¼ teaspoon almond essence
3 egg whites
pinch salt
1 tablespoon caster sugar
½ cup plain flour
1 cup whipped cream·
icing sugar

Grease and lightly flour a round 20 cm (8 in) cake tin.

Melt the chocolate with the rum over very hot water.

Cream the butter with the sugar until very smooth and light in colour. Beat the egg yolks together and then beat in gradually to the butter and sugar mixture. Fold in the melted chocolate, ground almonds and almond essence.

Beat the egg whites with the salt until they stand in soft peaks. Sprinkle with 1 tablespoon of caster sugar and beat until the egg whites are very stiff. Using a metal spoon fold in 2 tablespoons of the egg white to soften the basic mixture and then fold in the sifted flour. Add the remaining egg white, carefully folding and cutting it into the cake mixture.

Spoon the mixture into the prepared tin and bake for about 25 minutes in a moderate oven (350°F—170°C) or until a fine skewer or straw placed in the centre of the cake comes out clean. Cool the cake in the tin for 10 minutes. Run a knife around the edge of the tin and turn the cake on to a rack. When cold slice in half.

Fill the cake with whipped cream. Place 2.5 cm (1 in) strips of paper across the top leaving a 2.5 cm (1 in) space in between each. Dust with sifted icing sugar. Carefully remove the paper strips, leaving a striped effect.

Dundee Cake

Like all fruit cakes this Dundee cake improves with keeping and is best made at least 2 weeks before serving.

1 cup caster sugar
250 g (8 oz) butter
2 oranges
5 eggs
2½ cups of plain flour
1 teaspoon baking powder
½ teaspoon salt
½ cup blanched almonds, chopped
1 cup sultanas
1 cup currants
¼ cup glace cherries
¼ cup mixed peel
extra almonds

Grease a 20 cm (8 in) round tin and line with one thickness of brown and one thickness of greaseproof paper. Grease the paper. Set the oven temperature at slow (300°F—150°C).

Cream the butter and the sugar with the grated rind of the oranges. Beat in the eggs, one at a time. Sift the flour with the baking powder and salt. Mix into the fruit and chopped almonds. Stir into the creamed mixture with 1 tablespoon of orange juice. Turn into the prepared tin. Smooth the top and arrange the extra blanched almonds around the top. Bake in a slow oven for about 2½ hours or until a skewer placed in the centre comes out clean. Cool in the tin.

- Fruit cakes will keep for weeks, even months. So care must be taken to prevent them from drying out after they have been baked.
- There is a correct way to cut fruit cakes. Cut a half-inch slice from one side of the cake and continue slicing as needed. The cut surface is then covered with greaseproof paper **or** it stands on its end (the cut end) depending on the cake tin. It keeps freshest this way.
- An old trick is to put a wedge of apple in the tin to help keep the cake moist.

Chocolate Cream Roll

After a leisurely lunch in the sun everyone will be in the mood for coffee and this really super cake—Chocolate Cream Roll.

3 eggs, separated
½ cup caster sugar
2 tablespoons cocoa
1 teaspoon vanilla
½ teaspoon almond essence
¾ cup whipped cream
1 punnet strawberries
whipped cream for decoration

Generously brush a 30 cm × 25 cm (12 in × 10 in) jam roll tin with melted butter. Line base of tin with greaseproof paper and grease paper with melted butter too. Set oven temperature at moderate.

Beat egg yolks with a rotary beater or with an electric mixer until thick and creamy. Gradually beat in sugar. Sift cocoa, then fold into egg yolk mixture with vanilla and almond essence.

Beat egg whites stiffly and gently fold in. Pour at once into prepared tin and bake in a moderate oven (350°F—175°C) 15 minutes, or until cake draws away from sides of tin and springs back when touched lightly in the middle.

Have ready a tea towel or sheet of greaseproof paper liberally sprinkled with caster sugar. Turn cake out on towel, carefully peel away base paper by tearing off small strips at a time, and while still warm roll up, including towel, and leave on a wire rack to cool. When completely cold, unroll cake and spread with whipped cream. Wash, hull and slice strawberries and scatter evenly. Reserve several whole perfect strawberries for garnish. Roll cake up and chill in refrigerator for 30 minutes. Just before serving, pipe rosettes of well chilled whipped cream down centre of roll and garnish with reserved strawberries. To serve cut into slices.

Cup Cakes

Individual butter cakes cooked in paper cups. May be served plain or iced with glacé icing and decorated. They are also the base for small cream-filled butterfly cakes.

125 g (4 oz) butter
¾ cup sugar
1 teaspoon vanilla
2 large eggs, beaten
2 cups self raising flour, sifted
pinch salt
⅔ cup milk
whipped cream
icing sugar

Line patty tins with paper cases. Cream the butter and gradually add the sugar beating until smooth and creamy. Add the vanilla and the eggs gradually, beating well after each addition. Sift the flour with the salt 3 times and then fold lightly into the creamed mixture alternately with the milk. Spoon into the paper cases until three-quarters full. Bake in a moderately hot oven (375°F—190°C) for approximately 15 minutes.

Butterfly Cakes: For the peaked tops necessary for these little cakes increase the oven heat to hot (400°F—200°C). When cool cut a circle from the top of each cake. Fill with a spoonful of sweetened whipped cream and place the circle—cut in two —on top to resemble butterfly wings. Dust with icing sugar.

Croquembouche Nöel (see recipe overleaf)

Yule Log (see recipe overleaf)

Croquembouche Nöel

This is the traditional French wedding cake composed of a pyramid of tiny choux puffs. Each puff is filled with vanilla pastry cream and dipped in toffee before being arranged in circles one on top of the other. The crowning glory of many a Croquembouche is its web of finely spun sugar but whether or not you go to the trouble of making the spun sugar, it is still a most festive cake. Although commercially spun sugar is made with a metal comb, we find pulling it out with two wooden spoons is the most practical way of doing it. In most cases this is a touch of fancy and we don't recommend that you try it during the humid weather at Christmas, unless you have a daughter who can make it just before the cake is served.

The cherry and angelica decoration turns this wedding cake into a Christmas speciality.

Choux pastry:
$\frac{3}{4}$ cup of water
90 g (3 oz) butter
1 cup plain flour, sifted
3 whole eggs
Pastry cream:
2 egg yolks
$\frac{1}{2}$ cup caster sugar
2 teaspoons cornflour
3 teaspoons plain flour
1 cup milk
1 egg white
few drops vanilla essence
Toffee:
$1\frac{1}{2}$ cups sugar
$1\frac{1}{2}$ cups water
glace cherries and Angelica leaves for
    decoration

Choux pastry: Place the water and butter in a saucepan over a gentle heat until the butter has melted. Bring to the boil. Remove from the heat and add the flour all at once. Beat until smooth, place back on a gentle heat and beat until the mixture leaves the sides of the saucepan.

Turn the mixture on to a plate to cool. Whisk the eggs together lightly and then add by degrees to the cooled mixture, beating thoroughly after each addition. When all the eggs have been added the finished choux pastry should be smooth and shiny and hold its shape.

Using a piping bag with a 1 cm ($\frac{1}{2}$ in) plain tube, pipe small mounds (or drop in heated teaspoonfuls) on to a greased baking tray. Preheat oven to moderately hot (375°F—190°C) and then raise the heat to hot (400°F—200°C) and bake for 20 minutes until each puff is quite firm and the centre well dried out. Place on a wire rack to cool.

To assemble cake:

Cut a small slit in the side of each puff and fill with pastry cream, forcing the cream through a pastry bag fitted with a small round tube.

Pierce each choux puff with the point of a small, sharp, knife and dip it into the toffee.

With another small knife remove the toffee coated choux puffs to a flat plate, arranging them as you dip them in toffee in a circle about 18 cm (7 in) in diameter. Arrange the second row of puffs in the crevices of the first circle.

Continue to build the choux pyramid in decreasing circles until all the choux puffs are used up.

Pastry cream: Break the yolks into a bowl, add the sugar gradually and beat well. Add the sifted flours with about $\frac{1}{4}$ cup of the milk. Bring the remaining milk to the boil, pour on to the yolks, blend and then return to the saucepan.

Stir over a low heat until it comes to boiling point. Draw aside. Whip the egg white stiffly, put about a a quarter of the pastry cream in the egg white and fold in the egg white carefully. Return the mixture to the saucepan. Cook over a gentle heat for a few minutes, folding the mixture over occasionally to blend and adding vanilla essence. Turn into a bowl to cool.

For decoration: Dip the base of thin slices of angelica cut into the shape of leaves and red glace cherries into toffee and arrange around the croquembouche.

If finishing with spun sugar (see directions below) do this at the very last moment.

Spun Sugar

125 g (4 oz) loaf sugar
¼ cup water

Put the ingredients into a saucepan, allow the sugar to dissolve over a low heat, then bring to the boil and allow to cook rapidly without shaking or stirring until it reaches hard crack (320°F—158°C). Set the pan in a larger saucepan of hot water. Coat the backs of two wooden spoons with the toffee, put them back to back, then gently pull apart and as a thread begins to run when the spoons are raised begin to 'throw'. This is done with loose movements of the wrists, bringing the spoons back and forth together again. As you get a bundle of threads arrange on cake. Continue until all the syrup is used up.

Note: Do not attempt to make this spun sugar during very humid weather.

Yule Log

The origin of the Yule Log is believed to have been derived from the old custom of sending a log to the house to which you were invited on Christmas Eve so you could be sure to enjoy the Christmas dinner before a roaring fire.

½ cup plain flour
½ teaspoon baking powder
¼ teaspoon salt
60 g (2 oz) dark chocolate, chopped
4 eggs
¾ cup caster sugar
1 teaspoon vanilla
¼ teaspoon bicarbonate of soda
2 tablespoons cold water
caster sugar
chocolate butter cream

Grease a 38 × 25 × 2.5 cm (15 × 10 × 1 in) swiss roll tin and line with greased greaseproof paper.

Sift together flour, baking powder and salt. Melt the chocolate in a basin over hot water.

Break the eggs into a bowl, add the sugar and beat over hot water or on the highest speed of the electric mixer until the mixture is very light and thick and greatly increased in volume. Fold sifted flour, baking powder, salt and vanilla into egg mixture all at once.

Stir the bicarbonate of soda and cold water into the melted chocolate and fold quickly and evenly into the cake mixture.

Turn into prepared tin and bake in a hot oven for 15 minutes or until cake top springs back when the centre is lightly touched. Loosen edges and turn on to a tea towel thickly dusted with caster sugar. Peel off paper and trim edges of cake with a sharp knife. Roll immediately in the towel and leave to cool on a wire rack for at least 1 hour. When cold, carefully unroll cake and spread with one-third of the chocolate butter cream. Roll cake once more and cut off one end of cake at an angle. Place cake on plate or board, arrange the cut piece of cake to resemble a stump and cover Yule log with butter cream. Decorate with a fork and chill until serving time.

Chocolate Butter Cream

2 egg yolks
¼ cup caster sugar
½ cup sugar
½ cup milk
250 g (8 oz) unsalted butter, softened
60 g (2 oz) dark chocolate

Cream the egg yolks with the caster sugar. Dissolve the remaining sugar with the milk over a low heat and bring to the boil. Add gradually to the creamed mixture and then return to the saucepan and heat until the mixture will coat the back of a spoon. Strain and allow to cool.

Cream the butter until it resembles whipped cream and gradually beat into the cooled custard. Melt the chocolate over hot water, cool and then beat into the butter mixture.

Christmas Cake

Christmas Cake means a large, rich fruit cake which is made several months before Christmas so it will age gracefully, developing a rich luscious flavour.

This cake does not require the fruit to be macerated in alcohol or more alcohol to be added after cooking, yet its flavour is excellent and full of the promises of a rich and bountiful Yuletide.

315 g (10 oz) candied peel, finely chopped
315 g (10 oz) sultanas
250 g (8 oz) currants
155 g (5 oz) raisins
125 g (4 oz) glace cherries, cut in half
125 g (4 oz) angelica, finely chopped
2 cups plain flour
½ teaspoon baking powder
¼ teaspoon salt
250 g (8 oz) butter
220 g (7 oz) soft brown sugar
185 g (6 oz) ground almonds
4 eggs
3 tablespoons rum or brandy

Place the fruits in a bowl and sprinkle with 60 g (2 oz) of flour, tossing them to coat the pieces evenly. Set aside and sift the remaining flour with the baking powder and salt.

Cream the butter and then add the sugar gradually, beating until the mixture is light and fluffy. Add the ground almonds. Beat the eggs lightly and add to the butter mixture, gradually beating the mixture well to prevent it curdling. If using an electric mixer the eggs may be added whole—one by one, beating in between each addition.

Fold in the flour (about 6 tablespoons at a time) and mix carefully until thoroughly incorporated.

Beat the fruit into the cake batter and then stir in the rum.

Spoon the cake batter into the 20 cm (8 in) lined tin and smooth the top making a slight depression in the centre so that the top of the cake will be level when baked. Place on the centre rack in a preheated slow oven (310°F—154°C) for about 1 hour 45 minutes, then lower the oven temperature to 290°F—140°C and bake for a further 2½ hours until a fine skewer inserted in the centre of the cake comes out clean. If the cake tends to brown too much during baking, place a double sheet of dampened brown paper over it.

Remove the cake from the oven and allow to cool in its tin for 30 minutes, then remove to a cake rack and allow to cool completely. Wrap securely in alfoil and store in a dark, cool place until ready to ice.

Lining the tin

Cut a strip of double thickness greaseproof paper 8 cm (3 in) higher than the cake tin and cut two circles of paper to fit the base of the tin—one in greaseproof and one in brown paper or kitchen paper. Grease the tin well and fit the paper strip and then the greaseproof paper circle in the base. Brush with melted butter.

Cut a strip of brown paper or kitchen paper 10 cm (4 in) higher than the tin and make a 1 cm (½ in) hem. Nick the hem with a pair of scissors at 2.5 cm (1 in) intervals and fit this strip into the tin, making sure the hem lies flat on the base.

Place second disc of paper into the tin giving a neat finish to the lining and then brush the whole paper lining with melted butter.

Note: Instead of fitting a brown paper strip inside the tin it may be tied around the outside, giving the same protection.

Icing the Christmas Cake

Almond paste:
375 g (12 oz) ground almonds
185 g (6 oz) caster sugar
185 g (6 oz) icing sugar
1 teaspoon lemon juice
1 large egg
$\frac{1}{2}$ teaspoon almond essence
Glaze:
4 tablespoons apricot jam
3 tablespoons water
1 teaspoon lemon juice
Royal icing:
500 g (1 lb) icing sugar
2 egg whites
1 teaspoon lemon juice

Almond paste: Sift the ground almonds, caster sugar and icing sugar into a large mixing bowl. Add lemon juice, egg and almond essence. Mix by hand to a fairly stiff paste and knead lightly until the almond paste is smooth and pliable.

Glaze: Place the jam and the water into a small saucepan and bring to the boil over a high heat. Boil for 4 minutes then strain through a sieve into a small bowl. Clean the saucepan, put the glaze back into it, add the lemon juice and boil until the glaze is thick enough to coat a wooden spoon lightly. Brush the hot glaze evenly over the top and sides of the cake.

Divide the almond paste in half and roll out one half into a circle about 1 cm ($\frac{1}{2}$ in) thick. Place a 20 cm (8 in) cake tin on top and cut out a perfect round in the almond paste with a sharp knife. Gently set this disc on top of the cake and press it lightly into place. Roll and cut the remaining almond paste into a 60 × 8 cm (24 × 3 in) strip. Wrap the strip of almond paste around the cake. Gently press the almond paste with the edge of a rolling pin on to the cake to secure it. If the strip overlaps the top, roll the rim down lightly.

Wrap the cake in alfoil and allow to stand at room temperature for at least 48 hours before icing.

Royal Icing: Rub the icing sugar through a fine sieve. Whisk the egg whites to a light froth and add the icing sugar, a spoonful at a time, beating thoroughly between each addition. When all the icing sugar has been incorporated, stir in the lemon juice and continue beating until the icing will stand in soft peaks.

Using a spatula spread the icing evenly over the sides and top of the cake, reserving a little for making the fir cones and inscribing the cake.

Smooth the surface of the icing with a ruler or large palette knife by running it across the top, levelling off the surface.

Rough up the icing around the sides and edge of the cake with a small palette knife to resemble drifting snow. The icing will harden to a crisp coating over the almond paste underneath.

Scottish Black Bun

Black Bun is the New Year cake of the Scots—a rich fruit cake perfumed with spices and encased in pastry. This recipe was sent to us all the way from Scotland by a Mrs Marion McArthur of Blairmore, Argyle.

Pastry:
3 cups self raising flour
pinch salt
125 g (4 oz) butter
cold water
beaten egg to glaze
Filling:
4 cups plain flour
1 teaspoon freshly ground black pepper
1 teaspoon each ground allspice and
   cinnamon
1 teaspoon ground ginger
1 teaspoon bicarbonate of soda
2 teaspoons cream of tartar
185 g (6 oz) almonds
125 g (4 oz) mixed peel
1 kg (2 lb) raisins
1 kg (2 lb) currants
1⅓ cups firmly packed brown sugar
1 to 1¼ cups milk

Pastry: Sift the flour and salt into a bowl. Rub in the butter until the mixture resembles fine breadcrumbs. Add enough cold water (about 3 tablespoons) to make a firm dough. Knead lightly until smooth, then form into a ball, wrap in wax paper and chill.

Grease a deep, round 25 or 30 cm (10 or 12 in) cake tin and set oven temperature at moderate (350°F—170°C). Roll two-thirds of the pastry dough thinly and line the bottom and sides of the tin, allowing pastry to overlap the sides a little.

Spoon the filling into the pastry-lined tin and pack down well, so that it is 1 cm (½ in) below the rim. Fold edge of pastry over the fruit filling and brush with lightly beaten egg. Roll out remaining pastry and place on top, pinching the edges together to seal.

With a skewer make a few holes right through the bun. Prick the top of the pastry with a fork and brush with beaten egg. Bake in a moderate oven for at least three hours. If the top browns too quickly, cover with damp brown paper. Remove from oven and allow to cool in tin before turning out.

Filling: Sift the flour, pepper, spices, ginger, bicarbonate of soda and cream of tartar into a large bowl. Chop the almonds, peel and raisins and add to the bowl with the currants and brown sugar. Combine all the ingredients and mix to a stiff consistency with milk.

Rum Cake

Cake:
185 g (6 oz) butter
¾ cup caster sugar
3 eggs, lightly beaten
1½ cups self-raising flour
pinch of salt
1 to 2 tablespoons milk
Rum syrup:
1 cup water
½ cup orange juice
¾ cup sugar
⅓ cup rum
For decoration:
¾ cup cream, half-whipped
¼ cup flaked almonds, toasted

Grease and lightly flour a plain round 6½ cup cake tin.

Beat the butter until soft, add the sugar a little at a time and continue beating until light and fluffy. Gradually add the beaten eggs, beating thoroughly after each addition. Fold in the sifted flour and salt alternately with enough milk to make a dropping consistency.

Spoon the mixture into the cake tin and bake in a moderate oven (350°F—170°C) for 40 to 45 minutes or until a skewer inserted in the centre comes out clean. Leave to cool in the mould for a few minutes and then turn out on to a wire rack.

When the cake is cold, place it back in the cake tin. Prick the surface with a thin skewer.

Spoon the hot rum syrup over the cake allowing it to absorb the syrup before adding more.

Cover the cake with plastic wrap or foil and place in the refrigerator for at least half a day.

When ready to serve the cake, remove from the mould and spread with the half-whipped cream, lightly stroking a palette knife up the sides to give a decorative finish. Sprinkle with toasted almonds and cut into portions to serve.

Rum syrup:
Place the water, orange juice, sugar and rum into a saucepan and heat until the sugar has dissolved. Boil for 5 minutes and then remove from the heat and spoon over cake.

Note: When soaking a cake with syrup, use either a hot syrup on a cooled cake or a cool syrup on a warm cake.

Basic English Sponge Cake

A soft sponge which keeps well and is suitable for filling with jam or cream and serving with fruit.

3 eggs
$\frac{1}{3}$ cup caster sugar
$\frac{3}{4}$ cup plain flour
pinch salt
$\frac{1}{2}$ teaspoon ground cinnamon
grated rind of $\frac{1}{2}$ lemon
Filling:
1 cup cream, stiffly whipped
vanilla essence
2 passionfruit

Grease and line the base of a 20 cm (8 in) sandwich tin. Dust lightly with flour and caster sugar. Preheat oven to moderate (350°F—170°C).

Break the eggs into a bowl and beat in the sugar gradually. Place the bowl over a saucepan of simmering water and whisk for about 10 minutes or until a little of the mixture lifted on the whisk will fall from it in a smooth steady ribbon on to the remaining mixture. Remove the bowl from the hot water and continue whisking until the mixture is cool—about 5 minutes.

Sift the flour with the salt and cinnamon. Using a metal spoon gradually fold the flour and the grated lemon rind into the egg mixture. Turn into the prepared sandwich tin and bake in a moderate oven for 20 to 25 minutes. Turn on to a rack to cool.

Whip the cream with a few drops of vanilla essence and a little sugar. Combine half the cream with the passionfruit pulp.

Split the cake in half and fill with the cream and passionfruit. Place it on a cake plate and decorate with rosettes of whipped cream and dust with sifted icing sugar.

Basic Sponge Sandwich

This is the basic sponge cake known so well to Australian women.

3 eggs
$\frac{3}{4}$ cup caster sugar
1 cup self raising flour
pinch salt
1 teaspoon butter, melted
3 tablespoons hot water

Grease two 18 cm (7 in) sandwich tins and dust lightly with a little flour. Set oven temperature at moderate (350°F—170°C).

Separate the eggs. Beat the whites until stiff, add the sugar gradually, whisking until thick. Add the yolks all at the one time and whisk until thoroughly combined.

Sift the flour and salt together twice. Now sift the flour once more into the egg mixture folding it in lightly and evenly. Fold in the melted butter and hot water quickly and lightly. Pour into the prepared sandwich tins and bake for 20 minutes. Turn out and cool on a wire rack.

When cold fill with jam of your choice and decorate with whipped cream or dust the top with icing sugar.

Top: Chocolate Sponge Belle Héléne
Above: Rum Cake (see recipe on page 348)

Chocolate Sponge Belle Hélène

60 g (2 oz) dark chocolate
$\frac{1}{4}$ cup water
3 eggs
$\frac{1}{2}$ cup caster sugar
$\frac{1}{3}$ cup plain flour
pinch of salt
Filling:
1 cup cream, stiffly whipped
2 tablespoons honey
2 ripe pears, peeled and cut into thick
    slices

Grease a 20 cm (8 in) sandwich tin, line the base with paper and then dust with flour and caster sugar. Preheat the oven to moderate (350°F—170°C).

Chop the chocolate roughly and melt it with the water over a saucepan of simmering water until it becomes a thick cream. Break the eggs into a bowl and gradually beat in the sugar. Place over a gentle heat and whisk until the mixture is thick and will fall in a ribbon. Remove the bowl from the heat and continue whisking until the mixture is cool, about 5 minutes. Sift the flour with the salt three times and fold into the mixture alternately with the melted chocolate.

Turn into the prepared tin and bake in a moderate oven for about 45 to 50 minutes. Turn out on to a rack to cool.

When the cake is cool, split in half. Fold the honey and pear slices into the whipped cream and fill the cake. Sandwich the cake together and dust with sifted icing sugar.

Victoria Sponge

This perfect golden sponge cake requires only to be sandwiched with the jam of your choice and lightly dusted with caster sugar. It keeps well and was a great favourite at tea parties in Victorian times.

250 g (8 oz) butter
1 cup caster sugar
4 eggs
vanilla essence
2 cups of self-raising flour
pinch of salt

Grease 2 tins of 18 cm (7 in) diameter. Line the base with a disc of paper. Grease once more and dust with flour. Sift the flour with a pinch of salt. Cream the butter and vanilla thoroughly and then beat in the sugar by degrees until light and fluffy. Lightly beat the eggs and add gradually to the creamed butter and sugar until thoroughly combined.

Take care, if the eggs are added too quickly the mixture will curdle which affects the texture of the cake. Fold in the flour carefully and spoon the mixture into the greased tins. Bake in a moderately hot oven (375°F—190°C) for 45 minutes. Remove to a cake rack and cool. Sandwich together with a good fruit jam (we chose strawberry) and dust the top with caster sugar.

- The success of this cake depends upon the air beaten into the mixture. (Cold air expands when heated.) You beat from the wrist, flicking the mixture up as you go—it takes time but practise it. Once you get the knack it's easier and much more effective than using your whole arm.

Of course you may want to use your good electric beater. It is important to use the right speed indicated on the dial.

Swiss Roll

This type of sponge is an exception to the rule and is cooked at a higher temperature than that normally used for other sponge cakes.

½ cup self raising flour
pinch salt
3 eggs
½ cup caster sugar
1 tablespoon hot water
4 tablespoons hot jam
caster sugar for dredging

Grease and line a 30 × 25 × 2.5 cm (12 × 10 × 1 in) Swiss Roll tin with greased greaseproof paper or make a paper case and place it on a greased baking dish. Set oven temperature at hot (425°F—215°C).

Sift the flour with the salt twice. Place the eggs and sugar in a bowl and whisk together over gently simmering water until the mixture is very thick and creamy. If using an electric mixer whisking over hot water is not necessary.

Remove the bowl from the heat and continue whisking until the mixture is cool. Sift flour over the mixture and fold it in as lightly as possible with a metal spoon and then fold in the hot water.

Pour into the prepared tin or paper case and shake into the corners then spread evenly with a metal spatula. Bake in a hot oven for 12 minutes until pale gold or until the cake springs back when lightly touched with the finger.

Sprinkle a tea towel generously with caster sugar. Turn out the sponge immediately on to the tea towel and strip off the lining paper. Trim the crisp edges with a sharp knife. Roll up in the towel and allow to cool.

Unroll the sponge carefully. Heat the jam in the jar in a saucepan of hot water and when warm, spread over the Swiss roll leaving about 2.5 cm (1 in) around the edges.

Lifting the edges of the sugared tea towel nearest you, roll the sponge into a neat firm roll. Stand on a cake rack with the join underneath. Leave until cold. Sprinkle with a little more caster sugar before serving.

Mocha Sponge

4 large eggs, separated
1 cup caster sugar
1¼ cups self raising flour
2 tablespoons cornflour
30 g (1 oz) butter
4 tablespoons water
1 tablespoon coffee essence
Filling:
1 cup cream, whipped

Grease 2 × 20 cm (8 in) sandwich tins. Set oven temperature at moderate (350°F—170°C).

Beat egg whites until stiff and gradually beat in the sugar. Whisk in the yolks until they are thoroughly combined, and mixture is thick.

Sift the flour and cornflour twice and then sift a third time over the surface of the egg and sugar mixture. Fold in lightly. Heat the butter, water and coffee essence over a gentle heat and fold into the sponge mixture. Pour into prepared tins and bake for about 20 minutes or until the sponge cakes spring back when lightly touched with the finger. Turn out on to cake racks and cool. When cool fill with whipped cream and spread top with the butter cream. Decorate with walnut halves or chopped almonds.

Top: Swiss Roll
Above: Cream Filled Butterfly Cakes (see recipe on page 341)

Griestorte

This light, crisp torte relies on the contrast of a tart-sweet sauce to bring it into the class of "classics".

3 eggs, separated
½ cup caster sugar
grated rind and juice of 1 lemon
⅓ cup fine semolina
1 tablespoon ground almonds
1¼ cups cream, whipped
icing sugar
fresh plum slices to decorate

Grease a 20 cm (8 in) sandwich tin and line with greased greaseproof paper. Sprinkle tin with a little caster sugar, then flour. Set oven temperature at moderate.

Beat egg yolks and sugar together until thick and creamy. Add grated rind and juice of a lemon, beating until combined. Fold in semolina and ground almonds. Beat egg whites until stiff and carefully fold into the mixture.

Turn into prepared tin and bake in a moderate oven (350°F—170°C) 30 to 40 minutes or until the torte shrinks away from the sides of the tin. Remove from the oven and leave for a few minutes before turning out on to a wire rack to cool.

To serve, split cake and fill with half the whipped cream. Dust top with icing sugar, then decorate with remaining cream, piped in rosettes and plum slices. Serve with plum sauce.

Plum Sauce

Use blood plums if possible. Wash 250 g (8 oz) plums and remove stones. Dissolve ⅔ cup of sugar in 1¼ cups of water over the heat, add plums and poach gently until tender. Remove from the heat and rub through a fine sieve.

If the sauce is too thin, return to the saucepan and add 2 teaspoons of arrowroot mixed with 2 to 3 tablespoons of water. Bring to the boil and cook for a few seconds, stirring all the time. Allow to cool.

Griestorte with Fresh Peaches (or pears): Peel and slice 2 fresh peaches (or pears). Fill cake with cream and fruit slices. Dust top with icing sugar and serve.

Griestorte with Strawberries: Wash and hull 1 punnet of strawberries (reserve 8 whole strawberries for decoration). Slice strawberries and fold through half the whipped cream. Fill cake with strawberry cream. Dust top with icing sugar and decorate with rosettes of cream and reserved strawberries.

Blowaway Sponge

This is an extremely light, soft sponge cake which is best eaten the day it is made.

4 eggs, separated
½ cup caster sugar
½ cup arrowroot
2 tablespoons plain flour
1 teaspoon cream of tartar
½ teaspoon bicarbonate of soda
1 teaspoon vanilla essence
sweetened whipped cream
sifted icing sugar

Grease and flour two 20 cm (8 in) sandwich tins. Preheat oven to moderate (350°F—170°C).

Beat the egg whites until they stand in stiff peaks, then beat in the sugar gradually. When the mixture is stiff and glossy—after about 5 minutes beating—add the egg yolks, beating them into the mixture. Sift the arrowroot, plain flour, cream of tartar and bicarbonate of soda and fold lightly into mixture with the vanilla essence.

Pour immediately into the prepared tins and bake in a moderate oven for about 25 minutes. Turn on to a wire rack to cool. When cold fill with sweetened whipped cream and sprinkle top with icing sugar.

Pastry and piemaking

Shortcrust Pastry

2 cups plain flour
pinch salt
125 g (4 oz) butter
3 tablespoons water

Sift the flour and salt into a large bowl.

Cut the butter into small pieces, adding it to the flour. Rub the butter and flour with fingertips until the mixture resembles breadcrumbs. Do not overdo this as the butter will be blended more thoroughly later.

Make a well in the centre, add half the water and mix quickly with a knife. Press together with the fingers, adding the extra water if necessary to give a smooth dough.

Turn on to a floured board and knead lightly until smooth.

Roll into a ball. Brush off excess flour. Wrap in grease-proof paper and chill for about 15 to 20 minutes before using.

Bake pastry in a moderately hot oven (375°F—190-200°C) until it is golden. Cooking time will depend on the thickness, filling and size of the case.

Rich Shortcrust Pastry

2 cups plain flour
pinch salt
185 g (6 oz) butter
1 tablespoon caster sugar
1 egg yolk
1½ tablespoons water

Follow the first 3 steps for shortcrust pastry.

Add the sugar. Make a well in the centre. Mix the egg yolk with the water and combine quickly with a knife. Press the dough together with the fingers. Continue as for shortcrust pastry.

Note: The pastry may also be used for a savoury pie in which case omit the sugar.

Sweet Flan Pastry

1 cup plain flour sifted with a pinch of salt
60 g (2 oz) butter
⅓ cup caster sugar
2 egg yolks
2 drops vanilla essence

Sweet Flan Pastry (pâte sucrée) is fine and crisp, and used for the most delicate sweet fruit tarts. Sift the flour with the salt on to the pastry board or marble slab and make a well in the centre. Place the remaining ingredients into the centre. Work the ingredients together with the finger-tips of one hand.

Using a metal spatula quickly draw in the flour. Knead the pastry lightly until smooth. Wrap in greaseproof paper and chill for 1 hour or more before using. Bake in a moderately hot oven (375°F—190°C) until the pastry is a pale biscuit colour.

Note: This is sufficient for 1 × 20 cm (8 in) flan case or 1½ dozen tartlets. It is best chilled before baking, and again after it has been rolled out. Prick the base just before placing in the oven.

Christmas Mincemeat Pies

Mincemeat Tart

A double quantity of rich shortcrust pastry will make one 20 cm (8 in) tart and 12 individual pies. Although mincemeat is tremendously sweet, the spirit and butter or suet make it rich, taking the edge off the sweetness. Chilled whipped cream or plain vanilla ice cream is the nicest accompaniment to a slice of Mincemeat Tart.

500 g (1 lb) rich shortcrust pastry
Christmas Mincemeat with butter or
   suet added
1 egg
caster sugar

Make the shortcrust pastry by rubbing 375 g (12 oz) of butter cut into small pieces into 4 cups of sifted flour and salt until it resembles breadcrumbs. Make a well in the centre, add 2 egg yolks mixed with a little water and quickly mix with a knife to form a dough. Knead lightly on a floured board, roll into a ball and chill for 20 minutes before using.

Divide the pastry in half, keeping one half for the mince pies and then divide this quantity into two. Roll out one piece into a round, lift over the rolling pin and place over a 20 cm (8 in) flan ring standing on a baking sheet or into a flan tin. Mould the pastry into the flan ring and then trim off any excess. Place in the refrigerator until ready to use.

Roll the second piece of pastry into a round, place a 20 cm (8 in) ring or tin on top and trim to form a perfect circle.

Using a pastry wheel cut the pastry into 1 cm ($\frac{1}{2}$ in) strips. Weave these pastry strips into a lattice on a piece of greaseproof paper. Place in the refrigerator until well chilled and the the pastry is firm.

Fill the pastry case generously with mincemeat and gently and carefully shake the pastry lattice from the paper on to the top of the tart. Press the edges of the lattice to the pastry case.

Glaze the prepared tart with lightly beaten egg and sprinkle with caster sugar. Bake in a moderately hot oven (375°F— 190°C) for 45 minutes until the pastry is golden brown.

Serve warm with whipped cream or vanilla ice cream.

Mincemeat Pies

Roll out the remaining half-quantity of pastry into a thin rectangle. Cut rounds to fit small tartlet tins or patty tins and line them. Cut rounds of pastry to cover the pies. Fill pastry cases with mincemeat and cover with pastry lid, pressing around edges with the handle of a teaspoon. Glaze and sprinkle with caster sugar. Place in a moderately hot oven (375°F—190°C) for about 25 minutes or until a good golden colour.

Serve warm or cold.

● Rich shortcrust pastry may be made at the same time as you make your Christmas Mincemeat and frozen until the day you intend to use it. Or make and store, wrapped in foil, for up to 2 weeks in the refrigerator.

Apricot Tart Bourdaloue

This is one of those lovely fruit tarts that tantalize you in the windows of pastry shops in France—but never for long. Just picture tender sweet pastry filled with a fluffy almond cream upon which there are ripe poached apricots and toasted almonds in a golden glaze.

125 g (4 oz) sweet flan pastry
few drops almond essence
12 whole apricots, freshly poached, bottled or canned
toasted blanched almonds
Cream Bourdaloue:
2 egg yolks
60 g (2 oz) caster sugar
grated rind of 1 orange
1½ tablespoons each of cornflour and flour, mixed together
1 cup milk
2 tablespoons ground almonds
2 drops almond essence
1 egg white
Glaze:
3 tablespoons apricot jam
1 tablespoon water
lemon juice

Make the pastry, flavouring it with almond essence instead of vanilla. Wrap in greaseproof paper and chill for at least 1 hour before using. Roll out and line a 20 cm (8 in) flan case with the pastry and bake blind in a moderately hot oven for 30 minutes. Place on a cake rack to cool.

Cream Bourdaloue: Beat egg yolks with 1 tablespoon of the sugar and orange rind. Add the sifted cornflour and flour and when thoroughly incorporated and the mixture resembles a thick cream, stir in the milk which has been brought slowly to the boil with the ground almonds. Return this cream to the saucepan. Place back on the heat and stir until boiling. Lower the heat and cook a few minutes longer, stirring all the time. Stir in the almond essence. Turn out the cream on to a plate and cool.

Beat the egg white stiffly, and gradually beat in the remaining sugar until it forms a meringue. Fold into the cold Cream Bourdaloue. Spread over flan ring.

Slice the apricots in half, remove the stones and arrange on the tart. Decorate with toasted almonds and brush with apricot glaze.

Apricot Glaze: Melt the apricot jam with the water and lemon juice over a gentle heat. Rub through a sieve. Brush over apricots and allow to cool.

Glazed Strawberry Tart

1 quantity sweet flan pastry
Filling:
2 × 125 g (4 oz) packets of cream cheese
½ cup sugar
1 teaspoon grated lemon rind
1 tablespoon orange juice
1 tablespoon cream
1 punnet strawberries
Glaze:
¼ cup redcurrant jelly
1 tablespoon water
2 teaspoons Cointreau or 2 tablespoons orange juice

Roll pastry out thinly and line a 20 cm (8 in) flan case. Chill for at least 30 minutes. Prick the base with a fork. Bake the the pastry case blind in a moderately hot oven (375°F—190°C) for about 20 minutes or until the pastry is pale biscuit colour. Allow to cool.

Filling: Hull the strawberries. Cream remaining ingredients together and chill.

Glaze: Heat the redcurrant jelly and water in a small saucepan stirring until smooth. Cool slightly. Stir in the Cointreau or orange juice.

To assemble: Put the cream cheese filling in the flan case and smooth the surface with a spatula. Carefully decorate with the strawberries. Spoon glaze over them and chill.

Berry Pie

3 cups fresh or frozen blackberries,
   mulberries, boysenberries
1 cup sugar
1 tablespoon plain flour
1 tablespoon lemon juice
pinch salt
1 quantity rich shortcrust pastry
1 tablespoon butter
milk to glaze

Combine berries, sugar, flour, lemon juice and salt. Line a greased 20 cm (8 in) pie plate with two-thirds of the pastry. Add the filling, dot with butter and cover with the remaining pastry rolled out thinly. Crimp edges and cut vents in top. Brush the pie with milk and bake in a hot oven (400°F—200°C) for 10 minutes. Lower heat to moderate (350°F—170°C) and bake for a further 25 to 30 minutes until the berries are cooked and the crust brown and crisp.

French Apple Tart

Flat open fruit tarts are a very welcome dessert for a luncheon. The most suitable fruits are the firmer fruits such as apples, plums and apricots, although apple is probably most people's favourite. The apple slices are cooked in butter and then arranged in concentric circles and baked until the edges are tinged a deep golden brown. An apricot glaze gives the tart a beautiful finish.

125 g (4 oz) sweet flan pastry
1 kg (2 lb) Granny Smith apples
60 g (2 oz) butter
2 tablespoons sugar
caster sugar
Apricot glaze:
$\frac{1}{2}$ cup apricot jam
1 tablespoon water
2 tablespoons orange juice

Pastry:
Make the sweet flan pastry with 1 cup of plain flour which is sifted with a pinch of salt on to a board with a well made in the centre. Place 60 g (2 oz) butter, $\frac{1}{3}$ cup caster sugar, 2 egg yolks and a couple of drops of vanilla essence in the well and work together with the fingertips of one hand. Draw in the flour with a metal spatula and then knead lightly until the dough is smooth. Wrap in greaseproof paper and chill for 1 hour before using.

Filling:
Peel the apples, core and cut them into quarters and then thick slices. Cook with the butter and the sugar for about 3 minutes over a low heat.

Roll out the pastry to fit a 20 cm (9 in) flan tin or ring standing on a baking sheet. Line the flan ring and fill with the apple slices reserving the best for the top. Arrange the reserved apple slices on top starting from the outside forming smaller and smaller concentric circles until the apples underneath are completely covered. Brush the top with a little of the butter in which the apples were cooked and then sprinkle with caster sugar. Bake the tart in a moderately hot oven (375°F—190°C) for 20 to 25 minutes or until the edges of the apple slices are tinged a deep golden brown.

Remove from the oven and while still warm, brush with apricot glaze.

Serve warm with vanilla ice cream or whipped cream. This tart may also be served cold but we think it's twice as nice when warm.

Apricot Glaze:
Heat the apricot jam and water in a small saucepan stirring until blended. Rub through a sieve and cool a little. Stir in the orange juice and use while still warm.

Fruit Tartlets

These tiny fruit-filled glazed tartlets may be made with any fruits in season.

1 quantity sweet flan pastry
500 g (1 lb) fresh fruit
Glaze:
1 cup jam (use apricot for pale fruits and
  redcurrant for red fruits)
3 tablespoons water
1 tablespoon lemon juice

Roll out pastry thinly and line six tartlet tins. Chill. Prick the base of each tartlet with a fork and bake blind in a moderately hot oven (375°F—190°C) for 8 to 10 minutes. Allow to cool. **Glaze:** Heat all the ingredients over a gentle heat stirring until smooth. Strain through a sieve.

Brush pastry cases with hot glaze. Pile the fruit into the cases. Brush the fruit carefully with the glaze until it glistens. Allow to set.

To prepare fruits for tarts:
Strawberries: Wash, dry them carefully and hull. They can be left whole if small, sliced or halved.
Apricots: Poach apricots in a light syrup (125 g (4 oz) sugar dissolved in 1 cup of water) until just tender. Drain. Remove the stones. Small fruits may be used whole, larger fruits sliced or halved. Good quality preserved fruit may be used.
Peaches and Plums: Prepare in the same way as apricots.
Grapes: Wash the grapes and remove the pips with the pointed end of a small sharp knife.
Pears: If using ripe pears peel them and slice finely and arrange in the tartlet cases. Sprinkle with a little lemon juice to prevent them discolouring. If the pears are not quite ripe, peel them and poach in a light syrup until tender. Drain before slicing.
Rhubarb: Young rhubarb must be washed well and cut into 3.5 cm (1½ in) lengths. Poach in a light syrup and drain well.
Mandarins: Peel the mandarin and separate the segments. Peel away the outside membrane and dry the segments on paper towels before using.
Cherries: Wash the cherries. Remove the stones with a small sharp knife. Dry before placing in the tartlet case.

Fruit Tartlets

Lemon Meringue Pie

Pastry:
185 g (6 oz) plain flour
pinch salt
125 g (4 oz) butter
1 tablespoon caster sugar
1 egg yolk
1 tablespoon water
Filling:
3 level tablespoons cornflour
pinch salt
$\frac{3}{4}$ cup sugar
$1\frac{1}{4}$ cups water
3 egg yolks
4 tablespoons lemon juice
1 teaspoon grated lemon rind
60 g (2 oz) butter
Meringue:
3 egg whites
pinch cream of tartar
$\frac{1}{2}$ cup sugar
sifted icing sugar

Pastry: Sift the flour and salt into a large bowl. Cut the butter into small pieces and rub into the flour with the finger-tips until it resembles breadcrumbs.

Add the sugar. Make a well in the centre, mix the egg yolk with the water and combine quickly with a knife. Press the dough together with the fingers.

Turn on to a floured board and knead lightly until it is smooth, then roll into a ball, wrap in greaseproof paper and chill for half an hour. Roll out on a floured board to fit a 20 cm (8 in) flan ring or pie plate.

Prick the base with a fork. Line the pastry with paper and then fill with dried beans or peas and bake blind in a moderately hot oven (375°F—190°C) for 25 minutes.

During the last 10 minutes remove the paper and dried beans or peas and allow the base to cook through. Place on a rack to cool.

Filling: Mix the cornflour, salt and sugar in a saucepan and blend in the water. Stir over a moderate heat until the mixture boils and thickens. Lower the heat and cook 5 to 6 minutes, stirring occasionally, to cook the starch in the cornflour.

Remove from the heat. Lightly beat the egg yolks, lemon juice and rind together. Whisk into the cornflour mixture and then place over a very gentle heat for 2 minutes, stirring all the time. Beat in the butter which has been cut into pieces and then pour immediately into the prepared pie crust.

Meringue: Beat the egg whites and cream of tartar until very thick and standing in peaks. Gradually add the sugar 2 tablespoons at a time. Beat until the sugar dissolves.

Spread the meringue over the filling shaping it into peaks. Dust with icing sugar and bake in a moderate oven (350°F—170°C) for about 10 minutes or until lightly browned. Allow to cool before serving.

Quiche Lorraine

This is the old recipe for quiche which originated in the province of Lorraine on the border of France and Germany. This region is famous for its rich dishes and lavish use of cream and butter. The savoury custard in its buttery short-crust is perfect in its simplicity and is marvellous served piping hot at the beginning of a meal.

1 quantity shortcrust pastry
Filling:
60 g (2 oz) butter
1 cup cream
3 eggs
salt

Line a 20 cm (8 in) flan ring with the shortcrust pastry. Chill. Bake blind for 10 minutes in a moderately hot oven (375°F—190°C). Allow to cool.

Filling: Beat the eggs with the salt and then beat in the cream. Cut the butter into small pieces and lay on the base of the flan. Pour in the filling and cook in a hot oven (425°F—215°C) for 20 minutes or until the custard is set.

Greek Cheese and Spinach Pie

The paper-thin pastry used for this pie is filo, a Greek pastry which can be purchased from delicatessens, especially those specialising in Greek foods. The feta cheese that combines so well with spinach is made from goat's milk. It is firm, white and rather salty. Crumble it into salads, too, for variety.

half a large bunch fresh spinach
3 tablespoons olive oil
2 onions, finely chopped
2 shallots, finely chopped
1 tablespoon finely chopped parsley
2 teaspoons dried dill weed
salt and pepper
90 g (3 oz) butter
125 g (4 oz) filo pastry
125 g (4 oz) feta cheese
½ cup thick sour cream
1 egg, beaten
good grinding of nutmeg

Wash spinach and remove stalks. Chop the leaves very finely. Heat oil and cook the onions and shallots until soft and transparent, stirring occasionally. Add the spinach and cook, covered, for 5 minutes.

Add parsley, dill, ½ teaspoon salt and a good grinding of pepper and cook, covered, for 10 minutes, stirring occasionally. If any liquid remains, remove lid and cook gently until spinach begins to stick to the pan. Cool.

Melt butter and use a little to grease a 17.5 cm (7 in) sandwich tin or pie plate. Arrange one sheet of the pastry in tin and fold back the overlap to form a double layer. Brush with melted butter and repeat with about three more sheets of pastry.

Crumble the cheese and add to the cooled spinach mixture along with the sour cream, egg and nutmeg. Spoon into the pastry lined case.

Top with 3 to 4 more sheets of pastry, brushing each one as before with melted butter. Brush the top sheet of pastry with butter also.

Trim off edges of pastry with a sharp knife and bake the pie in a slow oven (300°F—150°C) for about 45 minutes or until the pastry is crisp and golden. Serve warm, cut into wedges.

- Any leftover pastry may be rolled up, wrapped in a plastic bag, sealed and frozen for future use.
- Two 300 g (10 oz) packets of frozen spinach can be used instead of fresh spinach. Thaw the frozen spinach in a colander and squeeze with hands to remove all moisture. Proceed as described in recipe.

Prawn Quiche

1 quantity shortcrust pastry
Filling:
45 g (1½ oz) butter
2 tablespoons shallots, finely chopped
125 g (4 oz) prawns, shelled, de-veined
    and coarsely chopped
¼ teaspoon salt
pinch pepper
2 tablespoons dry sherry
3 eggs
½ cup cream
1 tablespoon tomato paste

Line a 20 cm (8 in) flan case with the shortcrust pastry. Bake blind for 10 minutes in a moderately hot oven (375°F—190°C). Allow to cool.
Filling: Sweat the shallots in butter until soft but not brown. Add the prawns and cook for 1 minute. Add the sherry and season with salt and freshly ground white pepper. Bring to the boil and cook for a few seconds. Beat the eggs with the cream. Add the tomato paste and season with salt and pepper. Stir in the prawn mixture and pour into the pastry case. Bake in a moderately hot oven (375°F—190°C) for 25 to 30 minutes or until the mixture is set and golden brown.

Quiche Lorraine (see recipe on page 362)

364

Greek Cheese and Spinach Pie (see recipe on page 363)

biscuits and bread

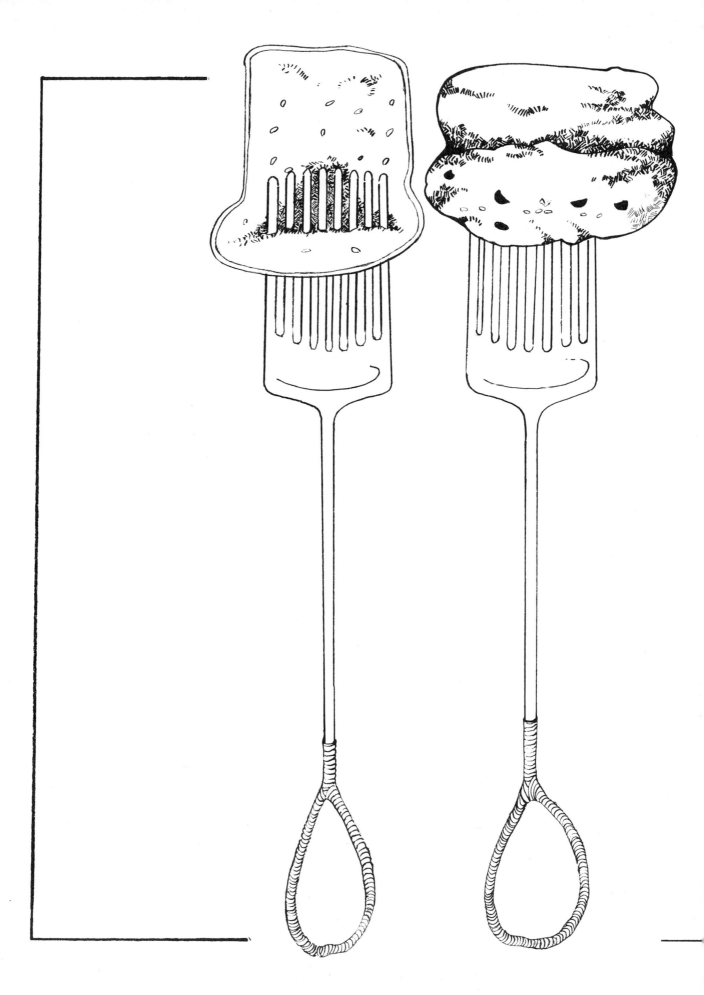

Clockwise left to right: Hazelnut Biscuits, Burnt Butter Biscuits, Afghans, Chocolate Fork Biscuits, Walnut Butter Biscuits, Refrigerator Biscuits

Biscuits

Afghans

Crunchy little chocolate mounds dipped in chocolate with a walnut on top.

220 g (7 oz) butter
⅓ cup sugar
¼ teaspoon vanilla
1½ cups plain flour
1 tablespoon cocoa
2½ cups cornflakes
Chocolate glaze:
125 g (4 oz) dark chocolate
1 teaspoon butter
walnut halves to decorate

Set oven temperature at moderate (350°F—170°C). Cream butter and then beat in the sugar with the vanilla. Stir in the flour which has been sifted with cocoa and add the cornflakes. Drop in teaspoonfuls on to greased baking trays and bake for 15 to 20 minutes. Cool on a wire rack.

Chocolate glaze: Chop the chocolate and melt in a bowl over hot water. Remove from the heat and stir in the butter. Dip each Afghan into the chocolate glaze and decorate with a walnut.

Burnt Butter Biscuits

Burnt butter adds its special flavour to these biscuits, but don't take this description literally. The butter should be only a light hazelnut colour.

125 g (4 oz) butter
½ cup caster sugar
1 egg
1 teaspoon vanilla
1½ cups self-raising flour
pinch salt
60 g (2 oz) blanched almonds

Grease baking trays and set oven temperature at moderate (350°F— 170°C).

Melt butter in a saucepan and allow to colour to a light brown over a low heat. Cool slightly, add sugar and beat well.

Stir in egg and vanilla. Fold in sifted flour and salt.

Roll into balls about the size of a walnut. Place on greased trays allowing room for spreading. Place a blanched almond on top of each one, then bake in moderate oven for 12 to 15 minutrs. Makes 2 dozen.

Chocolate Peanut Biscuits

Crisp little chocolate butterscotch biscuits studded with raw peanuts.

125 g (4 oz) butter
¾ cup firmly packed brown sugar
1 egg
1 tablespoon cocoa
1½ cups self raising flour
250 g (8 oz) raw peanuts

Grease baking trays and set oven temperature at moderate (350°F—170°C). Cream butter and add brown sugar. Add egg and beat well. Stir in cocoa sifted with flour, then add peanuts.

Drop teaspoonfuls on to prepared trays and bake in moderate oven 15 minutes. Makes approximately 30 biscuits.

Top left: Linzer Biscuits
Bottom left: Muesli Biscuits

Top right: Lemon Butter Biscuits
Bottom right: Old-fashioned Ginger Snaps

Old-fashioned Ginger Snaps

A plain ginger biscuit which has been a firm favourite for generations. Remember they are very hard.

90 g (3 oz) butter
¾ cup sugar
1 egg
½ cup debittered molasses
2½ cups plain flour
2 teaspoons bicarbonate of soda
2 teaspoons ground ginger
¼ teaspoon ground cloves
extra sugar

Set oven temperature at moderate (350°F—170°C). Grease baking trays. Cream butter, gradually add sugar. Beat in egg and molasses until light and fluffy. Stir in sifted flour, bicarbonate of soda and spices. Cover and chill 1 hour. Shape dough into balls the size of a small walnut. Roll in sugar to coat and place on prepared trays. Press biscuits down carefully with flat blade of a knife.

Bake in a moderate oven 12 to 15 minutes. Cool 1 minute on trays then remove to cooling rack. Makes about 3½ dozen.

Muesli Biscuits

Thin crisp biscuits crunchy with rolled oats, nuts and fruit. Ideal for a mid-morning snack.

1 cup muesli
1 cup sugar
1 cup plain flour
125 g (4 oz) butter
1 tablespoon golden syrup
3 tablespoons boiling water
1½ teaspoons bicarbonate of soda

Set oven temperature at slow (300°F—150°C). Combine muesli, sugar and sifted flour in a bowl. Melt butter with golden syrup over a very low heat. Mix boiling water and bicarbonate of soda and combine with butter mixture. Stir into the dry ingredients in bowl.

Place teaspoons of mixture on to greased baking trays and bake in a slow oven for about 20 minutes until golden brown.

Leave on baking trays for a couple of minutes before removing to a cake rack to cool. Makes 4 dozen.

Linzer Biscuits

Small continental biscuits filled with raspberry or red currant jam.

2 cups plain flour
1 teaspoon baking powder
¼ teaspoon each cinnamon and cloves
½ cup sugar
grated rind of ½ lemon
185 g (6 oz) unsalted butter
1 egg
raspberry or red currant jam
icing sugar

Sift flour and baking powder with spices into a bowl. Stir in sugar and lemon rind. Add softened butter, then egg. Mix well together to form a smooth dough, and knead on a well-floured board. Wrap in plastic film and chill 15 minutes.

Set oven temperature at moderate (350°F—170°C). Divide dough into three. Roll out on well-floured board to 3 mm (⅛ in) thickness. Stamp into rounds with 3 cm (1¼ in) fluted cutter, and using a smaller clover-leaf or round shaped cutter, remove the centres from half the biscuits.

Place on baking trays and bake in a moderate oven for 8 to 10 minutes until pale golden in colour. Store in an airtight jar. Just before serving, spread raspberry or red currant jam on plain biscuits, place cut-out biscuits on top and sprinkle with icing sugar. Makes about 6½ dozen.

Refrigerator Biscuits

This biscuit dough is rich and soft and when shaped in a roll, is refrigerated until firm and then cut into even slices. The biscuits are decorated with nuts, glace cherries or lemon peel.

185 g (6 oz) butter
1 cup firmly packed brown sugar
1 egg
1 teaspoon vanilla
2 cups plain flour
$\frac{1}{4}$ teaspoon salt
$\frac{1}{2}$ teaspoon bicarbonate of soda

Cream the butter and gradually beat in the brown sugar. Beat in the egg and flavour with vanilla. Sift the flour with the salt and bicarbonate of soda. Stir into creamed mixture. Shape into rolls about 5 cm (2 in) in diameter on a lightly floured board. Wrap in waxed paper or foil and chill until firm. Slice thinly and place on a greased baking sheet. Bake in a moderate oven (350°F—170°C) for 8 to 10 minutes. Makes 6 dozen.

Variations: Divide biscuit dough into three. To one third of the mixture add: 1 tablespoon chopped glace cherries and 1 tablespoon chopped almonds or hazelnuts. Roll up and chill. Cut into slices and decorate with a whole cherry.

Slice another $\frac{1}{3}$ of the basic mixture into biscuits and decorate each with a walnut half.

Add 3 teaspoons grated lemon rind to the rest of the basic mixture. Roll up and chill. Cut into slices and sprinkle with some chopped candied peel.

Chocolate Fork Biscuits

Rich chocolate flavoured fork biscuits.

125 g (4 oz) butter
$\frac{1}{4}$ cup caster sugar
1 cup self-raising flour
pinch salt
$2\frac{1}{2}$ tablespoons cocoa

Set oven temperature at moderately hot (375°F—190°C). Grease baking trays.

Cream butter until soft, then add sugar gradually and beat until white and fluffy. Sift flour with salt and cocoa and stir into cream mixture.

Roll mixture into balls the size of a walnut and place on greased baking trays.

Flatten each ball to a 5 cm (2 in) circle with a fork dipped in cold water. Bake in a moderately hot oven for 7 to 8 minutes. Cool on wire rack. These biscuits may be prepared in advance and kept in the refrigerator until you are ready to bake them.

Hazelnut Biscuits

Short crisp biscuits flavoured with hazelnuts.

125 g (4 oz) butter
1 cup sugar
1 egg
2 cups self-raising flour
$\frac{1}{2}$ cup ground hazelnuts

Set oven temperature at moderate (350°F—170°C). Grease a sandwich tin 20 cm (8 in) square.

Cream butter until soft and gradually add sugar, beating in well.

Add egg and beat well. Sift flour and stir into creamed mixture with hazelnuts. Press into prepared tin.

Bake in a moderate oven 20 to 25 minutes. Cool, then cut into fingers.

Lemon Butter Biscuits

Dainty lemon-flavoured shortbread biscuits sandwiched with lemon butter.

250 g (8 oz) butter
grated rind of ½ lemon
1 cup sifted icing sugar
2 cups plain flour

Set oven temperature at moderate (350°F—170°C). Beat butter and lemon rind until creamy. Add icing sugar and beat well. Stir in sifted flour. Roll level teaspoons of mixture into balls and place on ungreased baking trays. Press down well with a fork which has been dipped in cold water to prevent sticking.

Bake in a moderate oven for 10 to 12 minutes or until slightly coloured. Cool and store in an airtight tin. Just before serving, join shortbread in pairs with Lemon Butter.

Lemon Butter:
1 egg
½ cup sugar
¼ cup strained lemon juice
30 g (1 oz) butter

Beat egg with sugar until light and creamy. Add lemon juice and butter. Place in top of double boiler and stir over simmering water until thick. This takes about 20 minutes.

Remove from heat and allow to cool completely.

Walnut Crescents

Little walnut meringue crescents delicately flavoured with lemon rind and clove.

250 g (8 oz) ground walnuts
⅓ cup icing sugar
grated rind of ½ lemon
½ teaspoon ground cloves
3 egg whites
½ teaspoon vanilla

Grease and flour baking tray and set oven temperature at slow (300°F—150°C).

Mix the ground walnuts, icing sugar, grated lemon rind and ground cloves. Whip the egg whites until stiff then fold in walnut mixture and flavour with vanilla. Using a plain forcing pipe and bag, pipe mixture into crescent shapes on to a greased and floured baking tray. Bake in a slow oven for approximately 20 minutes or until lightly browned. Cool on a rack.

This mixture may be shaped into circles and decorated with a glacé cherry. Makes about 2½ dozen.

Kourambiedes

These little morsels pierced with a clove and coated with icing sugar are sometimes known as Greek shortbreads.

250 g (8 oz) butter
⅓ cup caster sugar
1 egg yolk
3 cups plain flour
½ cup finely chopped almonds
2 whole cloves
icing sugar, sifted

Cream the butter and gradually beat in the sugar. Add the egg yolk and beat well. Sift the flour and stir into the creamed mixture alternately with the almonds. Knead the mixture lightly and form into a ball. Roll small pieces of dough into balls the size of hazelnuts and press a whole clove into the centre of each. Place on greased trays and bake in a slow oven (300°F—150°C) for 25 to 30 minutes.

While still warm toss biscuits in sifted icing sugar and place on a wire rack to cool.

Cigarettes Russe

These crisp furled biscuits are a classic accompaniment for soft textured desserts such as Chocolate Mousse, ice creams and Strawberries Romanoff.

2 egg whites
½ cup caster sugar
90 g (3 oz) butter, melted
2 to 3 drops vanilla
½ cup plain flour

Brush baking trays with a little melted butter then dust lightly with sifted plain flour. Shake off excess flour. Preheat oven to moderately hot (375°F—190°C).

Beat the egg whites and sugar with a fork until smooth. Stir in the melted butter, vanilla and sifted flour. Place 1 small teaspoon of the mixture on the prepared tray and spread with a metal spatula into an oblong shape about 12.5 × 8 cm (5 × 3 in) in size. Place two teaspoons well apart on each tray. Cook only one tray at a time. Bake in a moderately hot oven for 5 to 6 minutes, until golden.

Immediately they are golden, remove from the oven and leave for 1 to 2 minutes then lift from the tray with a small thin-bladed knife and place upside down on the table. Wind closely around the handle of a wooden spoon working quickly. Remove at once and cool. Store in an airtight jar until ready to use.

- To test if the mixture is of the correct consistency, bake one cigarette russe first. If it is too firm and hard to remove from the tray add an extra 1 to 2 teaspoons melted butter. If the mixture is too soft and difficult to handle add 1 to 2 teaspoons of plain flour.

Vanilla Kippels

These crescent shaped almond shortbreads make a lovely Christmas gift especially for those people who have no time to do their own baking.

1¼ cups plain flour
pinch salt
155 g (5 oz) butter
¼ cup icing sugar
2 egg yolks
vanilla essence
155 g (5 oz) ground almonds
extra icing sugar

Sift the flour with the salt on to a board. Make a well in the centre and put in the butter, sugar, yolks and vanilla essence. Sprinkle the ground almonds on to the flour.

Work the ingredients in the centre with the fingertips until thoroughly blended.

Using a metal spatula quickly draw in the flour and ground almonds. Knead the biscuit dough lightly until smooth. Form dough into a ball, wrap in greaseproof paper and chill in the refrigerator for at least 1 hour.

Divide dough into small pieces and roll into balls the size of a small walnut.

Roll under the palm of the hand to form a small tube and then shape into tiny crescents. Bake in a moderate oven (350°F—170°C) for 10 to 12 minutes. Remove to a wire rack to cool, placing a sheet of paper underneath. Dredge the biscuits heavily with sifted icing sugar while still warm.

Cool and store in an airtight jar.

Vanilla Kippels

Wheatgerm Wafers

125 g (4 oz) butter
2 cups brown sugar
2 teaspoons vanilla
2 eggs
¾ cup buttermilk
1 cup wheatgerm
2 cups plain flour
1 teaspoon bicarbonate of soda
1 teaspoon salt

Cream butter and sugar, add vanilla and then beat in the eggs one at a time. Add the buttermilk and stir in the wheatgerm. Sift the flour with the bicarbonate of soda and salt, fold into the mixture. Drop in half-teaspoonfuls on to a lightly greased baking tray, flatten out with a fork and bake in a moderate oven (350°F—170°C) for about 10 minutes. This mixture will make about 10 dozen crisp little cookies.

Honey and Hazelnut Crisps

A flavourful variation of Wheatgerm Wafers.

125 g (4 oz) hazelnuts
125 g (4 oz) butter
¾ cup honey
1 cup raw sugar
2 eggs
2 teaspoons vanilla
1 cup wheatgerm
2 cups fine wholemeal flour
1 cup plain flour
1½ teaspoons baking powder

Toast hazelnuts in a moderate oven (350°F—170°C) for 20 minutes. Rub in a tea towel to remove skins. Crush lightly into coarse, chunky pieces. This can be done with a rolling pin on a wooden board.

Cream butter, honey and raw sugar. Add the eggs one at a time, beating well after each addition. Add vanilla. Fold in wheatgerm, sifted flour, baking powder and hazelnuts. Drop by half-teaspoonsful on to a greased tray and bake in a hot oven (400°F—200°C) 8 to 10 minutes. Cool on baking sheet, then store in airtight container. Makes about 6 dozen.

Walnut Butter Biscuits

Small butter biscuits flavoured with crunchy, mellow walnuts.

250 g (8 oz) butter
1½ cups sifted icing sugar
1 egg
1 teaspoon vanilla
2½ cups plain flour
½ teaspoon bicarbonate of soda
1 teaspoon baking powder
¼ teaspoon salt
1½ cups finely chopped walnuts
walnut halves

Set oven at moderately hot (375°F—190°C). Cream the butter and beat in the icing sugar. Add the egg and beat well. Flavour with vanilla. Sift the flour with the bicarbonate of soda, baking powder and salt and stir into creamed mixture with the chopped nuts.

Form the mixture into small balls and place on greased baking trays with a walnut on each. Bake until lightly browned.

Macaroons

Delicately brown and flavoured with almonds, Macaroons are one of the most beautiful biscuits. They keep well in an airtight container and are good to have on hand for that special treat.

Macaroons (1)

2 egg whites
1 cup ground almonds
¾ cup caster sugar
2 dozen split blanched almonds for decoration

Beat the egg whites until stiff but not dry and fold in the almonds and the sugar.

Grease a baking sheet and cut 5 cm (2 in) square pieces of greaseproof paper and arrange them on the baking sheet. Grease again.

Using a 1 cm (½ in) tube, pipe circles onto the paper squares. Decorate each with half a blanched almond. Sprinkle with a little caster sugar. Allow to stand for 4 hours.

Bake in a moderate oven (350°F—170°C) for 12 to 15 minutes until delicately browned. Remove from the oven and allow to cool before removing the paper.

Macaroons (2)

1 cup caster sugar
30 g (1 oz) granulated sugar
125 g (4 oz) ground almonds
15 g (½ oz) rice flour
2 large or 3 small egg whites
½ teaspoon vanilla essence
split blanched almonds for decoration

Mix the sugars together and combine with the almonds and rice flour in a mixing bowl. Add the egg whites and vanilla and beat together with a wooden spoon for about 5 minutes. Scrape down the sides of the bowl and leave to stand for 5 minutes. Cut the greaseproof paper into 8 cm (3 in) squares and place on a greased baking sheet. Grease once more. Beat the almond mixture for a further 5 minutes until it is thick and white.

Using a 1 cm (½ in) tube, pipe circles onto the paper. Place a split almond in the middle of each and bake in a moderate oven (350°C—170°C) for 20 to 30 minutes. Allow to cool and remove the paper.

- The success of these recipes depends on the quantity of egg white. Now that eggs come in so many different sizes the surest way is to measure a quarter of a cup. Don't forget to use the new 250 ml metric cup.

POEMS AND SONGS OF
ROBERT BURNS

A COMPLETELY NEW EDITION, IN-
CLUDING OVER 60 POEMS APPEAR-
ING FOR THE FIRST TIME IN A
COLLECTED EDITION, OF WHICH
SOME HAVE NEVER BEFORE
BEEN PUBLISHED

Edited and Introduced by
JAMES BARKE

Scottish Shortbread

Scottish Shortbread

Scottish Shortbread is famous all over the world but how many people really know how to make it, the Scottish way? The dough must be kneaded for about 15 minutes until it becomes smooth and very buttery before it is pressed into a tin or ring and decorated. If you do as the Scots do, you will have a superb shortbread, crisp yet tender.

375 g (12 oz) butter
½ cup caster sugar
500 g (1 lb) plain flour

Cream the butter until it resembles whipped cream and then add the sugar gradually, beating it until it is light and fluffy. Work in the flour gradually and then knead the dough for about 15 minutes until the mixture is very smooth.

Divide the dough into two pieces and press into 2 × 20 cm (8 in) flan rings standing on baking sheets or sandwich tins.

With the heel of the hand push the dough out until the mixture is very smooth, then smooth over surface with a palette knife.

Remove the flan ring and crimp the edges by pressing the edge of the pastry with the finger and then pinching the edge together. If using a sandwich tin, fork the edge for decoration.

Prick the surface of the shortbread with a fork and bake in the centre of a slow oven (300°F—150°C) for 19 minutes and then reduce the temperature to (275°F—140°C) and bake for a further 40 minutes.

- The surface of the shortbread is pricked with a fork to release the moisture as it cooks, making the shortbread crisp.

  When shortbread is gift-wrapped for any length of time it may soften a little. This can be remedied by placing it in a moderate (350°F—170°C) oven for 15 minutes.

Speculaas

These are special crisp biscuits rich in butter and flavoured with brown sugar, spices and rum made especially for Saint Nicholas' Eve in Holland. Sometimes the biscuits are in the shape of small rectangles sprinkled with almonds and sometimes the biscuit mixture is pressed into elaborate moulds in the shape of men and women or Saint Nicholas himself.

3 cups plain flour
4 teaspoons baking powder
1 tablespoon cinnamon
1 teaspoon each ground cloves and
    nutmeg
½ teaspoon each ground aniseed, salt and
    ground ginger or white pepper
250 g (8 oz) butter
1½ cups firmly packed dark brown sugar
3 tablespoons rum or brandy
1 egg white for glazing
125 g (4 oz) slivered blanched almonds
    for decoration

In a bowl sift together the flour, baking powder, cinnamon, cloves, nutmeg, ground aniseed, salt and ginger or pepper.

Beat the butter until creamy and then add the brown sugar gradually, beating until the mixture is light and fluffy. Stir in the rum or brandy.

Gradually add the flour and spices, stirring until well combined and then form dough into a ball. Knead the dough on a board sprinkled with about ¼ cup sifted flour and roll dough out into a rectangle about 5 mm (¼ in) thick. With a sharp knife or cutter cut dough into rectangles 6 cm × 3 cm (2½ in × 1½ in). Place on a buttered baking tray, brush with lightly beaten egg white and decorate with slivered almonds. Bake in a moderately hot oven (375°F—190°C) for 12 minutes or until they are browned and firm. Makes about 40 biscuits. Cool and store in an airtight tin.

Marzipan Sweetmeats

A European Christmas wouldn't be the same without the little Marzipan Sweetmeats. In many countries, the marzipan is moulded into little fruits and vegetables, pink pigs and other animals to ornament the Christmas tree. These little edible ornaments take a lot of time which isn't always available around the festive season. So we have made more simple sweets by moulding delicately coloured marzipan between two walnut halves, or pressing it into a plump date or prune and coating it in fine sugar. Placed in tiny paper cups and arranged in neat rows in a small box, these little sweetmeats make a very special gift.

500 g (1 lb) marzipan—an excellent Danish commercial brand called Odense is readily available in 227 g (8 oz) rolls
To flavour and colour:
sherry or rum and green colouring
rum and pink colouring

Divide marzipan into two portions. Flavour one portion with sherry or rum and colour it pale green and second portion with rum and pink colouring. Knead flavouring and colour into marzipan until perfectly distributed, adding the colour discreetly—a few drops at a time—a little more can always be added if the colour is not distinct. At this stage, the marzipan may be wrapped in waxed paper or foil and stored in the refrigerator.

Marzipan Walnuts

Roll small pieces of marzipan into balls about the size of a small walnut. Press a perfect walnut half into each side and roll in caster sugar. Place in paper cups and store in a box in the refrigerator if the weather is warm. The wooden chocolate boxes are ideal for this purpose.

Marzipan dates and prunes

Stone dessert dates and prunes by making a slit along one side—but not right through—and lift out the stone with the point of a knife. Roll some marzipan into a tube about 1 cm ($\frac{1}{2}$ in) thick and cut off in even-sized pieces with a sharp knife. Shape into oval pieces, press a blanched almond or a piece of glace ginger or orange peel in the middle and then insert the marzipan into each date or prune. Roll in caster sugar, place in small paper cups or tie in coloured cellophane and store.

Home-made Marzipan

In case you prefer to make your own marzipan we include this recipe which is more pliable than that used to ice the Christmas cake.

500 g (1 lb) granulated sugar
9 tablespoons water
375 g (12 oz) ground almonds
2 egg whites
1 teaspoon sherry
4 tablespoons icing sugar

Dissolve the sugar in the water in a large saucepan over a gentle heat and boil steadily without stirring for 10 minutes or until the mixture forms a soft ball when a little is dropped into a cup of cold water.

Remove from the heat and beat with a wooden spoon until the mixture looks slightly cloudy and stir in the ground almonds.

Beat the egg whites in a bowl with a fork until just frothy, add to the pan and cook mixture over a very gentle heat for 1 to 2 minutes. Add sherry, turn mixture on to a board dusted with a little of the icing sugar.

When mixture has cooled a little, knead until quite smooth, working in the rest of the sifted icing sugar as you go. While still warm, divide into 2 portions, colour and flavour as desired.

Cheese and Almond Biscuits

Piquant cheese biscuits are not only good with drinks, they are an excellent accompaniment to many soups, hot or cold. A batch may be made well in advance, stored and then put out at the last moment to make sure they are crisp.

250 g (8 oz) plain flour
½ teaspoon salt
185 g (6 oz) butter
60 g (2 oz) finely grated parmesan cheese
45 g (1½ oz) toasted almonds, finely chopped
1 egg, lightly beaten
45 g (1½ oz) slivered almonds for decoration

Sift the flour and salt, rub in the butter and stir in 45 g (1½ oz) of the Parmesan cheese and the almonds. Toss lightly together. Mix to a stiff dough with the yolk of the egg beaten with 1 tablespoon of water. Wrap in foil and chill for 1 hour then roll out on a lightly flavoured board to 5 mm (¼ in) thickness. Cut the pastry into rounds with a small fluted cutter and place on an ungreased baking tray. Brush the tops of the biscuits with lightly beaten egg white.

Sprinkle with the remaining cheese and the slivered almonds. Bake in the centre of a moderate oven (350°F—170°C) for 25 minutes. Cool on a wire rack and then store in an airtight container.

● If by chance biscuits become soft, just pop them in a moderate oven for 5 minutes, cool them on a wire rack and then store in an airtight container.

Cheese Daisies

Rich cheese pastry is the foundation of various cheese biscuits. These biscuits have a good bite to them and may be formed into straws or other attractive shapes.

2 tablespoons sesame seeds
1½ cups finely grated cheddar cheese
¼ cup grated parmesan cheese
185 g (6 oz) butter
1½ cups plain flour
1 teaspoon paprika
1 teaspoon salt
3 tablespoons poppy seeds

Toast sesame seeds in dry frying pan until golden and set aside. Set oven temperature at moderate (350°F—170°C). Cream cheeses and butter together until soft. Sift flour, paprika and salt together.

Stir flour into creamed mixture with sesame seeds. Mix well and put dough into a biscuit forcer fitted with a flower disc or use a piping bag fitted with a large star pipe.

Press mixture on to ungreased baking trays. Take tiny balls of biscuit dough and roll in poppy seeds. Place one into centre of each biscuit. Bake in a moderate oven 12 to 15 minutes.

Sesame Cheese Straws

Mixture can also be rolled out and cut into straws 8 cm × 5 mm (3 in × ¼ in) and baked for 10 minutes.

Savoury Caraway Biscuits

Delicious short-textured cheese biscuits flavoured with caraway seeds. For a plain cheese biscuit omit caraway.

1½ cups plain flour
salt, white pepper
pinch of cayenne
125 g (4 oz) butter
125 g (4 oz) finely grated cheese (half
    cheddar and half parmesan)
1 egg yolk
1 tablespoon water
1 tablespoon caraway seeds
1 egg white

Sift flour with seasonings into a mixing bowl. Cut the butter into the flour with a round bladed knife. When the pieces of butter are well coated with the flour rub them in with the fingertips until the mixture resembles breadcrumbs. Stir in the cheese and caraway with a knife. Blend the yolk with the water and mix quickly with the dry ingredients to form a firm dough. Turn on to a floured board and knead lightly until smooth. Chill for ½ an hour before rolling out.

Roll out the cheese dough thinly and cut into 3.5 cm (1½ in) rounds. Glaze with egg white. Place on a greased baking sheet and bake in a moderately hot oven (375°F—190°C) for about 10 minutes.

Coconut Cheese Roughs

Little savoury cheese biscuits to serve with pre-dinner drinks.

1 cup self-raising flour
1 teaspoon salt
½ teaspoon cayenne pepper
125 g (4 oz) butter
¾ cup grated cheese
about ½ cup desiccated coconut

Grease baking trays and set oven temperature at moderate (350°F—170°C).

Sift flour, salt and cayenne pepper into bowl. Rub in butter. Add cheese and mix to make a dough. Roll into small balls and toss in coconut. Place on prepared trays and flatten with a wet fork. Bake in moderate oven for about 20 minutes or until lightly browned. Makes about 24.

*A selection of savoury biscuits—Cheese Daisies, Sesame Cheese Straws
and Coconut Cheese Roughs*

Breads

Milk Bread

4 cups plain flour
1 teaspoon salt
15 g ($\frac{1}{2}$ oz) compressed yeast
2 teaspoons sugar
1$\frac{1}{4}$ cups milk
60 g (2 oz) butter
extra flour or milk as required

Sift the flour and salt into a large warm mixing bowl. Make a well in the centre. Cream the yeast with the sugar.

Warm $\frac{1}{2}$ cup of the milk to blood heat. Mix with the creamed yeast and place into the well in the flour. Mix well and stir in sufficient of the surrounding flour to make a light soft batter.

Cover the bowl with a cloth and stand in a warm place until the batter in the centre looks spongy and is full of tiny bubbles.

Melt the butter and add the rest of the milk and warm to blood heat. Pour on to the sponge in the bowl and mix to a soft dough using extra flour or warm milk if necessary.

Place dough on to a lightly floured board. Knead the dough until it is smooth and elastic. Shape dough into a ball and place into a clean warm bowl. Sprinkle with a little flour, cover with a cloth and place in a warm place to rise until it has doubled in bulk.

Test the risen dough with the fingers. It has risen sufficiently when a finger imprint fades. Punch the dough down and knead it lightly again.

Shape the dough into a loaf and place in a well-greased tin. Cover with a cloth and place in a warm place to prove for 30 minutes to 1 hour. When well risen bake in a hot oven (450°F—230°C) for 45 minutes or until the crust resounds when tapped with the knuckle. Wrap in a cloth and keep for at least half a day before using.

Wholemeal Bread

Prepare as for Milk Bread substituting 2 cups of wholemeal flour for 2 cups of the plain flour.

Bread Knots

$\frac{1}{2}$ quantity of Milk Bread dough
1 egg, lightly beaten for glazing
sesame seeds or poppy seeds

Divide the dough into 10 equal portions. Roll each under the palms of the hand on a lightly floured board until about 15 cm (6 in) long.

Tie into a knot and place well apart on a greased baking tray. Cover with a cloth and allow to rise in a warm place until these little buns have doubled in size.

Glaze with beaten egg. Sprinkle each one with sesame seeds or poppy seeds and bake in a very hot oven (450°F—230°C) for 10 to 15 minutes or until golden brown.

Sesame Crescents, Bread Knots and Caraway Seed Buns

Sesame Crescents

½ quantity of **Milk Bread dough**
soft butter
1 beaten egg, for glazing
sesame seeds

Roll dough into a 5 mm (¼ in) thick circle and spread with the soft butter. Cut in 8 wedges. Roll up each wedge from the wider edge towards the point. Stretch the dough gently and shape into a crescent.

Place the crescents well apart on a greased baking tray. Cover with a cloth and allow to rise in a warm place until the rolls double in size. Glaze with the beaten egg and sprinkle with sesame seeds.

Bake in a very hot oven (450°F—230°C) for 10 to 15 minutes or until the rolls are golden brown.

Caraway Seed Buns

½ quantity of **Milk Bread dough**
butter
1 egg, lightly beaten for glazing
caraway seeds

Keep the butter in the freezer until you are ready to use it. Divide dough into 10 portions. Roll each portion into a ball. Place on a greased baking sheet, cover with a cloth and allow buns to rise until doubled in size.

Using the floured handle of a wooden spoon make a small hollow in the centre of each bun and place a small piece of hard butter into it. Pinch the dough together to encase the butter and place the buns, smooth side up, on the greased tray. Glaze with beaten egg.

Sprinkle with caraway seeds. Bake in a very hot oven (450°F—230°C) for 10 to 15 minutes or until the buns are golden brown all over.

Note: Sesame or poppy seeds may be substituted for the caraway seeds.

Corn Bread

Corn was thought to have originated in Mexico and so important was it to the Indians that they built temples and held festivals to honour the goddess whose duty it was to look after it.

Today corn is still one of the staple foods of Mexico. Fresh corn grain is used in a variety of dishes and the dried corn is ground to make Corn Bread, for use in various prepared dishes, and to make the drink Atole. Nothing is wasted. Even the husks are used to make wrappers for tamales, the Mexican's favourite snack.

2 cups self-raising flour
½ **cup sugar**
2 tablespoons baking powder
1½ **teaspoons salt**
2 cups yellow cornmeal
4 eggs
2 cups milk
125 g (4 oz) creamed butter

Sift the flour, sugar, baking powder and salt into a mixing bowl. Stir in the cornmeal. Add the lightly beaten eggs, milk, and the creamed butter. Beat with a rotary or electric beater for about 1 minute until the mixture is smooth.

Pour mixture into a greased 33 × 23 cm (13 × 9 in) shallow tin and bake in a hot oven (400°F—200°C) for 30 to 40 minutes. Cut into 5 cm (2 in) squares and serve while still warm. Enough for 10 persons.

Note: Although the amount of baking powder seems excessive when self-raising flour is used, this quantity is necessary to give the Corn Bread its light, even texture.

Hot Cross Buns

Basic bun dough:
4 cups plain flour
1 teaspoon mixed spice
½ teaspoon cinnamon
1 teaspoon salt
60 g (2 oz) butter
30 g (1 oz) compressed yeast
½ cup caster sugar
½ cup lukewarm water } **mixed together**
½ cup lukewarm milk
1 egg, lightly beaten
Paste for Cross:
4 tablespoons self raising flour
2 tablespoons cold water
Glaze:
¼ teaspoon gelatine
2 tablespoons hot water
1 tablespoon sugar

Sift the flour with the spices and salt into a bowl. Rub in the softened butter. Cream the yeast with the sugar. Add a little warm water to the creamed yeast to dissolve completely.

Add the milk and remaining water to the yeast and add with the beaten egg to the well in the flour mixing to form a soft batter. Place on a lightly floured board and knead until smooth and elastic. Shape into a ball, place into a clean, greased bowl, cover and allow to rise in a warm place until it has doubled in bulk—about 1¼ to 1½ hours.

Turn risen dough on to a lightly floured board and press out to 1 cm (½ in) thickness.

Divide dough into 16 pieces and shape each into a small ball. Place buns on a greased baking sheet at least 2.5 cm (1 in) apart, cover and allow to rise in a warm place for a further 20 to 30 minutes.

Mix the self-raising flour and water and beat to a smooth paste. Fill into a greaseproof paper funnel or small piping bag. Make a slight indentation in the shape of a cross on the top of each bun with a sharp knife just before baking and pipe flour and water paste into the cross.

Bake the buns in a hot oven (400°F—200°C) for approximately 15 minutes. Remove from the oven and brush with glaze while still hot.

Glaze: In a small saucepan dissolve gelatine in the hot water over a low heat. Add the sugar and stir until dissolved. Remove from the heat and brush over the buns.

Note: When these buns are cool, they may be wrapped in foil and stored for weeks in the deep freeze. Reheat in a moderate oven for about 20 minutes before serving.

● Fruit may be added to the flour along with the batter. To this amount of bun dough add ¾ cup of currants or sultanas and ¼ cup mixed chopped peel.

Swedish Coffee Ring

half the quantity of basic bun dough
1 tablespoon soft butter
⅓ cup brown sugar
1 teaspoon cinnamon
⅓ cup raisins
White icing:
1 cup icing sugar, sifted
1 tablespoon hot milk

Roll out dough to a rectangle 37 cm × 23 cm (15 in × 9 in). Spread with butter and sprinkle with brown sugar, cinnamon and raisins.

Roll up tightly.

Place on a greased baking sheet, form into a ring and press ends together to seal.

Make cuts two-thirds of the way through the coffee ring at 2.5 cm (1 in) intervals.

Turn each slice on its side, cover with a cloth and allow to rise until doubled in bulk—about 30 minutes.

Bake in a moderately hot oven (375°F—190°C). for 25 to 30 minutes. Cool on a wire cake rack. Frost with white icing.

White icing: Sift the icing sugar into a bowl and gradually stir in the hot milk until it resembles a thick cream which may be drizzled over the coffee ring.

Hot Baps and Butter

Baps are morning rolls served all over Scotland although connoisseurs say the best come from Aberdeenshire. There are two sorts, the floury bap and the buttery bap, both light and white. Our recipe is foolproof so it's easy for everyone to enjoy this Scottish breakfast specialty.

500 g (1 lb) plain flour sieved with
  1 teaspoon of salt
1¼ cups milk and water mixed
60 g (2 oz) butter
15 g (½ oz) yeast
1 teaspoon sugar

Sieve the flour with the salt into a bowl. Heat the milk and water to blood heat, add the butter and when it has melted, remove from the heat.

Dissolve the yeast with the sugar and stir into the warm liquid. Make a well in the centre of the flour and pour in the liquid. Stir in a little of the flour from the side until it is the consistency of a thick batter. Cover with a folded cloth and place in a warm spot to sponge. When the yeast mixture has doubled and bubbles have formed, mix in all the flour.

Turn onto a floured board and knead until the dough is smooth—about 5 minutes.

Place into a clean greased bowl and turn the dough over so that the top surface is lightly greased. Cover with a cloth and leave in a warm place for about 2 hours until well risen and doubled in bulk—or leave in the refrigerator overnight. Knock the dough down and turn on to a floured board. Knead lightly, divide the dough into 12 pieces and shape each into a round ball. Place on to a buttered baking sheet cover and allow to prove in a warm place for 15 to 20 minutes. Bake in a hot oven for 12 to 15 minutes or until a very light golden.

May be served hot or cold with butter.

Note: If the dough has been left in the refrigerator overnight, remove the next morning and allow to warm slightly before kneading and shaping into Baps.

Puris (pronounced poo-rees)

Puri is a round, fried wheatmeal bread. It is delicious served with a dry type of curry such as the potato curry and is eaten with the fingers. Break off a piece and use it to spoon up a quantity of curry. In India puris are frequently served as part of a vegetarian meal with vegetable purée and lentil purée.

Wheatmeal flour is available from large grocery stores and many health food shops. It is different from wholemeal flour, although this particular recipe may be made with wholemeal.

1½ cups wheatmeal flour
1 cup self-raising flour
1 teaspoon salt
1 teaspoon ghee
1 cup warm water
oil for frying

Sift flours and salt. Rub in ghee, then add warm water and mix to a stiff dough. Knead for several minutes. The dough should be smooth and elastic. Cover and leave for 15 minutes. The dough should spring back into shape when pressed with a fingertip.

Divide into 12 equal portions. Shape each portion into a ball and roll out fairly thinly on a lightly floured board.

Heat 2.5 cm (1 in) oil in a frying pan and when smoking hot, fry each puri in it, separately and quickly. If oil does not cover puri, splash top with oil. Turn so that puri is well fried on both sides.

When golden brown drain well on crumpled kitchen paper. Serve hot.

Hot Baps and Butter

Glossary

Acidify: To add lemon juice or vinegar to water, a sauce or cooked dish.

Antipasto: Italian, "before the pasta". Appetiser of assorted vegetables, fish or cold cuts of meat.

Aspic: The culinary name for calf's foot jelly, or jelly made with bones of meat, fish or poultry. May be made from commercial aspic jelly crystals.

Au gratin: Food baked in a shallow ovenproof gratin dish, sprinkled with breadcrumbs, covered with sauce dotted with butter and browned in the oven or under the grill until a crisp gratin coating forms. Often contains cheese, but not essential.

Bain-Marie: A French kitchen utensil designed to keep liquids at simmering point without coming to the boil. It consists of a saucepan standing in a larger pan which is filled with boiling water. A bain-marie is a great help in keeping sauces, stews and soups hot without overcooking. In domestic kitchens, a double boiler can do double duty as a bain-marie.

Bake: To cook by dry heat in the oven. This term is usually used only for breads, cakes, biscuits, pies, tarts and pastries.

Baste: To pour or spoon liquid over food as it cooks to moisten and flavour it.

Batter: A mixture of flour and some liquid, beaten together, it is thin enough to coat food, pour or be dropped from a spoon.

Beat: To mix with a spoon, spatula, whisk, rotary beater or electric mixer; to make a mixture smooth and light by enclosing air.

Beurre manié: Equal quantities of butter and flour kneaded together and added bit by bit to a stew, casserole or sauce to thicken it.

Blanch: To heat in boiling water or steam. This can be done for several reasons: (1) to loosen outer skins of fruit, nuts or vegetables; (2) to whiten sweetbreads, veal or chicken; (3) to remove excess salt or bitter flavour from bacon, gammon, ham, Brussel sprouts, turnips, endive, etc; (4) to prepare fruits and vegetables for canning, freezing or preserving.

Blend: To mix two or more ingredients thoroughly, usually a powdered ingredient and a liquid mixed to a smooth paste using a wooden spoon.

Boil: To bring to boiling point and keep there, to cook in liquid which is boiling.

Boiling point: The temperature at which bubbles rise continually and break over the entire surface of a liquid—212°F at sea level.

Bone: To remove the bones from fish, chicken, poultry or game.

Bouillon: A clear soup, usually made from beef.

Bouquet garni: A bunch or "faggot" of culinary herbs, used to flavour stews, casseroles and sauces. Usually consists of sprigs of parsley, thyme, marjoram, rosemary, a bay leaf, peppercorns and cloves, tied in muslin.

Buttermilk: A fermented milk product from which fat has been removed in the process of churning.

Braise: To simmer gently in a covered casserole on a layer of mirepoix, in a small amount of liquid.

Broil: See grill.

Caramelize: To melt sugar in a small heavy saucepan, until it is a golden brown syrup.

Chaudfroid: A jellied white sauce made of butter, flour, chicken stock, egg yolks, cream and gelatine. Used to give a shiny white glaze to fish, chicken, ham, etc.

Canapé: A small piece of bread or pastry, biscuit or scone topped with meat, fish or cheese and served as a cocktail savoury.

Chill: To place in refrigerator or other cold place until cold.

Chop: To cut into very small pieces with a sharp knife or a chopper.

Chowder: A soup, usually using fish, clams or vegetables, made with milk.

Clarify: 1. To clear a stock or broth by adding slightly beaten egg whites and crushed egg shells and bring to the boil. The stock is cooled and strained before using.

2. To cleanse fat dripping for deep frying by adding water and melting very gently. When cool the clean fat is removed and the sediment is left at the bottom.

3. To melt salted butter and drain the oil off the salty sediment.

Cool: To allow to stand at room temperature until no longer warm to the touch.

Coat: To cover entire surface with a mixture such as seasoned flour, breadcrumbs, batter, or to cover vegetables with sauce.

Coddle: To cook slowly and gently in water just below the boiling point.

Compote: Fruits stewed in syrup and served as a dessert.

Consommé: A clear soup made usually with beef with an intensive flavour.

Courtbouillon: The liquid in which fish, poultry or meat is cooked to give added flavour. A simple courtbouillon consists of water to which you have added 1 bay leaf, 2 stalks celery, 1 onion, 2 carrots and salt and freshly ground black pepper to taste. Other additives: wine, vinegar, stock, olive oil, garlic, shallots, cloves, etc.

Cream: To cream butter and sugar by beating with a wooden spoon or an electric mixer until light, white and fluffy like whipped cream.

Crêpe: A very thin pancake served with a rich savoury or sweet filling.

Croûton: Fried or toasted cubes of bread used as a garnish or topping. Or accompaniment to soup.

Cut in: To combine fat and dry ingredients with two knives, scissor-fashion, or with a pastry blender, when making pastry.

Deep fry: To cook in deep hot fat or oil which covers the food, until crisp and golden.

Devil: To cook food by combining it with a highly seasoned hot sauce which contains worcestershire sauce and mustard.

Dice: To cut into small even cubes.

Disjoint: To cut poultry, game or small animals into serving pieces by dividing at the joint.

Dissolve: To mix a dry ingredient with liquid until it is absorbed.

Dredge: To coat food with a fine ingredient by dusting, sprinkling, or rolling the food in flour, cornflour, cornmeal, sugar, icing sugar, etc.

Dripping: The residue left in the pan after meat or poultry is cooked, usually including fat.

Dust: To sprinkle lightly as with flour or sugar.

Entrée: A single made-up dish, served before the main course of roast meat or game or poultry.

Escallop: See scallop. To bake food with liquid, usually white sauce, with a covering of breadcrumbs and sometimes cheese.

Fillet:
1. Special cut of beef, lamb, pork or veal; breast of poultry and game; fish cut off the bone lengthways.
2. To cut any of the above to use in cooking.

Fish fumet: A highly concentrated fish stock, made by reducing well-flavoured fish stock. Used to poach fish, fish fillets or fish steaks, and flavour sauces.

Flake: To break into small pieces with a fork.

Flame: To spoon alcohol over food and ignite.

Fold in: To add other ingredients to a mixture which has been beaten until light and fluffy, using a plastic spatula or tablespoon with a light cut and fold movement so that the air is not lost.

Fricassée: A stew made from white meats and vegetables and served in a thickened sauce.

Fry: To cook in a little fat or oil in a frying pan.

Fondue: A dish of Swiss origin cooked in a special pan over a flame at the table.

Frosting: A thick mixture of sugar and other ingredients used to ice a cake.

Garnish: To decorate food, usually with something edible.

Glaze: A thin coating of beaten egg, syrup or aspic which is brushed over pastry (beaten egg), fruits (syrup) or cooked fish, ham, tongue, chicken, etc. (aspic).

Grate: To rub a food against a grater to form small particles.

Gelatine: A protein substance found in the connective tissue of bones of animals.

Grease: To rub lightly with butter, margarine, oil or fat.

Grill: To cook by direct heat such as an open fire. Today, by charcoal, gas or electricity.

Homogenize: To process a food, such as milk, so that fats are completely integrated and will not separate.

Julienne: Cut into fine strips the length of a matchstick.

Knead: To work dough with hands until it is of the desired elasticity or consistency.

Lard:
1. Common cooking fat obtained by melting down of pork fat.
2. The strips can be threaded with a larding needle, or inserted in cuts made in the meat.

Lardons: Strips of fat or bacon used as above.

Liaison: To thicken a sauce, gravy or stew; 1: by the addition of flour, cornflour, arrowroot, rice flour, potato flour, or a beurre manié (flour and butter); 2: by stirring in egg yolk, cream or in the case of certain dishes of poultry or game, blood.

Macédoine:
1. A mixture of raw or cooked fruit for a fruit salad.
2. A mixture of cooked diced vegetables often garnished with a cream sauce, mayonnaise or aspic, and served as an hors d'oeuvre, salad or as a garnish.

Marinade: Usually a mixture of an oil, acid and seasonings in which food is marinated to give it more flavour and to soften the tissues of tough food.

Marinate: To let food stand in a marinade.

Mask: To cover cooked food with sauce.

Mocha: A combination of coffee and chocolate flavours.

Monosodium glutamate: A crystalline chemical product added to food to intensify the natural flavour.

Mince: To reduce to very small particles with a mincer, chopper or knife.

Mirepoix: Diced carrots, onion, celery (usually bacon or ham), simmered in butter until soft. Used to add flavour to dishes of meat, poultry and fish.

Oven fry: To cook meat, fish or poultry in fat in the oven, uncovered, basting food with fat from time to time.

Parboil: To boil until partially cooked.

Pare or peel:
1. To cut off outside skin or covering of a fruit or vegetable with a knife or vegetable peeler.
2. To peel fruits such as oranges or bananas without using a knife.

Parfait: A frozen dessert made with whipped cream usually layered with a syrup, or a fruit, in a tall narrow glass.

Pasteurize: To destroy certain micro-organisms by holding at a temperature of 140°F to 180°F for a stated length of time.

Pâté: A highly seasoned meat paste, usually served as a hors d'oeuvre.

Petit four: A small cake usually iced on top and sides and delicately decorated.

Pit: To remove pit, stone or seed, as from cherries.

Poach: To cook gently in simmering liquid.

Port wine cheese: A semi hard, blue veined, well matured cheese, usually stilton, that has port wine poured on to it and is left until the wine has soaked right into the cheese.

Pound: To reduce to very small particles, or a paste, with a mortar and pestle.

Praline: A confection made by preparing a syrup and adding nuts.

Preheat: To have oven or cooking appliance at desired temperature before putting in food.

Purée: To press through a fine sieve or put in a food blender to produce a smooth thick mixture.

Ragoût: A stew made from regular sized pieces of meat, poultry or fish, sautéed in fat until brown and then simmered with stock, meat juices or water, or a combination of these, until tender.

Ramekin: Individual baking dish.

Reduce: To cook a sauce over a high heat, uncovered, until it is reduced by evaporation to the desired consistency. This culinary process improves both flavour and appearance.

Roast: To cook meat by direct heat on a spit or in the oven, although "baking" would be a better term, for when meat is cooked in a closed area (oven) vapour accumulates and changes texture and flavour of true roast.

Roux: A mixture of fat and flour cooked slowly over a low heat used as a foundation for sauces, soups and thick gravies.

Sauté: To fry lightly in a small amount of hot fat or oil, shaking the pan or turning food frequently during cooking, usually until the fat or oil is absorbed.

Scald: To heat to temperature just below boiling point, with small bubbles rising occasionally to the surface.

Score: To make evenly spaced, shallow slits or cuts with a knife, on the surface of food.

Shred: To cut into thin pieces.

Simmer: To cook in liquid just below boiling point, with small bubbles rising occasionally to the surface.

Skim: To remove foam, fat or solid substance from the surface of a cooking, or cooked mixture.

Sliver: To cut in long, thin pieces.

Sour cream: A cultured, commercial product, usually 18% butterfat content. Used as a topping for vegetables and fruit, in sauces gravies and in meat dishes.

Steam: To cook food in vapour rising from boiling water.

Stew: A long slow method of cooking in a covered pan in a small amount of liquid, usually to tenderize tough meat.

Stir: To mix with a spoon with a circular motion.

Stock: A liquid containing the flavours, extracts and nutrients of bones, meat, fish or vegetables in which they are cooked.

Tamarind juice: Made by soaking dried tamarind fruit in hot water for 20 minutes, pressing through a sieve to make or purée and then diluting the purée with water to a pouring consistency.

Timbale: Individual baked custards made with minced fish, poultry or vegetables.

Torte: A rich cake made with crumbs and eggs, containing fruit and nuts.

Toss: To mix lightly, especially salad of fresh greens, using a fork and spoon.

INDEX